INSIGHT GUIDES
NORWAY

D0970967

APA PUBLICATIONS L
Part of the Langenscheidt Publishing Group

INSIGHT GUIDE
NORWAY

Editorial

Project Editor
Siân Lezard
Art Director
Steven Lawrence
Picture Manager
Tom Smyth
Series Manager
Rachel Fox

Distribution

UK and Ireland
Dorling Kindersley Ltd, a Penguin Group company
80 Strand, London WC2R 0RL, UK
customerservice@dk.com

United States
Ingram Publisher Services
One Ingram Blvd
PO Box 3006
La Vergne, TN 37086-1986
customer.service@ingrampublisher services.com

Australia
Universal Publishers
PO Box 307
St Leonards, NSW 1590
sales@universalpublishers.com.au

Worldwide
Apa Publications GmbH & Co. Verlag KG (Singapore branch)
7030 Ang Mo Kio Ave 5
08-65 Northstar @ AMK
Singapore 569880
apasin@signet.com.sg

Printing

CTPS – China

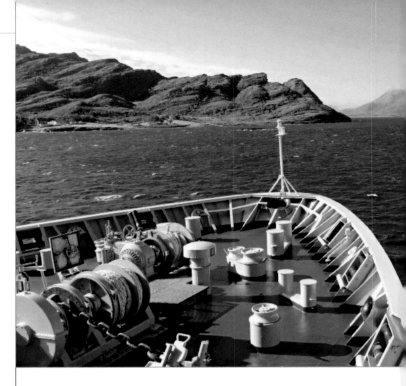

ABOUT THIS BOOK

The first Insight Guide pioneered the use of creative full-colour photography in travel guides in 1970. Since then, we have expanded our range to cater for our readers' need not only for reliable information about their chosen destination, but also for a real understanding of the culture and workings of that destination. Now, when the internet can supply inexhaustible facts, our books marry text and pictures to provide those much more elusive qualities: knowledge and discernment. To achieve this, they rely heavily on the authority of locally based writers and photographers.

Fjords, midnight sun and Vikings are the aspects most often identified with Norway. From the spectacular scenery of the west coast to the wilderness of the frozen north, Norway is a country that entices all those with an adventurous spirit and a desire for unspoilt nature.

How to use this book

This book is carefully structured to convey an understanding of Norway and its culture, and to guide readers through its sights and activities:

◆ The **Best of Norway** section at the start of the book gives you a snapshot of the country's highlights, helping you prioritise what you want to do.

◆ The **Features** section, indicated by a pink bar at the top of each page, covers the natural and cultural history of Norway, and includes illuminating essays on geography, wildlife, sports, traditional arts and why everything costs so much.

◆ The main **Places** section, with a blue bar, provides a complete rundown of all the attractions worth seeing.

LEFT: heading towards the Arctic Circle.

she's not working she loves cross-country skiing, hiking and taking photographs.

This edition builds on the work of the late **Doreen Taylor-Wilkie**. Other contributors include **Rowlinson Carter**, who wrote the history section, and **Inga Wallerius**, an eminent Swedish journalist who has a deep interest in ethnic cultures and wrote on the Sami people. **Bobby Tulloch**'s chapter on Svalbard was the result of an expedition there, while **Jim Hardy** contributed his knowledge on Scandinavian arts. **Karen Fossli** wrote on the oil industry, film and Norway's neighbours, and **Anita Peltonen** provided chapters on Oslo and its environs.

Full credits for the pictures are given at the back of the book, but the main photographer was **Glyn Genin**. The book was designed by **Andy Hunter**, proofread by **Neil Titman** and indexed by **Helen Peters**.

Map Legend

— · · —	International Boundary
— — — —	County Boundary
— · —	National Park
— — — —	Ferry Route
Ⓣ	Metro
✈ ✈	Airport: International/Regional
🚌	Bus Station
❶	Tourist Information
🕆 † 🕆	Church/Ruins
†	Monastery
∴	Archaeological Site
🏰 🏛	Castle/Ruins
☪	Mosque
✡	Synagogue
∩	Cave
𝟙	Statue/Monument
★	Place of Interest

The main places of interest in the Places section are coordinated by number with a full-colour map (eg ❶), and a symbol at the top of every right-hand page tells you where to find the map.

◆ The **Travel Tips** listings section, topped with a yellow bar, provides full information on transport, hotels, eating out, activities – from culture and shopping to cruises and outdoor sports – and an A–Z section of essential practical information. Information may be located quickly on the index printed on the back cover flap – and the flaps are designed to serve as bookmarks.

The contributors

This book was commissioned by **Siân Lezard**, edited by **Jane Hutchings** and updated by **Marie Peyre**. A journalist and editor, Marie moved to Norway in 2007 and has been there ever since. She has travelled extensively around Scandinavia in general, and Norway in particular, and covers this region for a number of publishers in the UK and the US. She speaks (almost) fluent Norwegian, and when

Contents

LEFT: giant lobster for sale.
RIGHT: the home of trolls.
BELOW: Heddal stave church.

Maps

Travel Tips

THE BEST OF NORWAY: TOP ATTRACTIONS

From the world's most spectacular fjords and stunning coastal scenery to historic old towns and the best in modern architecture, here, at a glance, are Norway's highlights

△ The route up to **Preikestolen**, or Pulpit Rock, is Norway's most popular hike, and with good reason. The views are stunning, but vertigo-sufferers should steer clear. *See page 215.*

◁ At **North Cape**, Continental Europe's northernmost tip and the last frontier, you can don a wetsuit and catch giant crabs which you then eat. *See page 324.*

△ **Oslo** has transformed itself into a vibrant capital, with child-friendly museums, great dining and shopping, and a stunning new opera house. *See page 145.*

▽ A slate stone tower in **Hardangervidda National Park**, Europe's largest mountainous plateau and a popular hiking destination in summer. *See page 191.*

◁ **Bergen**, Norway's second city, sits on a craggy shoreline on the west coast surrounded by islands. It's rich in history and sights, so allow a couple of days to make the most of its museums, galleries and restaurants. *See page 241.*

▷ **The fjords** are Norway's most spectacular attraction. Each has its own character and appeal – this is Geirangerfjord, to many the most beautiful. *See page 275.*

▽ **Røros**, a Unesco World Heritage Site, is a beautifully preserved old mining town famed for its turf-roofed wooden buildings and its church. *See page 184.*

▽ Its dramatic island scenery with rugged peaks and white sand beaches, and its traditional fishing industry make **Lofoten** well worth the trip north. *See page 311.*

◁ **Trondheim**, Norway's third-largest city, is still its historical and religious capital. Seen here is a monument to Olav Tryggvason, the city's founder. *See page 287.*

▽ The gateway to the far north, **Tromsø**, known as "the Paris of the North", has great museums and a beautiful cathedral, and appeals to adventurous types curious about the Arctic. *See page 318.*

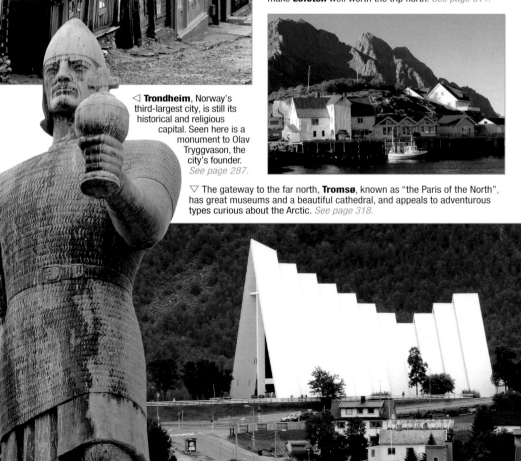

THE BEST OF NORWAY: EDITOR'S CHOICE

Beautiful fjords, breathtaking mountain landscapes, ultra-modern architecture and the widest range of outdoor pursuits – Norway is a haven for those who enjoy both culture and wilderness. Here we give you our selection of the best the country has to offer

BEST FJORDS (FROM NORTH TO SOUTH)

● **Geirangerfjord**
A Unesco World Heritage Site, Geirangerfjord is famous for its emerald waters and stunning waterfalls; it is arguably the most beautiful of the Norwegian fjords.
See page 275.

● **Nordfjord**
Snow-capped mountains and many shades of blue define the 100km- (62-mile) -long Nordfjord. Nearby you'll find the Jostedal Glacier, mainland Europe's largest, where you can take glacier walks and ski in summer.
See page 268.

● **Sognefjord**
Norway's deepest and longest fjord, and one of

its most spectacular. Here you'll find the newly renovated Urnes stave church and the Norwegian Glacier Museum. The Flåm railway ends in Aurland on Sognefjord, and is a must too. *See page 263.*

● **Nærøyfjord**
An arm of the Sognefjord, and only 250 metres (820ft) at its narrowest, the peaceful "Narrow fjord" is another Unesco World Heritage Site. The fjord freezes over in winter, but in summer it is popular with kayakers.
See page 266.

● **Hardangerfjord**
Visit this fjord in spring, when the many orchards

are in full bloom, or in summer to gorge on the delicious *moreller* (black cherries), then visit the manor house of Baroniet Rosendal, and the excellent folk museum at Utne. *See page 229.*

● **Eidfjord**
An arm of the Hardangerfjord, this small, peaceful fjord is within easy reach of both the 182-metre (600ft) -high Vøringsfossen, Norway's most famous waterfall, and the Hardangervidda. The Hardangervidda Nature Centre is located here.
See page 233.

● **Lysefjord**
Barren and windswept, Lysefjord is home to Prei-kestolen, a huge block of granite jutting out 600 metres (2,000ft) above sea level, and Kjerag, a big boulder precariously stuck between two mountain walls. A popular destination for extreme-sport enthusiasts and hikers. *See page 215.*

ABOVE: Lysefjord, Rogaland. **RIGHT:** at Naerøyfjord.

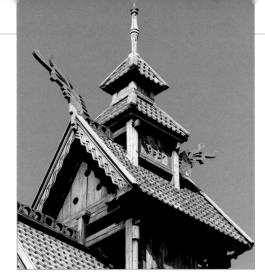

BEST ARCHITECTURE

● **Oslo Opera House**
This striking building in white granite and glass has made its mark on the Oslo waterfront since opening in April 2008, and is now one of the capital's top attractions. *See page 146.*

● **Ålesund**
When this town burned to the ground in January 1904 it was rebuilt in the *Jugendstil* style and today hosts a superb concentration of Art Nouveau buildings. *See page 273.*

● **Lysøen**
The residence of violin virtuoso Ole Bull, on an island outside Bergen, is a daring blend of styles that never fails to wow visitors. *See page 250.*

● **Stave churches**
There are 28 stave churches in Norway, two of the most striking being the newly restored church at Urnes, which is on the

Unesco list, and the Heddal stave church in Telemark, the largest. *See pages 207 and 265.*

● **Hamsun Centre, Nordland**
With its grassy roof and black wood exterior, the new Hamsun Centre towers over the island of Hamarøy, where the novelist Knut Hamsun spent his childhood. *See page 316.*

● **Sami Parliament, Finnmark**
An interesting exercise in modern architecture, with a design blending Sami culture and building traditions with modern technology. *See pages 86 and 325.*

● **Gardermoen Airport**
One of the most stunning airports in Europe, and a great introduction to Norwegian architecture from the minute you land in the country. *See page 343.*

BEST OUTDOOR PURSUITS

● **Hiking**
Norway is a hikers' paradise, and opportunities abound up and down the country, with Jotunheimen and Hardangervidda among the most popular walking haunts. *See page 97.*

● **Whale-watching**
This is a favourite activity for young and old between May and September off the coast of Nordland and in the Lofoten Islands. If you're lucky you might spot minke whales, orca and even sperm whales. *See page 315.*

● **Flåm railway**
One of the world's steepest and most spectacular railway lines, and a must for any rail enthusiast, with fantastic scenery at every bend. *See page 266.*

● **Northern lights**
There is nothing quite like witnessing the northern lights (aurora borealis), one of nature's most breathtaking spectacles. Visible anywhere north of the Arctic Circle in winter – Tromsø is a particularly good spot. *See page 306.*

● **Giant crab safari in Kirkenes** One of the most popular excursions in the Kirkenes region, where visitors swim in the Barents Sea and help

haul the day's catch on board before eating the crabs for dinner later on. *See page 326.*

● **Hurtigruten**
The Norwegian coastal voyage from Bergen to Kirkenes has been recognised as one of the best cruises in the world – this is the ideal way to experience the drama of Norway's extraordinary coastline. *See page 257.*

● **Sailing the Hvaler Archipelago**
There are few better ways to spend a hot summer's day than on board a sailing boat exploring some of the hundreds of islands that make up the Hvaler Archipelago. *See page 170.*

● **Cross-country skiing**
Come winter Norway turns into one of the best winter-sport destinations, and cross-country here reigns supreme, with thousands of kilometres of prepared tracks. *See page 100.*

ABOVE: Hallingdal stave church. **ABOVE RIGHT:** cross-country skiing. **RIGHT:** the northern lights over Kvaløya.

BEST MUSEUMS AND GALLERIES

● **Munch Museum, Oslo**
The most extensive collection of works by Edvard Munch in the world, a must-see for any art-lover. *See page 153.*

● **National Gallery, Oslo**
A great introduction to Norwegian art, focusing on the late 18th century to the early 20th, with works by artists such as Christian Krogh and J.C. Dahl well represented. *See page 151.*

● **Viking Ship Museum, Oslo**
Three carefully restored Viking ships and hundreds of artefacts draw the crowds to this ever-popular museum in Bygdøy. *See page 160.*

● **Maihaugen, Lillehammer**
One of the best folk museums in the country, with 200 buildings, wonderful handicraft and folk art, and activities for children year-round. *See page 180.*

● **Vilvite, Bergen**
Meaning "Want to know", the Bergen Science Centre brings the action back into technology with interactive displays and experiments. Fun for all. *See page 251.*

● **Norwegian Petroleum Museum, Stavanger**
A highly interactive, educational museum that will delight both grown-ups and children visiting the oil capital of Norway. *See page 223.*

● **Rogaland Museum of Fine Arts, Stavanger**
Modern art in a beautiful location. The first of Antony Gormley's *Broken Column* figures that wind their way down to the harbour can be seen here. *See page 225.*

● **Ringve Museum, Trondheim**
A superb collection of musical instruments that will fascinate anyone with even a passing interest in music. *See page 291.*

● **Polaria, Tromsø**
Everything you always wanted to know about the Arctic, in one neat package that combines a museum, an aquarium and a 3D cinema rolled into one. *See page 319.*

ABOVE: Akershus Fortress, Oslo, built in 1299 to protect the city from marauders.

BEST FOR KIDS

● **International Children's Art Museum, Oslo** (Barnekunstmuseet)
Drawings, paintings and sculptures by children from around the world – a great museum to visit with the little ones. *See page 150.*

● **Aquarium, Bergen**
Celebrating 50 years in 2010, the Bergen Aquarium is as popular as ever. Come here at feeding times to watch the penguins and the seals perform for visitors, or brave the underwater tunnel and see sharks swimming above your head. *See page 247.*

● **Zoo, Kristiansand**
Norway's largest zoo is a great place to spend a day, with 120 animal species from all over the world represented. *See page 203.*

● **Kongeparken, near Stavanger**
Western Norway's largest amusement park, located south of Sandnes in Rogaland, features 60 rides and attractions, including Norway's longest bobsleigh track and its biggest carousel. *See page 215.*

● **Hunderfossen Family Park, Oppland**
A very Norwegian theme park near Lillehammer, featuring, among other things, the world's largest troll. *See page 182.*

● **Bø Sommarland, Telemark**
Scandinavia's largest water park is the place to splash out on a hot summer's day. *See page 208.*

● **Tusenfryd, south of Oslo**
The name means "1,000 joys", and this amusement park lives up to the name, with water slides, carousels, bumper cars, ghost trains and several roller coasters, including a wooden one. *See page 364.*

LEFT: the Bergen Science Centre. **RIGHT:** taking part in the Molde International Jazz Festival.

BEST HISTORIC SIGHTS

● **Nidaros Cathedral, Trondheim**
Norway's oldest cathedral, and the resting place of St Olav, the king who brought Christianity to Norway. *See page 288.*

● **Old Town, Fredrikstad**
Scandinavia's best-preserved fortress town. Quaint, cobblestoned streets and period wooden buildings. *See page 170.*

● **Akershus Fortress, Oslo**
The pride of Norway's capital, perched on a bluff overlooking the harbour and fjord, this 1,000-year-old complex is an absolute must. *See page 147.*

● **Røros**
This perfectly preserved old mining town, with its 300-year-old wooden houses, is a remarkable survivor from a bygone age. The mines are open for tours. *See page 184.*

● **Rock carvings**
As many as 5,000 petroglyphs, the earliest dating from 4200 BC, are concentrated around Alta in Finnmark. Several carvings sites can also be found in Østfold, in southern Norway. *See pages 170 and 321.*

● **Håkonshallen, Bergen**
Norway's royal family still hold events at this legendary spot on the Bergen waterfront. *See page 245.*

ABOVE: seafood canapés.

BEST FESTIVALS

● **Holmenkollen Days, Oslo**
Norwegians gather in March to take part and spectate in this hugely popular event, where ski jumping and cross-country skiing take centre stage. *See page 105.*

● **Bergen International Festival, Bergen**
(Festspillene)
Celebrates a wide range of music and cultural activities, including opera, theatre and dance. Late May/early June. *See page 250.*

● **Molde International Jazz Festival**
Norway's largest jazz festival, held in July, attracts big names from around the world. *See page 278.*

● **St Olav's Festival, Trondheim**
Various cultural events commemorating the death of St Olav in 1030. July/Aug. *See page 293.*

● **Gladmat, Stavanger**
Norway's largest food festival brings hungry crowds to the harbourfront. Late July. *See page 221.*

MONEY-SAVING TIPS

Norway is an expensive country, and visitors need to be mentally, as well as financially, prepared. Try to avoid spoiling your visit by comparing the prices to those back home. There are also a few things that may ease the strain on your credit cards:

● **Hotel discounts**
Hotel rates in Norwegian cities can be lower than in other countries, especially at weekends and in summer, when the seminar- and conference-goers leave town. Check out individual hotel chains' websites to find the best available rate.

● **City passes**
Most of Norway's major cities offer passes that give the holder access to public transport and museums, as well as discounts on goods and services. They can be pricey, so do your own calculations before buying.

● **Taxis**
Single-fare public transport tickets are expensive, so four people sharing a taxi can save money on short hops. Be careful, though, as taxi rates jump in the evening, and at weekends and holidays.

● **Boat service**
There won't be a tourist guide on board, but commuter ferries are a cheap way of travelling between seaside towns.

NORTHERN CONTRASTS

Norway offers the visitor a beguiling mix of tradition and modern convenience, spectacular nature and city delights

The most accurate observation made about Norway is that it is a land of contrasts: majestic mountains tower above mysterious fjords; harsh winters are relieved by often glorious summers; and long polar nights give way to the radiant midnight sun. One of the oldest civilisations in Europe has become one of its youngest nations. The rapacious Vikings have turned into global peacemakers. It is a country where Grieg and Ibsen compete with the Eurovision and American sitcoms; where environmental concerns challenge over-consumption. Norway has urban excitement and rural tranquillity: shopping malls and Toyotas rub shoulders with compass and rucksack; high technology parallels tradition.

A thriving offshore oil industry has brought prosperity and, as a consequence, social habits are changing rapidly. Though, in a society where the divorce rate is high and cohabitation the norm, the home and family remain important. Politically, democracy and debate pervade all levels of society. Murray's *Handbook for Travellers in Norway* described the Norwegians in 1874 thus: "Great patriotism and hospitality are two of the leading characteristics of the Norwegians; they are often cold and reserved, and combine great simplicity of manner with firmness and kindness. 'Deeds, not words' is their motto" – 136 years later, little has changed.

Unexpected pleasures

Most people are pleasantly surprised when they visit Norway. Not only are the people friendly (with many speaking fluent English), the scenery is even more breathtaking in reality than any guidebook could ever hope to

inspire. Add to this the fact that communications and services are efficient, and that it is safe to go out at night, and you have all the ingredients for an enjoyable stay. As for prices, Norway remains expensive, so budgeting for your trip is a must *(see Travel Tips, page 365)*. But Norway's spectacular nature is free – another reason to make the most of its best playground: the great outdoors. ❑

PRECEDING PAGES: Geirangerfjord; gulls flock over a fish shoal; Museum of Decorative Art, Bergen. **LEFT:** Rorvik, capital of the Vikna island group. **ABOVE:** Alpine landscape; Lindesnes Lighthouse; street music in the town of Molde.

AN UNTAMED LAND

Throughout history, Norway's difficult topography has been both a challenge and a blessing for the country's inhabitants. It has also played a significant part in shaping the Norwegian character

From the thousand islands and skerries of the Skagerrak in the south to the sparsely vegetated Arctic tundra landscapes of the far north, from the dense forests of eastern Norway to the deep fjords in the west of the country, Norway's landscape is amazingly varied.

Covering the western and northern part of the Scandinavian peninsula, Norway (together with Svalbard and Jan Mayen) spreads over 385,155 sq km (150,000 sq miles), an area almost as big as California. Stretching 1,750km (1,090 miles) from south to north, the country is unevenly distributed in width, with the bulk of the landmass south of Trondheim. At its narrowest point near Narvik, it is only 6km (4 miles) wide.

Striking landscapes and seascapes

Peaks and plateaux dominate the landscape in many places. Norway is one of Europe's most mountainous countries, with four-fifths of the

One of Norway's remote outposts, and home to the polar bear, is the Svalbard archipelago, 600km (370 miles) north of the mainland. First used as a whaling base, then mined for its coal, Svalbard today lives from tourism and research.

landmass at an altitude over 150 metres (500ft). The highest summit, Galdhøpiggen in Jotunheimen (literally "Home of the giants"), culminates at 2,469 metres (8,100ft). The vast majority of Norway's highest peaks are concentrated

LEFT: Geirangerfjord, a Unesco World Heritage Site.
RIGHT: summer scene in Eidsbugarden, Jotenheimen.

in this area. Some of mainland Europe's largest glaciers can also be found in Norway – at 487 sq km (188 sq miles), Jostedalsbreen is the biggest of them all. Elsewhere, forests cover 23 percent of the territory, and cultivated land a meagre 3 percent, with the rest being lakes, bog, marshes and uncultivated land.

The bulk of the population is concentrated along the coast, and inland in the many valleys carved by glaciers during the last Ice Age – the same ones that formed Norway's many fjords. One of the largest valleys is the 230km (143-mile) long Gudbrandsdal, which stretches from Lillehammer in the south to Dovre in the north, and is a main traffic axis on the road from Oslo to Trondheim. South of Gudbrandsdal is Mjøsa, Norway's largest lake.

Another of Norway's striking features is its coastline, the world's most rugged, and Europe's longest, with a length of 25,000km (15,500 miles) – that is the mainland and fjords alone. It stretches to over 83,000km (51,500 miles) when you include outlying islands (there are 200,000 of these along the coast of Norway).

Fjords: the soul of Norway

Norway's long coastline is punctuated by fjords all the way from Oslo in the southeast to the Arctic north. The most dramatic are those found along the west coast, with steep mountain walls rising up from the water, and small farms clinging to every ledge and hectare of green. The fjords are beautiful, timeless, and everyone's idea of the soul of Norway.

The western fjords begin at Stavanger in the south, now Norway's oil capital, not far

> *The rugged Lofoten Islands, lying off Norway's northwest coast, have since pre-Viking times been the centre for the country's cod-fishing industry, which is still thriving today.*

VITAL STATISTICS

Highest mountain: Galdhøpiggen
Longest river: Glomma
Largest lake: Mjøsa
Largest glacier (on mainland Norway):
  Jostedalsbreen, 487 sq km (188 sq miles)
Town receiving the most precipitation: Bergen
Population density: 14 people per sq km
  (42 per sq mile)
Natural resources: oil, gas, iron, copper, fish, timber, hydropower
Land boundaries: Sweden (1,619km/1,006 miles), Finland (727km/452 miles), Russia (196km/122 miles)

from Preikestolen (Pulpit Rock), the great slab of rock standing a dizzying 600 metres (2,000ft) above Lysefjord. They stretch north to Hardangerfjord, one of the largest in the country and an early favourite, where the old traditions of music and storytelling influenced travellers such as the 19th-century composer Edvard Grieg.

Further north along the coast lies the port of Bergen, known as the gateway to the fjords; then Sognefjord (the longest and deepest fjord) and Nordfjord, in an area of glaciers, lakes and mountain massifs; Storfjord, parts of which bite far into the land; and, finally, the calm of the Geiranger, arguably the prettiest fjord of them all.

Human geography

The country's topography has shaped the Norwegian character: Norwegians have had to adapt to the difficult lay of the land and fight the elements to harness nature's bounty.

The fjords gave Norway its great seafaring tradition. For the early Vikings, who travelled to Scotland, Iceland and the rest of Europe, as much as for the modern traveller who chooses a ship as the most comfortable way to travel this magnificent coastline, the sea has provided the link. Today 15 percent of Norwegian households own one or more boats, and sailing is one of the nation's favourite pastimes.

> *Hardangervidda, a popular hiking destination in the southwest, is Norway's largest national park. It is home to wild reindeer, arctic fox and snowy owl. The park doubled as Planet Hoth in the Stars Wars film* The Empire Strikes Back.

to invent skiing, and then to excel at it. To this day the saying goes that Norwegians are born with skis on their feet, and anyone visiting Norway in winter will wonder whether to take this literally, such is the passion of Norwegians for winter sports.

The proximity of seas teeming with fish has also been a key factor in the development of the local fishing industry, going back 1,200 years to the first exports of stockfish to the Continent in the Viking age. More recently, it was the discovery of oil and gas in the North Sea which fuelled (literally) the huge economic boom that has seen Norway change from being a relatively poor country into one of the world's richest.

On land it was the cold winters with heavy snowfalls and the harsh terrain separating isolated valley communities that led Norwegians

When the snow melts, the mountains remain, and come summer Norwegians like hiking almost as much as they like cross-country skiing. The Jotunheimen, with its high peaks, has attracted serious mountaineers ever since the first tourists came to Norway in the 19th century, and the Hardangervidda, Europe's largest mountainous plateau, comes a close second among Norway's favourite places for hiking. Explorers Roald Amundsen and Fridtjof Nansen used the Hardangervidda to plan and prepare their polar expeditions.

Northern lights and midnight sun

Norway's climate is temperate along the coast, much milder in fact than its latitude would

LEFT: the Lysefjord, to the east of Stavanger.
ABOVE: climbing the glacier at Jostedal. **ABOVE RIGHT:** ski sailing in a storm, Hardangervidda.

In summer, days are noticeably longer throughout the country, but the midnight sun can only be observed above the Arctic Circle. It is a big attraction, drawing many tourists to Arctic Norway and the North Cape every year.

suggest. This is because the country benefits from the influence of the North Atlantic Current, warmed by the Gulf Stream, which keeps temperatures milder than they would otherwise be. Inland, winters can be harsh. Røros is one of the coldest places in Norway – record tem-peratures of –50°C (–58°F) have been registered here in winter, the coldest south of Finnmark. About one-third of Norway lies within the Arctic Circle. During the long winter nights it is not unusual for the northern lights (aurora borealis) to be visible in many places – a beautiful natural phenomenon that brightens up the skies of Nnorthern Norway from October to April. Tromsø is a very good spot from which to observe them.

Fauna and flora

The country stretches over many latitudes and, due to its varied topography and climate, it has

a greater variety of habitats than almost any other European country. As a result it possesses a very rich fauna and flora – as many as 60,000 species have been registered in Norway and its surrounding waters (*see Wildlife, page 93*).

Vegetation varies considerably, although the most common tree species are pine, spruce and birch. Timber is one of the country's main resources, providing paper for printing. Mosses and lichens are another component of local forests, and heather and berry bushes, most notably blueberry, are also abundant. ❑

GEIRANGERFJORD

The famed Geirangerfjord and its surrounding area were in 2005 added to Unesco's World Heritage List, which came as no surprise to the locals. It's a magical place, narrow and far from the open sea, with waterfalls crashing down steep mountain sides. Today, the Geirangerfjord is the second-most important cruise centre in the country. Its popularity comes at a price, with up to 100 ships visiting the fjord in summer, causing air pollution concerns. Efforts are being made to protect this environmentally sensitive area to prevent it from being damaged by the thousands of visitors arriving by ship and car every year.

ABOVE LEFT: reindeer graze by Porsangerfjord.
ABOVE: flowers in the Vesterålen Islands.
RIGHT: spectacular northern lights display.

DECISIVE DATES

Stone Age to Bronze Age

10,000 years ago
The first hunter-gatherers appear in the territory of what is now Norway, following the retreat of the great ice sheets.

5,000–6,000 years ago
Growth of agriculture around the Oslofjord.

1500–500 BC
Evidence of Bronze Age burial mounds and Iron Age workings.

Roman Age

AD 1–400
Burial sites indicate links with countries to the south. Latin-based runic letters appear.

AD 793
Norwegian Vikings loot English monastery of Lindisfarne, and raid, trade with and colonise parts of Western Europe.

Viking Age (AD 800–1030)

840–66
Vikings found Dublin (840), sack Paris (861) and control most of England by 866.

872
King Harald Hårfagre wins battle at Hafrsfjord, Stavanger.

1001
Sagas relate that Leiv Eiriksson discovers Vinland (America).

1028
King Canute of Denmark invades Norway.

1030
King Olav killed at the Battle of Stiklestad. Christianity arrives through trade with Europe.

1050–66
Harald Hardråde founds Oslo (1048). His defeat at the Battle of Stamford Bridge, England, in 1066, ends the Viking Age.

Middle Ages

1100
The first bishoprics include Nidaros (Trondheim) in 1152.

1130
Civil wars last until 1227. The population grows, towns develop and farmers change from freeholders to tenants.

1299–1343
Oslo becomes capital during the reign of Håkon V. Royal marriages produce a Norwegian-Swedish monarchy.

1349
Black Death reduces the population by 50 percent to about 180,000.

1380
Olav, son of Håkon VI, becomes king of Denmark and Norway.

1397
Trinity Sunday: union of the three crowns is formalised in Kalmar, Sweden.

Union with Denmark

1536
Norway loses its independence to the Danes, who take control.

1537
Reformation of the Norwegian Church imposed by Denmark.

1624
Oslo burns to the ground.

1660
Introduction of absolute rule under Frederik III. In the 1660s the population reaches 440,000; 900,000 by 1801.

1807–14
Norway and Denmark ally with France in Napoleonic Wars; resulting blockade causes shipping and timber exports to collapse and famine to spread.

Union with Sweden

1814
January: Secession from Denmark. 17 May: Norwegian constitution is formally adopted at Eidsvoll.
10 October: Treaty of Kiel places Norway in a union with Sweden.

1825
Great exodus to USA begins.

1850–99
The first railway line (1854), the first trade union (1872) and the first political parties (1884) are set up. Norwegian folkloric arts flourish with Grieg's music, Munch's paintings and Ibsen's dramas.

1905
August: national referendum ends union with Sweden.

FAR LEFT TOP: rock art. FAR LEFT BOTTOM: pendant of a man holding a sword and two spears. LEFT MIDDLE: 19th-century illustration of the Viking ship "Raven". LEFT: exhibit at Trondenes Heritage Centre, Harstad. TOP RIGHT: Petter Northug, gold medallist at the 2010 Winter Olympics. ABOVE RIGHT: oil rig.

Independence

1905
18 November: Storting (Parliament) elects Prince Carl of Denmark to be King (Haakon VII) of Norway.

1913
Universal suffrage is granted to women.

1920
Joins the League of Nations.

1939–45
Norway proclaims neutrality in World War II, but German forces invade in 1940. On 7 June 1945, King Haakon returns from exile. Birth of the social-welfare state.

1957
Haakon VII dies; Olav V is crowned king.

1960s
The start of oil exploration in the North Sea leads to new-found wealth for Norway over the following decades.

1972 and 1994
Norway votes against EU membership.

1991
King Olav V is succeeded by Harald V.

1994
Winter Olympics in Lillehammer.

2000
Oslo celebrates its 1,000-year anniversary.

2001
Norway elected to serve on the UN Security Council.

2005
Centre-left coalition wins national election.

2006 and 2009
Centre-left government led by prime minister Jens Stoltenberg of the Labour Party takes office. It is re-elected in 2009.

2008
The new Opera House opens on Oslo's waterfront.

2009
Norway is named best country to live in by a United Nations report. In a joint project with Sweden, Europe's first marine national park opens in Hvaler, southeastern Norway, and extends south across the border to the island of Koster.

2010
New Holmenkollen ski jump opens in Oslo.

BEGINNINGS

For two centuries the Vikings terrorised large parts of Europe, travelling far and wide in search of land, wealth and, when it suited them, trade

L ife in Norway has been influenced to an extraordinary degree by the terrain and the weather. The original inhabitants hugged the coastal areas which, warmed by the Gulf Stream, made life more bearable. With the gradual recession of the last Ice Age about 12,000 years ago, the hunters and fishermen inched northwards, but again only along the coast because the interior remained inhospitable.

The thaw was followed by mild weather, unknown before or since. Around 500 BC, however, just as iron was beginning to replace bronze and the Athenians were getting ready to build the Parthenon, the climate inexplicably deteriorated. The impact of suddenly colder, wetter weather was dramatic.

Taking a step back

During the preceding Bronze Age considerable progress had been made in weapons, ornaments and utensils made out of metal imported from Britain and Continental Europe. These developments were thrown into reverse by the climate change and the population declined.

Survival in the new Ice Age demanded cultural adjustments. Men, who until then had usually worn a kind of belted cloak, pulled on underwear and trousers. Instead of a semi-nomadic existence, all had to settle on farms in order to secure winter fodder and shelter livestock. People and animals occupied either end of the same house, an unhygienic but necessary form of early central heating.

In common with most of Europe, Norway was again struck by the weather in the 14th

century. The economic decline that followed was exacerbated terribly by the Black Death. The resulting acute shortage of labour led to the collapse of the aristocratic estates, demoting the owners to peasantry. The number of knights in Norway dropped from 270 to 60.

The people

But who were these people? The recorded history of Norway begins remarkably late, in about AD 800, and the archaeological pointers towards specific events in earlier times are comparatively scanty. The ancient world had curious opinions about the northerners: one, advanced by Pomponius Mela, was that, living on birds'

LEFT: the Gokstad ship, Viking Ship Museum, Oslo.
RIGHT: Odin, king of the Norse gods.

eggs, the people had hoofed feet, and ears so large that they covered their bodies, thereby dispensing with the need for any clothing.

Another, Greek in origin and containing an element of truth, had the territory populated by Hyperboreans, a jolly race who lived in forests and sang and danced their way to incredible longevity. When tired of life, they feasted, bedecked themselves with flowers and threw themselves off cliffs. Norwegians continue to live longer than many Europeans, and they remain energetic to the end. It is one thing for a foreigner struggling on skis to be overtaken by a blasé six-year-old, quite another if the speed demon

is a venerable grandmother. Lieutenant W.H. Breton, a 19th-century tourist, was amazed by reports of a man who married at 113 and lived until he was 146. Another visitor commented on four peasants who were the principal dancers at an entertainment for King Christian VI: all of them were over 100. One Derwent Conway, in 1820, asked a 74-year-old in Telemark for the secret of his robust health. Pouring himself a fifth glass of home-made corn brandy, he replied that it was due to this excellent drink.

New blood

That the original inhabitants of Norway received infusions of new blood, probably from the east, is indicated by artefacts which

have given their name to their respective cultures: Funnel-Beaker, Battle-Axe and Boat-Axe peoples. Changing burial practices are another reliable sign of influential immigration.

It was once thought that the Sami (Lapps of Finnmark) were the original inhabitants. Being Mongoloid and short of stature, they are very

> *Rock drawings from the Bronze Age show boats that were capable of carrying 30 men (although not yet with sails), warriors on horseback and either two- or four-wheeled carts drawn by horses or oxen.*

different from the familiar Scandinavian stereotype. However, it seems theirs was a relatively recent migration from Siberia, long after European types had moved in. The great majority of Norwegians are directly descended from the people who were occupying their territory long before 3000 BC, the date customarily taken as the beginning of Western civilisation.

Like a Nordic Rip van Winkle, Norway slept through the millennium in which Greece and then Rome flourished, although the runic alphabet did appear around the 3rd century AD. It was Latin in origin but dispensed with the curved Latin letters because, perhaps, straight lines were easier to cut into wood, stone and metal, as runic inscriptions invariably were.

Norway was ignored by the civilised world until the late 8th century. Nowhere in Pliny the Elder, Tacitus, Ptolemy or any of the celebrated descriptions of the then known world are the Norwegian people mentioned by name. Even the term "Scandinavia" is a misreading of a text by Pliny, who referred to the unknown land beyond Jutland as *Scatinavia*.

Development in secret

Foreign ignorance did not mean that nothing was happening locally. The evolution of ship design was the most potent of these hidden developments. Although the Phoenicians had undertaken stupendous voyages very much earlier, they routinely stayed within sight of land. The Norwegians were working on vessels capable of crossing oceans.

The Gokstad ship, found in a burial mound near Sandefjord in 1880, was a masterpiece. Made out of oak planks, it was 25 metres (82ft) long and 5 metres (16ft) wide. It had a mast and 16 pairs of oars. The crew handled one oar each, which left enough room for an equal number of marines. The *styrbord* or rudder, which hung on the right (hence, starboard) side, could be raised for fast beaching. A modern replica crossed the Atlantic in just four weeks. These ships represented a menacing mobility, and once the Norwegians had cause to take their unsuspecting neighbours to the south by surprise, they were able to do so with stunning efficiency.

The Norwegians introduced themselves to the rest of the world with deceptive tranquillity. The *Anglo-Saxon Chronicle* of 787 contains

down the coast in Northumbria, and the year after they arrived in southern Wales and Ireland with more than 100 ships. They were driven off by King Maredudd, and that, together with the resistance they had encountered in England, persuaded them, for a period of 40 years, to turn their attention to softer targets in Ireland.

Various opinions prevail about the origin of the name "Viking", but there was no doubt among their victims in the 9th and 10th centuries that it was synonymous with the term "pirate" or "sea robber". This is further confused by the tendency in English chronicles to call all Vikings "Danes", while many were actually

the laconic entry: "In this year King Breohtric married King Offa's daughter Eadburge. And in his days came the first three ships of the Northmen from Hereoalande" (known today as Hordaland, on Norway's west coast).

The Vikings appear

In 793 the Vikings opened their account in earnest by plundering the monastery of Lindisfarne off the northeast coast of England near the Scottish border, one of the great sanctuaries of the Western Christian Church. The next year they attacked the monastery of Jarrow further

In Arthurian romances the Vikings were described as being "wild and savage and had not in them the love of God nor their neighbours".

"Northmen", "Norsemen" or, in present terminology, Norwegians. In contrast, in Continental records Norwegians take all the credit (or blame) for what was usually the work of Danes. Swedish Vikings were busy, too, but they tended to direct their attentions overland via Russia.

Proper outside investigation into the geography and demography of Norway began with King Alfred the Great of England, who

LEFT: early sailing equipment.
ABOVE: a set of Viking keys.

had every reason to wonder about people who had become painful tormentors. He was enlightened by Ottar, a Norwegian chieftain from Hålogaland, at the same time as Alfred was waging war with other Viking chieftains. Ottar told the king that Norway was a very long and narrow country, full of rocks and mountains. The only places that could be pastured or ploughed were those close to the sea; the inhabitants kept sheep and swine and bred tame deer, which they called reindeer.

In reality, the Vikings were land-hungry adventurers for whom rich and undefended coastal abbeys were irresistible business opportunities. They had no scruples about violating their supposed sacrosanctity; on the contrary, they saw Christianity as a heretical threat to their own heathen beliefs.

Truculent population

While Christians put their faith in the sign of the cross, the Vikings trusted the hammer of Thor the Thunderer, defender of heaven against giants, men against monsters and themselves from the "Followers of the White Cross", as they called Christians. Small Viking raiding parties faced with a large and truculent population found that a reputation for uncompromising destruction and cruelty served their purposes well, encouraging the enemy to flee rather than put up a fight. Viking victory celebrations included the proven intimidatory tactic of drinking out of the skulls of fallen enemies.

The Vikings also have apologists who prefer to concentrate on their apparent managerial talents in occupied territory and an artistic streak manifested in the finely worked ornaments recovered from excavated ships. In the early 18th century, Baron de Montesquieu praised them as an army of free men in an age when armies were usually press-ganged.

The historian Snorri Sturluson is disarmingly indifferent to matters which others might consider to be grave flaws in their heroes. The royal pretender Harald Gille is summarised as "friendly, jovial, playful, unassuming, generous, accommodating and easily led". All this glosses over the fact, which Sturluson himself recounts, that he blinded and castrated a rival, hanged a bishop and died drunk in the arms of his mistress with his wife standing by.

The profits of piracy

The reason sometimes given for the sudden explosion of Viking activity abroad is that it was the result of another explosion, that of population because of uniform polygamy. Overpopulation was certainly the case in western Norway where agricultural land was so scarce. All sons, legitimate and otherwise, were entitled to equal shares of their father's inheritance, and as political power and social standing were invested in property, the aristocracy were reluctant to carve land up into small parcels. The surfeit of sons were thus encouraged to seek a fortune abroad.

Women and children often accompanied the men, but they were usually parked in fortified

PERMISSIVE ATTITUDES

Viking women made an impression abroad in a way that hints at the emancipated attitudes ascribed to them in the 20th century. In 844 a poet appointed to the court of a Norwegian king ruling in Dublin became enchanted by the queen. While keen to further their acquaintance, he was alarmed at the prospect of the king finding out. The queen reassured him that "it is not customary with us to be jealous. Our women stay with their husbands only as long as they please, and leave them whenever they choose." She seems not to have added that Viking husbands reciprocated in kind. Viking men traded wives or gave them away if they bored or displeased them.

camps while the men "harried". Occasionally the women did join in and one of them – an Amazon who rose to command her own army in Ireland – was acclaimed as the fearsome Red Maiden.

When the Vikings came across unoccupied land or, as in the Orkneys, rendered it so by annihilating the natives, they were keen to settle it. If that proved to be impractical, a raid might at least produce some slaves who could either be sold or put to good use at home. When piracy could not be made to pay, the Vikings were willing to engage in conventional trade. Profits from piracy and trade generated in

owners of guilt if a slave died through exhaustion or ill-treatment. Owners were permitted, when slaves died, to throw their children into an open grave to die from exposure. They were obliged, however, to step in and rescue the last one left alive.

> Some slaves, such as captured craftsmen, were prized, as were young women with whom masters could replenish the labour pool. Unlike in Sweden, the child of a Norwegian master and slave woman remained a slave.

Norway the nucleus of a merchant class which complemented the traditional structure of aristocratic earls, free men and thralls (or slaves). The pecking order was reflected in western Norway by *wergild*, a system which stipulated the compensation due in the event of murder. A slave was worth half the value of an ordinary peasant and a quarter of that of a landowner, who in turn was worth only a quarter of a chieftain and one-eighth of a king.

Slaves must have been worked hard, because there was a provision in law which absolved

LEFT: a confrontation from the *Frithiof Saga* by E. Tégnér, illustrated by Knut Ekwall. ABOVE: painting of a Viking selling a slave girl to a Persian merchant.

Protection money

The renewed Viking campaigns were launched from the west coast of Norway, from strongholds on the Scottish islands or from the Norwegian kingdom in Ireland, centred on a castle built in Dublin in 841 by Torgisl. The Vikings were overlords rather than settlers in Ireland, although some intermarried. Norway might still have overseas territories today if a Danish king, as we shall see, had not mortgaged the Orkney and Shetland Islands to raise money for his daughter's dowry.

The Viking raids into Europe were conducted like annual summer holidays, and year after year the fleets grew larger. An alarmed Charlemagne threw up military posts along his northern borders to guard against them. The defence of Paris against the Vikings was led by another King Charles, known as Charles the Bald. The city was attacked in 857 and sacked in 861. Charles offered one lot of Vikings 1,360kg (3,000lb) of silver to go and fight some of their compatriots instead of him. In 885 they were back, and it cost a further 318kg (700lb) of silver to get rid of them.

The most enduring Viking presence in France was in Normandy, which was named after them. Over the years the Viking armies on the Continent grew to massive proportions and were not finally driven off until 891, by the German

> The Viking kingdom on the Isle of Man lasted until 1263, when it was sold to Alexander III of Scotland along with the Western Isles. Remains of Viking forts can still be seen.

emperor Arnulf. Although geographical proximity recommended the British Isles, Vikings were active wherever the pickings looked good. At one point they laid siege to Lisbon, and they penetrated the Mediterranean as far as Constantinople. Nor did they restrict their territorial ambitions to Continental Europe. Vikings

THE VIKINGS IN BRITAIN

The Vikings attacked the British Isles in earnest from 834. The most spectacular effort was in 851 when they took 350 ships up the Thames, stopping off to capture Canterbury before storming London, only to be finally turned back by Ethelwulf at the Battle of Aclea. By 866 most of England was under their control, with only Wessex, ruled by Alfred the Great, staying independent. After the initial success of a winter campaign in 878, they were defeated by Alfred, but continued to rule large parts of England and a kingdom based in York. All further territorial ambitions were curtailed with the arrival of William the Conqueror in 1066.

sailed west to Iceland, Greenland and eventually to the American continent. As many as 20,000 Norwegians emigrated to Iceland; by the latter half of the 10th century there were no fewer than 39 petty kingdoms established there.

This surging mixture of colonialism, plunder, trade and adventurism lasted for two centuries between the fall of the Western Roman Empire and the First Crusade, and it nearly brought about the overthrow of Christianity in Europe. For those left at home, the period produced unprecedented wealth. ❑

ABOVE: a detail from a drawing by Halvfdan Egedins in Snorri Sturluson's *Sagas of the Norse Kings*. **RIGHT:** fierce mask carved on the side of the Oseberg cart.

KINGS AND CHRISTIANITY

Constant battles for the throne and the arrival of Christianity in a stubbornly pagan land were the unlikely precursors to Norway's "Period of Greatness"

With Snorri Sturluson, Norwegian history begins to speak for itself instead of relying on outsiders who observed or passed on fantastic tales about the land and its people. Sturluson's epic *Heimskringla (Sagas of the Norse Kings)* is a work of genius.

He visited Norway only twice, but, working on his remote saga island of Iceland, he compiled an almost inconceivable mass of information beginning in prehistory and continuing until 1177 (two years before he was born), by which time the Vikings had been tamed, Christianity had taken hold in Norway and the country had endured a century of civil war.

Amusing tale

Although Sturluson was himself a foreigner, he drew on the oral history of the skalds at the courts of the Norwegian kings. He was obviously a discriminating historian, although never one to exclude an amusing tale because he did not believe it. There are no fewer than 2,000 names of persons and places in his saga, and he gives his readers a vivid sense of what was happening, as it were, at home.

Sturluson introduces the Norwegian royal line in the person of Halvdan the Black, a king troubled by his inability to dream. He consulted Torleiv the Wise, who said he had suffered from the same complaint and had cured it by sleeping in a pigsty. The king followed his example "and then it always happened that he dreamed".

More prosaically, Halvdan was descended from the Swedish Ynglinger family, who ruled

LEFT: one of the oldest stave churches, Borgund.
RIGHT: Harald Hårfagre (*circa* 1200).

Sturluson's unlucky recompense for recording early Norwegian history in his famous sagas was to be put to death by the King of Norway's men in 1241.

in Uppsala. His branch had moved to Norway about a century before the Viking period, when the concept of Norway as an entity existed only in the term *Norovegr*, or North Way, the coastal stretch from Vestfold to Hålogaland.

A king dreaming in a pigsty might seem to belong to mythology rather than history, but he was real enough. The Oseberg ship unearthed in

Vestfold in 1904 proved to be that in which his mother, a Danish princess, was buried. When Halvdan died, his body was chopped up so that the pieces could be more widely distributed to bring good luck to the recipients.

Female demands

Halvdan's son, known as Harald Hårfagre (Fair Hair), was to become the first ruler of a united Norway. It was said of this subsequent unification that he was put up to it by a woman whom he wished to take to bed. Her reply to his proposition, conveyed by messengers, was that she could not possibly "waste her maiden-

hood" on a man who ruled over a kingdom that compared so unfavourably in size with those in Denmark and Sweden. His messengers nervously reported her comment but were relieved by the philosophical way in which he took it: "She has reminded me of those things", he said, "which it now seems strange I have not thought of before."

Harald advanced north from Vestfold to improve his conjugal prospects. He made contact with the powerful Earl Håkon, whose interests extended south from Trøndelag, the region surrounding what was eventually to become Trondheim. The cold facts, never as interesting as Sturluson's version, are that Harald and Håkon saw the mutual benefits of trade but first had to suppress unruly Viking bands along the coast who would have disrupted it.

Friendship with England

Harald needed assistance and set the precedent for cooperation between the Norwegian and English thrones by turning to Athelstan, King of England. As a pledge of friendship, accompanied by some mutual chicanery, he initiated what was to become another quite common practice: he sent his infant son Håkon to be fostered at Athelstan's court.

Harald's campaigns sent many of his dispossessed opponents into exile in Iceland, Shetland, the Orkney Islands and the Hebrides. The decisive battle was at Hafrsfjord, near present-day Stavanger, in southwestern Norway in AD 872. The victory made him, Sturluson says, the first king of the Norwegians, and also won him the postponed hand of the "large-minded maid", who proceeded to bear him five children. As a love story, however, the conclusion is not completely satisfactory. Sturluson writes: "They say that when he took Ragnhild the Mighty... he had divorced himself from nine other women."

Too many children

The awesome number of royal progeny was to prove a constant source of havoc in the matter of choosing a successor.

The English chronicler Roger of Hoveden wrote: "It is the custom of the kingdom of Norway... that everyone who is recognised to be the son of any King of Norway, even though he be a bastard and born of a serving wench, can claim for himself as great a right to the kingdom of Norway as the son of a wedded king and one born of a free woman. And so fighting goes on incessantly between them…"

Harald Hårfagre's umpteenth son, but the only one by Ragnhild, was the wretched Eirik Bloodaxe, who advanced his succession in AD 933 by murdering all but one of his legitimate half-brothers. The exception was Håkon, the boy who had been fostered by King Athelstan. Eirik had none of his father's authority, and the united kingdom degenerated into squabbling petty kingdoms ruled by various of Harald's bastard sons. On Håkon's return from England, Eirik was forced to flee in the opposite direction, ending up as King of Northumberland.

> When King Håkon attempted to introduce Christianity and urged his people to fast on the seventh day, they devised ploys to trick him into breaking his fast by eating horse flesh or making him drink a toast to their pagan gods.

more forcibly expressed than in Trondheim, which was then against any form of imposed authority, whether by Håkon or anyone else. Håkon urged people to "believe in one God, Christ, the son of Mary, and give up all blood offerings… and fast every seventh day". From

First Christian

Håkon den Gode (the Good) was more successful than Eirik at holding hostile factions together. Before he died (about AD 960), he was acknowledged as king over the whole coastal area from Oslo to Hålogaland. He was a notable reformer of law and defence; he was also the first Norwegian Christian king, having been baptised while in England. He imported an English bishop and missionaries with a view to converting his countrymen; but that wasn't easy. Nowhere was resistance to Christianity

LEFT: the monument at Hafrsfjord, where Harald Hårfagre first united Norway. **ABOVE:** 19th-century painting of Håkon the Good, by Peter Nicolai Arbo.

the typical audience "there was straight away a mighty uproar".

Missionaries' fate

Håkon's imported missionaries despaired. Their targets would not deviate from drinking to pagan gods morning, noon and night. They were concerned, too, that their potential parishioners would drink themselves into extinction; by instructing them in the cultivation of fruit and vegetables, they hoped to persuade them to consume at least some solids.

In the end the missionaries realised that pious sobriety was unattainable. The best they could hope for was to have the toasting converted to the Christian saints rather than pagan gods. They provided a long list of saints' names, and it seems that some of their parishioners were content to drink to them with undiminished frequency and pleasure.

The missionaries had less luck in suppressing traditions like blood sacrifices (usually animals but occasionally humans). In Trondheim the obdurate response to the message they preached was to send out four ships looking for tiresome missionaries: they "slew three priests and burned three churches; they then went home".

On the military front, Håkon was under constant threat from Eirik Bloodaxe's avenging

sons coming over from Northumberland. In defeat they turned to their uncle, the Danish king Harald Bluetooth, who wanted to regain old Danish territories at the mouth of Oslofjord. At a decisive battle in 960 Håkon was defeated and killed, paving the way for about 25 years of Danish rule, starting with 10 years under Eirik's son Harald II Gråfell.

Unlikely convert

Christianity had to wait for Olav Tryggvason, later King Olav I (AD 995–1000) and a monument in Norwegian history, for its next champion. Sturluson says he was a great sportsman who could walk on the oars along the outside of a ship, "smote equally well with both

hands" and could hurl two spears at a time. His personality changed through a chance meeting in the Scilly Isles, where he was resting after some strenuous atrocities. A wise old man took him to one side and explained the True Path. Transformed overnight, Olav returned to

> By the age of 12, Olav Tryggvason (the future King Olav I) was a full-blooded Viking, cruising the Baltic in command of five longships and later moving west to terrorise the English coast.

England "and now went about peacefully, for England was a Christian country and he was also a Christian".

He was not so peaceful when converting his compatriots at home. It is said that those who opposed him "he dealt with hard; some he slew, some he maimed and some he drove away from the land".

Olav Tryggvason was unlucky in love. In proposing marriage to the wealthy Queen Sigrid of Sweden, he insisted she would first have to be baptised. She refused, and Olav hit her with a glove. "That may well be thy death," she observed: so it proved.

She was a crafty enemy. Her wealth attracted a procession of proposals from minor kings, but King Swein Forkbeard of Denmark, son of Harald Bluetooth, was the type she preferred, and as soon as they were married she talked her husband into an alliance with the Swedish King Olav the Tax Gatherer against Norway. A great sea battle ensued, at the climax of which Olav I, who was being assisted by King Boleslav of Poland, was forced to jump overboard. He was never seen again and the victors, including the gratified queen, divided the spoils among themselves.

First saint

The man who would soon restore Norway's integrity had, like Olav Tryggvason, embarked on a naval career at 12. Olav Haraldson, later St Olav, was in England when the same Swein Forkbeard landed his forces and was responsible for the then King of England, Ethelred, being castigated evermore as "the Unready".

Olav allied himself with Ethelred in an anti-Danish war which came to a head at London

Bridge across the River Thames. The Danish forces looked, and probably felt, impregnable on their fortified bridge, but they reckoned without Olav's well-built Vikings. Having fastened ropes to the piles under the bridge, they heaved at the oars and brought the whole thing down. Several churches in England are still dedicated to St Olav for this remarkable feat.

A formidable enemy

Olav laid the foundations of the Church, even in petulant Trøndelag, but antagonised many potential rivals, none worse than the expansionist King Canute of Denmark and England, who

King Canute's kingdom fell apart after his death, the Scandinavian component re-forming into three distinct and generally hostile kingdoms. Norway was later ruled by Magnus I and then by Harald Hardråde.

Noble mercenary

Harald was typical of the young nobles who were forced to look abroad to enrich themselves. He signed up as a Varangian mercenary for the Byzantine emperor in Constantinople and saw service in Syria, Armenia, Palestine, Sicily and Africa. He was an enterprising warrior. During one siege he faked his own funeral

invaded in 1028 with overwhelming forces. Olav fled to Kiev until he learned that the earl whom Canute had appointed to rule Norway was dead. He returned to regain his kingdom but miscalculated his level of support in Trøndelag and was killed at the Battle of Stiklestad in 1030.

Olav was elevated to sainthood and his body placed in the church of St Clement in Trondheim (later to be moved). In spite of his insensitive missionary zeal, the memory of Olav kept alive the notion of a united and independent Norway through the troubled centuries ahead.

and, emulating the Trojan Horse, his men persuaded the townspeople to open the gates to admit his coffin which, they promised, would work powerful magic to their benefit.

All of this was immensely profitable because the mercenaries were entitled to keep as much treasure from captured palaces as they could grab with both hands.

Harald consolidated the kingdom of Norway. Troubled as Norwegian kings invariably were by the people of Trøndelag and its capital, Trondheim, he founded Oslo in 1048 as a counterbalance.

He provided the town with a patron saint, Hallvard, whose main claim to sainthood seems to have been the refusal of his body to sink after

LEFT: Norse marauders at Clonmacnoise, Ireland.
ABOVE: runic inscription on a Viking monument.

being thrown into a fjord with a stone tied around the neck.

Defeat in England

As King Canute's sovereignty over England (1017–35) was still within living memory, it was possibly inevitable that a confident Harald would develop similar ambitions. In any case, there had been so much toing and froing between the west coast of Norway and Britain that the affinities between them were as close, or closer, than those between scattered settlements in Norway. Harald therefore probably felt he was exercising a natural right in his inva-sion of England. His approach was from the north but his army was stopped at Stamford Bridge, in present-day North Yorkshire. Some historians argue that the English army's rush north to meet Harald weakened its ability to resist William the Conqueror when he materi-alised in the south.

After Harald's death in this abortive conquest of England, he was succeeded by his sons Magnus and Olav the Peaceful, the latter founding the towns of Bergen and Stavanger before ultimately being succeeded by his son – yet another Magnus, but in this instance unforgettably "the Bareleg" because, after visiting Scotland

(which he dearly wanted to annex), he took to wearing a kilt.

Magnus's death produced the familiar pattern of multiple heirs, in this case three simultaneously acclaimed kings who were all minors. One died young, Sigurd went off to the Holy Land to earn his title, "the Crusader", and Øystein mixed Viking raids with improvements to fisheries, harbours and roads and the establishment of monasteries. Sigurd had the throne to himself after Øystein's death, though he continued to be confronted by the complicated rules of succession throughout his reign.

These battles to occupy the Norwegian throne went on and on. There were brilliant interludes under a king like Sverre, but more

HANSEATIC HERITAGE

Norway became almost totally reliant on the Lübeck merchants as trade with the Baltic burgeoned in the 13th century. The merchants grew ever more powerful, and the trade privilege they were granted in 1278 provided them with concessions beyond even those enjoyed by native Norwegians. They were allowed to buy property in Bergen and settle there. If their demands were not met, they simply threatened to cut off corn supplies. Dependence on imported food was costing the country its independence, an unsettling vulnerability which persists in the current national obsession with subsidising agriculture (and refusing to join the EU in order to continue this policy).

often than not the succession was a squabble between the powers behind official contestants who might be children not yet six years old. With the stability of Håkon IV's 46-year reign and that of his son, Magnus the Lawmender, however, Norway achieved its 13th-century "Period of Greatness".

King Magnus the Lawmender introduced the first set of secular laws in the Western world. His law-making extended to his court, which was an unusually polite affair, with prescibed rules relating to court etiquette.

Cultural awakening

Money was spent on cathedrals and churches, the arts flourished and Norwegians assiduously studied and followed European fashions. This cultural awakening was to some extent through the creation of a wealthy upper class and the consolidation of state and Church. It was not so beneficial for the peasants; riches were not evenly spread, and the number of independent farmers dropped significantly as they defaulted on mortgages, leaving the Church and big land-owners free to repossess their land.

Norway's overseas empire contributed to a sense of greatness. Jämtland in Sweden was Norwegian, as were the Orkney and Shetland Islands. In 1262 Iceland accepted Norwegian sovereignty, as did Greenland. It was the period, too, which saw the growth of towns like Bergen with a rich trade in dried fish from the north. Foreign trade, to begin with, was mainly with Britain, but it then tilted towards the Baltic coast, especially Lübeck and the merchants of the Hanseatic League. The Germans had plenty of corn but a shortage of fish; a perfect trade balance with Norway.

The Black Death

A galley arriving in Sicily from the Far East in October 1347 brought the Black Death to Europe. Within a couple of years, a third of the European population was dead. The plague was carried north to Bergen in 1349 in the hold of an English ship. The effect on isolated Nor-wegian farming communities, especially, was catastrophic: farms which had been painfully created in conditions difficult at the best of times were reduced to waste.

The estates generating the wealth which was the necessary platform for general economic development could not be maintained while labourers dropped dead. The nobles who survived were reduced to scratching a living out of the land like everyone else. The effect of *force majeure* acting as a social leveller assumed a pattern in Norwegian history which cannot be discounted in explaining the easygoing class-lessness which remains today.

The decimation of the nobility removed the impetus behind the normally turbulent activity around the Norwegian throne. Unchallenged, two successive kings sat out long peaceful reigns, a foretaste of the comparative stability about to be foisted on Scandinavia in the late 14th century through the cunning manipulation of Margareta, widow of King Håkon, the "Lady King", who first persuaded the Danes to accept as king her son Olav, then aged five. With mother active behind the scenes, Olav also took over the crown of Norway at 10, and inherited the claim of the dispossessed Folkung dynasty in Sweden. He died suddenly at 17, and Margareta found a suitable substitute in Erik of Pomerania, her five-year-old nephew. ❑

LEFT: the Ring of Brodgar, Viking remains on the Orkney Islands off the northeastern tip of Scotland.
RIGHT: runic inscription in Orkney.

THE 400-YEAR SLEEP

A long spell under the control of its more powerful
neighbours brought Norway mixed fortunes and, ultimately,
something to celebrate – a constitution

The union of the three crowns was formalised at a coronation in the Swedish town
of Kalmar, close to the then border with
Denmark. The date, appropriately, was Trinity
Sunday, 1397. The coronation was performed
by the Danish and Swedish archbishops; Norway was represented by the Bishop of Orkney.

Although there may have been an attempt to
draft a constitution which would have united
the three realms for ever under a single king,
the rules of succession that were adopted left a
gaping loophole. Erik of Pomerania was given
full rights to dispose of the crown as he saw
fit, a recipe for reversion to the old royal uncer-
tainties after his death. In the event, the union
collapsed in his lifetime. His greatest difficulty

was paying for the court and administration in
Copenhagen. The united crown had no significant estates of its own; the nobility did and was
comparatively well off, but it was not inclined
to surrender its wealth.

Hanseatic blockade

While taking steps to undermine the authority of the nobility, Erik also tried to squeeze
the Hanseatic merchants for money. Their
response included an attack on Copenhagen,
where they were seen off by 200 examples of
a new invention, the cannon. He was less successful when the merchants retaliated with
a blockade. Those hardest hit were the nobility and wealthy merchants who, holding Erik

responsible for their misfortune, conspired to dethrone him. Erik retreated to the island of Gotland in the hope that they would change their minds. Norway would have done so, but the Danish nobles wanted to make a fresh start. The invitation went to Christian of Oldenburg, who thereupon rose from the title of count in an obscure part of Germany to found a dynasty which was to last for more than four centuries. Sweden resisted the choice, but Norway went along with it.

Christian I was almost as short of money as Erik had been. His attempts to make up shortfalls were notoriously at the expense of Norway, the weaker partner. Expected to hand over 60,000 guilders as a dowry for his daughter Margaret's marriage to the heir to the Scottish throne, he mortgaged the Orkney Islands to Scotland for 50,000. When the time came for the wedding, he was still 8,000 guilders short, and so mortgaged Shetland as well. To put 8,000 guilders into perspective, he spent three times that on a trip to Rome a few years later (which he had to borrow from the Hanseatics). The Scots gloated over the deal; not merely the trifling price, but that Margaret "deemed it a greater thing to be queen in Scotland than daughter of a king who wears three crowns".

European movements had little effect on Norway before the Reformation. Its peasant culture was deeply conservative, not to say backward, so much so that many scholars classify Norway as "medieval" until the early 16th century.

Treacherous murder

Norway's resentment at such exploitation eventually boiled over. On the turn of the 16th century, Knut Alvsson, a Swedish-Norwegian nobleman, led an uprising which created a potentially independent state stretching from Oslo to Bergen. Danish troops were sent to put a stop to it. The outcome, however, was thoroughly dishonourable. Alvsson had established himself in Akershus Castle in Oslo. He was invited to negotiate under a flag of truce and promptly murdered. In the poem *At Akershus*, Ibsen called his death a blow to Norway's heart.

LEFT: Sweden's Kalmar Castle, where the Kalmar Union was formalised. RIGHT: Queen Margaret.

Norwegian resentment at the treatment meted out to Alvsson was exacerbated by punitive taxes to pay for Christian II of Denmark's wars with the restless Swedes. Norwegians were not altogether sorry to see him toppled and bundled off into exile, but they were not ready to extend a welcome to his successor, Frederik I.

Norway was nominally Roman Catholic, and there was little interest in the forces of the Reformation which lay behind the tussle for the Danish throne. The country did not have the urban bourgeoisie who elsewhere were the first to adopt Lutheranism. It could be said that the Reformation, when it reached Norway, was

the first of the great European cultural swathes that had any real impact on the country. Feudalism passed it by (never a Norwegian knight in armour rescuing damsels in distress), as did the Renaissance. Most of rural Norway remained in the past, Christianity providing only a veneer on what were fundamentally old pagan ways.

A new leader

It was at this point that a new Norwegian leader emerged: Olav Engelbrektsson, the Archbishop of Trondheim (or Nidaros, as it was then known). Olav raised an army with a view to getting Christian II back. The exiled king was able to muster a fleet with Dutch help and in 1531 set sail for Oslo. A storm scattered the fleet so that only a small part of it went into action against Akershus Castle. The attack was futile. Christian was captured and imprisoned, and the Norwegians were forced to acclaim Frederik I as their king.

Christian II was still in prison when Frederik died and was replaced by Christian III, a Protestant. He rounded up the Danish bishops and then ordered the Archbishopric of Trondheim to be abolished, if necessary by force. Olav thought of resisting but, having weighed up the likely repercussions, fled to the Netherlands.

Any further hope of Norwegian independence was squashed by Christian III's 1536 edict

demoting the country to the status of a Danish province: "And it shall henceforth neither be nor be called a kingdom in itself." The humbled status was intended to last in perpetuity; in the event it lasted for less than 300 years, culminating not in independence but in takeover by Sweden in 1814 after Norway had become a coveted prize bobbing between its more powerful neighbours.

The loss of political sovereignty under Denmark could not obliterate Norway's separate identity at once. People went on speaking the same language as before and local administration retained many traditional features, but the creeping effects of the Reformation, and Christian III's determination to "Danicise" Norway, could not be postponed for ever.

Valuable assets

The Norwegian economy began to recover from its long decline, partly as the result of vast shoals of herring which materialised off the coast and partly because of the invention of the water-driven saw, which made exploitation of the timber forests lucrative.

Christian IV was far more positive about Norway than his predecessors. He visited the country at least 30 times, making a special trip on learning of the discovery of silver at what is now Kongsberg. He supervised the founding of the town, hence the name, which translates as "King's Mountain". He founded and attached his name to Kristiansand, as he did "Christiania" to the new city built on the site where the former Oslo had burned down in 1624. Christian ran the country as if it were a private company. He

THE DANISH INFLUENCE

By the 1530s Norway was being ruled by a Danish Protestant king, Christian III, whose influence, together with the imposition of the Reformation, was beginning to be felt among the population. Most of the new Protestant clergy were Danes. The revised version of the Bible was in Danish and so were the hymns. Official jobs were invariably given to Danes, who conducted them in the Danish language and reported back to Copenhagen. Danish noblemen also took over possessions as officers of the law in Norway, conducting (yet again) proceedings in their native Danish.

With the spread of schooling and therefore literacy in books imported from Denmark (the first printing press was late in arriving in Norway), the anomaly arose of people speaking one language among themselves but reading, albeit with characteristic Norwegian pronunciation, writing and conducting all official business in another. The result was a hybrid Dano-Norwegian and the genesis of a language dispute which has not been settled to this day *(see Language, page 74)*.

Norway won a measure of Danish respect in the latter's frequent wars with Sweden, in which the Norwegian contingents acquitted themselves well. Denmark began to realise that Norway could only be governed in its own way. Sweden was peering enviously over Denmark's shoulder at Norway. Too much antagonism could result in Norway accepting a more attractive offer of union with Sweden.

cracked down on the Hanseatic traders, making them take Norwegian citizenship, if they had not already done so of their own accord, or leave. Foreigners from other parts were encouraged to bring to Norway their skills, enterprise and, best of all, their money. Under his encouragement, former trading posts became towns in places like Drammen, Moss, Larvik, Mandal and Arendal.

The Norwegians did not always receive these foreigners with uncritical joy. In 1700, for example, a simple fight between two men in Arendal escalated into a brawl which pitched all 900 resident foreigners against everyone else. It

protected his Norwegian charges. He intervened to save peasants from the more rapacious taxes sought by Copenhagen, and he built up the Norwegian armed forces so that at Kvistrum in 1677 they were able to humiliate a far larger force of Swedes.

Hellfire and brimstone

As Norway belatedly shed the mantle of medievalism and got to grips with Protestantism, it adopted the faith as zealously as it had once defended paganism. The rural areas, especially, embraced Pietism, real hellfire-and-brimstone stuff which persuaded peasants that their

lasted a week. Nevertheless, a population which had been reduced by the Black Death to something like 180,000 picked up under Christian's energetic policies, reaching 440,000 in 1665 and nearly 900,000 by 1801.

Not all of Christian IV's successors shared his delicate touch with regard to Norwegian sensibilities. There were periods when the Danish crown was autocratically absolute, and respite depended on having an independently minded *Stattholder*, the crown agent with responsibility for Norway. Ulrik Frederik Gyldenløve, the illegitimate son of Frederik III, conscientiously

The legacy of the zealous Pietism that arrived in Norway in the 18th century can still be felt today, especially when it comes to attitudes towards alcohol.

austere existence was actually abominably frivolous. Gripped by a kind of manic fundamentalism, they despised their folk culture and, particularly in the 19th century when Pietism was still going strong, were encouraged to tear down the ornately carved, wooden stave churches. Confirmation and attendance at church on Sunday were made compulsory. Looking around them, the Pietists were appalled

---

LEFT: an old rose-painted *stue* (living room).
ABOVE: a traditional rural Norwegian Sunday.

by the realisation that in their midst, or at least within the national boundaries, there were still heathens. On the other hand, when a liberal wind blew in Copenhagen, it was also felt in Norway. For example, when Christian VII went mad the affairs of state fell into the hands of his physician, a German named Johann Friedrich Struensee. He believed in unrestricted trade and freedom of the press.

Norway was gratified to see the abolition of a trading system which placed an artificially low value on Norwegian iron imported into Denmark, whereas Danish corn exports to Norway were sold at whatever the market would bear.

Correcting the imbalance helped, but prospects of additional economic reforms ended abruptly when it was discovered that Struensee had been having an affair with Caroline Mathilde, wife of his deranged patient, and was executed.

Nelson attacks

Coexistence between Denmark and Norway was traumatised from the unlikely quarter of Napoleon Bonaparte. Britain had fallen out with Denmark (and hence Norway) over the Danish alliance with Prussia and Russia. A total of 149 Danish and Norwegian vessels were seized in British ports; in response, a Danish

ONE-MAN ENLIGHTENMENT

Against a backdrop of Pietism and the death penalty for sexual irregularity, one of the first rays of the Enlightenment shone through in the person of Ludvig Holberg. Born in Bergen, he later became a resident of Copenhagen; he was a playwright, historian and satirist (in Latin) who, according to the historian T.K. Derry, "in his own generation had no obvious superior in range of intellect except Voltaire". Holberg's impressive output included 26 plays for the newly founded Copenhagen Theatre between 1722 and 1727. It is a pithy comment on the difficulty of drawing a line between Norwegian and Danish history that both countries now claim Holberg as their own.

force marched into Hamburg and appropriated British property worth £15 million.

The British naval commander Horatio Nelson moved on Copenhagen with a powerful fleet. Danish and Norwegian crews manning a line of blockships put up a spirited defence, and after a six-hour battle Nelson urged the Danish crown prince regent to capitulate, failing which he would have to destroy the blockships "without having the power to save the brave Danes who have defended them". The prince agreed.

A few years later Napoleon insisted that Denmark-Norway join his Continental System and close their ports to British ships. A large British fleet demanded the handing-over of the Danish Navy, which Napoleon sorely needed after losing his at Trafalgar, and when this met with refusal, Copenhagen was bombarded with at least 14,000 rounds over three days. British troops occupied the capital for six weeks, after which they went home with the Danish fleet. The enormity of such an attack on what was a neutral country put Denmark and Norway firmly into Napoleon's camp, a position that required them to join him in attacking Sweden.

The division thus rendered between Sweden and Denmark was bound to have serious consequences. The inevitable began in 1810 when Sweden's King Karl XIII appointed as his heir (of all people, considering the events that had just

> On 17 May 1814 Norway became a "free, independent and an indivisible realm" as stated in the new constitution, but it would take 91 years for these words to become a reality.

the Peace of Kiel (following Napoleon's defeat at Leipzig) in 1814.

Battle for the throne

Christian Frederik was not going to surrender Norway without a struggle. He entertained the idea of getting himself popularly acclaimed as

passed) Jean-Baptiste Bernadotte, one of Napoleon's marshals. Bernadotte improved his Swedish credentials by changing his name to Karl Johan and succeeded to the throne in 1818.

Karl Johan conceived a plan whereby Russia and Britain would support Swedish claims on Norway. They agreed, with the result that Norwegian ports were blockaded to secure a "voluntary" union with Sweden. The Danish crown prince, Christian Frederik, tried to rally Norwegian loyalty. In the end, the decision did not rest in either Norwegian or Danish hands. Union between Sweden and Norway was imposed by

LEFT: the British defeat the Danish, First Battle of Copenhagen. ABOVE: Admiral Nelson. ABOVE RIGHT: Karl Johan.

king (he thought his chances best in Trondheim) but the feeling among the population at large was that the Danish line had renounced its sovereignty and the Norwegians were now entitled to choose their own king.

In April 1814, an assembly of 37 farmers, 16 businessmen and 59 bureaucrats met in Eidsvoll to decide what that future should be. The constitution they prepared was signed on 17 May, today Norway's national day. On the same day a new king was elected; it was the tenacious Christian Frederik. Sweden would have none of it. The Norwegians fought well in a one-sided contest but Christian Frederik soon had to sue for peace. Karl Johan stepped forward to occupy his double throne. ❑

UNION WITH SWEDEN

 uch artists as Ibsen, Grieg and Munch, the voice of
singly restless and independent-minded Norway
could be heard beyond its own borders

Divorce from Denmark was followed by a quarrel over the division of joint assets and liabilities. The assets were Iceland, Greenland and the Faroes, which Norway claimed were Norwegian colonies long before marriage with Denmark. The liabilities were the Danish-Norwegian national debt.

Who owed what? The Norwegian position was not only that Denmark alone should shoulder the burden, but that compensation was due to Norway for centuries of exploitation. Assuming powers granted under the Treaty of Kiel in 1814, which had brought about the union with Sweden, Karl Johan declared that Norway would pay off some of the debt. The matter of the colonies was not finally resolved until 1931, when the International Court at The Hague found in favour of Denmark.

Two kingdoms

Friction between Karl Johan and the Norwegian half of his kingdom was present right from the start: he envisaged a gradual merging of the two kingdoms, while Norway was determined to consolidate the independence ratified by the 1814 constitution.

A constitutional battle took place over a bill to abolish all noble titles and privileges. Again and again the Norwegian Storting (Parliament) presented the bill and the king refused to sanction it. The constitution said he could refuse a bill only twice; the third time it automatically became law. Karl Johan objected strongly to this limitation on his authority, which did not exist in Sweden. A fundamental principle was

at stake and the dispute was not to be resolved easily. Indeed, it remained the biggest bone of contention for the life of the union and, as much as anything else, was the cause of its eventual dissolution.

Norwegian pride was prickly. Merchant ships could fly the Norwegian flag close to home, but not in waters notoriously under the sway of North African pirates. Sweden had bought off the pirates, but the immunity extended only to the Swedish flag; if Norwegians wanted to take advantage of the immunity, then they had to switch flags.

Sweden's dogged refusal to allow Norway its own diplomatic and consular representation

---

LEFT: Eidsvoll, where the Norwegian constitution was signed on 17 May 1814. **RIGHT:** King Karl Johan XIV.

The Great Exodus

Poverty and lack of prospects at home pushed many Norwegians to emigrate to America and settle in the Midwest

One thousand years after the first Norwegian Vikings turned their longships towards the west, pushing out as far as North America, a second wave of Norwegians began to cast their eyes in the same direction. The motives of these

new emigrants were similar – lack of opportunity and poverty – but they had none of the warlike excitement of the earlier exodus. These new "Vikings" sought a place where they could work and prosper in peace rather than a place for exploration and conquest.

Yet the first emigrant boat, the 16-metre (54ft) sloop *Restauration*, crammed full with 52 crew and passengers, must have been scarcely more seaworthy than the superbly built longships. But these early "sloopers", who sailed from Stavanger in July 1825, were idealistic and highly motivated. The leader, Lars Larsen Geilane, was a Quaker, and there were members of the religious Haugeans sect among the crew. Their intention to found a classless society where they could follow their own

religion had been further encouraged when the previous year another Norwegian pioneer, Cleng Peerson, returned with reports of the promised land. The *Restauration* reached New York in October of the same year, and these farming people, mostly from Rogaland, lost no time in settling on land bought for them by Cleng Peerson at Kendall on the shores of Lake Ontario.

When the *Restauration* left in 1825, Norway's population was only 1 million, yet the next three generations sent 750,000 Norwegians to North America, reflecting a population increase at home rather than an emptying of the Norwegian countryside, though early industrialists began to campaign against such a dribbling away of potential labour. The main motive among the second and later waves of country people was good land and good farming prospects rather than religious or political repression. To be an *odelsbonde*, who owned his own land, was to be a free man and the goal of every Norwegian peasant. The American merchant fleets were also eager to make use of skilful Norwegian seamen.

The newcomers prospered, and regular letters home, reports and Norwegian visitors from the New World increased the fever. The letters were printed in newspapers all over the country, and one or two Midwestern American states began to use agents to encourage emigration.

By the middle of the 1830s new emigrants and some of the original "sloopers" had moved on to Illinois. Forty years later, their numbers had increased to more than 12,500. The 1862 Homestead Law, which granted land to immigrants, turned the early trickle into a steady flow, and Cleng Peerson founded Norwegian settlements in Iowa.

For many patriotic Norwegians it became *de rigueur* to help the expansion. The violinist Ole Bull had a well-intentioned but crashing failure with a planned settlement, "Oleana", in Pennsylvania. He was too far from his Norwegian farming roots. The soil was ungrateful, communications impossible, and Bull lost more than US$40,000.

Later, Norwegians also settled in Canada, but by the 1930s emigration had dwindled to a trickle. Yet the Norwegian influence was strong in the places where they settled. Today, the overt "Norwegian-ness" may have gone, but anyone who doubts it still exists need only read Garrison Keillor's winsome tales of life around Lake Wobegon. ❑

LEFT: this boy, aged eight, crossed the Atlantic alone in 1907 after his mother died.

abroad was not only an insult but a practical handicap, because the Norwegian merchant fleet was well on its way to becoming, by 1880, the third-largest in the world. Its far-flung crews wanted and needed a purely Norwegian diplomatic service.

Oslo once again

Karl Johan was adept at making a timely concession to court popularity, and the welcome he received on visiting Christiania in 1838 was probably sincere, as was the public grief when he died six years later. Although changing Christiania's name back to Oslo obliterated a

against the royal veto. Its leader, Johan Sverdrup, was a lawyer who worked at creating an alliance between urban radicals and wealthy farmers. Their interests were too divergent, however, and the party split, leaving room for the strong labour movement that characterised most of the 20th century. It dawned on poorer farmers

> The Norwegian peasant farmer was portrayed as the salt of the earth. The farmers' grip on the national heartstrings and purse has never been relinquished.

Danish memory, the capital was, and is, content to leave its main street named after Karl Johan.

Oskar's concessions

Karl Johan's successor, Oskar I, immediately tried to placate Norway through gestures such as his title which, locally, was changed to King of Norway and Sweden, rather than vice versa. He also agreed to the introduction of a new flag which gave equal prominence to the Swedish and Norwegian colours.

Norwegian politics in the 19th century were dominated at first by the Venstre Party, which carried the banner of separatism and rallied

and peasants, who had previously let the landowning and merchant classes get on with government, that their special interests, especially a reduction in taxes, could be advanced only if they too became involved in the political process. They were assisted by a general mood in the country of national romanticism, a Nordic adaptation of the French philosopher Rousseau's belief in the nobility of savages.

Emigration to the New World

Putting peasants on a pedestal did not ameliorate the hard facts of life. Emigration to the United States began in 1825, although statistics reveal the irony that emigration was highest when the economic conditions at home were

ABOVE: emigrants leave Stavanger for the New World.

good, and lowest when they were bad. Perhaps it was a case of being too poor in the lean times to pay the fare.

In 1882 a record 29,000 Norwegians left, and by 1910 there were more than 400,000 people of Norwegian birth in the United States, their numbers growing right the way through to World War I.

The arts flourish

The rise of nationalism throughout Europe produced in Norway an unprecedented, and subsequently unequalled, flowering of the arts. Henrik Ibsen (1828–1906) and Alexander Kiel-

land (1849–1906), giants among an extraordinarily talented assortment of writers – not forgetting composers, such as Edvard Grieg (1843–1907), and the painter Edvard Munch (1863–1944) – presented the world with a clearer insight into Norway than was available from the bestselling romantic writers.

The violin virtuoso Ole Bull was also caught up in his country's rising tide of romantic nationalism, and was another active promoter of Norwegian culture, helping revive old Norwegian folk songs and co-founding Det Norske Theater in Bergen, the first theatre in which actors spoke Norwegian, rather than Danish.

HENRIK IBSEN

Henrik Johan Ibsen was born in Skien in Telemark *(see page 206)* and was apprenticed at an early age to a chemist. His first poems, with titles such as *Resignation, Doubt* and *The Corpse's Ball*, give a clue to the majestic gloom – punctuated by delicious wit – of his later writing.

After working in the theatre in Bergen, he joined the Christiania Norske Theater in Oslo, which had been founded to promote Norwegian theatre. He fared miserably, with one failure after another, poor health and no money. In the depths of depression he began to question the deplorable position of the artist in Norwegian society, and that, ironically, put him on the road to better things. *The Pretenders*, first performed in 1864, was a success and helped him to obtain a travelling

scholarship. He went abroad, first to Italy, and did not live in Norway again for another 27 years.

The plays for which he is best remembered include *Pillars of Society*, which broke new ground in dealing with the humbug of a small provincial town. Ibsen touched on subjects that audiences were not ready for. According to the *Daily Telegraph* in London, the first overseas production of *Ghosts* was "positively abominable… a dirty act done publicly, a [lavatory] with all its doors and windows open… gross, almost putrid indecorum… crapulous stuff". George Bernard Shaw, however, summarised Ibsen's importance to the English theatre with: "The Norman Conquest was a mere nothing compared with the Norwegian Conquest."

> According to George Bernard Shaw, Ibsen's influence in England "is almost equal to the influence which three revolutions, six crusades, a couple of foreign invasions and an earthquake would produce".

Creative agitators

Henrik Ibsen and others such as the playwright and novelist Bjørnstjerne Bjørnson (1832–1910) were leading lights in agitation against Danish domination in the arts. They demanded, for example, that Danish actors should no longer

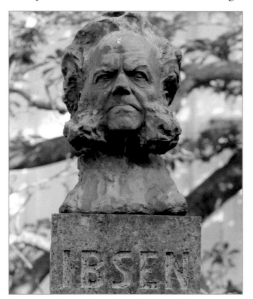

be employed on the Norwegian stage, and Bjørnson in particular championed efforts to revive the Norwegian language.

While the Norwegian element in the work of the great playwright Ludvig Holberg in the previous century could hardly be told apart from the Danish, there was no ambiguity about Ibsen's contribution. As a curious footnote, Ibsen once wrote to a friend in England saying that "there are very strong traces in me of Scotch descent. But this is only a feeling – perhaps only a wish that it were so."

LEFT: an early drawing of Oslo's Storting (Parliament).
ABOVE: bust of the playwright Henrik Ibsen.
ABOVE RIGHT: King Oskar. II.

Battle of wills

Ibsen's strong sense of national identity was mirrored in the political events swirling around him. Problems within the union with Sweden came to a head in 1905 over the long-running dispute about diplomatic representation. The government wanted its own consular service; King Oskar II refused.

The government then argued that, if it resigned and the king was unable to obtain an alternative government, his royal power would effectively have lapsed. It would then revert to the Storting, which would choose a new king. The Storting agreed to this plan.

Oskar was hurt and the Swedish government outraged. Neither would have been placated by a plebiscite which showed 368,208 in favour of breaking away from Sweden and only 184 against. The "compromise" reached in 1905 was a surrender to Norwegian demands: Oskar's abdication and Norway's independence. The king's parting shot was that no member of his house would be allowed to accept the vacated throne even if it were offered. This was only in part petulance. Oskar was privately convinced that an independent Norway was bound to collapse and whoever was then king would thus be discredited. When that happened, an unsullied member of his house would, of course, be standing by to answer the call. The call never came. ❑

AN INDEPENDENT, MODERN COUNTRY

Invaded by Germany, then caught up in the Cold War, Norway has passed through difficult times to emerge as an international peace-broker

The prime minister who led Norway to independence was Christian Michelsen, a Bergen solicitor who founded one of the biggest shipping companies in Norway and was by 1903 a member of the government. In the meantime, he had formed a breakaway group in Bergen of "liberals" from the radical left. Michelsen's initial modest aim was to settle the issue of whether Norway should have its own consuls abroad, which would finally destroy the union with Sweden; but by 1904 he was warning the Swedes not to assume that if negotiations failed this time, they could be resumed.

Michelsen at the helm

Michelsen had recognised the way Norwegian public opinion was running and the support the cause was getting from such famous Norwegians as the explorer Fridtjof Nansen (who later became Norwegian Ambassador in London) and the writer Bjørnstjerne Bjørnson. Soon

NANSEN AND THE LEAGUE

During World War I the Scandinavian monarchs met to discuss and set up committees to review the position of neutral countries when hostilities ceased. Under Fridtjof Nansen, polar explorer turned diplomat, Norway formed an Association for the League of Nations and drafted a potential constitution. But, as the war ended, the Great Powers were not inclined to take much notice of mere neutrals. Instead, they themselves laid down the rules and allowed the neutral countries just two months after the League was founded to seek membership.

Norway, temperamentally against alliances, was fiercely divided, and it was not until 1920 that the Storting finally voted for membership of the League of Nations. This was

Norway's first real move into internationalism. In fact, 16 of the Storting's 20 votes against membership of the League had come from the steadily growing Labour Party, which at the time took most of its principles and goals from the ideas behind the Russian Revolution.

Nansen, who had been so influential in the struggle for Norwegian independence, now had international links to the US, the Soviet Union and elsewhere, and became active in the League, particularly in the slow repatriation of nearly half a million prisoners-of-war from Russia. Later, he donated his own Nobel Peace Prize money for similar work for Russian and Armenian refugees. He was still working on this at the time of his death in 1930.

Michelsen was heading a cabinet that included ministers from a wide range of parties and of many shades of opinion.

With independence established in 1905 and King Haakon VII on the throne, Michelsen quickly left the stormy waters of politics for a calmer and more profitable life in his shipping business, though he remained an active elder statesman until his death in 1925.

No foreign policy

In the long years of struggle, Bjørnson had claimed that "the foreign policy of Norway should be to have no foreign policy", and imme-

willing to pay top prices for all the fish Norway could supply, which attracted British attention and led to a secret agreement, backed by the threat to cut off supplies of British oil and coal, under which Britain would buy most of the fish itself. Norway, in return, would not export vital copper pyrites to Germany, but otherwise it was free to trade with both sides.

Those lucky enough to get a share of this trade, and of the domestic black market, flaunted their overnight fortunes in such a way that workers on fixed wages, which were forever falling behind rampant inflation, became rebellious. Employers retaliated with lockouts,

diately after independence, the aim of all parties was to avoid entanglement in the affairs of the Great Powers. But, despite Norway's determined neutrality, World War I had the ironic effect of throwing it and Sweden back into one another's arms. "A new union, not of the old sort, but a union of heartfelt understanding," was the Swedish king's description, "to maintain the neutrality of the respective kingdoms in relation to all the belligerent powers."

Norway did well out of its neutrality, at least for the first two years of the war. Germany was

PRECEDING PAGES: paraglider with the Norwegian flag. **LEFT:** King Haakon VII. **ABOVE:** the royal family with their ski instructor.

and the government was forced to introduce compulsory arbitration.

Wartime losses

German submarine warfare put a damper on profiteering. Most of the Norwegian merchant fleet was under charter to Britain, and by the end of the war half of it, together with 2,000 crew members, was lost. In absolute terms only Britain lost more of its shipping. The intervention of the United States also made matters worse. The Americans demanded big cuts in trade with Germany before agreeing to make supplies available to Norway.

At the end of World War I the neutral countries had little say in deciding the terms of peace. Despite its heavy maritime losses the Norwegian Merchant Navy received no compensation in the shape of ships from the confiscated German Navy, and it was another 10 years before injured seamen and the families of those killed received any form of compensation from the German government.

Devised by Fridtjof Nansen, the Nansen "passport" offered those people who had been made stateless by World War I a means of official identification.

The steadily growing Labour Party became more revolutionary in its beliefs, and passed a resolution reserving the right to use "revolutionary action in the struggle for the economic liberation of the working classes". The point having been made, militancy declined and by the end of the decade the party had turned its attention back to parliamentary rule. In the 1927 elections, in spite of fragmentation, it became the biggest party in the Storting.

The Wall Street crash of 1929 compounded the economic misery. A third of all trade unionists were already out of work when employers tried to reduce wages which, in spite of nearly

The rise of Labour

Although Norway was one of the creditor nations when the war ended, the cavalier business atmosphere of the war years carried over as financial recklessness, if not ignorance. In very short order the country was further into debt than it had so recently been in credit.

By 1921 conditions had deteriorated into a full-blown economic depression, with more than a million tonnes of shipping laid up, free-spending local authorities in difficulty and, unthinkably to Norwegians, one of the biggest banks going bankrupt in spite of receiving secret state support.

Storms and controversies over prohibition caused the downfall of three different cabinets.

a decade of economic turmoil, were still very high compared to most European countries.

A lockout at Norsk Hydro produced not only the most notorious incident in the history of Norwegian industrial relations (police and troops fighting demonstrators), but also the rise to prominence of a figure as shameful in Norwegian memory as anyone since Eirik Bloodaxe. The defence minister who ordered in the troops was Vidkun Quisling, and he was soon accusing Labour of plotting an armed revolution. Quisling was largely discredited in his own country by 1939. At that time he was in Berlin for reasons that were soon to become very clear.

By 1933, the economic crisis was so bad that the unlikely alliance of the Labour Party with the Agrarian (Farmers') Party put a Labour prime minister into power. He was Johan Nygaardsvold, who had had lengthy experience in the Storting. He was prime minister from 1935 and had a direct responsibility for creating employment. By 1939, the average day's wage had risen by 15 percent.

Precarious neutrality

When World War II broke out in September 1939 Norway proclaimed immediate neutrality, but had taken almost no precautions to defend itself. Perhaps Nygaardsvold was too immersed in his economic renaissance. He remained

prime minister until 1945, but in the recriminations and resultant inquiry that followed the end of the war, he was deemed partly to blame for not having made adequate preparations when the threat of conflict loomed.

The first warning signs came from the Allied side, with Britain complaining that its ships were being sunk by Germany in Norwegian territorial waters. Also, German ships were being given free access to strategic iron ore from the port of Narvik. The ancient Norwegian fleet

LEFT: the meeting between Vidkun Quisling and Adolf Hitler prior to World War II.
ABOVE: strategic map from World War II.
ABOVE RIGHT: the struggle for Narvik, 1941.

was in no position to keep territorial waters neutral, so the British suggested mining them.

The dilemma was highlighted by the *Altmark* affair. The *Altmark*, an auxiliary to the battleship *Graf Spee*, was on its way to Germany with 300 captured British seamen when it sought refuge in Norwegian waters near Egersund. The British Royal Navy was alerted to its presence and charged into the fjord to rescue the men while two small Norwegian vessels looked on, making vain protests. The Norwegian government complained to Britain about violation of its neutrality. The British government asked why Norway had been unable to prevent German abuse of its neutral waters, and Germany posed the same question, but the other way round.

Invasion by sea

Britain unilaterally began laying mines along the Norwegian coastline and, on the very day Norway lodged a protest – 8 April 1940 – German forces were on the high seas bound for Norway. Once the invasion was under way, the German minister in Oslo sent a note to say that Germany was only occupying a few strategic points to keep the British out.

At last the Norwegian government woke up to what was going on. The German heavy cruiser *Blücher* was sunk by the Oscarsborg fortress in the Oslo fjord near Drøbak, and two

The Heroes of Telemark

The Norwegian Resistance fought the Nazis during World War II, but it was the Heroes of Telemark who captured the people's imagination

The most celebrated act of resistance in Norway during World War II was the sabotage of the Vemork heavy-water plant at Rjukan, in Telemark, in February 1943. No visitor to Rjukan, dwarfed and darkened by mountains all round, could fail to be awed by the audacity of the saboteurs. More importantly, the production of heavy water in the plant, if it had not been stopped, could conceivably have aided the German development of an atomic bomb. The operation was originally planned for a joint force of Norwegian volunteers and British commandos in two towed gliders. It ended disastrously when both gliders and one of the aircraft towing them crashed 160km (100 miles) from Rjukan.

The next attempt was an all-Norwegian affair. "Gunnerside", the code name for six men who had been trained in Scotland, parachuted onto a frozen lake where they were supposed to join up with "Swallow", an advance party on the ground. The first person they bumped into was a reindeer-hunter. He was later released with food and money on the promise that he would reveal nothing. Once the parties had linked up, they skied to the ridge above Rjukan for the perilous descent on foot. They slithered down, up to their waists in snow. Just after midnight, the covering party took up positions while the six-man demolition team cut a chain on the gates and crept forward to the basement of the concrete building where the most vital equipment and the heavy-water storage tanks were located. All wore British uniforms and agreed that no lights would be carried; weapons would be unloaded to avoid the accidental discharge of arms, and anyone captured would take his own life.

As the basement was locked, the best way in appeared to be a funnel carrying cables and piping. Two of the men went through it. The solitary Norwegian guard was astonished, but agreed to lead them to vital components.

"I had placed half the charges in position when there was a crash of broken glass behind me," one of the pair wrote later. The other members of the team, not realising that their leaders had managed to get in, had decided to smash in through a window. With the rest of the charges laid, the six began a rapid withdrawal. They were nonplussed by the cooperative guard who, understandably getting out as well while the going was good, implored to be let in again. He had forgotten his glasses! The request was granted, but the delay meant that the party had only gone a few yards when there was what members later variously described as "a cataclysmic explosion" and "a tiny, insignificant pop".

Five members of the parachute team reached Sweden after a 400km (250-mile) journey on skis in indescribably difficult conditions; the sixth stayed on in the area for another year before eventually he was able to escape. In due course he turned up in Britain, reporting for further duties. ❏

LEFT: Kirk Douglas in the film *The Heroes of Telemark*.
ABOVE: monument to the resistance fighters at Rjukan.

creaking Norwegian destroyers boldly took on a much larger German force at Narvik.

The Storting granted the government full powers "to take whatever decisions might be necessary to ensure the best interests of the country", the point on which many a debate would later hinge. On 10 April the Germans

> *Max Manus (1914–96) was a Norwegian Resistance fighter who earned fame as a saboteur during World War II. His life became the subject of a film of the same name that was a huge box-office success.*

showed their hand. Quisling, whose National Unity Party commanded all of 1.8 percent of the electorate, was their choice as new prime minister. The government, which had moved itself from Oslo to Trysil, repeatedly refused to comply, and its defiance was repaid with a German bombing attack on the meeting place.

Help from the Allies

Norway's only hope against such lopsided odds lay in the Allies. From Britain's point of view, Narvik was the key because of the iron-ore traffic. The British Royal Navy went into action against German naval units in the area and destroyed them. A combined force of Norwegians, British, French and Poles fought to regain control of the city itself and on 28 May succeeded in doing so.

Earlier, on 14 and 15 April, other Allied troops had landed near Trondheim. They were joined by small Norwegian units. They put up a plucky fight but, practically without any air cover against the Luftwaffe, took a pasting from above. Towns where there was a British presence were bombed to ruin: Åndalsnes, Namsos, Steinkjer and Mosjøen.

The fight for Norway was overshadowed by the German steamroller in Western Europe and, with what were seen to be greater needs there, the Allied forces withdrew, leaving Norway alone.

The king and government, evacuated to the north and ready to fight on, decided to decamp to Britain; on 7 June 1940 they boarded a British cruiser.

RIGHT: the traitor Vidkun Quisling inspecting German troops in Berlin.

Reprisals begin

A Nazi, Josef Terboven, was despatched to Norway as Reichskommissar. Quisling was appalled; he had expected to be appointed Führer, in which capacity he would then conclude peace with Germany and mobilise Norwegian forces on its side.

Terboven had little time for Quisling, but the latter had friends in Berlin who arranged to have him appointed "minister president". As such, Quisling ordered all children between the ages of 10 and 18 to join his version of the Hitler Youth. His plans for the Nazification of the civil service, courts, all professional bodies

and trade unions were in every instance fiercely rejected. Resistance met with grim reprisals. Two trade union leaders, Viggo Hansteen and Rolf Wickstrøm, were shot; the rector of Oslo University was arrested. A steady flow of prisoners, including 1,300 uncooperative teachers, arrived at Grini, the prison camp established outside Oslo.

The most summary reprisals were meted out to members of the military underground, Milorg, a nucleus of survivors of the 1940 fighting augmented by volunteers and armed by clandestine shipments from Britain.

Telavåg, a village near Bergen, was razed to the ground when the Germans discovered it to be an assembly point for a clandestine ferry

> *During World War II, the old Viking character could be seen in the number of small boats that regularly made the crossing between Shetland and Norway, keeping links open with the exiled king and government in Britain.*

service known as the "Shetland Bus", which operated between Norway and Britain. The village men were deported to Germany, the women and children interned. A group of 18 men waiting in Ålesund for the trip to Britain were found and shot.

held in Oslo. It was still going strong a week later when Crown Prince Olav returned, five years to the day after his reluctant departure.

Cleaning up after the war concentrated on Quisling's prosecution. Charges were brought against 50,000 people, many for petty crimes rather than full-scale collaboration. The courts were not considered unduly harsh, perhaps sensing that participation in Quisling's so-called "NS" would remain a stigma. Some 25 were executed, including Quisling and two of his ministers.

After that necessary purging, Norway's most pressing needs were to replace what had been

Celebration party

The final chapter of the occupation was played out by German troops retreating from Finland through Finnmark in northern Norway. They adopted a scorched-earth policy which utterly destroyed many towns and villages. The inhabitants were herded into fishing boats to find their own way to the south.

The Germans were still very strong in Norway while their forces elsewhere capitulated – the army alone numbered 350,000. Fears that the whole country might be put to the torch were laid to rest only when they surrendered on 7 May 1945. The gates of Grini were thrown open and thousands streamed out to join what was undoubtedly the biggest street party ever

destroyed during the war, and to modernise and expand industry and the economy. The whole of northern Norway had been so heavily devastated that in some cases areas of hasty rebuilding are only today being replaced, and many of the small northern towns still have an austere anonymity about them.

Rising standards

Fast economic expansion and many crash programmes led to large-scale investment and over-employment, but it provided a rising standard

Above: Crown Prince Olav (later King Olav V) returns to Norway from exile at the end of the war.
Right: Oslo's Nobel Peace Center.

of living that climbed faster and further than that of most countries in Europe. By the early 1960s Norway used more electricity per head than any other country in the world, and only three people in every thousand in remote areas had no supply. The merchant marine had made good its wartime shipping losses by 1949 and tonnage tripled within 15 years.

Then fortunes changed quickly when oil was found in the North Sea, and by the 1970s Norway was almost overwhelmed by the riches it was receiving from the oil industry.

All this went along with over 20 years of socialist government, which introduced com-prehensive social-welfare services, Scandinavian-style, and much state control of industry. But this was no far-left Labour Party in the style of its post-World War I predecessors, and many shared its belief in an equal society and care for all. In keeping with similar parties in Sweden and Denmark, post-war Norwegian social-

> *As NATO's most northeasterly outpost, with a short 196km (122-mile) border with Russia, Norway inevitably walked a tightrope between the superpowers.*

AN OFF-THE-SHELF MONARCHY

Imported from Denmark in 1905, Norway's popular monarchy has passed through a number of trials on its way to acceptance by the nation. The various monarchs, from Haakon VII to the current king, Harald V, have managed to win their people's heart with their unassuming manner and their love of sport. Olav V, although born in England, proved he felt at home in Norway by winning prizes on the Holmenkollen ski jump (as daunting a test of Norwegian authenticity as could be), and Harald V has made a name for himself as a competitive sailor, something that went down well in a nation of seafarers.

King Harald married a commoner, Sonja Haraldsen (the current Queen Sonja), and Crown Prince Haakon did the same in 2001 when he controversially married an unwed mother and former waitress, Mette-Marit Tjessem Høiby. Like his father, Haakon chose to "marry the girl he loves rather than love the girl he marries".

In 2002, Princess Märtha Louise also married a commoner, author Ari Behn, reinforcing, once again, the national unity symbolised by the royal family.

Like the flag and the 17th of May celebrations, the Norwegian monarchy symbolises independence from the life under the rule of first Denmark and then Sweden. What often appears to be fervent nationalism is, in fact, no more than national pride and a desire to hold on to a hard-earned self-determination.

ism had been middle-of-the-road, led first by Einar Gerhardsen, who had been a prominent Resistance worker, then Oscar Torp, and Trygve Bratteli.

In recent years, the best-known Norwegian prime minister, ranking high in international esteem, has been Gro Harlem Brundtland. She was appointed prime minister for the first time in 1981. That tenure was short, lasting only until a historic conservative-led victory at the polls that autumn; but at 41 she was the youngest person ever to hold the office, and the first woman. In total, she held the post for more than 10 years before stepping down in 1996. In

1998 she became Director-General of the World Health Organiszation. In 2001, a new centre-right coalition won the national election, followed by a centre-left coalition in 2006, This centre-left "red-green" coalition was led by Jens Stoltenberg (Labour Party), who was re-elected for a second mandate in September 2009.

Maintaining independence

In recent years Norway has been planning for the future, often ambitiously. The state's investment in big road-building projects is one example. Nothing has deterred Norwegian engineers from tackling the harsh terrain, whether it's digging the longest tunnel in the world, the Laerdal Tunnel *(see page 267)*, or building bridges (no fewer than eight) along Atlanterhavsveien (the Atlantic Road).

Oslo has been making international headlines of late, and attracting visitors with a mix of inspiring new architecture *(see page 126)*, a growing number of music events and festivals (the highlight of which was possibly its successful hosting of the Eurovision Song Contest in May 2009), revamped shopping and dining, and more.

Gordon Ramsay officiating as guest of honour at the Gladmat festival in Stavanger in 2010, and President Barack Obama's visit in January for the awarding of the Nobel Peace Prize cere-

> In 2001, Norway signed the Schengen Agreement allowing citizens of other Schengen countries to travel without the need for passports.

mony, are telltale signs that Norway now wants to play with the big boys.

But Norwegians have also started thinking about new challenges lying ahead, such as what to do now the oil is running out; issues related to the environment have often been at the forefront of the debate, as with the proposed drilling for oil off the coast of the Lofoten Islands, or the building of high-power electric cable lines in the Hardangerfjord area. Both are areas of outstanding beauty, and popular tourist destinations, and the debate continues to divide. ❑

PEACEKEEPERS

In 1945 Norway was one of the founding signatories of the United Nations, and a former Norwegian foreign minister, Trygve Lie, became its first secretary-general. Lie held the office during the first hopeful years and continued to do so into the Korean War, in which United Nations troops took an active fighting role for the first and last time. Norway provided and staffed a field hospital in Korea. Since then some 32,000 Norwegians have worn a UN blue beret. Norway has continued its commitment to internationalism and peace, notably as broker in the 1993 Israeli-Palestinian peace proposals. It concentrates on human rights, humanitarian help and environmental issues.

LEFT: Mother Teresa receiving the Nobel Peace Prize in 1979.

Black Gold

The discovery of oil and gas in the North Sea has made Norway rich, but resources won't last and plans are being made for the future

I t became clear in the 1970s that vast oil and gas riches lay beneath the ocean floor off the Norwegian coast, and yet the full extent of these resources is still being determined today. Current estimates predict that without major new oil discoveries oil production will gradually decline this century, but as a major gas exporter Norway can count on a longer perspective.

It all started in 1962 when, prompted by a gas find off Holland, the American Phillips oil company acquired the right to explore in Norwegian waters. Other companies soon followed. After clarification of legal problems and territorial rights with Denmark and Britain, drilling started in earnest in 1966. Four years later, Phillips announced the discovery of a giant oil field, Ekofisk. The 1970s saw a series of major discoveries: French Elf found Frigg; American Mobil found the world's largest offshore oilfield, Statfjord; Shell confirmed the giant Troll gas field off Bergen. The Norwegians learned quickly, and two Norwegian oil companies joined the fray. The state-owned Statoil discovered Gullfaks, and the semi-nationalised Norsk Hydro became the operator at Oseberg.

Oil production at the Ekofisk field started modestly from a floating rig in 1971. Permanent installations and a pipeline to Teesside in northeast England were commissioned in 1975. By the end of the 1970s Norway had built a gas-processing plant at Kårstø, near Stavanger, and was exporting dry gas to the rest of Continental Europe, and the Norwegian shipbuilding industry was entering a golden age as far as contracts were concerned.

After several years of discussing production levels, and with low oil prices, the offshore industry was finally forced into a 3 percent production cut, with the hope that this would help oil prices rise once again.

International terrorism and wars later sent oil prices skyrocketing, fuelling a new exploration boom that focused attention on the Barents Sea. Norwegian companies were keen to team up with

ABOVE RIGHT: oil drilling platform.

Russian oil interests in the development of the Stockman field, while massive investment was also made in the Snow White field and its ground facilities at Hammerfest. Today, the big question is whether or not to look for oil off the coast of the Lofoten Islands, an area of stunning natural beauty and a popular tourist destination.

The Norwegian state has three sources of revenue from its offshore industry: taxes and duties levied on the oil companies; the state's direct economic involvement; and share dividends from its ownership stakes in Statoil and Norsk Hydro. Since the late 1990s, much of Norway's oil revenue has been stashed into what initially was called the

state's Oil Investment Fund (now the Government's Pension Fund). By 2006, its value equalled that of all the real estate on Manhattan, and it had become a serious player in international stock and bond markets. As of March 2010, its value is estimated at NKr 2.763 trillion (US$443 billion). With 1.78 percent of European stocks, it is the largest stock owner in Europe. The money is earmarked for future pension demands, a key concern in a country that is among the most expensive in the world.

Despite Norway's supplies of oil and gas, much of it is exported, and the country remains concerned about a looming energy crisis. Heavy investment is being made in solar power and heat pumps, and in wind energy, not least because hydroelectric plants often suffer from a lack of rain. ❑

WHO ARE THE NORWEGIANS?

Ask a visitor what defines a Norwegian and you might get a general description of a Scandinavian. While some of the stereotypes ring true, differences abound

One character in a Hans Christian Andersen story proclaims: "I'm a Norwegian. And when I say I'm Norwegian, I think I've said enough. I'm as firm in my foundations as the ancient mountains of old Norway… It thrills me to the marrow to think what I am, and let my thoughts ring out in words of granite."

Andersen was, of course, a Dane, and he was teasing the Norwegians, as their Scandinavian neighbours are apt to do. In much the same way as Italians are satirically reduced to being tearful opera and ice-cream fiends, and Frenchmen become obtuse philosophers in garlic necklaces, so the typical Norwegian has often been portrayed as a simple, stubborn peasant who needs a comforting pat on the head.

Naturally, Norwegians see themselves rather differently. A Gallup poll once asked 200 people from each of 12 countries to rank themselves in terms of culture, food, living standards, beauty, *joie de vivre* and national pride. The Norwegians gave themselves top marks in virtually every category. This sweeping victory for the home side was surpassed only by the conceit of the American entry.

Generous hospitality

The Norwegian character is, of course, far more complex than Andersen would allow or Gallup could measure. It is sometimes said that Norwegians are xenophobic. While this may be an exaggeration, it is often the case that they do not accept outside criticism. Yet the hospitality shown towards foreign visitors far exceeds the

demands of mere good manners. An English visitor arriving late was whisked off spontaneously to a wedding party in Oslo. As the only foreigner among 200 guests, he was disarmed when the bride's father, advised of his surprise presence, gave away his daughter in English. Although the younger Norwegian guests were, as usual, fluent in English, some older ones were left in the dark, but they thoroughly approved of the gesture.

A welcome candle

Other signs of welcome are given without thinking. A visitor in the house is the signal for lighting candles, probably a throwback to the

---

PRECEDING PAGES: national pride at the Holmenkollen ski jump. **LEFT:** Royal Guardsmen outside the Royal Palace. **RIGHT:** National Day parade.

> Peer Gynt, Ibsen's (anti-) hero, is seen as a satire of the Norwegian character, displaying weaknesses such as self-delusion. The play's popularity says much about Norwegians' ability to laugh at themselves.

days when, compounded by the long hours of winter darkness, houses shuttered against the cold were rather gloomy. Most of Norway's population was thinly scattered across a vast landscape in a patchwork of tiny communities, so visitors invariably arrived after a long

and exhausting journey, sometimes on skis. The assumption was that they arrived hungry, and restorative food and drink still appear as if by magic.

Ten Commandments (Jante Law)

The more enigmatic aspects of the Norwegian psyche – including the Nordic gloom which descends after a drink too many – have been famously scrutinised by native Henrik Ibsen. He was brought up in small communities and, during a long exile, turned his critical eye on the experience. One of the themes running through his writings is the double-edged nature of life in

A MULTICULTURAL SOCIETY

Norway is an increasingly multicultural society. As of 2009, there were 459,000 immigrants and 93,000 Norwegian-born citizens with immigrant parents living in Norway. Together they represent 11.4 percent of Norway's population. Oslo has the largest proportion of immigrants (27 percent), with 160,500 people. Poles have recently overtaken the Swedes as the largest immigrant group in Norway, followed by Pakistanis, Iraqis and Somalis.

Until the 1960s, immigration to Norway had mainly consisted of Europeans and people from other Nordic countries. The first labour migrants arrived from Pakistan in the 1960s, followed in the 1970s by Thai, Filipino and Russian women who had married Norwegian men, and refugees

from developing countries such as Chile and Vietnam. The mid-1980s saw an increase in asylum-seekers from countries such as Iran and Sri Lanka, joined by war refugees from the Balkans in the 1990s and, since the end of that decade, from Iraq, Somalia and Afghanistan.

The arrival of these immigrants has not been without its challenges (the debate about Muslim women wearing the *hijab*, for example, has received extensive coverage in the Norwegian press of late), but it has also been a force for change and, as a result, Norway is a more tolerant society than in the past. Their influence can also be felt in the media, on the cultural scene and in the culinary diversity on offer, in both supermarkets and restaurants.

such a community: mutual support in adversity weighed against a suffocating lack of privacy.

The lesser-known Aksel Sandemose wrote Ten Commandments (Jante Law) for village life, the essence being humility bordering on self-abasement. They included: "You must not think that you are worth anything; you must not think that you are better than anyone else; you must not think yourself capable of anything worthwhile; and you must not think that you are in any way exceptional."

Jingoistic chest-pounding of the sort noted by Hans Christian Andersen is derived to some extent from Norway's peculiar position as both the imperial powers in the 19th century. Having been relegated to a back seat in Scandinavian affairs for hundreds of years, these distant descendants of the illustrious Vikings need to pinch themselves – or blow a trumpet – as if they nervously expect to find that their independence was a cruel dream.

Free to show the flag

Well-deserved national pride makes Norwegians ardent flag-wavers. This could be construed as a rude gesture to the Swedes who, under the union, decided when, where and how the Norwegian colours were to be shown in

one of the oldest, if not the oldest, nation in Europe and at the same time one of the youngest. It is the oldest in the sense that the Norwegians can trace an unbroken line of descent from people who inhabited their territory in prehistoric times, a homogeneity whose origins predate the beginnings of Western civilisation in the Aegean.

Yet the present state of Norway was reconstituted only in 1905, which makes it younger than many of the junior members in the United Nations, themselves pasted together by

Many houses have flagpoles and every home possesses a flag which is hoisted on the slightest pretext, if only to indicate that the owner is in residence.

foreign waters, relegating them to a mere patch on a much larger Swedish flag. The flag flown on Norwegian ships was, like separate consular representation and the establishment of a national bank, a perennial bone of contention before independence.

Their dignity as a sovereign state is not to be trivialised. The Swedish king who reluctantly oversaw Norway's independence predicted that

FAR LEFT AND LEFT: part of a multicultural society in Bergen, the second-largest city in Norway. **ABOVE:** ski jumping in Holmenkollen.

Language

Did you know that Norway has three official languages? This has created problems over the years as well as enriching the cultural scene

Bokmål? Nynorsk? Sami? Language was a burning issue in Norwegian politics until the 1950s, even causing a prime minister to resign in 1912. The long-running controversy started as a form of agitation against Danish rule, throughout which Danish was the language of the civil service, schools and the Church. For a long time after the Reformation the revised Bible was available only in Danish. Denmark got its first printing press in 1480 but Norway had to wait until 1643, so books were imported and in Danish.

When reading aloud, Norwegians modified standard Danish through the use of their own pronunciation and intonation, eventually producing the hybrid known as bokmål (book language).

The 19th-century nationalists saw it as fundamentally Danish and wanted a national language that was authentically Norwegian. Unfortunately, there was no single Norwegian substitute as the language had developed many distinct dialects.

The early language reformers – including Ivar Aasen and Knut Knudsen, the latter a schoolmaster

driven by his pupils' frustration in trying to decipher Danish spelling – concentrated on developing a composite. They worked on what became known as landsmål or nynorsk, but their efforts were not unreservedly welcomed. Danish was the language of society and the theatre, and if Norwegian had to be spoken, a "Danicised" pronunciation was fashionable. These tendencies eroded as intellectuals like Ibsen lent respectability to the campaign for the revival of a purely Norwegian language.

In 1929 bokmål and nynorsk were recognised as dual official languages, the hope being that they would drift towards a blend to be known as samnorsk. Progress towards samnorsk was given a nudge in the 1950s with a proposal to have school textbooks converted into it. There was such an outcry, however, that the government backed down. Subsequent policy has been to treat the two languages even-handedly, still hoping that they will one day converge. But nynorsk is today used by only about 15 percent of Norwegian primary school children. As a language based on rural culture, nynorsk suffered because of 20th-century urbanisation, and today, in spite of attempts to shore it up through radio and television, it is losing ground to bokmål, although nynorsk literature remains popular.

Educated speech is distinctly that of the southeast, although that does not prevent country-dwellers on a visit to the capital, say, from laying on their regional accents thick for effect. The Bergensere, at the heart of the nynorsk area, are certainly proud of their individualistic tongue.

The third language, Sami (Northern Sami, the most widely spoken of the Sami languages), is currently used by nearly 25,000 people in Scandinavia, most of whom live in Finnmark and Troms in northern Norway (see The Sami, page 83). ❑

LEFT AND ABOVE: fortunately you don't need to know Norwegian to get by, as most Norwegians speak English.

bureaucratic incompetence would soon have Norwegians begging to be returned to the fold. The response, even now, is a reluctance to admit (to outsiders) that they are capable of making a mistake.

As long as authority was vested in foreigners, Norwegians did not regard it too highly. On assuming it themselves, authority took on the aura of divine right before which loyal citizens should willingly prostrate themselves. Norwegian history is full of swings from one extreme to another. Pagans who held out against Christianity until a surprisingly late date became, and in some cases remain, doggedly fundamen-

> *The klem, a typically Norwegian embrace that consists of putting your arms round someone while simultaneously touching cheeks, but not kissing, is reserved for good friends, and is a common way of showing one's affection.*

that sober Norwegians aren't big on small talk. They are, however, open and considerate people. And they are polite, too, even if they do not say *takk* (thank you) as frequently as English-speaking people, and if there is no word in their language for "please". The only thing remotely

talist after seeing the light. And a nation once thought in danger of drinking itself to death has by no means buried the bottle, even if alcohol consumption is now kept mainly for the weekend and Norwegians are adopting more Continental customs – wine sales are up, hard liquor down.

Friendships worth forging

While drinking customs are becoming a little more moderate, there's no question that Norwegians become less reserved after a *skål* or two. Foreigners moving to Norway discover quickly

ABOVE: women are more economically independent in Norway than in most other European countries.

WOMEN'S EQUALITY

Norway's main strategy in achieving gender equality has been to strengthen women's economic independence through increasing their labour market participation, with a welfare system ensuring childcare and parental leave for all. Today, the percentage of women in the workforce is among the highest in Europe. Norway was the first country to appoint a Gender Equality Ombudsman, and its governments have always had a high proportion of women ministers. Women increasingly occupy top positions in business (40 percent of board members in public limited companies are women), but at grassroots level there are still more women than men in low-paid employment.

unruly in Norwegian manners occurs in the busy streets of Oslo. People jostle each other with impunity, as they tend to do in most big cities the world over: don't be offended if you don't get an apology after someone bumps into you – as long as it's gentle. Of more concern are the mad darts people make across streets, without regard for traffic lights.

Although young people tend to be a lot less formal than their parents, Norwegians do still go about life with some surprisingly rigid rules of behaviour. And everyone, young or old, likes to dress up, and finds an excuse to do so for any occasion – 17 May being the biggest one.

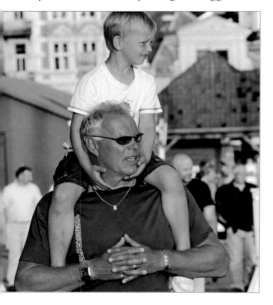

A language instructor at the University of Oslo claimed that "Norwegians are like a Thermos bottle, hard and cold on the outside, but nice and warm once you open them up". Society is very closely tied to family and long-term friends from school days. Many do not feel inclined to extend their relationships to outsiders, and establishing friendships can take time. Once formed, genuine friendship is taken very seriously.

A generous people

The Norwegians' penchant for sharing their wealth is also legendary, both at home and

ABOVE: society tends to place a high value on family and long-term friends.

abroad. Many Norwegians say they pay their high taxes with pleasure, firmly believing that no one should be too rich or too poor, while their generosity in donating money to worthy causes and international relief efforts leads all other countries on a per-capita basis.

Norwegians can also be remarkably generous where they might be expected to be most possessive. There is little alarm about the predatory impact of, say, satellite television on a language which hardly exists outside Norway. Far from resenting visitors who presume to address them in a foreign tongue, Norwegians positively relish the challenge, usually responding with fluency.

> *Norwegians are great hand-shakers. Strangers meeting always shake hands and exchange names. When meeting casual acquaintances, you shake hands as you arrive and leave.*

Confidence in the hardiness of their language is curiously at odds with its historical background (*see Language, page 74*).

Autonomy and self-sufficiency

The regional fragmentation at the heart of the language debate extends to most facets of cultural and economic life. While Norway has since Viking times been a single nation, it has been a confederation of many parts. Norway can be divided north–south, east–west, or a dozen different ways. Like the Renaissance, the Industrial Revolution hardly intruded, so there was not the rapid urbanisation that occurred elsewhere. Trondheim, Bergen and Oslo were towns rather than cities. A later creation, Stavanger owed its existence to the arrival of vast shoals of herring, which were the basis of jobs and trade. Most of Norway remained rooted in subsistence agriculture.

Rural families tended to be isolated and self-sufficient. Their lives depended on agriculture, and the land was not good enough to support more than a family or two in a single valley. Separated from their neighbours by mountains, which were easier to cross in winter (on skis) than in summer, they effectively lived in different worlds. There were hardly any villages where tradesmen could be found and paid in cash. The versatile family managed on its own, a resourcefulness which still runs in the blood. ❑

Norway and Its Neighbours

While outsiders talk about "Scandinavians", there are marked differences between Norwegians and their neighbours

If you walked into a room and met three Scandinavians, it would be hard to tell which was the Norwegian, which the Dane and which the Swede. They look alike, have similar interests and seem to speak the same language, even if the accent is somewhat different.

The written languages, all based on Old Norse, are so similar they are generally understood by all, and SAS, the airline shared by the three countries, allows its crews to use their own language. This works well when a crew is Norwegian, but less well with Danes and Swedes, who sometimes find each other incomprehensible.

This Scandinavian family is often taken to include Finland, though the Finns are of a different race with a language related to Hungarian. In any event, all four countries are part of the Nordic group, which includes Iceland, the Faroes, Greenland and the Åland Islands in the Gulf of Bothnia.

Like all families, Scandinavians have the usual squabbles and false images of one another that come out of close proximity. To other Scandinavians, Norwegians are "blue-eyed" or naive, often the butt of innocuous jokes, yet both Swedes and Danes are astonished to learn that similar jokes are told by Norwegians against them. The family analogy continues in that the Danes tend to look on Norway as a younger brother, with all that that implies.

Sweden, with which Norway shares a 1,700km (1,000-mile) border, is often looked on by Norway (and to a lesser extent by Denmark) as an elder brother, with allegations of arrogance and insensitivity from the smaller countries and a tendency for the larger to think it "knows best". But since Norway discovered oil in 1969, the big-brother attitude has taken a knock, and left Sweden looking at Norway with a degree of wonder and envy. The image of Norway as the junior partner is partly due to the fact that, after 500 years ruled

first by Denmark and then Sweden, the present Norwegian state is just over a century old, though Norway has been a nation for as long as any Scandinavian country.

Norway's only non-Nordic neighbour is Russia. The two countries coexist without much friction on Spitsbergen (Svalbard), the remote northern islands, best known for coal, bird- and plant-life, and the sealers and whalers of former days.

In the days of the Soviet Union they were at odds over their joint border in the far northern Barents Sea. Norway favoured a border on the median line equidistant between the two countries, but their Russian neighbours wanted to adopt a sector

principle, giving them control of larger fish areas and oil reserves. In April 2010, the two countries agreed on a line straight through the grey zone that had been a bone of contention since the 1970s.

During World War II, when only Sweden was neutral, the Scandinavian countries did their best to help one another, although neither Norway nor Sweden has yet managed to forget that Sweden allowed German troops to pass through its country on their way to attack Norway. Many Finnish children left for homes in Sweden, and that country also became an escape route from Norway. At the end of the war, Norway, Denmark and Iceland joined NATO, Sweden remained non-aligned, and Finland (in an uneasy position between the Eastern and Western Blocs) declared itself neutral. ❏

RIGHT: the Swedish and Norwegian royal families, with Norwegian Princess Mette-Marit on the right.

EPIC EXPLORERS

Whether because of exile, scientific exploration or wanting to be the first, Norwegian explorers have travelled the world from the North to South Poles

A lthough exploration is most often associated in modern times with rocket journeys into space, the names of at least two Norwegian explorers are as evocative now as at the time of their epic achievements: Roald Amundsen (1861–1930) is for ever remembered as the man who beat Captain Scott to the South Pole, and Thor Heyerdahl (1914–2002) for the *Kon-Tiki* expedition.

Their fame steals some of the limelight which ought to be apportioned to a much larger cast of intrepid Norwegians, beginning with Bjarni Herjulfsson who, in 986, lost his way while sailing from Iceland to Greenland and ended up, according to an ancient saga, as the first European to sight the American continent.

Early migrations

A 19th-century Norwegian explorer, Fridtjof Nansen (1861–1930), set the pattern for the investigation of human migration. He established his reputation in 1888 with a hazardous crossing of Greenland from east to west. A few years later he was excited by the discovery near the southern tip of Greenland of some wreckage whose origins were traced to the New Siberian Islands. How had it got there?

Nansen determined to find out. His vessel, *Fram*, was designed to lift herself under the crushing pressure of the drift ice in the Arctic Ocean. She was set adrift off the New Siberian Islands in September 1893 and, two years later, emerged near Spitsbergen – but without Nansen. He had left the ship in charge of

his second-in-command in a heroic but vain attempt to reach the North Pole with dog-drawn sledges. He and his companion survived a winter in Franz Josef Land, living in an ice hut and eating whatever they could shoot. They reached safety on practically the same day as *Fram*, and Nansen's six volumes of findings are the basis of the science of oceanography.

The purpose of the 1947 *Kon-Tiki* expedition was to test a theory about the origins of the Polynesian people and culture. Heyerdahl demonstrated that a balsawood raft set adrift off the coast of Peru could eventually – it took him about four months – reach the Tuamotu Archipelago 8,000km (5,000 miles) to the west.

LEFT: Hanssen, one of Amundsen's expedition members to the South Pole, next to the flag.
RIGHT: Roald Amundsen.

In the 1960s he successfully conducted a similar experiment – the *Ra* expedition – to discover whether West African voyagers using rafts may have reached the West Indies before Columbus.

Viking explorers

The father of Norwegian exploration is Erik the Red, a man who seems to have had a liking for slaughter. In the 10th century he was banished from Norway to Iceland for murder, and then from Iceland for several more killings. Unwelcome anywhere, he sailed west with a shipload of livestock and discovered the world's largest island – a lump of ice, more than 3km (2

miles) thick in places. A keen angler, Erik was so engrossed by the excellent catches to be had in summer that he neglected to collect enough animal fodder for the winter. His livestock starved to death. He resolved to risk violation of his ostracism to collect replacements from Iceland and to persuade others to join him on his return.

Erik trumpeted his new-found land with the zeal of an unprincipled estate agent. It was so wonderful, he said, that he had decided to call it Greenland. By 985 he had acquired animals and enticed enough colonisers to fill 25 ships, of which 14 reached the destination.

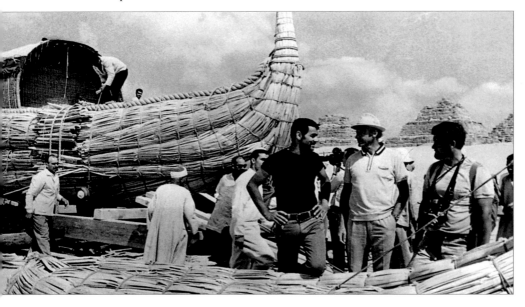

AMERICAN PROOF

The discovery of America by Christopher Columbus in 1492, a significant landmark in world history, was not contested for several centuries. The Italian explorer, however, was not the first European to set foot on the American continent – the Vikings had got there first, as it turned out.

The existence of "Vinland" was known to Adam of Bremen, a chronicler in the 1070s, and to writers of the sagas, but it was through a typically bizarre quirk of archaeology that Eiriksson's discovery of America *(see page 81)* is put virtually beyond doubt. Excavations on the site of a Greenland farm belonging to a member of the

Vinland expedition produced a lump of coal that proved to be anthracite, a material unobtainable in Greenland but plentiful on the surface in Rhode Island.

The case was strengthened in 1960 by Helge Ingstad, who thought about the likely landing place on the American continent of an expedition from Greenland. Working like a detective, he backed a hunch and at L'Anse aux Meadows, on the northern tip of Newfoundland, discovered that six buildings had once stood on the site. Carbon dating proved they were medieval, and the archaeological remains left no doubt that the occupants had been Norsemen.

It was in one of the settlements founded by Erik the Red that his son, Leiv, having heard Bjarni Herjulfsson's strange tale, prepared to find out for himself what it was all about. His 35-man expedition left Greenland about the year 1000. They landed first at "Markland", a wooded region on the coast of Labrador, and then continued south to "Vinland".

An inscription on a map probably drawn by a monk in Basel in 1440 describes Leiv Eiriksson's discovery of "a new land, extremely fertile, and even having vines... a truly vast and very rich land". Attempts to settle the land were defeated by the hostile natives.

Liv Arnesen (born 1953) was the first woman to reach the South Pole alone in 1994, and Monika Kristensen (born 1950) led a South Pole expedition in 1986–7, following in the footsteps of Roald Amundsen.

was more concerned with reaching the North. Nevertheless, faced with the shattering disappointment of the news that Robert Peary had pipped him to the post, in 1910 he secretly went south instead in Nansen's old ship, *Fram*. But not until he reached Madeira did he let any-

Race for the Pole

Roald Amundsen had served a rigorous apprenticeship for his famous assault on the South Pole, which came about as a last-minute change of plan. Although he had taken part in a Belgian expedition to Antarctica, his first interest was the Arctic. He was stuck for two years off King William Island in a seal-hunting boat, *Gjøa*, and applied his time to studying the Inuit inhabitants and making reckonings on the magnetic pole.

Amundsen knew about Captain Scott's ambitions to reach the South Pole, but he himself

LEFT: Thor Heyerdahl's *Ra* under construction in Egypt. **ABOVE:** Monika Kristensen.

one know what his intentions were. Amundsen decided to dispense with all scientific work in his sprint to the South Pole. Scott had a head start but discovered too late that his Siberian ponies were useless in the conditions. He and his team had to pull their sledges. Amundsen took a shorter, rougher route and had the benefit of dog teams. In the event, he beat Scott by a month.

The dispirited English team perished on their return, and this unlucky fate took some of the lustre off Amundsen's feat. At last, though, the director of London's Royal Geographical Society, which had backed Scott, paid tribute to Amundsen's effort as "the most successful polar journey on record". ❑

THE SAMI: PEOPLE OF FOUR NATIONS

Behind the popular image of the Sami with their colourful costumes and large herds of reindeer lies a rich, complex culture that is an important part of modern Norway

The Sami (or Lapps, as they are sometimes called despite its derogatory overtones) have lived in Norway from time immemorial. Traces of their presence stretch back more than 8,000 years. The name Sami comes from the Sami *sápmi*, denoting both the people themselves and their traditional territory. Sami-land extends from Idre in Sweden, and adjacent areas in Norway, south to Engerdal in Hedmark; to the north and east it stretches to Utsjoki in Finland, Varanger in Norway and on to the Kola peninsula in Russia. It covers a larger area than Norway and Denmark combined, and the population is cautiously estimated at 70,000, of which around 45,000 live in Norway, mainly in Finnmark.

Norwegian Sami divide roughly into three groups. The Mountain Sami are the most widespread, ranging from Varanger to Femunden. They live mainly by breeding reindeer. The River Sami live around the waterways in the interior of Finnmark and have turned to

Reindeer-herding is at the heart of Sami culture and influences all aspects of life, including the concept of time – the Sami people count eight seasons, related to the annual behavioural pattern of their reindeer.

agriculture and animal husbandry, though hunting, fishing and berry-picking still add to their income. The third group, the Sea Sami, is the largest, making a living from fishing and

LEFT: traditionally, Sami women like to smoke a pipe.
RIGHT: Sami Easter festival, Karasjok.

farming in a lifestyle that differs little from that of other northern Norwegians.

Ancient culture

The Sami people have been particularly successful in conserving their rich cultural heritage and many unique traditions. Not the least important is the Sami language, which derives from the Finno-Ugric branch of the Uralic family and is closely related to the Baltic Sea-Finnish languages.

From ancient times, the sea has been of great importance as an abundant source of fish, and of seal to provide the Sami with valuable hides. Walruses, with their precious tusks, were also highly prized, particularly by the Sami crafts-people who produced all sorts of tools and utensils including needles, buttons, spoons, cups and a variety of musical instruments.

Nomadic lifestyle

Samiland is a mighty land, rich in lakes, rivers, small streams, grandiose mountains and bound-less hills, which in some places reach as far as the Atlantic coast. Besides fishing, hunting also used to be important, and there was much game, big and small. Squirrels, martens, foxes, even bears were all hunted, but the most impor-tant animal was – and to a certain extent still

is – the reindeer. About 10 percent of Norway's landmass is used for reindeer-grazing (mostly in Finnmark). While the economic value of this industry is minor on a national scale, it is important both financially and culturally to the Sami, with about 40 percent of the population living from herding reindeer.

Very few of the truly nomadic Sami people are left. Most Sami have settled down in the sense that they have a permanent address but move with their herds to the high ground in the summer. During late summer and in the autumn the reindeer are driven down to the woods near the foot of the summer mountain

SINFUL SINGING

Of great importance when trying to get inside the world of the Sami people is to understand the importance of the *yoik*, a kind of primitive singing comparable with unaccompanied humming or melodic scanning. To outsiders, it is particularly difficult to grasp since the words can be isolated or subordinated to melody and rhythm, followed by long sentences of meaningless sylla-bles, such as *voia-voia*, *ala ala*, or *lu-lu-lu*.

The *yoik* probably originated as a way of keeping rein-deer quiet and at the same time frightened wild animals away. But it is also used as entertainment, when people are

gathered together. In Finnmark, *yoiking* has grown strong, and each Sami has his own personal melody. Traditionally, a young Sami boy will compose his own *yoik* for the girl he is courting. However, today a suitable *yoik* can be composed to order for almost any occasion.

Like many other Sami traditions, the *yoik* was forbidden by the missionary Christians. At a time when the only decent song was a hymn, the *yoik* was seen as sinful. But a *yoik* could not be burnted like a troll-drum. Many of the old melodies are still alive, handed down from one generation to the next.

pastures where there is plenty of lichen. There they stay during winter, roaming in freedom until the spring when it is time once more to move up the mountain to the high slopes, now covered with succulent, nourishing vegetation.

Brilliant colours

Perhaps the vivid colours of the land all around them have been a source of inspiration for the traditional Sami costume. In days gone by, this dress was for daily use; now it is kept for festivals, weddings, funerals and other important occasions. Easter is *the* big feast, particularly in Kautokeino, with traditional reindeer racing and other events. Then the richly ribboned skirts and frocks, with red their most outstanding colour, are fetched from drawers and chests.

There are no bounds to this richness and colour, which makes a magnificent sight. With these lavish dresses go jewellery in silver, exquisitely worked into neckchains and elegant pendants. Another speciality is pewter embroidery, in which very thin threads of pewter are sewn in ingenious patterns on fine bracelets or on bags made of reindeer hide.

The old religion

Like many other people living in close contact with nature, the Sami had, and still have, a religion related to shamanism, in which nature and its forces are of the greatest importance. Beaive (the Sun) and Mannu (the Moon) were the supreme gods; next came Horagalles, the god of thunderstorms. Under these main gods there were many lesser gods and spirit beings, who ruled over fertility and over wild animals and the hunt, as well as over lakes and their fishes and other inhabitants. There were evil spirits as well. One was Rota or Ruta, the demon of illness and death; another was the Devil himself, Fuadno. In many areas Sami religion was related to Norse mythology: Horagalles corresponding to the Norse god of Thunder, Thor.

Christianity did its best to combat and extinguish this popular belief and Swedish Laestadianism did much to destroy the Sami religion. Many of the ceremonial "troll-drums", of great importance in Sami culture but anathema to

LEFT: Sami women and child in traditional costume.
ABOVE RIGHT: Coastal Heritage Centre in Foldalbruket, on the Arctic coast.

the would-be missionaries, were burned. The most effective Christian missionary was King Christian IV. He travelled to Finnmark around the turn of the 17th century and in 1609 introduced the death penalty for Sami who refused to give up their traditional faith. He followed

Famous artists of Sami descent include actress Renee Zellweger (her Norwegian-born mother's family originally came from Lapland) and singer Joni Mitchell, whose paternal grandparents also emigrated from Norway.

this with an order to build the first Christian church in Varanger. To go to church regularly was, nevertheless, impossible for many of the nomadic Sami, who had to travel over mountains and vast lakes. It was the great festivals which gathered the Sami together and so it is today, with New Year, Easter, Lady Day, and the spring and autumn equinoxes.

Language revival

Traditionally, Sami culture possessed an extensive oral "literature", including a vast number and variety of legends and fairytales, many of which were written down earlier last century by J.K. Ovigstad in his *Sami Fairytales and Legends*. This literature also includes a distinctive form of poetry designed to accompany the traditional Sami "song" or *yoik (see box, page 84)*. In the first half of the 20th century, it was government policy to encourage the "Norwegianisation" of the Sami people and their language. This led to the irony that one of the greatest writers of Sami descent, Mario Aikio from Karasjok, wrote only in Norwegian, though today a number of younger writers are once again using the Sami language.

As has happened with many minority languages in recent times, Norway now has a policy of encouraging the Sami language. It is taught from the start of schooling, and Sami

people can pursue higher education in their own language in various establishments such as the universities of Oslo and Tromsø, and their their own teachers' training college in Alta. There is also a Sami TV channel, and several Sami radio stations.

Towards home rule

The Norwegian Sami have also fought for political control over their own affairs and for the preservation of their way of life, which has continued to be eroded by the opening up of the northern areas through improved roads and other forms of communication.

The establishment of national parks, for example, can lead to the protection of wild ani-

mals that prey on the reindeer herds, and Sami people have been successful in gaining compensation for reindeer-grazing areas and recognition of the right to hunt and fish. Sami have also succeeded in curtailing some electricity development projects that would have flooded whole districts and jeopardised the local reindeer economy.

> The Sami singer Mari Boine, whose music is rooted in the Sami heritage, is known all over Europe, and her success has brought new life to Sami music and culture.

Today, the Sami people have their own Sameting (Parliament), based in Karasjok, which was opened in 1989 with great ceremony. Parliament is an elected body, and to vote you must have a grandparent speaking the Sami language or "feel that you are a Sami". Further progress was made in 1990 when Norway ratified the ILO Convention, which dealt with the rights of indigenous and tribal peoples.

The Sameting deals with all matters pertinent to the Sami people and has gradually been given more autonomy. It has developed a plan of action for Sami coastal and fjord areas, an agricultural plan, and has participated in a Sami fisheries committee. In addition, it has endeavoured to boost local employment (in which tourism is playing an increasingly important role). Nordic cooperation is also a central part of its activities. The Sami parliaments in Norway, Sweden and Finland collaborate through a special parliamentary council.

In the summer of 2006, the people of Finnmark finally won the right to administer their own lands. Crown Prince Haakon and several government ministers travelled north for celebrations marking a new law that shifts power from the state to the Sameting and local county councils. It was the biggest land transfer in Norway's history, encompassing an area the size of Denmark that is rich in natural resources. Local Sami, who had long made it clear they wanted their share of the area's potential wealth, are also keen on their share of offshore oil and gas riches from the Barents Sea. ❑

LEFT: Sami singer Mari Boine.
RIGHT: Sami woman in traditional dress.

FOLKLORE: SAGAS AND FOLKTALES

Among the treasures of Norwegian heritage is its rich legacy of legends and sagas. This form of popular storytelling is an important part of the national psyche

The Norwegian word for folktale, *eventyr*, crops up as early as the 12th century in the form *ævintyr*, borrowed from the Latin word *adventura*, meaning event or strange occurrence. These folktales were imaginative stories passed from one storyteller to another, and depicted relationships expressed in fantastic and symbolic terms. Narrators were often clergymen who used folklore as a moralistic vehicle. The folktale style was, above all, objective; however fantastic the subject, the narrative was always believable.

Country legends
A constant topic in Norwegian legend is its landscape. Many of the stories connected with the sea involved mythical creatures, the best known of which are the Lake Mjøsa monster and Draugen, the personification of all who have died at sea. In lakes and rivers lives the sprite Nøkken (Nixie). Many mythical creatures inhabit the mountains and forests, and tales about landmarks supposedly created by trolls exist all over the country. Marks said to have been left by trolls show their size, such as the Giant Cut (Jutulhogget) in Østerdal.

ABOVE: a 13th-century legend tells how two warriors carried the infant King Håkon to safety from rebel factions trying to claim the throne.

ABOVE: the *Völsunga* saga involves Odin punishing the Valkyrie Brunnhilde for disobedience.

LEFT: the Oseberg ship, formerly used for sailing and as a burial vessel, dates from *c.* AD 815–20.

RIGHT: the rock carvings at Hjemmeluft, in the far north, date back as far as 6,000 years ago.

BELOW: Julenissen ('Norway's Santa Claus, second from right) is said to live in Drøbak.

THE GOLDEN AGE OF LITERATURE

On 17 May 1814, after almost 400 years of Danish rule, Norway signed the constitution at Eidsvoll. This event heralded a revival of the Norwegian language. Per Christen Asbjørnsen (1812–55) and Jørgen Moe (1818–82) were part of this "golden age". Inspired by the German Brothers Grimm and Norwegian Andreas Faye, who published *Norske Sagn (Norwegian Legends)* in 1833, Asbjørnsen and Moe began compiling the first collection of Norwegian folk-tales, *Norske Huldre-Eventyr og Folkesagn (Norwegian Ghost Stories and Folk Legends)*. Their first volume appeared in 1845, the second edition in 1852. Asbjørnsen went on to publish an illustrated version, commissioning some of the best Norwegian painters of the time, including Erik Werenskiold and Theodor Kittelsen *(work seen above)*.

Asbjørnsen and Moe's collections have become classic Norwegian folktales; Kittelsen and Werenskiold's illustrations have given the troll its visual image.

ABOVE AND BELOW: 11th century Viking arm ring. RIGHT: harness mount from Gotland, one of a pair known as Odin's Birds, with exaggerated beak and talons.

WILD NORWAY

Aside from the stunning scenery and the many outdoor activities, spotting wild animals in their natural habitat often features high on a traveller's agenda. While some of the rarer species might remain elusive, you don't need to venture far off the main road to find others

You may be unlikely to spot one of Norway's last remaining brown bears unless you travel all the way to Øvre Pasvik National Park, on the border with Finland and Russia, and although wolves are present in parts of the country, mainly in the east and south, few visitors ever see them.

Elk, "the king of the forest", can be found throughout Norway, except in the very far north, where reindeer, which are herded by the Sami people, take over. Despite liberal hunting quotas, the elk thrives in Norway, and the current population averages 120,000.

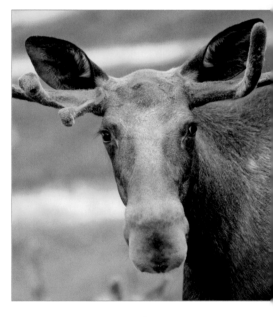

Norway's national parks offer one of the best ways to spot wildlife. Rondane, a four-hour drive north from Oslo, is home to wolverine, marten and lynx, as well as a small population of bears, while golden eagles circle overhead.

Only males, known as bulls, have antlers, which they drop after the mating season each year to conserve energy for the winter. Your best chance to spot one is in summer, when they come out of the forest to eat ripe crops before the harvest.

Mountain resident

Other mammals of note include lynx, wolverine, deer, hare, beaver, otter, fox, lemming and the fascinating musk ox, a survivor of the last Ice Age and once close to extinction. It was

PRECEDING PAGES: sea eagle above Trollfjord. **LEFT:** halibut-fishing off the coast. **RIGHT:** elk can reach up to 2.1 metres (7ft) high at the shoulder.

imported into Norway from Greenland in 1932, and since then there has been a herd in the Dovre National Park *(see page 186)*, one of only a handful of places in the world where you'll be able to see it.

This mountain giant, famed for its thick coat and the male's pungent odour (to attract females during the mating season), feeds on grasses, reeds and moss, and can withstand particularly hostile climate conditions.

Endangered species

For many, however, it is the Arctic animals that are the most fascinating. Sadly they are often the most endangered too, as is the case with

> Norway was, as early as 1974, one of the first countries to ratify the Ramsar Convention, an international treaty whose aim is the conservation of wetlands. Ramsar areas are good places to observe wading birds.

the cute Arctic fox for example (the population estimate for the whole of Norway, Sweden and Finland is a mere 120 adult individuals), and the polar bear, Europe's largest predator, which can be found in the northerly archipelago of Svalbard.

Safaris are organised throughout the country to give animal-lovers a chance to see the local fauna at close range, whether it's a bird-watching and photography trip to popular birding colonies, a king-crab safari in Kirkenes, or a whale-watching boat tour off the coast of the Lofoten or Vesterålen islands, where orca, minke and sperm whales are often spotted (see also page 315).

Fishing is a national pastime, whether salt-water angling on the coast or freshwater angling on the lakes and the rivers – some of which are favoured by Atlantic salmon for spawning. (For more on fishing, see page 107.) ❑

LEFT: Norway is the world's largest producer of Atlantic salmon, seen here leaping up a waterfall.
ABOVE: husky dogs.

UNDER THREAT: THE *RED LIST*

The Norwegian *Red List* is a record of the country's threatened species. Currently 1,988 species feature on the list, and include 78 types of birds, 44 fish species, 31 mammal species and 5 species of reptiles and amphibians.

Beetles (802 species) and fungi (744 species) top the list, followed by butterflies and moths (430 species).

The highest concentration of threatened species can be found in forest and woodland, closely followed by agricultural landscapes *(kulturlandskap)*, which is perhaps hardly surprising – increased agricultural activity and forestry destroy habitats, as do the building of roads and houses.

Pollution and climate change also form important pressures on biological diversity.

Published in 2006, the *Red List* was compiled by 23 teams of experts who assessed a total of 18,500 species in mainland Norway, on Svalbard and in Norwegian seas. The list helps to draw attention to threatened species not only at a national level, but also among regional and local authorities. The aim is to make sure species do not disappear from the country and to maintain viable and healthy plant and animal communities. The *Red List* also has an important role to play in long-term planning and environmental protection.

A Bird-Watcher's Paradise

Snowy owls, golden eagles, puffins, wild swans and many more species thrive in Norway's pristine coastal, mountain and wetland habitats

Some 470 bird species are found in Norway, 260 of which regularly breed here, making it a great country for bird-watching year-round. Witness the impressive capercaillie mating display every spring in the deep forests in eastern Norway, or spot wild swans, geese, ducks and other waders resting in wetlands and marshes up and down the country during the great migration. Jæren, south of Stavanger, is one of the largest such areas, but there are others scattered around the country, the Ramsar sites being the best *(see panel opposite)*.

With such a lengthy coastline, opportunities to observe seabirds in their natural habitat are many, whether in the Hvaler Archipelago in the south or in the rock cliffs around North Cape – and all the stretch of west coast in between.

The Femundsmarka National Park, southeast of Røros on the Swedish border, is a good place to spot falcons, while white-tailed eagles, the largest raptor in Scandinavia, can be found along the Nordland coast. Golden eagles inhabit mountainous areas. Norway also counts four different owl species,

including the pretty snowy owl (known as the Arctic owl or the great white owl in North America).

Seabird colonies

The islands of Runde and Røst are both famed for their huge seabird colonies. Hundreds of thousands of birds nest on Runde, off the Ålesund coast, between February and August every year, including huge colonies of puffins, but you will also see kittiwakes, fulmars, shags, skuas, razorbills and guillemots here, making this one of the best bird sanctuaries in northern Europe. Gannets are also present – indeed the colony at Rundebranden is the biggest and oldest in Norway, one of only about 40 gannet colonies in the world.

The steep and towering islands of Røst, at the very southern tip of the Lofoten Archipelago, are home to the largest number of nesting birds in all of Norway, with approximately one-quarter of the country's seabird population. Boat trips to both Runde and Røst are available.

Arctic species

If you're heading north in the summer, the Varanger peninsula in Finnmark is another compulsory stop, where you will see true Arctic species such as eiders (including the rare Steller's eider), guillemots, red-throated pipits, northern hawk owls, Siberian jays and great grey owls, among other species. The rare osprey can also be seen in the nearby Øvre Pasvik National Park.

Yet further north, Svalbard is another great place to observe puffins, purple sandpipers, little auks, kittiwakes, fulmars and Brünnich's guillemots. Most of the birds on Svalbard are migratory birds, and the Svalbard rock ptarmigan is the only species not to leave the archipelago in winter. ❑

LEFT: gulls shadow a fish shoal by the fishing village of Havøysund, north of Hammerfest. **ABOVE:** on a sea-eagle safari by the Raftsundet strait.

AN OUTDOOR LIFE

In Norway you are free to roam, through forest or over mountain; but wherever you end up, however remote, you can rely on the homely comforts of a *hytte*

As a nation, Norwegians are quite at home in their wild, unspoilt country, and have a great feeling for its mountains. Composer Edvard Grieg, who did much to capture the Norwegian landscape in his music, wrote with passion of the Jotunheimen range in central Norway: "When I contemplate the possibility of a future visit to the mountains, I shudder with joy and expectation, as if it were a matter of hearing Beethoven's Tenth Symphony." There are higher, more remote, more exotically named countries with arguably more photographically stunning landscapes, yet few can claim a population so attuned to its great outdoors.

One Norwegian in four counts outdoor recreation as a first pastime, and Norwegians excel at sports evolved from outdoor pursuits such as cross-country running or skiing, orienteering and cycling. Everyone takes part: urbanite and ruralist, commoner and king tramp the terrain, year-round. Foreign visitors, unaware of this, often find the mass migration to the open air unnerving, especially if they arrive on business at Easter or during July, the prime times of the year for moor and mountain, sea and shore.

Free to roam

Centuries of that view evolved into one of the country's shortest laws – and the *allemannsretten*, or right of access for all, made official with the 1957 Outdoor Recreations Act – which states succinctly that: "At any time of the year, outlying property may be crossed on foot, with consideration and due caution." The few restraints imposed are for environmental or

The Rodøy Man, a 4,000-year-old rock carving in Nordland, is evidence that skiing in Norway dates back to the Stone Age.

safety reasons. Camping isn't permitted in the immediate watersheds of drinking-water reservoirs, and bonfires are forbidden during summer dry spells that can turn forests to tinder.

This liking for untethered roaming seems an integral part of the national character. Among the country's real-life heroes are Fridtjof Nansen and Roald Amundsen, towering figures of polar exploration around the turn of the 20th century,

LEFT: tackling a frozen waterfall.
RIGHT: climbing a glacier in the Jotunheimen.

Morgedal and Telemark Revival

It was in this mountainous region of southern Norway that skiing was honed into an art form and winter sports were born

Morgedal, in the southern county of Telemark, is a hamlet that long remained an entry only found in history books pored over by scholars of the sport of skiing. Today, that has all changed because of a reawakening of interest in the style of skiing called Telemark, which evolved in Morgedal.

In the mid-19th century, there were even fewer people than the 168,000 who live in Telemark today – a hardy breed of woodsmen, small farmers, hunters and traders, who fashioned their own implements, including the skis they needed to get about on winter snows. Morgedal is in the mountains, so the ski-makers there sought designs that would perform well in the surrounding rugged terrain, both in everyday winter skiing and for impromptu sporting meetings.

Among the most visionary in the mid-1800s was Sondre Norheim, a young tenant farmer. He excelled not only in village ski meetings, but also in ski-making skills.

Norheim devised bindings (devices that hold ski boots to skis) that were firm and were the first to give the feet control over the skis. He also gave the skis what is known as "sidecut", the slight hourglass profile of a ski seen from above. Sidecut is what enables skis to run true and turn easily.

Norheim and his fellow Morgedal skiers used the new designs to perfect new skiing manoeuvres, including ways of turning and stopping on snow, and ways of landing from airborne flights off snow-

covered rooftops and natural outcrops. Their fame spread and, by 1868, Norheim and his farmers from Telemark were ready to show off their new skills. He led them on skis for the 180km (112-mile) journey from Morgedal to Christiania (now Oslo), where the city crowds turned out to greet and applaud the peasant skiers and their miraculous new techniques. This led to the start of the big ski-jumping contest at Husaby near Oslo in 1879, where 10,000 spectators led by the king cheered the skiing pioneers from Telemark. Around the same time, the Telemark skiers established the world's first ski school in Oslo.

While Telemark skiing originally meant a bent-knee stance with one ski trailing, in modern Telemark skiing, the heel is free to lift up from the ski, and turns are steered, with one ski trailing and at an angle to the other. From the side, the manoeuvre looks like a genuflection in motion. Although competitive Telemark ski races are now held on packed slopes, as are Alpine ski races, true Telemark skiing is a throwback to the skiing of Sondre Norheim's time. The rebirth of the Telemark turn has revived another old skiing practice – skiathlon – in which competitors must ski-jump, ski through a slalom course, and run a cross-country ski race, all on the same pair of skis.

The name is new, but the combination of manoeuvres dates to the times when the men from Morgedal first mastered the ski-jumping meets in Christiania some 130 years ago. A ski-jumping performance required the competitor to jump through the air, come to a stop after landing, ski back uphill to the top of the ski jump, and jump again before finishing. ❑

LEFT: traditionally, Telemark skiing uses only one pole.
ABOVE: in cross country skiing the heel is raised.

and Thor Heyerdahl, probably the most widely known Norwegian abroad.

Encounters with nature thread the fabric of everyday life. A family returning from an autumn hike to collect wild mushrooms will drop into a public mushroom check station to verify their edibility. In the winter, city-dwellers heading for a ski tour in a nearby forest look for the snow report on the same website they checked the previous summer for the water temperatures at local bathing areas.

Norwegian kindergartens and day-care centres are usually small buildings attached to extensive outdoor playgrounds, designed

(www.turistforeningen.no). Even the simplest cabins put to rest any thought of a hut, while the larger make the title ludicrous.

Well-marked walking trails connect the lodges that stand at crossroads on networks so extensive that DNT's trail marker, a red painted letter "T" on cairns, is synonymous with serious

> *"There is no such thing as bad weather, only bad clothing"* – goes a popular Norwegian saying, and only extreme conditions prevent Norwegians from enjoying the great outdoors.

for day-long activity. Only in extreme weather, defined in most places as below –10°C (14°F), do the kids stay indoors. Yet Norwegians see no valour in doing battle with nature. As the British polar exploration chronicler Roland Huntford pointed out, that's more the British psyche: Norwegians are much more likely to meet nature on its own terms and seek or make their own comfort wherever they go.

Following the red "T"

Supreme on that scale are the *hytter* run by Den Norske Turistforeningen (DNT), called "the Norwegian Trekking Association" in English

HOME FROM HOME IN A *HYTTE*

In a country where winter days are short and nasty weather can crop up any time, comfort translates to secure shelter. A quarter of households own a holiday home, or *hytte*. The word *hytte* translates as "hut", but a *hytte* is by no means a rough structure; most are well-appointed small wooden houses. Indeed, *hytter* in parts of the country sell for as much as other houses. A few, particularly in remote locations, do not have running water and therefore feature a *utedo* (outside toilet). For those without a *hytte* of their own, clubs and associations often own one, and one of the standard business perks is liberal use of the company *hytte*.

ABOVE: Norway is a hiker's paradise.

walking. When winter snows cover the cairns, poles in the snow serve the same purpose.

The bulk of the trails and lodges are conveniently in the middle of the triangle bounded by the cities of Oslo, Bergen and Trondheim. A central entry point is Finse, situated above the timberline at 1,200 metres (4,000ft). Finse's main street is the station platform; there are no cars because there are no roads. When a train has gone and the last passengers have left, Finse returns to normal, a speck in a seemingly infinite expanse of rock, ice and snow.

A few hundred metres from Finse railway station is the DNT *hytte*, with its 114 bunk beds in two- and four-person rooms, hot showers, a staffed dining room serving three meals a day, a snack bar and three lounges. Other DNT lodges are still larger: Gjendesheim in Jotunheimen has 129 bunks. The DNT also has unstaffed self-service accommodation. Here you can prepare your own food or purchase from a pantry. You pay upon leaving, by putting money in a box on the wall. The honour system works well.

Skiing

Skis have been a source of benefit and pleasure to Norwegians for thousands of years, with much of local community life in winter dependent on

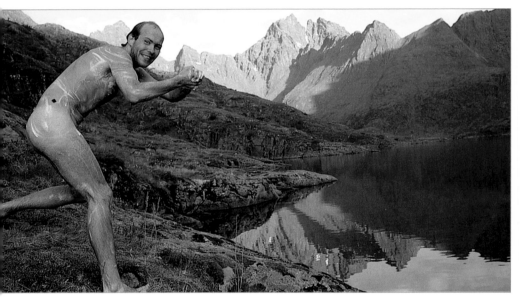

ACCESSIBLE MOUNTAINEERING

To the north of Finse lie the Jotunheimen Mountains, the range that took its name from Norse mythology, literally "Home of the Giants". The name is appropriate: peaks jut a kilometre and more skywards from lake-studded, moraine-strewn flats, all above the timberline. Nonetheless, even the loftiest of the Jotunheimen peaks, Galdhøpiggen and Glittertind, which are the highest in northern Europe with summits more than 2,400 metres (7,900ft) high, rank low on the international scale of noteworthy mountains where sheer altitude, not challenge, is the main criterion. Though this fact has led to relative anonymity – few Norwegian peaks appear in the classic mountaineering literature – it does mean that you can ascend the equivalent of the Mat-

terhorn or Mont Blanc without having to cope with the problems of altitude.

Most Jotunheimen trails meander from 900–1,200 metres (3,000–4,000ft) above sea level, and there are few or no acclimatisation problems at that height.

Some of the glaciers that hewed the Norwegian landscape left offspring. One, Jostedalsbreen (the Jostedal glacier), is the largest on mainland Europe. Jostedalsbreen and its siblings throughout the country are the places to see crampon-shod parties wielding ice axes from spring until autumn. Contact with the ice that shaped their land is currently the Norwegians' fastest-growing wilderness recreation, and many centres organise specialist courses.

So ethereal yet so accessible is Finse that it was chosen as a location for the space adventure film The Empire Strikes Back, *the sequel to* Star Wars.

skis. In the 19th century skiing evolved into a mass sport, urged on by the Morgedal pioneer Sondre Norheim. The first skiing competitions were arranged in the mid-1880s – the term "slalom" originated in Morgedal from the Norwegian words *sla*, meaning slope or hill, and *låm*, depicting the track down it. Norwegians have

nities have a locally prepared piste. Major ski resorts include Trysil in Hedmark, Hemsedal and Geilo in Buskerud, Voss in Hordaland (which is a year-round resort) and, of course, Lillehammer in Oppland, the location of the 1994 Winter Olympics. Ski jumping has again surged in popularity in recent years. There are some 600 ski jumps in Norway.

In the total absence of snow, there is always skating or ice hockey. In winter, municipalities up and down the country convert sports fields and playgrounds into ice rinks by getting the local fire brigade to spray them with water. These are then used for ice hockey and speed

practically unlimited access to skiing and skating facilities. About 30,000km (18,600 miles) – three times the distance between Norway and Australia – of marked ski trails wind their way through unspoiled scenery. Cross-country skiing in the mountains may be enjoyed up until May, although Easter usually marks the end of the season. The winter darkness is no obstacle, with some 2,500 illuminated tracks providing for a bit of serious exercise after work.

Alpine skiing has gradually increased in popularity in Norway. Though by no means as universal as cross-country skiing, most commu-

skating. When the fjords freeze over, whole families take Sunday "walks" on skates among the rocks and islets.

Outdoors in reach

In travelling time, even the remote wilderness areas are close to the bulk of the population: the wilderness itself is still closer. Oslomarka, just outside the capital, is a vast area of forests (larger than Greater London) set aside for outdoor recreation. Likewise, Bergen has its Vidden, Trondheim its Bymarka, Tromsø its Tromsdalen. No Norwegian city is without nearby natural surprises. But to Norwegians, who are as likely to shoulder rucksacks as to carry a briefcase, that's no surprise. ❑

LEFT: going for a quick dip in the fjord. **ABOVE:** near the Holmenkollen ski jump.

SPORTING PASSIONS

To Norwegians, sport is almost a religion, permeating every
aspect of life all year round, and there is room for everyone,
from Olympic champions to Sunday goalkeepers

Put the question "Are you a skier?" at almost
any social gathering anywhere in Europe,
and you could expect a few positive
responses and perhaps a lecture or two on the
virtues of the sport. Put the same question to
someone you meet on a Sunday afternoon at
one of the ski-trail lodges in Norway, which you
can only reach on skis, and the answers will be
quite different: "No, I'm a bank clerk"; "Who
me? Never dream of it!"

A way of life

Why the disparity? The answer lies in a tradition that has woven sport deeply into the fabric
of Norwegian life. It is even reflected in the language. While English has just one word, "sport",
Norwegian has two: *sport* and *idrett*. The Norwegian *sport* is the umbrella word that covers
all sporting events, so that a sports journalist
in Norway plies exactly the same trade as his
or her foreign counterpart. The word *idrett* is
reserved for events in which the limits in performance are determined by the capabilities
of the human body. Horse-riding is not *idrett*,
while scuba-diving is. There is a further nuance:
aktiv (active) means a person currently competing in a sport classified as *idrett*.

This explains why, when you ask skiing Norwegians "Are you a skier?", you have asked if
they currently compete in the sport. Ask often
enough, and you unearth the astonishing fact
that one Norwegian in three is *aktiv*.

Mad about sport

This amazing statistic reflects the high priority Norwegians give to sport. Oslo has numerous statues of living Norwegians in sporting
poses: a statue of King Olav V skiing, near the

Holmenkollen ski jump, one of marathon
runner Grete Waitz running, of course, at the
marathon gate of Bislett Stadium, and statues of
speed-skater Oscar Mathisen and figure-skater
Sonja Henie near the Frogner Park Stadium. All
new high-rise flats are obliged by law to include
"sports gear storage rooms".

Within the Ministry of Church and Education there is a department for "Youth and *Idrett*".
City newspapers vie with each other for sales
on the strengths of their sports sections, and
almost 15 percent of the Norwegian Broadcast-
ing Corporation's output is devoted to sports.

ABOVE: Norwegians love their football. **RIGHT:** there's
plenty of opportunity for all kinds of sports.

So pervasive is sport that visitors sometimes ask "Where is the flash, the excitement?"

The answer is that the pinnacles are there, as high and sometimes higher than elsewhere, but the surrounding plateau of sporting achievement is so high that it makes the peaks appear less prominent.

Norges Idrettsforbund (NIF), the Norwegian Confederation of Sports, is the umbrella organisation for 55 separate national sports federations with, in total, more than 2.1 million registered memberships. It spotlights this fact in its motto "Sport for All", and the pinnacles are grouped and designated "elite". So, for the Confederation

and its member associations, competitive sport is both egalitarian and elitist.

International competition

From the broad base of people for whom sport is a major leisure-time activity come the elite, competitors who enter the many national

> Handball is a favourite team sport in Norway, with the women's national team scooping a gold in the 2008 Olympic Games, and winning the European Championships the same year.

THE WINTER OLYMPICS

It might have a population of only 4.8 million, but Norway has won the most medals in the history of the Winter Olympics: a whopping 303 medals to date, well ahead of the United States in second position with 253, and the former Soviet Union with 209. Norway has won a total of 107 gold medals in the Winter Olympics, again ahead of the US and the former Soviet Union (87 and 81 respectively).

In terms of gold medals, the best games to date for Norway were at Salt Lake City in 2002, when the country scooped an impressive 13 gold medals out of the 25 medals

they brought home. The most successful games overall were at Lillehammer in 1994, when Norway, which was competing on home turf, beat all the other participating countries and topped the table with a remarkable 26 medals, 10 of which were gold.

Norwegians also did well in the 2010 games in Vancouver, where they won 23 medals – nine gold, eight silver and six bronze. Cross-country skiers were once more making headlines, with Marit Bjørgen scooping five medals in total (three gold), and Petter Northug four (of which two were gold).

championships and represent Norway in international sports meetings. The results speak for themselves. For a country with such a small population, Norway has always been disproportionately strong in sports.

Traditionally, Norwegian competitive prowess has been in winter sports and in sailing, but Norwegians have also won international medals in a wide range of other events. Such pervasiveness and prowess have their price. The annual turnover in sports, excluding the sports equipment sector, is more than NOK1,400 million (£120 million), and sports are supported through many channels: the NIF receives a

major chunk of its revenue from the government, and sport receives one-third of the profits of the state-run football pools and the national lottery. The 5,000-odd clubs use extra-curricular activities, such as bingo and local lotteries, to raise up to 40 percent of their income.

Football

As in other European countries, football (soccer) is the biggest sport in Norway, with more than 1,800 clubs and a total of over 280,000 players. The national team had its golden age in the 1990s, when Norway twice reached the World Cup finals and even beat Brazil. A number of Norwegian players have become famous internationally, among them Ole Gunnar Solskjær

(Manchester United's "baby-faced assassin") and John Arne Riise, a Liverpool player for several years before he moved on to play in Italy.

Women's football is also big in Norway, with some 110,000 registered members. There are 12 clubs playing in the top division, and another 12 in the first division (each football club in Norway, has both a men's and women's team).

The country also hosts the Norway Cup – the world's largest football tournament for children and young people – held every year in the first week of August. The tournament, which dates back to 1972, attracted some 30,000 participants in 2009, with 1,371 teams from 49 countries.

> Wherever you go in Norway, you are besieged by young people selling lottery tickets to support the local sports club.

Winter sports

Number two in the statistics and, its supporters contend, spiritually number one, is the country's traditional stalwart, skiing, with more than 1,500 clubs and a total membership of more than 200,000. Together, the five skiing disciplines – cross-country, Alpine, ski jumping, biathlon (a cross-country skiing and rifle-shooting combination event), and combined (ski jumping followed by a cross-country competition) – receive as much funding as football.

Grassroots support

The backbone of Norwegian sports is, of course, people's involvement. A great deal of work on sports facilities is local and voluntary – and that includes raising funds, too. One persistent reminder of this involvement is the seeming ubiquity of sports facilities and sports instruction. There are 10,000–12,000 sports centres in Norway, from the most modest local football field to major stadiums and indoor halls.

In summer and autumn, these centres are hatcheries for future football and track-and-field athletic talents. In winter, their iced surfaces swarm with figure and speed skaters and serve as mini-arenas for ice hockey and *bandy*, a related sport played with a ball instead of a puck, to rules more closely resembling those of field hockey. ❑

LEFT: the women's football team is very successful.

The Great Ski Jump

No Norwegian icon enjoys quite the same status in the heart of the population as the Holmenkollen ski jump, the nation's top jumping hill

The Holmenkollen Ski Festival is the oldest in the world, taking place in March and attended by 1 million people each year. At the climax on Holmenkollen Sunday, more than 50,000 people gather at this famous ski-jump hill to watch ski jumping in the country that invented it. Although the Nordic skiing competitions (cross-country and ski jumping) and the newer events attract top competitors eager for World Cup points, Holmenkollen is much more than yet another international winter competition. This is very much a citizens' festival, a chance for ordinary Norwegians and visitors to take part in the events.

The idea of sitting or strolling as a spectator all day in the middle of a Norwegian winter might sound like the best way of catching a cold, but the excitement is high. Wrapped in boots, anoraks, gloves and hat, with the necessary extra of a warm cushion to sit on, you need no more than a regular quick coffee, best laced with aquavit, to keep out the cold.

Norway was the first country to introduce ski competitions when Norwegian soldiers began to compete as early as 1767, and the first civilian event took place in 1843 at Tromsø. By the 1880s, the Norwegian Society for the Promotion of Skiing already held a winter competition and in 1892, this transferred to Holmenkollen. That year, the longest ski jump was 22 metres (72ft). Today, it is 139.5 metres (457ft).

In the very first days the competitors were all Norwegians, but even by 1903 Swedes had arrived, and were soon joined by French and German skiers. Since World War II, foreigners from most skiing countries have taken part – and won. Women first competed in 1947, when Alpine skiing events were introduced, but they weren't admitted to the cross-country race until 1954.

The fact that women are still not able to take part in the ski-jumping competition, because there are allegedly too few athletes to compete at this level, is an issue that has made the head-lines in Norway recently, and this is likely to change in the next few years.

Norway's King Olav V, a first-class sportsman, made his debut on the Holmenkollen jump in 1922, and was a faithful spectator for nearly 70 years. His son, King Harald, has inherited this keen interest in the sport. Norwegian members of parliament – fitter perhaps than their counterparts elsewhere – and local politicians, also take part. On Children's Day more than 5,000 children swarm into the arena for events to mark the end of the season at the children's ski school, and the Holmenkollen March attracts around 7,000 to 8,000 people, many just ordinary skiers, to ski either 21 or 42km (13 or 26

miles) through the Nordmarka forest finishing beneath the jump.

The atmosphere of Holmenkollen Sunday is electric. They call it Norway's second national day, after Constitution Day on 17 May, and when the new ski jump opened in March 2010, thousands of Norwegians spent the night outside, braving the cold winter air to secure a good view of the action.

The huge crowd packed into the arena hushes as the first skier appears. Up there, on the top platform, he looks like a being from another world. The silence lasts until the tiny, bright figure takes off and, in a second, is flying through space with an ease that makes it look simple. Then, as skier follows skier in graceful arcs, a roar loud enough to cause an avalanche fills Holmenkollen. ❏

RIGHT: Holmenkollen ski jump.

FISHING: SPORT AND SUSTENANCE

Norway's fjords, rivers and coastline are a veritable anglers' paradise. And when it comes to eating fish, Norwegians have a dish for every occasion

To Norwegians, fish is the standby staple. Even in modest markets, the variety of fish and fish products is amazing, and Norwegians look on a proper wet fish shop as an asset to a community. Fish is both humble fare and holiday cuisine. Fish balls in white sauce are the Norwegian dining-table stalwart, and steamed cod is a favourite for Sunday dinners. On festive occasions, herring in myriad forms takes its place with other delicacies such as *gravlaks* (cured salmon), *rakfisk* (half-fermented trout) and *lutefisk* (dried codfish marinated in a lye solution, a dish few foreigners appreciate).

An angler's paradise

Angling in Norway is done both for the sport itself and as part of other outdoor pursuits. Fishing tackle is among the paraphernalia of camping trips, just as it is the prime equipment for avid anglers.

The long coastline is a mecca for saltwater angling, yet freshwater angling is the more popular pastime, and there are a quarter of a million fishable inland lakes and ponds. The most common of around 40 freshwater species are trout and char; in the northernmost parts, and in lakes and ponds at higher elevations, they are the only fish. Grayling and pike are more common in larger lakes and rivers in eastern and central areas. Local legends about lakes rich in pike hold that the fish are descended from stocks set out in the late 18th century by the ruling Danes.

Bream, whitefish, perch and carp are found in most lower lakes in the southern part of the

LEFT: salmon smoked in the traditional way.
RIGHT: fishing is hugely popular.

country, as well as in eastern Finnmark in the far north. Reliable varieties in salt water include cod, coalfish, haddock, whiting, halibut, herring and mackerel.

Salmon rivers

The stars on the angling scene are the Atlantic salmon and sea trout, related varieties which are both popular game and commercial fish. The commercial varieties now come largely from fish farms, but the game fish still swim the rivers until they are two to six years old, migrate to the sea, and then return to spawn in some 400 rivers. Norwegians argue about the best rivers, but five in the northern part of the country stand out – the Alta and Tana rivers in Finnmark, and the Gaula, Namsen and Orkla rivers in Trøndelag, all of which draw anglers from around the world. There, the sport is so popular that you have to apply for licences as much as a year in advance. Fly-fishing is also a favourite pastime.

> The minimum permissible sizes for keeping caught fish are 25cm (9¾ins) in length for salmon, sea trout and sea char, and 30cm (11¾ins) for all other fish.

of a lake, whether private persons or communities. These vary in price, and are valid for specific dates and periods. You can buy them from local hotels, sports shops or tourist offices.

Baiting the hook

Even youngsters start fishing using artificial bait. Theories abound as to why this is so, but the most plausible ascribes it to Norway's location and topography. In the north, there are few insects large enough to use as bait, and worms are hard to find on rocky shores. Minnows and other live fish are prohibited as bait, primarily to curtail the spread of diseases. For the same

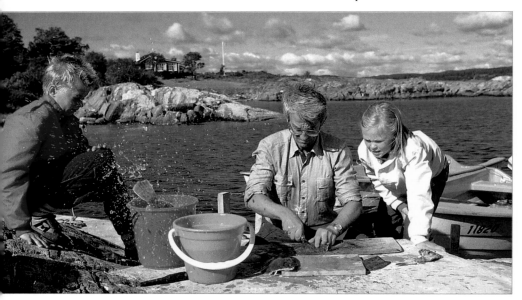

Gaining a licence

You need two types of angling licence to keep within the law. The first one is the annual *Fiskeravgift* (fishing fee) that helps to offset the costs of overseeing fishing and the aquatic environment (particularly adding lime to the water). The *Fiskeravgift* can be obtained at a post office and covers freshwater fish and crabs, but not salmon and sea trout. The latter two are, however, included in the annual fishing licence, which is usually twice the cost of the fishing fee. Fishing in sea water is free, whereas fishing in lakes and rivers requires a further local licence. Freshwater fishing licences come from the owners of the fishing rights, usually the property owners along the banks of a river or the shores

reason, the transfer of live fish, water, or wet fishing boats or other equipment, from one watercourse to another is prohibited.

Just as winter does not deter Norwegians from walking (they switch to cross-country skis), frozen lakes do not halt fishing. Ice fishing is a prime wintertime hobby, a simple and straightforward form of angling, which requires only a baited hand line or short pole and line, an ice-drill, warm clothing, and patience. Ice anglers must hew holes in the ice by hand as motorised augers are prohibited. It's a sport for the hardy, but ice-angling contests are popular. ❑

ABOVE: cleaning the catch outside the family *hytte*.
RIGHT: a huge catch of plaice *(flyndre)*.

NATURE'S LARDER

Norway's culinary traditions have evolved from two key ingredients: its wild nature and its mild climate

Magnificent landscapes and climatic contrasts have helped to create a natural larder from which Norwegians have helped themselves for centuries. Norway's long, varied coastline has provided ample opportunity for harvesting both "wild" and farm-raised fish; the slow ripening process of everything that grows during the light summer imparts an extraordinary aroma to berries, fruits and vegetables; and the animals that graze on the verdant grass provide meat with a distinctive full flavour. Today Norwegian comestibles such as apples, pears, cherries and strawberries, not to mention the famed smoked salmon and Jarlsberg cheese, are in demand the world over. Although eyebrows are raised when the nation's chefs win international awards (like Geir Skeie being awarded the prestigious Bocuse d'Or in 2009, for example), it is not the first time that foreigners have been impressed by Norway's fare.

PAPAL SURPRISE

When papal envoy Cardinal Wilhelm Sabina attended the coronation of King Håkon IV in Bergen in 1247, he arrived with apprehension, having been forewarned about the food. However, in his speech following the banquet he lavished praise on the meal he had been served. Sadly, the historical record of his speech makes no mention of the menu, but visitors to Norway in the 18th and 19th centuries speak highly of the salmon, fowl, game and strawberries with cream – treats which modern-day tourists may also experience.

ABOVE: cloudberries (or *multebær*) are found in mountain marshlands in late summer/early autumn. Rich in vitamin C, *multer* is used as a jam, a liqueur and in desserts.

ABOVE: fresh prawns *(reker)* are a favourite among Norwegians, often served with white bread *(loff)*, mayonnaise, lemon and an ice-cold pils.

BELOW: the Bergen fish market is no longer the bustling hub it once was, but it's still a good place to pick up picnic food to eat on the waterfront – freshly boiled shrimps are popular.

AKEVITT – THE WATER OF LIFE

Akevitt (aquavit or "water of life") is the national spirit of Norway. The most famous aquavit, Løiten Linie, is matured through a 150-year-old process that includes a sea voyage in oak casks across the equator and back (each bottle carries details of its voyage on its label). This story originates from 1840, when the Norwegian ship *Preciosa* rounded Cape Horn; on board was aquavit, which the crew swore had improved in flavour.

Distilled from Norwegian potatoes, this blend of spirit, caraway and other herbs and spices is matured for several months in sherry casks. The result is a smooth spirit of about 45 percent proof by volume. Norwegians regard Linie as an accompaniment to pork *(ribbe)*; it also goes well with seafood and the Christmas *lutefisk* dish.

ABOVE: *klippfisk* (dried, salted split cod) is a major Norwegian export.

RIGHT: chanterelles are found in forests throughout the country from July to October, and are a delicious complement to reindeer and game.

ABOVE: popular brands of Aquavit, Norway's favourite tipple.

RIGHT: logo of the Løten brewery in the Hamar region of Norway.

THE TRADITIONAL ARTS

Tradition is strong in Norway, especially when it comes to the folk arts; but to an inquisitive eye, that tradition contains some unexpected influences

In AD 793 "dire portents appeared over Northumbria and sorely frightened the people. They consisted of immense whirlwinds and flashes of lightning, and fiery dragons were seen flying in the air. A great famine followed those signs, and a little after that in the same year, on 8 June, the ravages of heathen men miserably destroyed God's church on Lindisfarne, with plunder and slaughter."

So the *Anglo-Saxon Chronicle* documented the destruction of the monastery at Lindisfarne, now Holy Island, just south of Berwick-upon-Tweed in Northumberland in the northeast of England. It was the first major impact on Christendom by the Vikings, the pagan men of the north who were to make their mark on European culture for the next three centuries. But in the end, it was a reciprocal cultural exchange. An early Viking king, Olav Haraldson, converted to Christianity, was baptised in Normandy, and returned to his homeland to introduce the faith. By the year 1030, when he fell in battle, he had firmly rooted Christianity in most areas as Norway's future religion.

Today, the legacy of the Vikings is neither blurred nor buried, but still highly visible in a myriad of forms, collectively termed the folk arts, which include woodcarving, rustic painting, national costumes and decorative painting.

Woodcarving

The Viking Age owed its very being to superior sea power. The Viking craft, or longships as they became known, were at once extremely

seaworthy and boldly beautiful. They were clinker-built (overlapping planks held together with iron rivets) on long keel planks that swept up to a stem at either end. The Vikings carved elaborate decorations on the prows down to the waterline, often with dragon heads and figures. They also carved elaborate designs on everyday items, from the handles of implements to the lever of the aft-right mounted *styrbord*, or steering board.

On land, the details of buildings were similarly enhanced. Pillars were carved, not just at their capitals, but over their entire surfaces. There were ornate friezes, interior mouldings were decorated and gable ends became display

PRECEDING PAGES: carving on Heddal stave church.
LEFT: Tidemand's *The Grandmother's Bridal Crown.*
RIGHT: scene from Torndelag Folk Museum, Trondheim.

points. Woodcarving was a highly developed art, executed primarily for, and partly by, the Viking aristocracy.

A passion for the past

With the arrival of Christianity, medieval woodcarvers focused their attention on creating wonderfully ornate stave churches *(see below)*. At home, people decorated chairs, beds, tables, ladles, bowls and other household items with intricate carving.

Some of the best-preserved examples of the work of Norwegian medieval artisans are the carved portals, window surrounds and other details of farm buildings. The traditions survive to the present day, and the current nostalgia in home furnishings, nowhere better expressed than in the timber *hytte*, is not for the lavish designs of the courts of the past, but rather for peasant pieces of native spruce or pine, the

The Frognerseteren Restaurant, built in 1891 on a hillside overlooking Oslo and remodelled in 1909, is one of the best examples of the more modern dragon style of decorated wooden buildings.

STAVE CHURCHES

By the 12th century, Christianity had supplanted the Viking aristocracy as the prime patron of the arts, and the wooden *stavkirke* (stave church) became the foremost outlet of woodcarving as an art form. About 1,000 of these magnificent structures were built in Norway, the majority in a 100-year period

from 1150 to 1250, and 28 survive to this day, making them among the world's oldest wooden buildings.

Their ornately carved portals serve the same purpose as original book illumination in England. They form one of the country's "manuscripts". If you look closely, first, there are the animal heads of Nordic mythology, documenting the remnants of the Viking Age; then the classical tendril of Christian art appears, springing from the jaws of a beast; and finally, tendrils and flowers assert themselves, sometimes solo and sometimes interwoven with other motifs, partly but not completely replacing the beasts.

Some of the best stave churches to visit include Heddal (pictured) in Notodden, Telemark, which is the largest and best preserved, and Urnes in Luster, Sognefjord, which dates back to the first half of the 12th century. The church at Urnes, listed as a Unesco World Heritage Site, is believed to be the oldest of its kind.

more ornately carved the better. "Collecting old houses is something of a family mania," says one shipowner (the nearest Norway comes to an aristocracy). "My father, brother and I have been combing the back country for 40 years for hand-crafted dwellings and objects, homesteads, barns, cabins and huts complete with their country beds, chests, baskets and cupboards. Each must be unique to its own valley and period."

Typical of the national mania for folk art, this family's collection began simply by barter-ing with valley farmers for small items, such as handcrafted butter and porridge *tine*. These colourful wooden caskets, often a first gift to a betrothed, form an unbroken tradition from Viking times to the present. Always highly dec-orated, the *tine* are still used by country lads to show off their carving and rose-painting skills.

Rose painting

Much as woodcarving evolved from the urge to decorate functional items, the art Norwegians call *rosemaling* or "rose painting" sprang from humble surroundings. The two were often used together: carved building details and household furnishings and implements were frequently painted, both as enhancement of, and in con-trast to, the carved wood. The name misleads: roses appear only in a few of the traditional pat-

> Rose painting survives today, like woodcarving, as a nostalgic link with the past, and throughout the country amateur rose painters keep that link alive.

terns; it would be more correct to term it "rus-tic painting", which denotes its agrarian roots, far removed from the cities.

True *rosemaling* is not limited to flowery designs, although variations of the tendril motif are its strongest themes. It also includes geometric figures, portraits, and even an occa-sional landscape.

The earliest decorations have survived less well than the carvings on which they were painted, so the beginnings of rose paint-ing remain an enigma. The oldest surviving

LEFT: grass-roofed houses in Torndelag Folk Museum, Trondheim. **RIGHT:** rustic painting in Kvernes stave church in Møre og Romsdal.

examples date from around 1700, centuries after the necessary paints were first available.

Imported styles

Rose painting evolved and, in its own right, became a record of its times. The earlier rose paintings of interiors and household articles clearly show that the art of the Renaissance reached as far as the Norwegian countryside. The colours are the peasant stalwarts, blue, green, red and yellow, but the patterns are defi-nitely imported.

The prosperity of the late 18th century brought more clerics and more functionaries

to rural districts, and with the new profession-als came their belongings, decorated household furnishings and implements. What the peasants saw they replicated as best they could in their own style.

Most were untutored, and the commonest way of learning the skills was either from trav-elling artists or from local practitioners. The relative isolation of the valleys, cut off from their neighbours by the high mountain ranges, meant that every valley became its own art centre for a particular style of painting.

Hallingdal farmers were partial to delicate S-curves applied to everything from walls to spoons and bowls. In affluent Gudbrandsdal, the locals carved their decorations into built-in benches and box beds. The most isolated districts, such as Setesdal, have a very simplified *rosemaling* tradition.

So individual were the styles, today's experts can identify the age and origin of almost any item with uncanny accuracy. Their knowledge is currently much in demand, as rose-painted period furniture commands the highest of prices for Norwegian antiques.

The national costume

Norway's *bunad* is as colourful as the national costume of any country. It is not just worn by folk dancers or for fancy-dress parties, but is in

FOLK REVIVAL

In the mid-19th century, factory-made garments began to replace homespun products. As people moved from farm to town, the *bunad* (national costume) was heading for extinction. It was rescued by Hulda Garborg, a prominent author, who saw a need to preserve the rural traditions. In the late 1800s, she founded a folk dance group in Oslo. Folk dances should, she believed, be performed in folk costumes, which led her to compile the first anthology of *bunads*, published in 1903. It was a bestseller, and Garborg and one of her dancers, Klara Semb, succeeded in starting the folk dance movement and a *bunad* renaissance which continues to the present day.

regular use as formal attire at weddings, official ceremonies and gatherings on national holidays. Many claim that the *bunad* is Europe's most often worn national costume.

The *bunad* is a throwback to the clothing of times past, and the word itself means simply "clothes". It has developed variations in style, cut, colouring and accessories according to locality and the skills and tastes of its makers. There were costumes for men, women and children, everyday *bunads* and dress *bunads*. As with rose painting, every area of the country had its own style.

Despite these differences, the *bunad* has common characteristics that identify the dress as Norwegian. Women's costumes characteristically have skirts or dresses of double-shuttle woven wool and bodices or jackets of similar or contrasting material worn over blouses with scarves. Sashes, purses, beautiful silver accessories and traditional shoes and stockings complete the costume. Men's *bunads* are essentially three-piece knickerbocker suits, with matching or contrasting waistcoats, white shirts, long socks and traditional shoes.

Although *bunads* are no longer daily wear, the number of known types and varieties is greater than ever. Some, like those from Setesdal, date back 300 years or more. Others, such as the costume from Bærum, a suburb of Oslo, have been designed in the past 40 or so years.

Who should wear the *bunad*?

Its current popularity is matched only by the range of opinions about how it should be worn. Traditionalists contend that a *bunad* from a particular district should be worn only by a person born and bred there. Moderates maintain that correct style outweighs the circumstances of the wearer's birth and upbringing, and the radicals view the *bunad* as a style to be copied piecemeal in modern clothes.

While the standard dark suit has, like in so many other countries, become the bastion of the Norwegian male wardrobe, women still face the dilemma of what to wear for formal occasions. In Norway, a *bunad* is always correct. It is timeless and may be passed on from generation to generation, while the traditional silver belt is often a gift from a parent to their son's wife. ❏

LEFT: Hulda Garborg *(left)* in a traditional *bunad*, 1899.
RIGHT: national dress in the Norwegian Folk Museum.

ART AND CULTURE

Norwegian artists, writers and musicians dug deep into the country's rural past in search of a new national identity

The cultural scene in Norway has been experiencing a significant revival in the past few decades, fuelled in part by money from the oil boom. This new-found confidence was perhaps best illustrated with the opening of the stunning opera house on the Oslo waterfront in April 2008, which put Oslo under the limelight, and Norway firmly on the international cultural map. For if until recently glittering gala soirées were the preserve of rare occasions such as the annual Nobel Prize award ceremony in Oslo Town Hall, things have since changed dramatically, with top events now taking place year-round throughout the country. Bergen hosts Scandinavia's largest annual cultural event, Festspillene, a huge showcase for art, music, theatre and dance in northern Europe; Stavanger was in 2008 named European Capital of Culture; and in spring 2010 Oslo welcomed tens of thousands of pop music fans to the Eurovision Song Contest, on top of an already charged music festival programme.

Home-grown culture

Historically, Norwegian culture is something far more fundamental – folksy, a reaction to foreign domination. As a political entity, Norway was established in 1905 after centuries of Danish and Swedish rule. All Norwegian "dialects" were forbidden by the Danes for official documents and communications. Such cultural imperialism was crushing to Norwegian self-esteem and national identity.

Ordinary Norwegians turned to rural tradition, folk costume and the old ways as a cultural

refuge and eventually the treasuries of Norway's national personality. Culture with a capital "C" was something the overlords brought with them from foreign capitals. And it was something they took away with them when they left.

While politicians could elect a king and parliament, it fell to writers, musicians and artists to revive the national identity. They turned for inspiration to the traditions of those isolated valleys with their ancient farmsteads and their equally ancient verbal customs, telling heroic sagas about an expansive Norway of earlier days and of the greatness of native Viking lords.

Henrik Wergeland (1808–45), a richly talented poet and prose writer, became an early

LEFT: Henrik Ibsen. **RIGHT:** in Ole Bull's villa on the island of Lysøen.

and passionate propagandist of this sort of Norwegian nationalism. Following the same call, artist J.C. Dahl (1788–1857) left his studio for the wilds of Norway's hinterland. His shimmering, majestic views of the mountains are major attractions at the National Gallery, which he helped to found in 1836.

On the dark side, the epoch's fears of isolation and rampant anxiety of the future inspired the violent, emotionally charged style of painter Edvard Munch (1863–1944). Death and desolation are his recurring themes, most strongly expressed in *The Scream* (1893), *The Kiss* and *The Vampire* (both 1895). Munch's art has come so close to the national heart that his works have been enshrined in their own museum in Oslo as well as several rooms in the National Gallery.

Equally loud cries for freedom came from Henrik Ibsen (1828–1906), whose poetic drama *Brand* was a spirited indictment of Norwegian authority at home. It put Ibsen on the cultural map for the first time even outside Norway.

He was not the only one, at the close of the 19th century, to turn homewards for inspiration. Nobel laureate Knut Hamsun's (1859–1952) chilling novel *Hunger* (1890) is an exposé of the abuses of bourgeois Swedish rule. His masterpiece, *The Growth of the Soil* (1917), reflects a

A Doll's House *and the much-loved* Peer Gynt *are among Henrik Ibsen's most famous plays. For more on Norway's influential playwright and cultural icon, see page 54.*

deep love of nature and concern for the effects of material conditions on the individual spirit, themes that still dominate Norwegian writing. Dramatist Bjørnstjerne Bjørnson (1832–1910) also helped promote home-grown themes and talent (*see box below*).

Even architects abandoned continental idioms to embrace a native "Viking Romanticism". They began building in heavy timber and turfed roofs. Eaves and gables sprouted carved and polychromed dragon heads, in an unabashed folkloric, wildly romantic style.

Works by major authors such as Amalie Skram (1847–1905) and Alexander Kielland

BJØRNSTJERNE BJØRNSON (1832–1910)

Dramatist, novelist and poet Bjørnstjerne Bjørnson is, together with Henrik Ibsen, Alexander Kielland and Jonas Lie, known as one of the Four Greats (*De Fire Store* in Norwegian), a term referring to the four most influential Norwegian writers of the late 19th century. Perhaps not as well known as Ibsen outside his homeland, Bjørnson is nonetheless widely acknowledged for having championed the Norwegian cause, working his entire life to free the Norwegian theatre from Danish influence.

While director of Bergen's Ole Bull Theatre (1857–9) and the Oslo Theatre a few years later, he commissioned new, saga-like dramas drawing on Norway's epic past, such as *Kong Sverre* (1861) and the trilogy about *Sigurd Slembe*

(1862). His efforts helped to revive Norwegian as a literary language.

He became poet laureate, and his poem *Yes, We Love this Land of Ours* became a rallying point in the struggle for political independence from Sweden. The poem is now the national anthem of Norway. Other works include his greatest plays, *Beyond One's Powers* I and II (1893, 1895).

Bjørnson, the son of a Norwegian pastor, was born in Kvikne in Österdalen. He was awarded the Nobel Prize for Literature in 1903, and his statue today stands proud outside the National Theatre in the capital, together with that of Henrik Ibsen, one of his fellow students at school in Christiania, as Oslo was then called.

(1849–1906), who abandoned a promising international career to write about old Norway, were front-page news in Oslo, Bergen and Trondheim. Critics and politicians publicly debated new works; plays became issues, even national causes. Literature became the smithy where the nation's identity was being forged.

Post-war art

As with other cultural forms, Norwegian art began to drop its nationalist style after World War II. Gone (but certainly not forgotten) were the fairytale illustrations of Theodor Kittelsen (1857–1914) and morbid subject matter of

(1903–79), and the team responsible for the Oslo Rådhus murals.

There was also the inevitable reaction to the modernists. When Odd Nerdrum (born 1944) applied for a place at the National Academy of Fine Arts he submitted three works; two of these

> *Norway has a wealth of talent to continue the traditions of the prolific sculptor Gustav Vigeland (1869–1943). There are more 20th-century sculptures/statues per capita in Norway than in any other country in Europe.*

Edvard Munch, and in came the modernists. Impressionism inspired such landscape artists as Gladys Nilssen Raknerud (1912–97) and Thorbjørn Lie-Jørgensen (1900–61); Expressionism found its place through the likes of Arne Ekeland (1908–94) and Rolf Nesch (1893–1975); and Abstract Expressionism appeared in the early 1960s through the work of Sigurd Winge (1909–70) and Jakob Weidemann (1923–2001). However, the old nationalist style continued well into the 1950s with such artists as Hjalmar Haalke (1892–1964) and Søren Steen Johnsen

had been long-term projects, but he was selected on the basis of his third work, an abstract image thrown together the night before. With his scepticism towards the establishment and doubts about abstract art reinforced, the young Nerdrum turned to the great masters, in particular Rembrandt, in whom he saw "eternal tranquillity". However, his subject matter was always on the controversial side – *Amputation* (1974), *Hermaphrodite* (1976–81) – and it took until the late 1980s for the Norwegian public to catch on to his postmodern classicism.

There is growing interest in the moderns, which had hitherto been the domain of the avant-gardist Swedes. The focal point of the Norwegian art calendar is the Autumn Exhibition

LEFT: Edvard Munch's *Midsummer* (1915).
ABOVE: writer and nationalist Bjørnsterne Bjørnson at the dinner table.

in Oslo, and the city's three main contemporary art galleries, which exhibit the works of national and international artists, have been growing in popularity in recent years.

New concerns

The 1980s produced a sort of realistic novel, written in sociology textbook style, directly opposed to the older, bourgeois psychology novels, "a die-hard heritage from Hamsun, Cora Sandel and Torborg Nedreaas". Most readable among these "revolution" works are Dag Solstad's (b. 1941) trilogy about World War II, *Svik (Betrayal)*, *Krig (War)* and *Brød og Våpen (Bread*

third novel, *The Story of Eli*, explores sex roles in society. The 1990s saw a general literature boom. Whodunnits by Gunnar Staalesen, Jo Nesbø, Karin Fossum, Ingvar Ambjørnsen and Anne Holt are popular. The first prize, however, must go to a book on the history of philosophy written for adolescents: *Sophie's World* by Jostein Gaarder. He is the most famous Norwegian writer since Knut Hamsun.

Leading the way

If there is one area where Norwegians have the edge it is in furniture (consider Peter Opsvik's classic TrippTrapp chair for kids, for example)

and Arms). This revival of social realism allowed an author such as Asbjørn Elden (1919–90) to produce essentially modern yet "back to our roots" sagas about the inconspicuous lives of ordinary people, such as his *Rundt Neste Sving (Around the Next Bend)*.

Women have come to the fore of Norwegian writing. Cecilie Løveid (b. 1951) and Kari Bøge (b. 1950) crashed onto the literary scene in the late 1970s with audacious, even shocking works. Ignoring male-dominated social realism, they picked apart purely female problems using "street language" and spoken modes of expression. Løveid's lyrically erotic *Sug (Suck)* rocked the staid Oslo critics but has brought her international recognition. Liv Køltzow's (b. 1945)

OLE BULL (1810–80)

Born 200 years ago, "The Nordic Paganini", as Ole Bull was known, became a model for musicians and writers such as Grieg, Bjørnson and Ibsen. A virtuoso violinist and composer, famed for his charismatic personality and his way with the ladies as much as for his musical brio, Bull was Norway's first superstar, performing in front of adoring audiences in packed concert halls at home and abroad. He died, aged 70, on his island at Lysøen, near Bergen, and his funeral procession was one of the most spectacular in Norwegian history, with countless smaller boats following the ship carrying his body – a nation's fitting farewell to one of its beloved sons.

and architecture, which in recent years has responded to increasing demands for sustainable development.

Probably the most internationally renowned Norwegian architect is the "concrete poet" Sverre Fehn (b. 1924), whose main materials have been concrete, wood, glass, and the Nordic light. In 1997, Fehn became the first Nordic architect to win the American Pritzker Architecture Prize, the "Nobel Prize" of architectural awards, and the award cited "a marvellous, lyrical and ingenious architectural form… both forceful and extremely rational". To see his work, visit the Norsk Bremuseet (Glacier Museum) in Fjærland, or the Norwegian Museum for Architecture in Oslo. Snøhetta is another architect firm that has made a name for itself recently, most spectacularly with the new Opera House on the Oslo waterfront.

Norway's Paganini

Norway has a long tradition in music. The skaldic poems of the Viking Age provide a medieval link to the music traditions of Central Europe; Gregorian chants used in the worship of St Olaf are very similar to the Parisian school of the 13th century.

While higher forms of music stagnated during the 450 years of Danish rule, folk music unfolded freely, encouraged by the ecclesiastical centres and travelling musicians of the time.

Norwegian music developed for the first time in the early 1800s, mainly as a result of the union with Sweden and the influence of the Royal Swedish Court, but also because of the international breakthrough made by violin virtuoso Ole Bull (1810–80) (*see box, opposite*).

The 1870s and 80s became known as the Golden Age of Norwegian music, with such prominent composers as Halfdan Kierulf (1815–68), Edvard Grieg and Johan Svendsen (1849–1911). Music took on a national flavour, urged on by Ole Bull's promotion of the Hardanger fiddle and Ludvig Mathias Lindeman's collection of Norwegian folk tunes. Many composers incorporated some element of folk music in their works.

With the end of the union with Sweden in 1905, Norwegian composers found the need to define a national identity, and reverted back to

LEFT: Norsk Bremuseet (Glacier Centre), Fjærland, when first built. **RIGHT:** the novelist Liv Køltzow.

> *Norwegian movies* Pathfinder, *by Nils Gaup (1988), and Petter Næss's* Elling *(2002), were both nominated for an Oscar. In 2008,* Max Manus, *about Norway's World War II saboteur, was also a big box-office success.*

the music of the Norwegian Middle Ages. Seeking inspiration in medieval poetry, German Romanticism and French Impressionism, David Monrad Johansen (1888–1970) tried to create a monumental kind of music based on musical archaisms. This national Romanticism contin-

ued until just after the war, when a new generation of composers went to study in Paris or the United States, consciously aware of the need to internationalise their musical language.

Festivals

The Norwegians' yearning for culture is most explicit, however, in the myriad of annual festivals (*see also page 358*). There is a festival, big or small, to cater for every taste, from the northernmost jazz festival, in Svalbard, to the Notodden Blues Festival, the biggest of its kind in Norway, not to mention the Ice Music Festival in Geilo, where every instrument is carved out of local ice, or the Øya Festival in Oslo, one of Scandinavia's best-loved rock events. ❏

ARCHITECTURE

Visionary new projects are gracing the skyline, from the Opera House in Oslo to a seed bank in Svalbard, with wooden stave churches and a complete *Jugendstil* town along the way

The stunning Olso Opera House might be the best known, but is only one of many innovative and exciting new buildings to have appeared in Norway over the past two decades. From the new Holmenkollen ski jump in Oslo to the Global Seed Vault in Svalbard, the country is littered with such gems. There are hotels, like the glimmering steel-and-glass "Sail" in Molde, or the new Preikestolen Mountain Lodge, part of a project promoting environmentally-friendly timber technology in modern architecture; public and religious buildings, such as the Sami Parliament in Karasjok and the Arctic Cathedral in Tromsø; and, of course, museums and galleries, like the Petter Dass Museum and the new Hamsun Centre, both in Nordland, to name but a few.

It is not just about new buildings, though. The stave churches, which date back to the Middle Ages, are masterpieces in their own right, and the *stavkirke* at Urnes has been on the Unesco World Heritage list since 1979. Also on the list are Bryggen, the Hanseatic merchant houses in Bergen, and the old mining town of Røros, famed for its church and colourful wooden turf-roofed buildings. Nidarosdomen, Norway's oldest and largest cathedral in Trondheim, and the town of Ålesund, whose entire centre was rebuilt in the *Jugendstil* style after the town burned to the ground in 1904, are equally impressive.

ABOVE: designed by Norwegian architect firm Snøhetta, Oslo Opera House has won several awards since its inauguration in 2008, including the prestigious Mies van der Rohe Prize.
RIGHT AND LEFT: Trondheim's cathedral has been an important pilgrimage destination since construction began in 1066. The cathedral houses the relics of St Olav, Norway's patron saint.

RIGHT: Ålesund's town centre has an impressive 320 Art Nouveau *(Jugendstil)* buildings.

THE NATIONAL TOURIST ROADS PROJECT

It all started in 1994, as a trial project aimed at improving the driving experience in Norway by offering motorists an alternative to the main roads, and with superb architecture along the way. A special council was set up, a team of international architects assembled, and before you knew it really interesting buildings were beginning to pop up at the roadside.

The focus throughout has been on quality, and many of the 200 or so buildings and structures (most of them information centres, rest areas or observation platforms) have already won awards in their field. The jaw-dropping Stegastein viewpoint *(pictured above)* at Aurlandsvegen, a wood-and-glass platform jutting out 650 metres (2,133ft) high over the green waters of the fjord below, might be the most photographed, but there are many other striking structures.

This visionary project, which covers 1,850km (1,150 miles) on 18 roads nationwide and will have been 20 years in the making when completed in 2015, is financed by the Norwegian government. The final bill is expected to be in the region of 2.3 million NKr, a big but smart investment that is already giving a real boost to Norwegian architecture.

ABOVE: the design of the Sami Parliament in Karasjok, Finnmark, as based on techniques and materials that reflected Sami culture nd building traditions.

RIGHT: the intricately decorated wooden stave churches are an important, and unique, part of the Norwegian heritage. Dating back to the Middle Ages, as many as 28 stave churches survive today.

WHY DOES EVERYTHING COST SO MUCH?

Norway's high standard of living has its price, but the country is not as expensive as it used to be

Let's get this straight right from the start: day-to-day living used to be exorbitantly expensive in Norway, about 30 years ago, but there has been a gradual levelling out of prices in comparison with other European countries. Today, some food items are generally less expensive than elsewhere, such as coffee and butter, but these are the exception rather than the rule. Visitors are often surprised at the relatively high prices for meat and, amazingly enough, fish. Staple vegetables are reasonable; exotic types, for which there is less demand, are expensive. Fruit follows the same pattern. You can find imported apples or tomatoes at normal European Union (EU) prices. To reduce costs, it's worth looking out for *lavpris* (low-price) shops.

Somewhat surprisingly, Norway produces a reasonable tomato crop, less because of sunshine and high temperatures and more because of encouragement from the Norwegian Ministry of Agriculture, which sees independence from other countries as its main aim. The tomatoes don't always have much taste though, and their price shoots up when imports are restricted.

"Made in Norway"

Norway's desire to be self-sufficient has blossomed in unusual areas. The farmers in some tiny valleys in the west of the country live in grand style because their tomatoes, cucumbers, Chinese cabbages or cattle are highly subsidised. Only 3 percent of the land is used for agriculture, so variety is essential. Cattle farmers are proud of their beef and pork, vegetable

At 25 percent, VAT (known as MVA or "moms" in Norway) is one of the highest value-added taxes on goods in the world.

farmers praise their organically grown produce. Around 95 percent of the grain consumed is harvested in the country, and cattle is almost entirely reared for the domestic market.

As far as foodstuffs are concerned, the logo "Made in Norway" is more an expression of a political principle than of exceptionally high quality. Things are changing though. The higher standard of living has stimulated a demand for

LEFT: fine dining in Norway is a luxury.
RIGHT: much of the farming is still in traditional style.

a richly laid table. Admittedly, prices in Norwegian hotels are high – but so is the standard of the breakfast buffet. Anyone sampling a fully laden breakfast table can only start the day in a good mood: fruit juice, smoked salmon, pickled herring, fresh bread, fruit and muesli. This meal can easily get light eaters through the day and save them the expense of lunch.

Taxed to the hilt?

Not so long ago, it was fashionable to blame rich farmers and a false subsidy policy for high taxes. In reality these subsidies are cut each year and many smallholdings have been given up.

PRICE CHECK

Room for two in a mid-range hotel: NOK 1,200*
Campsite plot for the night: NOK 160
Main course in a restaurant: NOK 120–200
Hot dog in a kiosk: NOK 40
Glass of beer in a bar: NOK 80
Bottle of red wine in Vinmonopolet: NOK 100
Car rental per week: NOK 4,000; 1 litre petrol: NOK 12
Bus ticket: NOK 25; cinema ticket: NOK 90
1 litre milk: NOK 12; bread: NOK 25
Ice cream: NOK 20
Newspaper: NOK 25–30; paperback: NOK 150
Postcard: NOK 10; stamp (Europe): NOK 11
*All prices approximate at time of going to print.

Income is subject to 30–45 percent income tax. But that's it. Social security, health insurance and pension payments are all included, and even the Church is funded by the state.

Other state revenue comes from oil and gas sales as well as taxes on various luxury items – which explains the high prices for cars, alcohol and cigarettes. Luxury costs money, and Norwegians aren't supposed to enjoy luxury items – or at least they should do it in a different way.

The debate on cigarette and alcohol prices is an inevitable item in the annual budget discussions, and only two of the eight political parties in the Storting ever vote to reduce

> To encourage Norwegians to recycle, the "money back" system is often used: a deposit of NOK 1 (pant) may be charged when buying bottles, either glass or plastic, and the money is refunded on return of the bottles.

these taxes; the rest squeeze yet a little more out of them every year.

What is the reasoning behind these constant tax increases? The government insists that the treatment of alcohol and cigarette-related illnesses costs billions. And the budget discussions are also enlivened by the Christian Democratic Party, which rallies against these habits. Norwegians, however, have long learned to live with the link between vice and illness, and have stopped arguing about prices – these days they drink their beer in peace.

Paying for the roads

It's no exaggeration to claim that car drivers have financed their own infrastructure. Here, as with alcohol and tobacco, Norwegians believe in the principle of cause and effect, which is paid for through high car prices (Norway doesn't have its own car industry), a large tax on petrol and toll charges: if you want to drive through Oslo (and there are few ways to circumnavigate it), Bergen, Trondheim or Stavanger, you have to pay a toll.

The road system, on the other hand, has been considerably upgraded and now, with numerous bridges and tunnels (including under the sea), reaches the tiniest villages. ❑

LEFT: fresh produce "Made in Norway".

To Drink or Not to Drink

From Viking mead-drinking sessions to 20th-century prohibition, the consumption of alcohol has always been a subject of heated debate

The question of alcohol and its corollary, teetotalism, have long been burning issues in Norway, and are discussed so keenly that visitors might like to familiarise themselves with the background. The climate is often blamed for Norwegian drinking. There may be some truth in this, since long winters used to put a premium on the art of preserving and storing food. Salt was the key, and it was consumed in such quantities that great thirst followed. At one time, the "normal" consumption of beer and mead was between 6 and 10 litres (10–18 pints) a day.

The 19th century produced a rash of travel books about Norway, and all of them drew attention to a weakness for drink. Even boys of 12 and 14 years, according to the Reverend R. Everest, indulged in the "odious vice", drinking quantities of brandy "that would have astonished an English coalman".

Today's statistics show that Norwegians actually consume less alcohol than almost any other European nation. These statistics also reveal that beer and wine have supplanted harder spirits. But unreported numbers are higher: Norwegians like to travel and certainly buy the complete quota of duty-free items, and some still brew their own schnapps.

The situation was very different in the early 20th century. In 1917 the Norwegian government decided to prohibit the sale of alcohol. Large parts of the Norwegian population were struggling to feed themselves during World War I, so it seemed unreasonable to use grain and potatoes for the production of alcohol. Prohibition was only supposed to last as long as the war raged in Europe, but as it had worked well and helped to reduce social problems related to alcohol consumption, the Norwegians decided in a referendum in 1919 to keep it.

Interestingly, it was the prohibition issue that mobilised women politically. They came out in droves to vote for prohibition in 1919 because they had had enough of their drunken husbands spending their weekly wages on alcohol. But trouble with trade partners such as Spain, Portugal and France

– who threatened to stop buying Norwegian fish if Norway stopped buying their wine – and widespread smuggling, led to the ban being lifted in 1926.

Until the late 1990s, the import and sale of wines and spirits was a state monopoly. Government buyers decided what was to be made available (and the price) in the chain of *Vinmonopolet* shops, as well as in most hotels and restaurants. It was said that by this act the Norwegian state had made itself the biggest single buyer of alcoholic drinks in the world, a painful irony for the numerous prohibitionists who were still beating the drum.

In 1997, the Norwegian government made a major concession to the EU by deregulating the

import, wholesale and distribution side of the market. This means that hotels, restaurants and bars may now do business with independent importers, although *Vinmonopolet* maintains its monopoly on retail sales.

One of the results of this, as visitors find out, is that drinks are freely available in major cities, albeit at numbing prices. Today, it is easier to be served a drink in Oslo at 2am than it is, say, in London. Laws affecting the sale of alcohol are decided at the *kommune* level (by town and rural councils), so outside the cities, and especially on the southwest-coast *bibelbeltet*, it is a matter of luck whether a particular place is completely dry or not – although such conservative attitudes seem to be increasingly on the way out. ❏

RIGHT: a glass of aquavit, Norway's spirit of choice.

PLACES

A detailed guide to the entire country,
with principal sights clearly cross-referenced
by number to the maps

Norway is a long narrow strip of a country, stretching north from mainland Europe far into the Arctic. In the ancient capital of Trondheim, you are 500km (350 miles) from the modern capital of Oslo, but only a quarter of the way up the country's jagged coast. Oslo is as far from Monaco as it is from Nordkapp (North Cape), with Norway's northernmost outpost, the islands of Svalbard (Spitsbergen), hundreds of kilometres further on. With a population of only 4.8 million, Norway has, above all else, space.

Yet travel is not difficult. From early times, the Norwegians (as Vikings) were magnificent sailors, and this old way of travel continues today through the Hurtigruten coastal express and other ferries that link coastal communities. On land, the Norwegians have connected even the most isolated settlements by building railways, roads and bridges across their fjords and by tunnelling deep into the mountains and under the sea.

The scenery is dramatic and the land changes constantly, from mountain to sea, fjord to forest. Oslo, Stavanger, Bergen, Trondheim and Tromsø are small, manageable cities that make good use of the surrounding countryside. Neither the Norwegian climate nor the people are as chilly as the

northern latitudes might suggest. The Gulf Stream warms the western coastline so that the seas are ice-free all the year round, and the great distances between villages, towns and farms have encouraged an age-old tradition of hospitality.

In the 1970s, oil brought wealth to Norway, and now these deeply patriotic people enjoy one of the highest standards of living in the world. But

money hasn't changed Norwegians' deep-rooted love for nature: they are first and foremost an outdoor people, and Norway is a country where inhabitants and visitors alike can make the most of limitless space for walking, skiing, touring and breathing in the clear air – the ultimate active-holiday destination. ❑

PRECEDING PAGES: old wooden houses at Bergen; Svinoy lighthouse on the West Cape; atmospheric landscape of the West Cape. **LEFT:** Trollfjord. **ABOVE:** the Atlantic Road in Møre og Romsdal; monument marking the Arctic Circle on the island of Hestmannoy; "King Neptune" anoints passengers as they cross the Arctic Circle.

Norway

Norwegian Territory

Svalbard

OSLO, NORDIC CITY OF LIGHT

With its idyllic setting, a multitude of galleries and museums and a magnificent new landmark overlooking the Oslofjord, the capital of Norway is a great introduction to the country

Travellers to Norway once gave Oslo no more than a passing nod as they steamed through on their way to Bergen and the more spectacular scenery of the west-coast fjords. But if Oslo once lacked the vitality of Copenhagen or Stockholm, prompting Munch and many of his contemporaries to leave the country for the Continent, today the city bears little resemblance to its 1880s, or even 1980s self. The small capital by the fjord, which celebrated its 1,000th birthday in the year 2000, has come of age in quite a spectacular way, and its new-found confidence can be felt on every street corner.

On the world stage

Oslo has a vibrant city centre, heaving with shoppers, visitors and business-people day and night, with a stunning new opera house, a revitalised water-front area, world-class museums and the world's most modern ski jump, standing proud on the hills above the buildings. An array of festivals draw big international names and music fans from far and wide, while top restaurants rival the very best in the world. The list goes on...

It still ranks as one of the world's most expensive cities, but at least Oslo

has awakened to the attractions of city fun, and developed into a metropolis with a revitalised cultural life and a diverse and lively nightlife. In 2010 Oslo was the only Scandinavian city to make it into the top 10 city-break destinations at the World Travel Awards, the industry's biggest and most prestigious award worldwide. Oslo's cultural rebirth in recent years has been in part conscious, in part a natural outcome of infusions of money in the right places.

On the back of the oil boom came more money for the arts. Suddenly

Main attractions
OPERA HOUSE
CITY HALL
AKERSHUS FORTRESS
AKER BRYGGE
NOBEL PEACE CENTER
KARL JOHANS GATE AND ROYAL PALACE
NATIONAL GALLERY
MUNCH MUSEUM
VIGELAND SCULPTURE PARK
HOLMENKOLLEN SKI JUMP
VIKING SHIP MUSEUM
NORWEGIAN FOLK MUSEUM

PRECEDING PAGES: Vigeland's *Fountain* in the sculpture park named after him. **LEFT:** standing before *Monolitten*, Vigeland Sculpture Park. **RIGHT:** dining at Aker Brygge.

there were sufficient goings-on at home to make artists curious enough to return. And since the opening of the magnificent waterside **Opera House** ❶ (Operahuset) in Bjørvika in April 2008, they have been lining up to perform here. Oslo's new landmark, which has in itself spearheaded the redevelopment of the entire downtown area around the central train station, was designed by Norwegian architects Snøhetta, and the white marble and glass structure, which has already won an array of prestigious architectural prizes and awards, has been an instant success with both locals and tourists. An impressive 1.3 million people visited it in the first year of opening alone, making this Oslo's most popular attraction in 2008.

Oslo from the water

Oslo is at the head of a fjord shaped like a swan's neck; it is surrounded by low hills. Your initial impression will depend on how you arrive. The ideal way is by boat, for then you get the most complete picture, though arriving by car from the south along the Mosseveien also offers some impressive views.

There are a few tall buildings in Oslo, but your view from the fjord will still be dominated by the **City Hall** ❷ (Rådhus; tel: 23 46 12 00; daily 9am–6pm; charge May–Aug, otherwise free; guided tours Mon and Wed at 10am, noon and 2pm, and of the clock tower in summer). It is a large, mud-coloured building topped by two square towers, known as the "goat's cheese" (geitost)

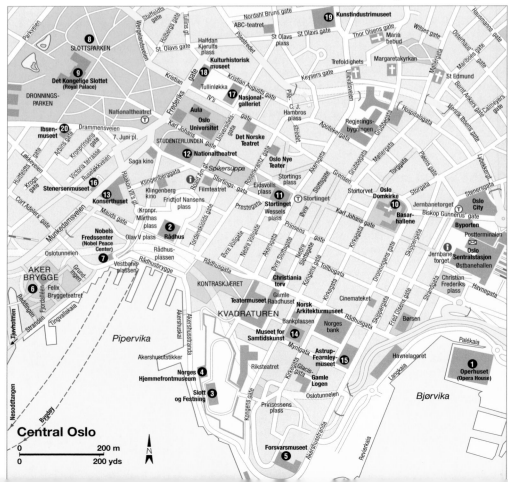

Central Oslo

0 ___ 200 m
0 ___ 200 yds

N

by locals because of its striking resemblance to blocks of Norwegian brown goat's cheese.

The courtyard is adorned with fantastic figures and symbols from Norwegian mythology; note the **astronomical clock**, the **Yggdrasill frieze** by Dagfin Werenskiold and Dyre Vaas' **swan fountain**. The murals inside the main hall are based around more modern themes, and this is where the Nobel Peace Prize is awarded every year on 10 December. The south-facing clock, at 8 metres (30ft) in diameter, is one of the largest timepieces in Europe.

War and peace

Walking south from the Rådhus along the fjord is the medieval **Akershus Castle and Fortress** ❸ (Slott og Festning; tel: 23 09 32 12; May–Aug Mon–Sat 10am–4pm, Sun 12.30–4pm; Sept–Apr weekends only noon–5pm; fortress grounds daily 6am–9pm; charge for castle). Built originally in 1299, it helped to protect Christiania (as Oslo was called until 1925) from marauders throughout the periods of Danish and Swedish rule. The Nazis took over Akershus during World War II and shot several Resistance fighters by the old magazine. When the war was over, the traitorous Norwegian chancellor, Quisling, was shot on the same spot.

The **Resistance Museum** ❹ (Norges Hjemmefrontmuseum; tel: 23 09 31 38; June–Aug Mon–Sat 10am–5pm, Sun 11am–5pm; Sept–May Mon–Fri 10am–4pm, Sat–Sun 11am–4pm; charge) in the grounds illustrates the intense story of occupied Norway, while the **Armed Forces Museum** ❺ (Forsvarsmuseet; tel: 23 09 35 82; May–Aug Mon–Fri 10am–5pm, Sat–Sun 11am–5pm; Sept–Apr, Tue–Fri 10am–4pm, Sat–Sun 11am–5pm) covers Norwegian military and political history from the Vikings to the present day.

Thrusting up on the opposite side of the Pipervika inlet are the glass, chrome and neon buildings of **Aker Brygge** ❻. Centred around an open-air sculpture court, this renovated shipyard and harbour-side development is the setting for shopping arcades, trendy bars and restaurants, food stalls, theatres and galleries, as

TIP

The Oslo Pass gives free entry to over 30 museums and attractions in Oslo, free parking in municipal car parks, free public transport in the greater Oslo area, and other discounts in the city. Available for 24, 48 or 72 hours. Buy online at www.visitoslo.com.

BELOW: Oslo's Opera House.

A statue of Karl Johan XIV stands on the steps of Det Kongelige Slott, the Royal Palace.

well as outdoor summer festivals. Buzzing with activity round the clock, this pedestrian area is hugely popular with both tourists and locals, and on a hot summer day there are few better things to do in Oslo than to sit at one of the many outdoor terraces and watch life go by on the waterfront.

West of Aker Brygge is the swanky newer development of Tjuvholmen, which also has its fair share of restaurants and expensive apartments. A luxury hotel will open here in 2013, which will be the first hotel in Oslo with a location right on the water. Between Aker Brygge and City Hall is the **Nobel Peace Center ❼** (Nobels Fredssenter, Rådhusplassen; tel: 48 30 10 00; www. nobelpeacecenter.org; daily June–Aug 10am–6pm; closed Mon rest of the year; guided tours in English at 1pm every weekend; charge), telling the history of the prize and offering exhibits on war, peace and conflict resolution. Housed in a renovated train station, it's an ultra-modern account of world affairs since the late 1800s. There are also changing temporary exhibitions and a popular café on site.

In summer, greenery encroaches on Oslo from every side. From the fjord approach you'll see the tops of the trees of the **Palace Gardens ❽** (Slottsparken), and several parks stretching north beyond them to the wooded hills at Oslo's back. There your eye will inevitably be drawn to the impressive new Holmenkollen ski jump on one of the city's highest hills *(see page 105 for more information).*

Royal avenue

Oslo city centre is large enough to be interesting yet compact enough to cover on foot. The main axis is **Karl Johans gate**, originally designed in 1826 by the royal architect H.D.F. Linstow. It was widened some 30 years later to become Oslo's answer to the Champs Elysées. Its western end merges into the broad avenue leading to the doors of the **Royal Palace ❾** (Det Kongelige Slott; guided tours in the summer, tickets sold at local post offices and online at www.billettservice.no; if you haven't pre-booked try your luck at the main entrance, where remaining tickets are sold on the day) and

BELOW: Nobel Peace Center.
BELOW RIGHT: Karl Johans gate leading to the Royal Palace.

the focal point of the National Day celebrations on 17 May. In the east it runs to Jernbanetorget, the location of **Oslo S station** (Oslo Sentralstasjon). To the south, the centre extends to the fjord.

Cathedral of art

Parallel to Karl Johans gate to the north is **Grensen**, another busy, shop-lined street. **Oslo Cathedral** ❿ (Dom-kirke; daily Mon–Thur 10am–4pm, and throughout the weekend from Fri 3.30pm until Sun 7pm; tel: 23 62 90 10), sparkling new after a three-year renovation project, dominates the Stortorvet (square) at the east end of Grensen. Completed in 1697, its exterior is of darkened brown brick, while inside artists of the 18th, 19th and 20th centuries have contributed to the cathedral's adornment, including stained-glass windows by Emmanuel Vigeland and ceiling paintings by Hugo Lous Mohrs, which took over 14 years to complete. They are the largest of their kind in Norway. Look out for the massive bronze doors by artist Dagfin Werenskiold, the baroque altar panel, pulpit and organ's facade, and the silver altar piece by Italian sculptor Arrigo Minerbi, famous for his work on Milan Cathedral. Behind Domkirke is **Basarhallene** – a round, colonnaded market with food and handicraft stalls. Lille Grensen leads south to the **Parliament** ⓫ (Storting; tel: 23 31 35 96, www. stortinget.no; late June–late Aug guided tours 10am, 11.30am, 1pm, free; rest of year by appointment) on **Karl Johans gate**, from where **Eidsvollplass** spreads out in front of the Storting.

A big open-air ice rink is erected here every winter, while in summer it's a popular lunchtime spot for nearby office workers, who come and sit by the fountains while enjoying their *matpakke* (packed lunch). **Studenter-lunden**, the small park around the university, contains the main university building, **Aula**, which is decorated with murals by Edvard Munch.

The **National Theatre** ⓬ (National-altheatret), the country's main scene, which stages a mix of classical drama and groundbreaking contemporary productions, opened its doors in 1899, and is flanked with statues of national

TIP

Fancy a ski? Tryvann Vinterpark, only 20 minutes north of downtown Oslo, has 14 slopes (floodlit at night), seven lifts, a terrain park, and more. Accessible by tram and bus from the city centre, it's open from early December to April. www.tryvann.no.

BELOW: outside the National Theatre.

Children in Oslo have their own museum of art, Barnekunstmuseet (Lille Frøens vei 4; Tue–Thur and Sun; closed mid-Aug–mid-Sept). Works by youngsters from 180 countries are on display, and artistic activities are a regular feature.

icons Henrik Ibsen and Bjørnstjerne Bjørnson. It is just opposite Studenterlunden, and Slottsparken is immediately west.

Music venues

Norwegians, with their seagoing past, have always had a fine awareness of faraway cultures. But it has always been hard to entice foreign artists they admired to their own shores: Norway was too remote, the population too small. Riotously enthusiastic receptions can make up for a lot, however, and that's how Oslo now gets its favourites back year after year. The Oslo Philharmonic, whose home is the **Konserthuset** ⓫ (tel: 23 11 31 00; see www.oslokonserthus.no for programme) on Munkedamsveien, performs with a dazzling sequence of guest conductors and soloists.

Away from the classical, the variety of music to be heard in Oslo's clubs and concert halls is vast, from world music to indie rock and black metal, and everything in between. International rock stars now regularly add Oslo to their world-tour calendar,

RIGHT: berry picker.

and two of the best venues to see them are the **Oslo Spektrum**, Sonja Henies plass 2 (tel: 22 05 29 00; www. oslospektrum.no), and **Rockefeller**, Torggata 16 (tel: 22 20 32 32; www. rockefeller.no). The music festival calendar is also a busy one, kicking off at Easter with the Inferno Metal Festival, while summer highlights include the Norwegian Wood rock festival, held in Frogner every June, and the Øya Festival, Oslo's largest rock festival, in August – the international jazz and chamber music festivals also take place in August. Later in the year, the Ultima festival features contemporary music (and a lot of impro), and the World Music festival draws artists from far and wide (for more on festivals, *see page 358*).

Christian's town

The simple need for space to accommodate all these artistic ventures has also played a role in reviving neglected parts of Oslo. It has helped to breathe life back into **Christian IV's town** (Kvadraturen), a historic area bounded to the north by Råd-

Weekends Outdoors

A typical city-dweller from Oslo spends huge amounts of time outdoors. In summer, people are likely to plan outdoor activities after work, anything from swimming, berry-picking, walking, boating or cycling at home in the suburbs in the light of the evening sun. Norwegians treasure their space and contact with nature, and many people who work in Oslo live a fair distance from the city; in winter, this means they can get quickly onto the floodlit slopes and cross-country ski trails after work.

Come the weekend, there is a widely followed pattern for the 48 hours. Friday night is usually a night out on the town. Saturday morning is given over to shopping, followed by gardening or watching football, and Saturday evening tends to be dinner or a party at someone's home. No matter how wild or calm the Saturday night, Sunday is *tur* day. The *tur* is a walk or ski tour, and a formidable tradition. Depending on a person's age, fitness and the number of accompanying children, the *tur* can be anything from a one- to six-hour affair. Some walks will include café stops in one of the 70-odd cabin lodges in the **Nordmarka** area of Oslo; if not, coffee and hot chocolate come along in a vacuum flask.

Then home to change for an early dinner before going off to the cinema. And thereby hangs a weekend.

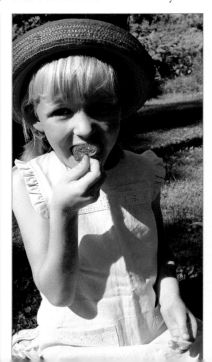

husgata and to the south by Akershus Slott, and characterised by old customs and shipping houses and grand open plazas. At one time this area was frequented only by prostitutes and their pursuers. The district's history as a redoubtable part of Oslo is reflected in its former nickname, "Little Algeria" – see the painting in Engebret Café on Bankplassen, an artists' haunt since the early 1900s. **Gamle Logen** on Grev Wedels plass is now a serious concert venue, and there's also the **Cinemateket** (repertory film theatre) a few blocks away.

The original Central Bank (Norges Bank) building on Bankplassen houses the **Museum of Contemporary Art** ⓮ (Museet for Samtidskunst; tel: 21 98 20 00; Tue–Fri 11am–5pm, Thur until 7pm, Sat–Sun noon–5pm; free), showing an extensive collection of 20th-century Norwegian art. Also worth a visit is the **National Museum for Architecture** (Nasjonalmuseet – Arkitektur, Bankplassen 3; tel: 21 98 21 00; Tue–Fri 11am–5pm, Thur until 7pm, Sat–Sun noon–5pm; free). Here you will find models of some of

Norway's most significant buildings, as well as exhibitions covering a range of related topics. The purpose-built pavilion housing the changing exhibitions was designed by Sverre Fehn, one of Norway's most acclaimed architects.

Just around the corner is the **Astrup Fearnley Museum of Modern Art** ⓯ (Dronningensgate 4; tel: 22 93 60 60; Tue–Fri 11am–5pm, Thur until 7pm, Sat–Sun noon–5pm), featuring work by the likes of Olafur Eliasson, Damien Hirst, Jeff Koons, Charles Ray and Andy Warhol, among many others.

Galleries across the city are full of art in every medium, and established museums have opened their doors to the works of contemporary artists. Try the **Stenersenmuseet** ⓰ (Munkedamsveien 15; tel: 22 49 36 00; Tue, Thur 11am–7pm, Wed, Fri–Sun 11am–5pm; charge Apr–Sept only), which shows Norwegian art from 1850 to 1970.

A multitude of museums

The National Gallery ⓱ (Nasjonalgalleriet, Universitetsgaten 13; tel: 21 98 20 00; Tue–Fri 10am–6pm, Thur

BELOW: National Gallery.

TIP

You can save on accommodation and sightseeing by booking an *Oslo Pakken* (Oslo Package) offered by travel agents. A room with breakfast at a choice of 42 hotels and the Oslo Pass *(see page 147)* are included.

until 8pm, Sat–Sun 11am–5pm) is for anyone who has never heard of any Norwegian artist apart from Edvard Munch. The sheer size, if not the content, of the forest and fjord paintings of the Romantic artist J.C. Dahl (1788–1857) will impress you. You'll also see the work of his prolific contemporaries Adolph Tidemand (1814–76) and Hans Frederik Gude (1825–1903). There is a wonderful series of etchings depicting barn dances, village scenes and festivities. The display of Impressionist works is excellent. And don't forget the Munch room.

Behind the National Gallery is the **Historical Museum ⑱** (Kulturhistorisk Museet, Frederiksgate 2; tel: 22 85 19 00; mid-May–mid-Aug Tue–Sun 10am–5pm; rest of the year 11am–4pm; free), which retraces Norwegian history from the Stone Age to the present time. The museum contains Norway's largest collection of gold treasures from Viking times, and an interesting exhibit of Norwegian coins. Other exhibitions, both temporary and permanent, cover the Arctic, East Asia, Africa, Latin America and Ancient Egypt. A little further northeast is the **Museum of Applied Art ⑲** (Kunstindustrimuseet, St Olavs gate 1; tel: 21 98 20 00; Tue–Fri 11am–5pm, Thur until 7pm, Sat–Sun noon–4pm). It is graced by two earthenware urns at its entrance and has superb displays of Norwegian textile, fashion and furniture design. The most famous tapestry it owns is the *Baldishol*, dating from 1180, and one of the most popular exhibits is of the royal costumes. On the uppermost floor is a collection of Scandinavian design for the home ranging from bent-wood chairs to streamlined kitchen gadgets.

Ibsen at home

West along Drammensveien from the National Gallery is the **Ibsen Museum ⑳** (Ibsenmuseet, Arbins gate 1; tel: 22 12 35 50; www.ibsenmuseet.no; charge), with guided tours of the apartment where Henrik Ibsen lived from 1895 until his death in 1906.

For the technically minded, 8km (5 miles) to the north there is the **Norwegian Museum of Technology** (Norsk Teknisk Museum, Kjelsåsveien

BELOW: shop at the Ibsen Museum.

143; tel: 22 79 60 00; 20 June–20 Aug daily 10am–6pm; rest of year Tue–Fri 9am–4pm, Sat–Sun 11am–6pm; suburban train, trams 12 or 15, buses 22, 25 and 37 to Kjelsås; charge). This is a great day out for children, with lots of hands-on exhibitions about energy, industry, transport and telecommunications. Nearby is a watermill that feeds the Akerselva River.

Showcasing Munch

Combining a museum visit with a stroll is a relaxing and usually a cheap way of spending part of a day or evening. Once you leave behind the bigger hotels and restaurants where businesspeople wine and dine, food and drink prices drop significantly. The suggestions that follow focus on sights outside the very heart of Oslo.

One of Norway's best-known museums is **Munch Museum** in the east of the city ㉑ (Munch-museet, Tøyengata 53; tel: 23 49 35 00; www.munch.museum. no; June–Aug daily 10am–6pm; Sept–May Tue–Fri 10am–4pm, Sat–Sun 11am–5pm; charge; T-bane Tøyen/ Munch-museet). The largest collec-

tion of Munch's works in the world is housed here, all donated by the artist himself.

The life of Edvard Munch (1863–1944) was permeated by sickness – a theme reflected in his paintings. Himself a sickly child, both his mother and sister died at an early age from tuberculosis. Festive renderings of gypsy families and blazing autumn landscapes counteract these gloomier works. The famous *The Scream* (*Skrika, 1893*) stolen in 2004 but recovered two years later, is darkly riveting, as is the *Death of Marat* series (*Marats død, 1907*) in which Munch portrays himself bleeding from gunshot wounds inflicted by an angry mistress.

After a series of breakdowns, Munch returned to Norway, having spent most of his adult artistic life in Paris and Berlin. He sought peace, but continued working, in his cottage at Åsgårdstrand in Vestfold.

The Munch Museum is flanked by parks. The one to the east contains the **Tøyenbadet** (public swimming pools), including a lido, water slide and saunas. To the west is **Tøyen Botanical**

A stroll round the Tøyen Botanical Gardens makes a pleasant change from culture.

BELOW: *Separation* (1896) at the Munch Museum.

Strømsdammen Lake • **Tryvannstårnet** • Øvresetertjern

Lillevann • Voksen-kollen • Frogner-seteren

Skogen

Bogstad camping-plass

Bogstad Manor

Voksenlia

Holmenkollen kapell

29 Holmenkollen bakken

Midtsuen

Holmenkollen

Ankerveien

Besserud

↓ Oslo

Strømsdalsveien • Jonsrudveien • Gustav Vigelands vei

Tryvannsveien • Lillevannsveien • Ullveien • Voksenkollveien • Holmenkollveien • Mattrostveien

BLINDERN • Kringkastingen • Wilhelm Færdens vei • Kirkeveien

Grefsen • Frøen • Apalveien • Gydas vei • Gardeveien • Suhms gate

VESTRE GRAVLUND • Borgen • Slemdalsveien • Thaulows vei • Trudvangveien

Majorstuen • Aalis • Suhms gate • Fagerborggata

Colosseum senter • **Sporveismuseet** • Schønings gate • Lyder Sagens gate • Bogstadveien

Misjons-kirken • Jacob Aalls gate • Hammerstads gate • **Døvekirken**

Colosseum kino • **Majorstuen** • Ole Vigs gate • Sorgenfri- • Industrigata • Vibés gate

VIGELANDS-PARKEN • **26**

Fridtjof Nansens vei • Essendrops gate • Bogstadveien • Gjørstads gate • 168 • Rosenborggata

MAJORSTUEN • Majorstuveien

Monolitten • **1** • **27** • Frogner stadion

FROGNERPARKEN • HEGDEHAUG • Bogstadveien • Ole Vigs gate

Frogner- dammene • Kirkeveien • St Dominikus • Professor Dahls gate • Industrigata

Oslo Bymuseet • **28** • R2 • Fuglehauggata • Fearnleys gate • Prof. Dahls gate

Vigeland-museet • Munthes gate • HOMANSBYEN • Uranienborgveien • Oscars gate • Grenner

FROGNER • Nordraaks gate • Gyldenløves gate • Holtegata • Josefines gate • Hegdehaugsveien

Halvdan Svartes gate • Solheimgata • Tidemands gate • Eckersbergs gate • Briskebyveien • Josefines gate • Uranienborgveien

Kristinelundveien • Thomas Heftyes gate • Gimleveien • BRISKEBY • Arno Bergs plass • Eilert • Uranienborg • Kunstn

Eckersbergs gate • Nobels gate • Odins gate • Løvenskiolds gate • Camilla Colletts vei • Oscars gate • Werge

Olav Kyrres plass • Bygdøy allé • Eilisenbergveien • Gyldenløves gate • president Harbitz gate • Skovveien • Riddervolds plass • Ridderv

Olav Kyrres gt • Nobels gate • Thomas • Frognerveien • Niels Juels gate • Meltzers gate • Parkv • SLOTTSPARK

Frøyas gate • Drammensveien • Tostrups gate • Frogner • Gimle kino • Gabels gate • Colbjørnsens gate • Inkognitogata • **Slottet**

Båthavn • Bygdøy allé • Mogens Thorsens gate • Bygdøy allé • Oslo Energi • Parkveien • DRONNINGS-PARKEN

American Lutheran Church • Sophia Lies gate • Niels Juels gate • Skovveien • Frognerveien • Hansteens • Drammensveien

E18 • Thomas Heftyes gate • Stangs gate • Hydro • Solligata • Løkkeveien

Wedels vei • Drammensveien • Frederiks gate • Niels Juels gate • Observatorie terrasse • Observatoriegata • Reichweins gt • RUSELØKKA

SKILLEBEKK • Universitets-biblioteket • Munkedamsveien • Parkveien

Bygdøy • Frognerkilen • Båthavn • Rikstrygdeverket • Frammensveien • Munkedamsveien • Oslotunnelen

Oscarshall slott • Oscarshallveien • Ferry port • Hjortnesskaia • AKER BRYGGE

Dronninghavnveien • Båthavn • **Kongen** • Filipstadveien • Munkedamsveien

Mellbyedalen • Dronningen • FILIPSTAD • Filipstadkaia • Piper

34 Norsk Folkemuseum • **35** The Holocaust Center • Langviksveien

Langviksveien • Christian Bennaches vei • Filipstadutstikker • Tjuvholmen

30 Vikingskipshuset (Viking Ship Museum) • Kon-Tiki Museet • **32** • **31** Frammuseet

Oslo • Nørsk Sjøfartsmuseum (Maritime Museum) • **Oslofjord**

0 — 500 m
0 — 500 yds

Denmark, Germany ↓ • **36** Hellviktangen Manor, Nesoddtangen

One of Oslo's many statues, overlooking the water in Eidsvollplass.

Gardens ❷ (Tøyenhagen), with the Zoological, Mineralogical, Geological and Palaeontological Museums at its north end (all year). In September and early spring this is the site of Norway's largest traditional circus.

Vibrant Grünerløkka

A few streets northwest of Munch-museet, across Trondheimsveien, is the **Grünerløkka** district, a former working-class neighbourhood now densely populated with artists and writers. The most interesting street in Grünerløkka is **Markveien** ❷, painted in muted pastel colours and lined with galleries and boutiques. Parallel to Markveien is Thorvald Meyers gate, with many restaurants and bars open until 3am. On long, warm summer nights, locals like to sit alfresco at one of the many terraces, and getting a table outside can prove tricky.

Continuing north on Markveien, you'll find a cross street called Grüners gate. From here up to Schleppergrells gate are some magnificent residential courtyards: peer inside for a look at tranquil urban living in Oslo.

Futuristic design

Just to the southwest of Grünerløkka, across the Akerselva River, **The Norwegian Centre for Design and Architecture** ❷ (DogA, Haussmans gate 16; tel: 47 23 29 28 70; www.doga.no; Mon–Fri 10am–5pm, Wed–Thur until 8pm, Sat–Sun noon–5pm) has taken up home in a restored transformer station next to Jakob's church. This is the place to see the latest in Nordic contemporary design – furniture, lighting and graphics – with new exhibitions every couple of months, a shop selling choice items, and a restaurant.

Multicultural Grønland

Lying southeast of Grünerløkka is one of Oslo's biggest ethnic commercial neighbourhoods, **Grønland** (T-bane to Grønland station). It's largely Pakistani, but other cultures are evident in the shops, cafés and the dress of those out strolling. The **Grønland Basar**, at the corner of Tøyengata and Grønlandsleiret (Mon–Fri 10am–8pm, Sat until 6pm), offers everything from a halal butcher's shop to Middle Eastern sweets and Persian carpets. The

BELOW: *Monolitten* at the Vigeland Sculpture Park; busking in the park.

old Grønland Police Station next door at Tøyenbekken 5 now houses the **International Cultural Center and Museum** (tel: 22 05 28 30; Tue–Fri 10am–4pm, Thur until 8pm, Sat–Sun noon–4pm), with exhibits on immigration, a gallery and a café.

Kampen ㉕, whose northern limit is Kampenparken (on the southeast side of Munch-museet), is a district of gorgeous wooden houses brilliantly painted in sienna, gold, pastels and vibrant blues. Some of the streets in lower Kampen are overhung by trees and are supremely quiet; look up, too, at the dormer windows above the street corners, hung with macramé and lace curtains.

Vigeland's vision

West of the city centre is **Frogner Park** (Frognerparken) or **Vigeland Sculpture Park** ㉖ (Vigelandsparken; all year). The park, containing the life's work of the famous Norwegian sculptor Gustav Vigeland (1869–1943), is a 40-minute walk from the centre. One way of getting there would be by continuing on northwest from the Royal Palace to Hegdehaugsveien, which becomes Bogstadsveien – a long, lively street of art galleries and enticing shops – or hop on a bus (Nos 20, 45 or 81) or tram (No. 12) in the direction of Frogner. Any westbound T-bane from the Nationaltheatret stops at Majorstuen, the end of Bogstadsveien, from where it is only a short walk to the main entrance of the park.

Once inside the intricate wrought-iron gates, you'll come across **Vigelandsbroen** (bridge), bedecked with 58 bronze figures of men, women and children, including the famous *Sinnataggen (Angry Boy)*. Next is *Fontenen (Fountain)*, six male figures raising a giant bowl. Vigeland was obsessed with the cycle of life, which he depicts here in 20 reliefs around the edge of the fountain pool.

Above the fountain, on a raised plateau, and surrounded by 36 groups of granite figures, is ***Monolitten*** ㉗, a great spire 17 metres (55ft) high and comprising 121 figures sculpted out of one solid block of Iddefjord granite. The last of the major sculptures, the *Livshjulet (Wheel of Life)* is a continuum

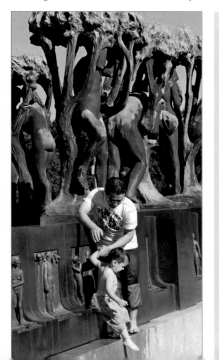

LEFT: cooling off at the Vigeland Sculpture Park.

Oslo's Nightlife

Oslo's streets are tangibly alive, especially in summer: festivals come fast and furious, and the crowds at restaurants and cafés brim onto the pavement. The city's nightlife owes much to the extension of licensing hours to 3am.

The influx of immigrants has resulted in a wide variety of **restaurants** being opened, which complement the Norwegian and fish menus traditionally on offer. Other dining options include the more casual and often cheaper *kafé*, *gjæstgiveris*, pubs, *kros*, bistros, *spiseris* and *kafeterias*. Seattle-style coffee shops are also popular.

Bars and **clubs** are spread throughout the city, and range from underground to upmarket. The "in" scene can be identified by the queue out front, which will certainly not disperse until after 1am. Since eating and drinking in restaurants and bars is expensive, many people invite friends into their homes for "before" drinks *(vorspiel)*. Likewise, after a night on the town it is not unusual to invite friends back to polish off the remaining contents of the house bar *(nachspiel)*.

Nobel's Peace Prize

Out of dynamite came peace: Alfred Nobel amassed a great fortune in his lifetime, which he left to endow the Nobel prizes

One of the great ironies is that the Swedish armaments manufacturer Alfred Nobel should have been the founder of the world's most prestigious prize for peace. Was it the realisation that his invention of dynamite in 1866 could and had been easily turned from peaceful rock tunnelling to war that led him to include the peace category alongside prizes for physics, chemistry, medicine and literature? Or was his conscience troubled by the thought that his great riches were built on weapons of war? It may have been no more than a tribute to the Norwegian reputation as workers for peace.

It is almost as strange that when he set up his trust fund, Nobel chose the Norwegian parliament (Storting) to make the peace award. It was a time when the near century-old union between Sweden and Norway was collapsing. Perhaps Nobel hoped that, by passing the Peace Prize into Norwegian jurisdiction, he might help to keep the two nations together. If this was his aim, he failed. The union was dissolved less than 10 years after his death in 1896, and Norway was already a year-old sovereign state at the first ceremonies in 1906.

Except for the Peace Prize, the other categories are judged in Sweden and presented in Stockholm to those who, in Nobel's words, "shall have conferred the greatest benefit on mankind". The Nobel Peace Prize ceremony takes place in Oslo's City Hall (Rådhus) on 10 December every year.

Nobel's early instructions were that the Peace Prize should be used to award efforts to reduce the size of military forces and standing armies, but the prize broadened its remit to the promotion of peace in general. This vague brief can lead to controversy, as it did when the Israeli and Egyptian leaders, Menachem Begin and Anwar Sadat, received the Peace Prize jointly for their 1978 efforts to open up talks and communication between their two countries. Dr Henry Kissinger's award in 1972 also aroused controversy, particularly when his Vietnamese co-recipient, Le Duc Tho, turned down his own award for their joint efforts in ending the Vietnam War.

However, few begrudged Nelson Mandela and F.W. de Klerk their joint award in 1993. There were no dissenters when the Red Cross received the prize in 1917 for its work amid the battlefield carnage of World War I. The explorer Fridtjof Nansen regarded the Nobel Peace Prize as the greatest of the tributes to his years as internationalist, humanitarian and head of the Norwegian delegation at the League of Nations.

Among the many other recipients were Martin Luther King, Dr Albert Schweitzer, Amnesty International, the Dalai Lama, Kofi Annann and more recently US president Barack Obama, whose high profile and much publicised visit to Oslo to pick up his prize in 2009 was in stark contrast to that of Mother Teresa, who 30 years earlier had accepted her award in her customary habit and sandals despite the Norwegian winter.

Women's campaigns for peace have not gone entirely unnoticed, with awards being made to Betty Williams and Máiread Corrigan in 1976 after they and thousands of other women demanded an end to military and paramilitary bloodshed in Northern Ireland, and to Shirin Ebadi in 2003, who has worked tirelessly for human rights in Iran.

Learn more about the Nobel Peace Prize at the Nobel Peace Center in Oslo (see page 148). ❏

LEFT: Alfred Nobel (1833–96).

of human figures in a kind of airborne ring dance.

The **Vigeland Museum** (Vigelandmuseet; tel: 23 49 37 00; Tue–Sun noon–4pm, summer 11am–5pm; charge), containing the rest of his work, is at the southern end of the park. Vigeland spent 40 years of his life designing and constructing the park, all financed by the taxpayer, something Munch found reprehensible; he made his own feelings clear by donating all his own work to the city.

Oslo in the making

Frogner Park also contains the **Oslo City Museum** ㉘ (Oslo Bymuseet; tel: 23 28 41 70; Tue–Sun 11am–4pm; free), which traces the city's history. Founded in 1050 by Harald Hardråde, Oslo was originally bounded by the (now subterranean) Bjørvika, Alna and Hovin Rivers. It took another 250 years before it attained capital status during the reign of Håkon V (1299–1319). The town had just 3,000 inhabitants at the time.

Following a great fire in 1624, which caused immense destruction, Christian IV decided to move the city settlements to where Akershus Festning (fortress) now stands, and the town became known as Christiania (Kvadraturen). What was the centre is now called **Christiania torv**, where in 1997 a statue of Christian IV's index finger was erected to commemorate the historic event.

With its strict grid plan, Christiania had little in common with medieval Oslo. The greatest change, however, has happened over the past 150 years due to growth in its population. In 1880, Christiania had 120,000 inhabitants; by 1910 the population had doubled. By popular consensus the town reverted to its original name in 1925.

From 1945 to 1955, Oslo went through a new period of growth, and surpassed the half-million mark in 1997. Today the city counts 580,000 inhabitants, and the greater Oslo area about 1 million.

Norway's national jump

For the striking new **Holmenkollen** ㉙ ski jump and **Ski Museum** (Skimuseet; tel: 22 92 32 00; June–Aug 9am–8pm; Oct–Apr 10am–4pm; May and Sept 10am–5pm; charge) take T-bane 1 to Holmenkollen. The jump is only used in February and March, and the crowning event of the ski-jump season is the competition on the second Sunday in March (see page 105).

Holmenkollen is a national symbol, as well as Norway's most popular attraction, with more than 1 million visitors every year. The ultra-modern jump, which was rebuilt for the Nordic World Championships in 2011, has an observation platform at the top of the tower (accessible by lift), which affords fantastic views of the city and beyond.

The Ski Museum, situated inside the jump itself, is a monument to "One Thousand Years of Skiing". Very old skis and snowshoes are on display, as well as gear carried by such Norwegian explorers as Fridtjof Nansen, who crossed Greenland on skis. There is also a popular ski simulator, which recreates the thrill of a Holmenkollen

Norway's top female ski jumper, Anette Sagen (25), officially opened the splendid new Holmenkollen ski jump on 3 March 2010.

BELOW: Holmenkollen ski jump.

BELOW:
Norwegian
Maritime Museum.

jump. The same metro line to Holmenkollen (T-bane) ends at **Frognerseteren** (with a restaurant of the same name, famous for its home-made apple pie). The area is thickly forested and popular for walking and skiing. If you choose to go back to Holmenkollen on foot, the walk is signposted and takes 15 to 20 minutes.

Bygone days on Bygdøy

Oslo hugs the fjord, and the city limits extend quite far down its sides. Just west of the harbour is the **Bygdøy peninsula**, where the old Viking ships and the more recent explorer ships are kept, and where Norway's maritime past is commemorated (bus No. 30 or from Apr–early Oct boat No. 91 from Rådhusbrygge 3 in front of City Hall).

Bygdøy is home to the **Viking Ship Museum ③** (Vikingskipshuset; tel: 22 13 52 80; daily May–Sept 9am–6pm; Oct–Apr 10am–4pm; charge), where the three best-preserved Viking ships found in Norway – the *Gokstad*, the *Oseberg* and the *Tune* – all of which had been buried for over 1,000 years in royal burial mounds around the Oslofjord, as was the tradition, are now displayed with other artefacts found at the sites.

The **Fram Museum ③** (Frammuseet; tel: 23 28 29 50; June–Aug daily 9am–6pm; Sept–May daily hours vary; charge), houses Fridtjof Nansen's polar sailing ship *Fram*. Launched in 1892, it was a remarkable vessel that sailed further north and further south than any other on three acclaimed polar expeditions.

Nearby, the **Kon-Tiki Museet ③** (tel: 23 08 67 67; June–Aug daily 9.30am–5.30pm; Sept–May daily hours vary; charge), contains both the *Kon-Tiki* raft on which Thor Heyerdahl travelled from South America to Polynesia, and *Ra II*, a fragile-looking reed barque on which he sailed from Morocco to Barbados. There is also a collection of his Easter Island artefacts.

Almost opposite, the **Norwegian Maritime Museum ③** (Norsk Sjøfartsmuseum; tel: 24 11 41 50; mid-May–Aug daily 10am–6pm; Sept–mid-May daily 10.30am–4pm, Thur until 6pm; charge) presents the history of Norway as a seafaring and boatbuilding nation, including a unique collection of vessels and maritime-themed paintings, countless models of ships, and a stunning panoramic film taking visitors on a cruise along Norway's extraordinary coastline.

Also on Bygdøy is the **Norwegian Folk Museum** ❸❹ (Norsk Folkemuseum; tel: 22 12 37 00; mid-May–mid-Sept daily 10am–6pm; rest of the year Mon–Fri 11am–3pm, Sat–Sun 11am–4pm; charge). The Folk Museum, established in 1894, is an indoor/outdoor museum devoted largely to Norwegian rural culture. The collection of outdoor buildings, including a stave church from Hallingdal, gives a good idea of what old villages and agricultural settlements looked like. Other exhibits include Sami ethnography, a pharmacy museum, a delightfully quaint "colonial shop" (grocery) still in use, and a renovated Oslo apartment building featuring flats as they have evolved since the 1800s.

A 15-minute walk to the south brings you to **The Holocaust Center** ❸❺ (Huk Aveny 56, bus No. 30; tel: 22 84 21 00; daily mid-June–mid-Aug 10am–6pm; rest of the year 11am– 4pm; charge). Housed in the mansion occupied by traitor Vidkun Quisling during World War II, the museum offers a permanent exhibition on the Holocaust and the tragic fate of Norwegian Jews, while serving as a centre for studies of the Holocaust and religious minorities.

Exploring the Oslofjord

Other exploring possibilities are provided by the islands and peninsulas of the Oslofjord, most of which are accessible by ferry from Aker Brygge quay or Vippetangen near Akershus Fortress. Many of the ferries are operated by the same public transit service that runs the bus and tram network, and the same tickets can be used. Mini-cruises of variable duration are also available.

At the tip of a hilly, wooded peninsula jutting from the east side of the fjord is **Nesoddtangen**. Local artists exhibit at **Hellviktangen Manor** ❸❻ (May–Sept; weekends out of season; charge), where a café serves coffee and waffles on Sundays. The house is surrounded by apple trees and gives directly on to the fjord. ❏

BELOW:
at the Norwegian Folk Museum.

Ferry to the Islands

Only 15 minutes by boat from Vippetangen (on the Akershus Fortress-side of the harbour, next to the DFDS and Stena terminals) is **Gressholmen**, one of the prettiest islands in the Oslofjord and best-known for its popular café. It makes an ideal excursion for those who are more interested in a walk than a dip in the sea. As many as 160 species of birds have made their home here. If it's a swim you fancy, **Hovedøya** is where most people head to, particularly with children. Here you will find one of the best sand beaches in the area, as well as fantastic views of the city. There are a myriad of walking trails, too. Or you can venture a bit further to **Langøyene**, the last island on the 94 ferry route, and the only one on which it is permitted to camp. There is a big lawn and another fine sand beach here.

AROUND OSLO AND ITS FJORD

The charms of the Oslofjord may need some searching out, for this is Norway's industrial heartland, but it is rich in natural beauty and Viking history, and the surrounding area echoes to its pulse

At dusk the islands of the fjord that leads to Oslo look like hunched prehistoric animals about to sink into a subaquatic sleep. In the colder months, the sky at sunset grows from lavender to purple while the islands turn slate-grey, then ominous and black. Summer sunsets bring twisted pink clouds underlit by a huge red sun that drops only briefly behind the fjord's western cliffs before rising again in the east.

Daytime along the 100km (60-mile) long fjord reveals a high concentration of industry down both the eastern and western sides. With Oslo at its head, the fjord is the capital's workhorse, its roads travelled by juggernauts with cargoes of timber and oil, its ports and waterways busy with yachts and barges. Outside its working ports, Oslofjord is a magnificent expanse of water, sprinkled liberally with islands, skerries, natural marinas and swimming beaches, and is a popular playground for Oslo residents.

The lungs of the city

Akershus, **Vestfold** and **Østfold** are the three main counties to touch Oslofjord. Akershus county contains parts of the Oslo metropolitan area, the national Gardermoen Airport, plus a

broad swathe of agricultural and forest land reaching to Sweden. At its northern reach lies the Mjøsa lake town of Eidsvoll, where the Norwegian constitution was signed and the modern state born in 1814.

Østfold (east) and Vestfold (west) spread down from Oslo like a pair of lungs. Some of Scandinavia's oldest ruling families were found buried in Vestfold along with Viking ships loaded with booty, while Østfold is rich with ancient rock paintings and stone circles. Both of these counties contain

Main attractions
OSLOMARKA
HADELAND GLASS WORKS
HENIE ONSTAD ART CENTRE
EIDSVOLL
DRØBAK
OLD TOWN, FREDRIKSTAD
HVALER ARCHIPELAGO
FREDRIKSTEN FORT, HALDEN
ÅSGÅRDSTRAND
TØNSBERG
VERDENS ENDE, TJØME

PRECEDING PAGES: Norwegian wood.
LEFT: a summer's evening on the fjord.
RIGHT: Moses with the Ten Commandments, Drøbak church.

Around Oslo and Its Fjord

0   20 km
0   20 miles

N

towns of major historic significance: Fredrikstad and Halden in Østfold, two magnificent fortress towns, and Tøns-berg in Vestfold, the oldest extant Scandinavian city, founded in 872. Remains of **Kaupang**, the oldest Nordic town yet discovered, were found a couple of kilometres from Tønsberg and are now in Oslo's Historical Museum (Kulturhistorisk Museet, *see page 152*). Corroboration of its early existence appeared in a world history by England's 9th-century monarch King Alfred the Great. All are accessible within a couple of hours from Oslo.

Despite its rich history and good travel links, the Oslofjord area doesn't get as many tourists as western Norway; the scenery isn't as dramatic. There are, however, more habitable islands than in any other fjord, many with sports centres and hotels offering everything from tennis to windsurfing and swimming. Inland, the sloping countryside is punctuated by forests, orchards and tilled fields, and appeals to cyclists.

A trail through Akershus

There are fantastic walks in **Oslomarka** (the forests surrounding Oslo) accessible by bus, train or tram (*see box*). By car you can explore further. If you're a fan of Norwegian rural architecture you will have your fill in outer Akershus. Take route E16 in a westerly direction towards Tyrifjorden and Sundvollen into the **Krokkleiva** district. The paths cross wooded hills 400–500 metres (1,300–1,600ft) high. The **King's View ❶** (Kongens Utsikt) gives panoramic views across Steins-fjord and Tyrifjord.

Afterwards, rejoin the E16 north-bound, direction Hønefoss. Leave it before Hønefoss, direction Jevnaker. There you can visit **Hadeland Glass Works** (Hadeland Glassverk; daily, all year) and the countryside of Hadeland. South of Highway 35 is a wilderness of pine marshland, secluded lakes, oak forests and stream-bordered fields. Road 4 south returns you to Oslo and the junction with the E6; northbound

it leads to Gjøvik on the western side of Lake Mjøsa.

After all that walking you'll want to take a rest. The **Henie Onstad Art Centre ❷** (Kunstsenter; www.hok.no; Tue–Fri 11am–7pm, Sat–Sun until 5pm) at Høvikodden, about 10km (6 miles) west of Oslo on a headland jutting into the Oslofjord, contains over 4,000 works spanning the 20th century. Housed in a striking neo-expressionist building, and surrounded by a vast sculpture park, it is one of Norway's foremost galleries for the modern arts, founded by figure-skater and actress Sonja Henie and her husband in 1968.

Around Eidsvoll

If you go east from the junction of Road 4 and the E6 along Road 170 you come to the small village of **Fetsund**, just past Lillestrøm, and the **Lumber Museum** (Fetsund Lenser; tel: 63 88 75 50; June–Aug Tue–Sun 11am–4pm; May and Sept Sat–Sun 11am–4pm; charge), a timber-floating centre celebrating the industrial activity on the banks of the Glomma River. The museum includes a nature trail, a

On the outskirts of the capital, Oslomarka (Oslo's fields) contain 2,500km (1,550 miles) of ski trails, 110km (68 miles) of which are illuminated at night. Trail use is free, and there are lodges and cafés along the way.

BELOW: shopping at Østfold.

nature centre (weekends only, all year) and boat trips to the North Øyeren Nature Reserve, a haven for migratory bird species.

Heading northeast, a road to the left will bring you to **Sørumsand ❸**, where there is a narrow-gauge "Tertitten" railway (tel: 63 86 81 50; Dec, July–mid-Sept Sun only 11am–3pm). From here, Road 171 will bring you back to the E6. Travelling north you come to Jessheim near **Gardermoen ❹** and **Rakni's Mound** (Raknehaugen; all year), a 77-metre (253ft) diameter barrow, centre of an ancient kingdom.

Continuing in a northerly direction, at the southern end of Lake Mjøsa is **Eidsvoll ❺**, about 80km (50 miles) from Oslo. Eidsvoll is a lake town of old wooden houses and churches, and nearby, on the other side of the E6 at Eidsvoll Verk, is a national landmark: **Eidsvoll Memorial Building ❻** (Eidsvollsbygningen; tel: 63 92 22 10; 1 May–30 Aug daily 10am–5pm; times vary rest of the year; charge), a mini-museum to the Norwegian constitution which includes the room where the document was signed. The nearby **Rural Museum** (Eidsvoll Bygdetun; June–Aug Tue–Sun noon–4pm; charge) consists of a collection of 26 farm buildings and a World War II museum, all set in beautiful countryside. Then tour Lake Mjøsa on the old paddle steamer *Skibladner* (tel: 61 14 40 80; late June–mid-Aug Tue–Sun). The round trip takes 12 hours, with the halfway point at Lillehammer (*see page 180*).

Fjordside Drøbak

Heading south out of Oslo on the east side of the fjord, the quiet way to Fredrikstad is via the old **Mossveien**, which hugs the fjord as near as topography allows. Having taken the E6 or E18 out of the city, turn right off the main road at Vinterbru and head for the tip of Bundefjord. Take the road signposted to Nesoddtangen and you will come across a signpost to **Drøbak ❼**.

The village of Drøbak was once a fishermen's settlement. Fishing vessels still arrive here and sell fresh prawns and fish on the quayside. Places of interest include the **Heritage Museum** (Follo Museum; tel: 64 93 99 90; mid-

BELOW: Eidsvoll Memorial Building. **BELOW RIGHT:** Heritage Museum, Drøbak.

May–mid-Sept Tue–Fri 11am–4pm, Sun noon–4pm; charge), the small **Aquarium** (Akvarium; tel: 95 90 39 27; daily June–Aug 10am–7pm; Sept–May 10am–4pm; charge) and **Oscarsborg Fortress** (Oscarsborg Festning; tel: 81 55 19 00; www.nasjonalefestningsverk.no/ oscarsborg; tours in summer) out in the fjord from where gunfire sunk the German cruiser *Blücher* in 1940 (guided boat trips from Drøbak's harbour).

Another point of pride is the cross-timbered **Drøbak Church** (Kirke) from 1776 (all year). The church has an elaborately carved model of a ship, a common piece of church decoration in seafaring towns. Rococo touches include wooden busts of Moses and Aaron. Gospel and jazz concerts are held here in summer. Jazz and blues cruises depart from Drøbak on Thursdays and Saturdays respectively (7pm; details Krambua, tel: 64 93 36 31).

The road out of Drøbak takes off just before the ferry terminal, from where small car ferries run every half-hour or so to the Hurum peninsula. Soon the road passes through fertile farmland and forest, first to Hvitsten and then to **Son**

❽ (pronounced *soon*), a fetching artists' village hugging the edge of a sheltered sound. Son is a popular summer resort for boating enthusiasts. The surrounding countryside and shoreline here provided inspiration for the likes of Theodore Kittelsen and Edvard Munch.

The **Coastal Heritage Centre** (Son Kystkultursenter; tel: 64 95 82 13; mid-May–mid-Sept Tue–Sun) explains how this one-time Dutch freeport (the original name was Zoon) has thrived on timber, ice and fishing. The unusual elevated building at the edge of the marina is the last remaining fishing-net-drying structure in the Oslofjord.

South to Østfold

Østfold is a long funnel through which Norwegians drive on their way to cheaper shopping in Sweden. Despite its industrial towns such as Halden, Sarpsborg and Moss, Østfold buzzes with outdoor pursuits: canoeing and cycling are popular, and the area is dotted with hiking and skiing centres. There are also golf courses, and the Mysen racetrack. Then there's the draw of the fjord. Jeløy peninsula is the

BELOW: Oscarsborg Fortress.

RIGHT: Hvaler Marine National Park.

site of **Galleri F15** (all year; charge) at **Jeløy ❾**, which has fjord-side trails and stupendous lawns. Exhibitions are laid out through a light-filled house. Its cafeteria is a beloved coffee pit stop. Down the coast is the royal enclave of **Hankø**, Norway's regatta centre. The summer home of Princess Martha Louise's grandfather is located here.

Cobbled Fredrikstad

The **Old Town** (Gamlebyen) in **Fredrikstad ❿** is a gem among Østfold towns, and Scandinavia's best-preserved fortress town, dating from 1567. The cobbled streets of the Old Town were laid by prisoners; wooden stocks still face the former prison on the main square. Here you'll also find the former military barracks, now a school (Gamlebyen was a garrison town until as recently as 2002), and a statue of Frederick II, the Danish king who founded the town. Other buildings of interest include the drawbridge, at the entrance to the town, the former arsenal (which today houses the tourist office and the museum) and the Provianthus, the Old Town's oldest building, whose walls are

4 metres (13ft) thick in places. Go for a stroll on the leafy ramparts for a good view over the Glomma River, and the moat that surrounds the fortress. Some of the 200 cannons that once defended the town can still be found here. Then indulge in a bit of browsing in the many art galleries and small boutiques before enjoying a cup of coffee or lunch in one of several little cafés.

History and prehistory figure largely in Østfold's attractions. The **Highway of the Ancients** (Oldtidsveien), along Rv110 between Fredrikstad and Skjeberg, is dotted with dozens of 3,000- to 4,000-year-old rock paintings (*helleristninger*) and burial sites like **Hunn**, covered with stone circles.

Hvaler marine haven

Another great drive is the road to the island community of **Hvaler ⓫**, which crosses the water at some points. It ends at the charming village of Sjær-halden on **Kirkeøy**, where you'll find one of Norway's oldest stone churches, **Hvaler Kirke**, dating back to the Middle Ages. The population of Hvaler increases almost ten-fold in the sum-

Trekking in Oslomarka

Oslo is surrounded by hills and forests known as *marka*. Larch, birch, pine, aspen and several deciduous species dominate; the colour contrast in autumn is worth a special trip. The Trekking Association, Den Norske Turistforening (Storgata 3, Oslo; tel: 22 82 28 00; www.turistforeningen.no; weekdays only) has maps of trails in these areas. Most walking trails double as cross-country skiing trails in winter, and many are floodlit. Access to the trails from the centre is easy via public transport. For **Grorud** and the **Lillomarka** area to the northeast, take either T-bane 5 or bus No. 30 from Jernbanetorget. Trails begin just west of the Grorud T-bane. Due north is **Grefsen**, along a suburban train line (information from Trafikanten at Oslo Sentralstasjon), or via tram 11 and 12 (Grefsen/Kjelsås), or take the bus to Grefsenkollen. **Maridalsvannet** is parkland with a lake fed by clear-water brooks. **Sognsvann**, the lake west of Maridalsvannet, is at the end of T-bane 5. The most heavily used trails start from Sognsvann and **Frognerseteren**.

For walks in the **Holmenkollen** area and northwest, part of Nordmarka, take T-bane 1 to Frognerseteren (not to be confused with Frognerparken) and stay on until the end of the line. In winter, you can rent a sled (*akebrett*) to take on a 3km (2-mile) downhill trail (the Corkscrew). All trails are sign-posted, but if you get lost, seek help from other walkers.

mer, going from 3,700 permanent inhabitants to 30,000 between July and August. The outer part of the archipelago became Europe's first marine national park, jointly with its counterpart on the Swedish side of the border, when it opened in 2009.

Halden ⓬, situated south of Skjeberg and close by the Swedish border, is dominated by **Fredriksten Fort** (Festning; tel: 69 19 37 00; all year, free; museum and tours May–Aug 10am–5pm; charge), a largely intact ruin with many of its buildings serving as small themed museums, including a historic pharmacy (1870), bakery and brewery. The streets below were laid out along the cannons' blast lines to give the fortress's defenders freedom to fire. Local residents famously torched their town to drive out the Swedes in 1716, a heroic feat commemorated in the Norwegian national anthem. The views from the top of the fortress are stunning, and open-air concerts often take place here in summer. Between June and mid-August a passenger boat makes regular trips along the Halden Canal (one of only two inland water-way systems in Norway), navigating through the massive Brekke locks, the highest in Scandinavia, which rise to 26 metres (85ft).

Throughout Østfold, St Olav's Day (29 July) is celebrated with a great show of folk costumes, music and dance. One of the best displays is at the **Borgarsyssel Museum** (June–Aug Tues–Fri 11am–3pm, Sat–Sun noon–4pm; Sept Sun only; free) in **Sarpsborg** ⓭, a town founded by St Olav himself in 1016.

Across to Vestfold

The Moss–Horten car ferry connects Østfold and Vestfold in less than an hour. There is much shared history between Østfold and Vestfold. It was the fast action of troops on both sides of the fjord that led to the sinking of the *Blücher*, scuppering Hitler's plans for an easy invasion.

The **Naval Museum** (Marinemuseet; tel: 33 03 33 97; May–Sept daily noon–4pm; Oct–Apr Sun noon–4pm; free) at **Horten** ⓮ documents this event and hundreds of others in displays bulging with weird and wonderful artefacts

WHERE

The publication *Highway of the Ancients*, free from the tourist office (Tøihusgaten 41, Gamle Fredrikstad), is a useful guide to the ancient history and sites along Rv110, the road between Fredrikstad and Skjeberg.

BELOW LEFT: at Fredriksten.
BELOW: Fredriksten Fort.

TIP

If you're booked on a plane landing at Torp Airport, near Sandefjord, why not sample fjord life at Åsgårdstrand? Once home to Munch, the little town comes alive in summer with a festival, dance and music concerts, barbecues (the Wiener schnitzel barbecue is a favourite), and is a centre for boat trips.

including a full-size submarine open to the public. There are also museums of photography and veteran cars in Horten (both all year; charge).

Heading southwards, tranquil **Løvøy** island has a solemn medieval stone church. This was Viking country, and **Borre National Park** ⓯ (Nasjonalpark; all year; free access to grounds), en route to Tønsberg, contains enormous turf-covered humps concealing Viking kings' graves. Borre also has an extensive network of trails, and the largest collection of Iron Age burial sites in Scandinavia.

Munch's retreat

Keeping to the coastline along Road 311, **Åsgårdstrand** ⓰ is the site of Munch's House (**Munchs Hus**; June–Aug Tue–Sun 11am–6pm; May and Sept Sat–Sun; charge; tel: 33 08 21 31), where the artist lived when he returned to Norway from abroad. Munch painted *Three Girls on a Bridge* here. Åsgårdstrand Hotel is the town's only hotel. In summer a great gush of activity emanates from here, including a festival and boat trips, barbecues,

and the Åsgårdstrand Festival. You can spurn these organised activities to cycle, swim in the fjord, fish in Borre's lake, or watch the fishermen come in each afternoon with the fresh catch.

Viking burials

Between Åsgårdstrand and Tønsberg is **Oseberg Burial Mound** ⓱ (Oseberghaugen; all year), the most important Viking site yet discovered. Oslo's Viking Ship Museum (Vikingskipshuset, *see page 160*) contains the finds, including the 20-metre (65ft) arch-ended wooden ship. Only the mound itself, near Slagen church, remains, but as a symbol Oseberghaugen has a subtle, magnetic power.

Just to the south is history-rich **Tønsberg** ⓲, established in the 9th century and said to be Norway's oldest settlement. On the 65-metre (200ft) high **Slottsfjellet** are the fortress remains and tower. The main street, Storgata, is flanked by Viking graves. These were excavated and incorporated, under glass, into the ground floor of the new library. Across the street are the walls of one of only two medieval round churches in Scandinavia. The most renowned king to hold court in Tønsberg was Håkon Håkonson IV (1240–63). The ruins of his court can be seen on Nordbyen, a street with old houses hunched along it.

To the south of Tønsberg, along the eastern side of the fjord, the islands of **Nøtterøy** and **Tjøme**, and the skerries, are fantastic summer hangouts. **Verdens Ende** (World's End) is, naturally, at the end – but for a few boulders – of the chain. The old lighthouse is a beautifully simple structure made of stone.

On the other side of Tønsbergfjord lies **Sandefjord** ⓳, once the whaling capital of the world. The sea still dominates life here, and one of the main industries is marine paint production. But today the town is better known for its restaurants: it's home to the well-established Midtåsen and Solvold. Restaurant Geir Skeie, run by the local young chef who won the Bocuse

BELOW: Oseberg Burial Mound.

d'Or in 2009, is scheduled to open here in November 2010. The town centre is compact, and the cosy old Kong Carl Hotel is one of its more handsome buildings. Near Badeparken are the former spa and the Old Town, along Thaulowsgate. Preståsen is the hilly park above it. Torp Airport is located here.

Just outside Sandefjord are the **Gokstad Burial Site** (Gokstadhaugen; all year; free), in which the Gokstad ship, now in Oslo's Viking Ship Museum, was discovered in 1880; and the **Vesterøy** peninsula, a supremely peaceful place, ideal for walking, cycling and boating. The film star Liv Ullmann's summer house is in the vicinity.

Larvik waterfront

Larvik ⓴ was home to two legendary boat-lovers: Thor Heyerdahl, and Scotsman Colin Archer, designer of the polar ship *Fram*. Archer's first house was at Tollerodden, on the fjord. At Larvik's back is the huge Lake Farris. Unsurprisingly maybe, there are many fine waterside spots around Larvik, such as **Mølland** beach, stacked with sea-rounded pebbles, and **Nevlunghavn**, an exquisite fishing cove tucked around the bay west of Stavern.

Inner Vestfold's rivers run with salmon and trout. **Brufoss** is a favourite anglers' haunt (accommodation and day licences available; tel: 33 12 99 20). In winter, this is a popular downhill ski district. You will find a number of ceramic works which offer tours in outer and inner Vestfold and, in common with Østfold, every little hamlet seems to have an art gallery.

Fjord people's pride

People who live around Oslofjord have a strange modesty-pride complex. They are the first to point out the area's shortcomings – smallish mountains, the stink of some pulp and paper plants – then the superlatives begin to flow. The birthplaces of the most intrepid explorers are here, as are the best sailing races, the warmest summers, the finest archaeological discoveries, the best drinking water, summer resorts… the list goes on; for when it comes to this part of Norway neither the modesty nor the pride is false. ❏

Learning to sail on Oslofjord.

BELOW: Paradise beach Oslofjord

THE HEART OF NORWAY

Away from Mjøsa and its lakeside towns, central Norway extends east into the wilds around the old copper-mining town of Rorøs, and north towards the quintessentially Norwegian Dovre Mountains

Norway's heartland is centred on the counties of Oppland and Hedmark, and is characterised by three main features: Lake Mjøsa, the country's largest lake; the great massif of Dovrefjell to the north; and the long, slanting valleys of Gudbrandsdalen and Østerdalen.

In this widest part of Norway, these great valleys lie straight and narrow from southeast to northwest, their rivers like veins cutting between the mountain ranges. Alongside the rivers are fertile farms, which climb up the valley sides to forests. Then, above the treeline come the bare slopes of tussocky grass and rocks, a playground for skiers and walkers.

Despite Norway's busy network of rural buses, it can be difficult to reach some of the remoter corners; but this region makes wonderful country for touring by car. Each new vista is more magnificent than the last as the road climbs, dips and circles. Nevertheless, for some of the higher plateaux, it can be simpler and quicker to push further into the wilderness by train, which stops at many small stations along the main line between Oslo and Trondheim – this route is almost as spectacular as the famous Oslo–Bergen line in the west.

Mjøsa and Mjøsabyen

Lake Mjøsa ① also lies southeast to northwest some 160km (100 miles) north of Oslo. One of the best ways to enjoy the lake and its surroundings is a trip on the old paddle steamer SS *Skibladner* (tel: 61 14 40 80; late June–mid-Aug Tue–Sun). Built in 1856 as a continuation of Norway's first railway line between Oslo and Eidsvoll, she now plies the lake carrying tourists and is based in Gjøvik on the west side.

Around Mjøsa lies some of the most fertile agricultural land in Norway,

Main attractions
LAKE MJØSA
LILLEHAMMER
TRYSIL
RONDANE NP
RØROS
DOVRE NP

PRECEDING PAGES: the colourful opening ceremony of the 1994 Winter Olympics, Lillehammer. **LEFT:** snow angel.
RIGHT: Lake Mjøsa.

The Heart of Norway

```
0            50 km
0                    50 miles
```

N

NORWEGIAN
SEA

and throughout the gently undulating countryside are large farms, encircled by thickly forested hills. Where Lake Mjøsa is at its widest, some 17km (10 miles) across, is the attractive island of **Helgøya**. At its southern tip, the island has a burial mound, part of the historic Hovinsholm, a royal estate from Viking times until 1723.

Three main towns lie along the lake: Hamar and Lillehammer are on the eastern shore and Gjøvik on the west. A bridge across the lake about halfway between Hamar and Lillehammer links the municipalities and, in a commercial sense, has combined the area into what has been christened **Mjøsabyen**.

Hamar ② was the centre of Roman Catholicism in Norway in the Middle Ages and the seat of the bishop. It enjoyed great prosperity and had an impressive cathedral. The town's downfall came in 1537 when the Danes carried off the bishop, and 30 years later when the Swedes burned Hamar to the ground. Now the cathedral ruins at **Cathedral Point** (Domkirkeodden) are part of the **Hedmark Museum** (Hedmarksmuseet; tel: 62 54 27 00; mid-May–mid-Sept; charge). They are enclosed in a superb glass structure designed by renowned Norwegian architect Sverre Fehn. There is also an **Emigration Museum** in Hamar (tel: 62 57 48 50; summer only Mon–Sat 10am–4pm, Sun noon–4pm, guided tours daily at 1pm; charge) and the **Kirsten Flagstad Museum** (Kirsten Flagstadmuseet; tel: 62 54 27 00; mid-June–mid-Aug Wed–Sun 11am–4pm), the childhood home of opera star Kirsten Flagstad, who made her debut at New York's Metropolitan Opera in 1935.

Not until the 19th century and the coming of the railway did Hamar regain a measure of importance, as a railway junction with a locomotive-building works. The works have gone, but the **National Railway Museum** (Norsk Jernbanemuseet; tel: 62 51 31 60; July–mid-Aug daily 10am–5pm; Jan–June and Aug–Dec 11am–3pm, closed Mon; charge), established in 1896, serves as a reminder. A highlight of this collection is the early steam engine *Caroline*, built by George Stephenson in

The paddle steamer SS Skibladner, sails between Hamar, Eidsvoll, Gjøvik and Lillehammer on Lake Mjøsa during the summer months.

1861. There are regular excursions on a narrow-gauge railway.

The landmark Olympic **skating arena** (all year; charge), in the style of a Viking ship, was built for the 1994 Winter Olympics, which were held in and around the Mjøsabyen towns. Seven of Norway's eight distilleries are located in the region. About 18km (11 miles) east of Hamar towards Elverum is the **Løten Brewery** (Brænderi; tel: 90 18 99 05; guided tours; charge), which is famous for Løten aquavit. Løten is also the town where artist Edvard Munch was born.

Lillehammer winter sports

The largest of the three Mjøsabyen towns is **Lillehammer ❸**, situated at the northern end of the lake where it narrows to become the Lågen River and crosses Gudbrandsdalen. Lillehammer is known as the capital of Gudbrandsdalen and was the site of the 1994 Winter Olympics. A downhill ski area on nearby **Hafjell** and

BELOW: skier at Lillehammer.

500km (300 miles) of cross-country skiing tracks were built for the occasion. Other facilities included an ice-hockey rink at Gjøvik, built inside a mountain, Scandinavia's only artificially frozen bobsleigh and luge track (near Hunderfossen) and a ski-jumping arena over Lillehammer itself, all of which are still in use.

Open-air Maihaugen

For summer visitors, the biggest attraction is Norway's remarkable open-air museum, **Maihaugen** (tel: 61 28 89 00; June–Aug daily 10am–5pm; Sept daily 11am–4pm; Oct–May Tue–Sun 11am–4pm; guided tours throughout the day in summer, booking required at other times; charge). Some 120 buildings have been brought into the 40-hectare (100-acre) site from all over Gudbrandsdalen, including a stave church and two farms. The museum was the life work of Anders Sandvig. A dentist by profession, he came to Lillehammer in 1885 suffering from tuberculosis and with a life expectancy of a mere two years. Whether or not it was the interest of the museum he founded in 1887 which kept him going, Sandvig lived for another 65 years and died in 1950. Apart from the buildings, which range from the medieval to the 19th century, Maihaugen has some 30,000 artefacts, all collected by Sandvig, and the many demonstrations of old skills and rural crafts give the museum a real sense of being alive.

For the motoring enthusiast, the **Museum of Vehicle History** (Norsk Veg Museum; tel: 61 28 52 50; all year; free) at Fåberg, to the north of Lillehammer on the E6, has everything from horse-drawn sleighs, gigs and carioles to motor cars. There are some unusual examples, including steam and electric vehicles, a strange six-wheeled Mustad and a 1922 Bjering, which seated two people in tandem and could have its front wheels replaced by skis in winter. There is also the Troll, which ended its production run of 16 vehicles in 1956.

GAIASTOVA

HAFJELLSNUEN

Artistic light

The quality of light in Lillehammer and its surroundings has attracted many artists to the area over the years. As a result, the town has an impressive art gallery, the **Lillehammer Art Museum** (Kunstmuseum; tel: 61 05 44 60; July–Aug daily 11am–5pm; Sept–June Tue–Sun 11am–4pm), which includes works by J.C. Dahl, Hans Gude, Adolph Tidemand, Christian Krohg, and Norway's most famous artist, Edvard Munch.

One of Lillehammer's most revered names is Danish-born Sigrid Undset, winner of the 1928 Nobel Prize for Literature, who took up residence at in the town in 1919. "Bjerkebæk", **Sigrid Undset's home** (Sigrid Unsets hjem, Gamle Nordseterveg 1; tel: 61 25 94 00; late May–Aug daily 10am–5pm, Sept Tue–Sun 11am–4pm; charge), was created from two wooden farmhouses which had been moved from Gudbrandsdalen. Her statue stands on Lillehammer's main shopping street.

Aulestad ❹ (tel: 61 22 41 10; May–Sept; charge), about 11km (7 miles) northwest from Lillehammer, is the home of another notable Norwegian author and playwright, Bjørnstjerne Bjørnson (1832–1910; *see page 122*), one of the writers who inspired the nationalist movement in the 19th century. He wrote Norway's national anthem, *Ja, vi elsker dette landet (Yes, we love this land of ours)*, in 1870, promoted Norwegian plays in the theatre in preference to Danish and won a Nobel Prize for Literature in 1903. His house is just as it was when he died.

Alongside these literary attractions, Lillehammer has not neglected its younger visitors. On the outskirts of the town is **Lilleputthammer** (May–Aug; charge), with its quarter-scale version of the centre of Lillehammer as it was in 1930. You walk down the main street, peer in the shop windows and find some are open to the public. There is also the popular **Hunderfossen Family Park** ❺ (Familiepark; tel: 61 27 55 30; May–early Sept; charge) north of the town, featuring the world's largest (fibreglass) troll.

Nearby is the **Lillehammer Olympic bobsleigh and luge track**, built

TIP

If you're interested in learning more about the history of the Olympic Games, visit the Norwegian Olympic Museum in Håkons Hall, Lillehammer (Norges Olympiske Museum; tel: 61 25 21 00; June–Aug daily 10am–5pm; Sept daily 11am–4pm; Oct–May Tue–Sun 11am–4pm; charge).

BELOW:
sledging at
Lillehammer.

for the 1994 Winter Olympics, which offers dry runs for tourists during the summer (tel: 61 05 42 00; times vary).

Østerdalen

To the east of Lake Mjøsa lies **Øster-dalen**, which cuts through the mountains on a line roughly parallel to Gudbrandsdalen. At times the valley is narrow, with seemingly endless forests on either side, broken only occasionally by patches of farmland. The valley starts at **Elverum** ❻ in the south and continues northwards for 250km (150 miles), becoming broader and more open further north. Throughout its length flows Norway's longest river, the **Glomma**, kept company by the railway and the E3.

Elverum is one of the essential crossroads of Norway, and lies at the junction of many valleys, with routes to Hamar to the west, Kongsvinger to the south and Trysil to the northeast. It has the well-preserved **Terningen bastion**, built in 1673, and a climb to the top of the water tower provides a good view. The town's most famous episode is commemorated in a monu-

ment to the fierce battle fought in April 1940 which delayed the German Army for long enough to allow the king and members of the government to escape further north before finally crossing to Britain to continue the fight in exile.

By far the most important of the town's attractions are two major museums. The **Glomdal Museum** (tel: 62 41 91 00; daily mid-June–Aug 10am–5pm; rest of the year 10am–4pm; between Christmas and New Year noon–4pm; charge), opened in 1911 on a large natural site, has 88 old buildings of many kinds, brought in from Østerdalen and Solør. The indoor exhibition is divided into three sections – the farming year; transport and communication; and handwork and crafts – and it shows what life was like in Østerdalen from 1870 to 1900. There is also a collection from the Neolithic age and Viking era, as well as an open-air theatre.

The **Forestry Museum** (Norsk Skogmuseum; tel: 62 40 90 00; daily late June–Aug 10am–5pm; rest of the year 10am–4pm; charge) encompasses forestry, hunting and fishing. The main building also has exhibits devoted to geology and wildlife, and children usually head for the aquarium. The outdoor collection is mainly situated on the small island of Prestøya in the middle of the Glomma River.

Skiing and more at Trysil

To the northeast, **Trysil** ❼, in Hedmark near the Swedish border, is Norway's largest ski resort. In summer, Trysil is a centre for paragliding, rafting, canoe tours and mountain tours with pack dogs to carry the luggage.

But it goes without saying that almost anywhere in the heart of Norway you need to go only a short way for the sort of outdoor recreation that mountain, river and lake can provide. North from Elverum along the E3 there are few places of any size or importance, but the whole of this area is well off the tourist track and ideal for exploration.

At **Koppang**, about halfway along the length of Østerdalen, you can take an alternative route north, along Road 30 past the long thin Storsjøen (lake), rejoining the E3 at **Tynset**. North-

west of Tynset you come to Kvikne and near it the rectory at Bjørgan, the birthplace of Bjørnstjerne Bjørnson.

Alternatively, try Road 219, which turns west at **Atna**, some 30km (20 miles) north of Koppang, for a drive into the foothills of the wild and mountainous region of **Rondane**, where the peaks rise up to 1,800 metres (6,000ft) high. At Enden, the road is joined by Road 27, which has taken the parallel route north from Ringebu. Called the **Rondevegen** ❽, the road climbs steeply from Gudbrandsdalen to some superb views of the Rondane Mountains. After coming this far, it is well worth continuing from Enden to Folldal, past the great peaks that include Rondeslottet at 2,178 metres (7,144ft) high, with the **Rondane National Park** to the west. Established in 1962, this was Norway's first national park and offers a wide range of trails of varying difficulty.

Road 27 ascends to nearly 915 metres (3,000ft) before reaching **Folldal**, itself one of the highest permanently inhabited communities in Norway. The community's history began when cop-

BELOW: skiing at Trysil.

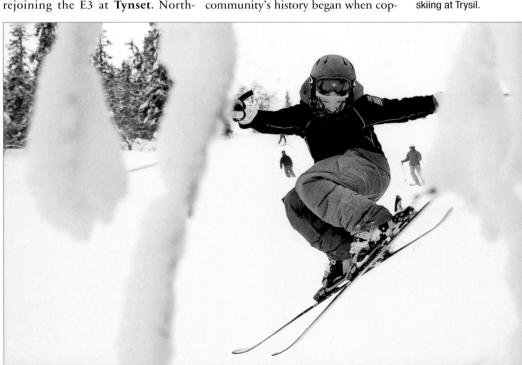

Røros and the Old Copper Country

The copper-producing town of Røros, active until 1972, is now preserved in its entirety as a World Heritage Site

Røros was the archetypal company town, with life and society revolving around the mining of copper. Isolated, exposed, nearly 600 metres (2,000ft) above sea level and surrounded by mountains and enduring winter cold, its existence was entirely due to the discovery of copper, which was first mined here over 300 years ago and was worked until 1972. The town was hardly beautiful, and slag heaps and the smelter provided the backdrop to the miners' houses. These were usually small and overcrowded, but many workers also possessed a small patch of land and one or two animals as a source of food.

Further away from smelter and slag lived those higher up the company pecking order – in the executive area. By some miracle, Røros escaped the fires which so often laid waste to the wooden buildings of many other Norwegian towns. Today, Røros has a unique townscape, and almost the entire older part of the town is preserved by law. Doors, windows and colour schemes all have to conform, buildings have to be lived in, and there is strict control of advertising signs and notices. As a result, Røros is in a time warp, retaining much of its mining-town atmosphere, and is on the Unesco World Heritage list (www.worldheritageroros.no).

The most noticeable feature in Røros is the stone church (Bergstadens Ziir; tel: 72 41 00 50; June–Sept Mon–Sat; Oct–May Sun only; charge) – "the pride of the mining town" – which was dedicated in 1784 and replaced a wooden church built in 1650. The interior reflects the mining society, with paintings of clergymen and mining officials. Prayers were said every Sunday for the company and its directors.

The smelting works (*smelthytta*; tel: 72 40 61 70; www.rorosmuseet.no; all year; charge) were the heart of the copper-mining company and the focal point of the town. Its bell was rung at the start and end of each shift and is still in place today. The smelter has been restored as a museum: the exterior resembles the building as it was in 1889, but the interior is now given over to a series of exhibitions depicting life in the town, mining techniques in Europe in the 18th and 19th centuries, cultural features of the southern Lapp society and aspects of Røros society and its environs. Small-scale models help to explain the production process.

One of the most interesting elements in the museum is the series of working models to one-tenth scale which demonstrate the arduous methods called for when the only power available was water, horses and human muscle. In the past it was usual to make such scale models to see if a new technique or piece of equipment would work, so today's replicas are following an old tradition.

Thirteen kilometres (8 miles) from Røros is the Olav Mine (Olavsgruva; tel: 72 40 61 70; all year; charge), which was opened as a mining museum in 1979. The guided tour takes visitors 50 metres (165ft) below ground. Until 1880, when dynamite was introduced, the miners used the heat from wood fires stacked against the rock face to crack the rock.

Back on the surface, the bare and bleak scenery surrounding the mine, even in the summer sun, is the most telling way to emphasise the wretched existence of those early miners. ❏

LEFT: both Rorøs church and the town's characteristic turf roofs are now preserved.

per was discovered in the area in the 18th century. Although the mine is no longer worked, the mining company is still based here to serve a new mine at Hjerkinn about 30km (20 miles) away. The buildings of the former **Folldal Mine** (Folldal Gruver; tel: 62 49 05 05; all year; charge) now form a museum, with train rides into the mine (mid-June–Aug Mon–Fri 11am–6pm, Sat–Sun 11am–5pm; charge).

Along the Copper Road

From Folldal, if you head east you return to the Glomma River valley and the E3 at Alvdal, all connected to and part of the system of valleys and rivers that spreads out from Øster-dalen. Along the way abandoned mine works indicate how important minerals were and, to some extent, still are to this area. North of Alvdal, rail, road and river head northeast, through Tolga and Os – which is the start of the **Kopperveien** (Copper Road) – before coming to the former copper-mining town of **Røros** ❾ (*see feature opposite*), a World Heritage Site east along Road 31.

Røros is also a junction for roads which lead through an eastern wilderness with little habitation: the first is Road 31 to the Swedish frontier, 45km (30 miles) away to the east, past several lakes, some artificial, dug to provide water for mining operations; another leads north to Ålen (Road 30), which has a small open-air museum, then through the fast-flowing gorge of the Gaula River until the valley broadens out near Støren; a third runs southwest to Femund Lake, Norway's third-largest, which offers good fishing.

Gudbrandsdalen

After Østerdalen, **Gudbrandsdalen** is the second-longest valley in Norway. The Lågen River runs its full length and the valley stretches for 140km (90 miles) northwest from Lillehammer to Dombås, the starting point for climbing trips into the Dovre rock formation. This huge plateau is very popular

The mining town of Røros still has its 17th- and 18th-century wooden houses, with their roofs covered in turf.

BELOW: stone church dominating the town of Røros.

Dovrefjell is one of only three places in the world where musk ox can be seen in the wild.

RIGHT: Lake Mjøsa.
BELOW: Peer Gynt, as depicted by P.N. Arboe.

with walkers, not least because it is framed by impressive peaks such as the **Snøhetta** (2,286 metres/7,498ft).

Perhaps because it was surrounded by mountains, which emphasised its sense of identity, the Gudbrandsdal valley has a long tradition of folk dancing and folk music; it is famous for its woodcarving and rose painting, and you can find good craftwork to take home. North of Lillehammer at **Ringebu 🔟**, you can visit the 13th-century **Ringebu stave church** (Stavkirke; late May–Aug; charge). Built of enormous upright timbers, it has a statue of St Lawrence, crucifixes and a baptismal font, all from medieval times.

Vinstra folktales

Vinstra 🔟 is the heart of what is known as "Peer Gynt country" *(see box)* after the legendary figure first written about by Peter Asbjørnsen in the 19th century, and then made famous by

both Ibsen and Grieg. Scottish visitors may also want to stop at **Kringen** to see the memorial to a battle of 1612, when an army of Scottish mercenaries was defeated by local farmers. Despite their defeat, the Scots (said to be Sinclairs) have another memorial in the checked cloth used in one of the local costumes, which looks remarkably like Sinclair tartan.

Dovrefjell

Travelling north from Vinstra, the E6 passes through Otta (where Road 15 heads west to the western fjords) on its way to Dombås. Here it turns northeast, accompanied by the railway, and climbs up and over **Dovrefjell 🔟**. The train stops at small stations such as Fokstua, Hjerkinn, Kongsvoll (with its excellent historic lodge) and Drivstua to disgorge walkers with boots, poles and backpacks.

The summit of Dovrefjell is at Hjerkinn, reputed to be the driest place in Norway, and for the rest of the way it is downhill across the **Dovre National Park** en route to Oppdal.

Oppdal 🔟 looks up towards the Dovre plateau, and to Trollheimen *(see page 282)* to the northwest. In winter it is a centre for skiing and in summer for walking, fishing, rafting and riding. The **cable car** takes walkers and skiers high above the village.

West of Oppdal, off Road 16, a small path leads to a peaceful place with trees and uneven mounds which are Viking graves. This is **Vang**, once the centre of the community until the railway brought Oppdal to life. There are 758 graves dating back to the early Iron Age.

A track branches north to **Gjevilsvassdalen** and its lake. It is here that Anders Rambech, an 18th-century country attorney and one of the negotiators of the 1814 constitution, built **Tingstua**. Today, the wooden building is a popular upland inn. Small and simple though it is, the inn has been favoured by Queen Sonja who made it her base for walking in Dovrefjell. ❏

Peer Gynt Country

The 19th-century Norwegian folklorist Peter Abjørnsen walked the country gathering material for a book of local folk tales, *Norske Folkeeventyr*, which he published with his friend Bishop Jørgen Moe in 1844. One of Abjørnsen's characters was Peer (Per) Gynt, a legendary marksman, ski-runner and braggart, who was often economical with the truth. The character inspired the dramatist Henrik Ibsen to write the play *Peer Gynt* (1867) and Edvard Grieg to compose his *Peer Gynt* Suite No. 1 (1888). Today, the play is performed with Greig's music every August in the outdoor amphitheatre at **Gålåvatnet**, southwest of Vinstra. One of the so-called Gynt cottages serves as the tourist information office in Vinstra (tel: 61 29 47 70).

The character has also inspired the creation of a mountain route, the **Peer Gyntvegen** (www.peergyntvegen.no; June–late-autumn; toll), through Gudbrandsdalen. The 60km (37-mile) round trip is accessible from Vinstra, Harpefoss and Hundrop on the E6. Passing through Gålå, it reaches an altitude of over 900 metres (3,000ft) and presents a panorama of mountains and lakes – stark but appealing.

PEAK AND PLATEAU

Whether on foot or by car, the peaks of Jotunheimen and the flat rocky expanse of the Hardanger plateau both mesmerise and stun the senses with their sheer size and magnificence

Jotunheimen ("Home of the Giants"), which includes Norway's mightiest mountain range, and Hardangervidda (*vidde* means highland plateau) together form an extensive area of outstanding natural beauty. Centres of population are few, and places of interest are also thin on the ground, but of superb scenery – mountains, glaciers, lakes and rivers – there is an excess.

Crossing Hardangervidda

The attraction of **Hardangervidda** resides in its wide open spaces. On average 900 metres (3,000ft) above sea level, it lies south of Jotunheimen with three main valleys – Begnadalen, Hallingdalen and Numedalen – cutting across it. The centre of the plateau with its lakes and streams (a paradise for anglers) forms the source of the mighty Hallingdal and Numedal Rivers. There are a number of magnificent waterfalls in the area, including **Vøringfossen** (*see page 233*) and **Valursfossen** , which drops 90 metres (300ft) into Hjelmodalen. To the south, Hardangervidda broadens out from **Hallingskarvet**, a rocky wall rising to a height of 1,700 metres (5,700ft).

Hardangervidda is in many ways unique as Europe's largest mountain plateau, covering an area of 10,000 sq km (3,860 sq miles), nearly a third of which lies within the **Hardangervidda National Park** ⑮. The flora and fauna of the plateau includes Arctic species and is hugely varied: several thousand reindeer roam freely, around 100 species of birds breed on these upland moors, and there are in excess of 500 different species of plants, an abundance due to the two distinct climates of Vidda – the gentle western coastal climate and the harsher inland climate of the east. There are tracks and trails

Main attractions
HARDANGERVIDDA NP
FINSE
GEILO
JOTUNHEIMEN NP
LAKE GJENDE AND BESSEGGEN
FAGERNES
BORGUND STAVE CHURCH
AURLANDSVANGEN
SOGNEFJELLET MOUNTAIN ROAD
LOM

PRECEDING PAGES: Aurland valley seen from the Norway in a Nutshell trip.
LEFT: footbridge in Hardangervidda National Park. **RIGHT:** keeping traditional tunes alive.

Dr Holms Hotel in Geilo was opened in 1909, the same year as the Bergen line, by Doctor Ingebrikt Christian Holm, a specialist in respiratory diseases. This historic hotel, all in wood and spread over four floors, is one of the largest in the area, and has the only Shiseido spa in Scandinavia.

BELOW: the Bergen line, part of the Norway in a Nutshell trip.

galore, and isolated cabins provide basic overnight accommodation.

The **Oslo–Bergen railway line** *(see box below)* cuts across Hardangervidda, keeping Road 7 company as far as Haugastøl, where it goes north of the Hardangerjøkulen through **Finse** *(see box, page 195)*, Myrdal and Mjølfjell. The road takes a different course, heading southwest across the wide, empty landscape with distant views of mountains, passing lakes and streams, before making a dizzy descent to sea level via a series of tunnels to Eidfjord.

Explore Geilo and around

Travelling northeast from Haugastøl, both road and railway are initially dominated by Hallingskarvet. The immediate surroundings become somewhat softer as you reach **Geilo** , which has a good strategic position at the head of the Hallingdal valley and the gateway to Hardangervidda. Though it lies at a height of 800 metres (2,650ft) above sea level, Geilo has grown into one of Norway's most popular winter sports resorts, with 20 lifts, three snow parks, 40 well-groomed downhill runs and

220km (135 miles) of cross-country tracks. With its range of hotels, Geilo has also become popular as a summer holiday centre and as a base for exploring the region by car (although the choice of roads is limited), on foot or horseback. In summer it still looks like a typical winter resort minus snow, with its spread-out, slightly unfinished appearance.

Hol's rural heritage

From Geilo, Road 40 goes southeast past **Hol Museum** (Hol Bygdemuseum; July–mid-Aug; charge), a rural museum which takes the usual form of a collection of old buildings. In this case it includes the Mostugu from 1750, the Hågåstugu from 1806 and a mill from 1774. Road 40 continues along the eastern edge of Hardangervidda before it follows the Numedal valley to Kongsberg.

Road 7, meanwhile, continues northeast to Hagafoss, where **Road 50** turns off it towards Lake Strandavatn. It leads along the north side of the long, clear lake dotted with small mountain huts. The landscape soon changes, allowing

The Bergen Line

A vital link between Norway's two biggest cities, Bergen and Oslo, the Bergen line (Bergensbanen; www.nsb.no) was established in 1909 to connect the rail networks in the east and west of the country. As many as 15,000 men worked on this daring engineering project, laying tracks, building bridges and carving out over 180 tunnels. The final bill totalled NOK 50 million.

The line covers a distance of 496km (308 miles), but it is the stunning stretch across the Hardanger plateau that has made the railway famous and earned it a place among the Society of International Railway Travelers' top 25 trains in the world. A must for any rail enthusiast, the trip between Oslo and Bergen takes about eight hours. Trains run year-round, with several departures daily.

a magnificent view, and a summer skiing centre is located nearby. Suddenly, the road begins to descend through a series of tunnels, including spirals, until the motorist is decanted into the Aurlands valley, which continues to the village of Aurlandsvangen at the head of Aurlandsfjord.

Art in Ål

After being separated by Strandfjord, Road 7 and the railway meet up at Ål ⑲, where the Norwegian-German artist Rolf Nesch (1893–1975) lived and worked for 25 years. The Rolf **Nesch Museum** (all year; charge) contains the largest exhibition of his work in the country. **Torpo** may not have a museum, but it does have a stave church (June–Sept; charge) which is the oldest building in Hallingdal. It dates back to the second half of the 12th century and has a splendid painted ceiling from the 13th century. The motifs include scenes from the life of St Margaret, to whom the church is dedicated.

Just past Gol, Road 7 turns south towards Nesbyen, site of Norway's oldest outdoor museum. Founded in 1899, the **Hallingdal Folkemuseum** (June–Aug; charge) has 29 buildings, the earliest – Staveloftet – dating from 1330. All come from different parts of Hallingdal. Some interiors are rose painted, and the exhibition building houses collections of furniture, textiles and weapons.

The two other roads at Gol both lead the traveller through more attractive scenery. Road 52 goes northwest along the Hemsedal valley through **Hemsedal**, another winter sports centre, with 24 lifts, 50 runs, five snow parks and 212km (131 miles) of cross-country tracks. The church (Mon) has an altarpiece from 1715 and a painting of *The Last Supper* from 1716.

The Panorama Way

From Hemsedal a minor road goes past a small open-air museum near the village of Ulsåk and, further on, a private toll road winds its way across superb scenery to Ulnes on Road E16. This is the **Panorama Way** ⑳ (Utsiktsveien; summer only), a popular route which links the Hemsedal and Valdres valleys. Although narrow and rough in parts,

TIP

Buskerud county has several stave churches worth visiting, in addition to the one at Torpo. South of Geilo, on Road 40 to Kongsberg, you will find *stavkirkes* dating from the 12th and 13th centuries at Uvdal, Nore, Rollag and Flesberg.

BELOW: winter in Finse.

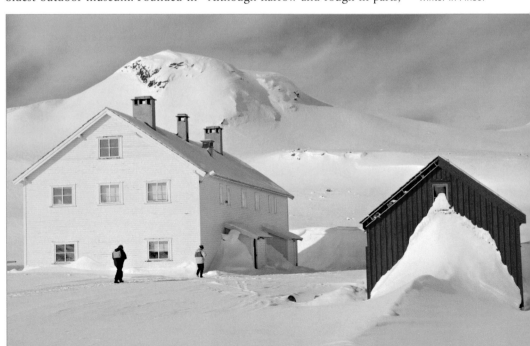

BELOW:
Jotunheimen National Park.

it lives up to its name, threading its way between lakes and providing fine views of the Skogshorn, known as the "Queen of the Hemsedal".

Jotunheimen National Park

Jotunheimen was, in Norwegian mythology, the home of trolls and giants, and it is here that the mightiest mountains are to be found. In the east is the **Jotunheimen National Park ㉑**, which includes the two highest mountains in the country: **Galdhøpiggen** at 2,469 metres (8,098ft) and **Glittertind ㉒** at 2,452 metres (8,043ft). In west Jotunheimen there is another range of crevassed mountains, the **Skagastøl- stindane** (2,000 metres/8,000ft).

The southern part of the Jotunheimen has some major lakes, including Gjende, which is particularly beautiful with its greenish glacier water and flanked by impressive peaks. Other major lakes are Bygdin, Tyin and Vinstri, while glaciers add to the superb natural attractions. Opportunities for walking abound in the area, from day walks to longer treks, and the Jotunheimen is the number one destination for

hiking in Norway. Try to go slightly off-season if you can, to avoid the crowds that flock here in summer.

The northern border of Jotunheimen is the Otta River valley, which acts as a natural boundary. From **Otta** in the east the river and Road 15 wend through fertile countryside, with farms and forests, but beyond Lom the scenery gradually changes. The green and lush surroundings give way to forests and rocky outcrops and the river grows more turbulent. Eventually, at the tree line, the scenery becomes bare and rather inhospitable.

Into the mountains

Grotli, which consists of little more than a large roadside hotel, cafeteria and souvenir shop, marks the beginning of Lake Breidalsvatnet. Shortly afterwards, at Langevatnet, Road 63 turns off and becomes a spectacular mountain road which skirts Djupvatnet and then descends steeply to Geiranger. Road 15 continues on its course through 15 tunnels until it reaches Stryn on Innvikfjord. An alternative to Road 15 from Grotli is the old **Road 258 ㉓**. Some 26km (16 miles) long, it climbs to a height of 1,139 metres (3,736ft) and, although narrow and unsurfaced in parts, provides a thrilling journey. West of the summit it passes a summer ski centre and **Snowland**, a summer activity area for the family – with snow thrown in.

Between Otta and Grotli there are only two roads that go south, bold enough to penetrate the heart of Jotunheimen. Road 51, the most easterly, leaves the Otta–Grotli road at Randen and heads into the **Valdres** region. It starts by climbing into an area of upland pastures with a distant backdrop of mountains. A further climb to Darthus brings **Ridderspranget ㉔** (Knight's Leap) close at hand, where the Sjoa River is channelled into a narrow gorge.

Lakes lie scattered across to the west, while beyond can be seen the peak of Glittertind. The most important stretch of water is **Lake Gjende 25**, long and narrow and curving slightly to the southwest. Beyond Bessheim there are more inspiring views, and this scenic feast continues for kilometre after kilometre.

Bygdin lies between two lakes: Lake Bygdin stretches like a long finger pointing to more distant mountains in the west; eastwards is the major expanse of Lake Vinstri. There are boat trips on several of the lakes, and Lake Bygdin has northern Europe's highest scheduled boat service, in waters 1,060 metres (3,477ft) above sea level.

The heart of the Valdres

Between Bessheim and Bygdin the road reaches its highest point – 1,389 metres (4,557ft). From here it descends, first to the tree line, then to more gentle scenery at **Beitostølen**. This winter sports resort got its first ski lift in 1964 and now has nine lifts, 12 runs and more than 325km (200 miles) of cross-country tracks. It is a typical village of its kind with several hotels – very popular for cross-country skiing – and with a school for disabled and blind skiers, who plunge down the slopes with unbelievable confidence.

Fagernes 26 is in the centre of the Valdres area. The focus of attention is the large **Valdres Folk Museum** (Folkemuseum; all year; charge), which features some 95 buildings built between 1200 and 1900. Of particular interest are a 16th-century tapestry, medieval chests, a collection of antique silver, folk-music instruments and hunting weapons. This area is scattered with **stave churches**, including those at Hedalen, Reinli, Lomen, Høre, Øye, Hegge and Garmo. Fagernes is also the birthplace of *rakfisk*, one of Norway's strangest delicacies – brine-cured fish, usually trout or char, that has been left to ferment for several months before being eaten.

In one direction the E16 heads southeast through the Begnadal valley and eventually to Hønefoss. In the opposite direction the road goes west through more exciting scenery on the southern edge of Jotunheimen. At Tyinkrysset a road goes off to Øvre Årdal on Årdalsfjord while the E16 turns south, descending through forested scenery to **Borgund 27**. Borgund

BELOW: Valdres Folk Museum.

Finse

To the south of the Jotunheimen lies the hamlet of Finse, the highest point at 1,225 metres (4,000ft) on the Oslo–Bergen railway line. Its main street is the station platform, as there are neither cars nor roads. It's a small speck in a seemingly boundless expanse of snow and ice in winter, and a gateway to some of Norway's most beautiful wilderness.

Finse has the country's largest *hytta* (holiday lodge) for hikers and skiers, and a hotel. It is the starting point for two giant trail networks, stretching as the crow flies 225km (140 miles) north to the Jotunheimen and 100km (60 miles) south to Hardangervidda. In summer the region offers more than 5,000km (3,000 miles) of T-marked hiking trails. At Easter-time, 2,000km (1,240 miles) of ski trails are marked by poles in the snow.

stave church (May–Sept 10am–5pm,; mid-June–mid-Aug 8am–8pm; charge) is regarded as the most typical and best preserved in Norway. Built in 1150, it is dedicated to St Andrew.

A few kilometres past Lærdalsøyri, a minor road goes to **Aurlandsvangen** ㉘. It starts to climb almost immediately through lush scenery, but this gradually changes as the narrow road ascends higher and higher, unfolding a series of stunning panoramas until the summit at 1,305 metres (4,284ft). It then begins an increasingly steep descent to the village of Aurlandsvangen. "Breathtaking" is an overused description, but on this road it is justified, especially the view over Aurlandsfjord from several thousand feet above it. It is not for the fainthearted. Stop at the Stegastein viewpoint to take in the scenery before completing your descent towards Aurland.

Across Sognefjell

The second route south from the Otta–Grotli road is Road 55 from Lom to Lustrafjord, which is the part of Sognefjord furthest from the sea.

The Sognefjellet is one of only six National Tourist Roads in Norway (roads famed for their scenic beauty) and was named by the *Guardian* as one of 10 top bike rides in the world in January 2007. **Lom** ㉙ is a typical Norwegian "junction" village with its couple of hotels, shops and garages, but it also has a fine stave church. The **Stone Centre** (Fossheim Steinsenter; all year) in Lom contains stones, rocks and gems from all over Norway, and it has a collection of minerals from Jotunheimen, while the associated **Mountain Museum** (Norsk Fjellmuseum; all year; charge) focuses on mountain life throughout Norway.

Starting out from Lom, you drive through the deceptively placid Bøverdal valley, passing small farms and villages, but the view gradually changes as it gains height and the mountains become more noticeable. At **Galdesand** there is a toll road to Juvashytta, which is the nearest point by car to the Galdhøpiggen mountain.

At 640 metres (2,100ft), **Elveseter** ㉚ (May–Sept) is one of Norway's most unusual hotels. The Elveseter family has owned the property for five generations, gradually converting it into a hotel but retaining many of the old buildings. The oldest is from 1640 and has survived as a wooden building because of the dry mountain air. The first visitors arrived in the 1880s, but it was the opening of the Sognefjell road in 1938 that led to the expansion of tourism.

Krossbu summit

The road continues its upward ascent past the isolated Jotunheimen Fjellstue to the summit at **Krossbu** at a height of 1,400 metres (4,590ft) amid superb mountain scenery. From there, make the steep descent to **Turtagrø**, where the hotel (which is about all there is to Turtagrø) is a popular base for walkers and climbers; continue the downward course to softer surroundings at Fortun and, a few miles on, to sea level, at the end of **Lustrafjord** at Skjolden. ❑

BELOW: Elvester Hotel. **RIGHT:** hiker in Jotunheimen National Park.

TELEMARK AND THE SOUTH

Norway's southern coastline is a magnet for summer visitors with its beaches and picturesque seaside towns. Inland, the scenery is starker and life in the mountain valleys lingers in the past

As they are proverbially advised to do "when in Rome", visitors to Oslo – or, equally, to Stavanger and Kristiansand – could usefully do what the locals do for recreation. The choice is either mountains and lakes, in which case they steer a course for **Telemark**, or the sea, which draws them to **Aust-Agder** and **Vest-Agder**, jointly known as Sørlandet (south land).

Locals would usually travel in their own cars, a definite advantage in trying to make the most of Telemark but not so necessary on the coast, along which it is possible to leapfrog from port to port on ferries, which are sufficiently frequent to permit an improvised itinerary.

Oslo, Kristiansand and Stavanger, the principal cities along the southern rim of Norway, have good connections, including flights, so they all serve as practical starting or finishing points for a tour, and you can combine Telemark and Sørlandet on one of several bus excursions. One from Oslo, for example, covers nearly 1,200km (750 miles) by road and ferry and lasts five days.

Designed by a king

In 1639 King Christian IV of Denmark-Norway had the sort of whim which is the privilege of kings and very few others. He wanted to found a town and name it after himself.

In the event, the choice of the site where **Kristiansand ❶** now stands was not entirely capricious. It was an admirable base from which to control the approaches to both the North Sea and the Baltic. The town had to be fortified, and much survives of the first of many forts to be built on the site, **Christiansholm Festning** (fortress; tel: 38 07 51 50; mid-May–mid-Sept 9am–9pm). Through nearly three turbulent centuries, however, none of the

PRECEDING PAGES: fountain sculpture, Kristiansand. **LEFT:** *Boy riding Bear* in the sculpture gardens. **RIGHT:** pedalling through the streets of Kristiansand.

Southern Norway and Its Fjords

NORTH SEA

HARDANGERVIDDA

Hordaland

Rogaland

Vest-Agder

Setesdal

Ryfylke

Hardangervidda Nasjonalpark

0   20 km
0   20 miles

N

forts ever fired a gun in anger (not until 9 April 1940), and gradually Kristiansand changed from being a military town to a trading and administrative centre.

Present-day Kristiansand is a pleasant city, laid out in a grid according to Christian IV's directive, and the sort of place that invites visitors simply to stroll about. The weather is more reliably sunny than anywhere else in Norway, the port and central market are always busy, the **Posebyen** is a picturesque quarter of old wooden houses, and one never has to look far for a spot to sit down and watch the world go by. "A total of more than 10,000 seats in cafés and restaurants" is the city's proud claim.

Kristiansand Zoo (Kristiansand Dyrepark; tel: 38 04 97 00; www. dyreparken.no; all year, times vary; charge), which includes the miniature town of Kardemomme By, is the most visited family park in Norway. The fictional town is out of a popular children's story by Torbjørn Egner, and besides the large zoo there are water chutes and other attractions. The zoo itself contains 800 animals, including Scandinavian fauna such as wolves and elk, exotic wild animals such as lions and tigers, and even a few endangered species such as the red panda. There is also a large breeding ground for camels.

Just north of the city centre, the **Ravnedalen Park** is set in attractive, hilly grounds. The **Gimle Mansion** (Gimle Gård; tel: 38 10 26 80; mid-June–Aug Tue–Fri 10am–5pm; Sat–Mon noon–5pm;mid-May–mid-June noon–5pm; closed rest of the year; charge) across the Otra River is a magnificent symbol of 19th-century Norwegian capitalism. It was built by a shipping tycoon, Bernt Holm, and passed down the family until it was bequeathed to the town and opened to the public in 1985.

Also worth visiting are the **Railway Museum** (Setesdalbanen), with its narrow-gauge steam railway (sum-

A possible sighting of the Seljord Monster, as depicted here in an early illustration, draws many to the small Telemark village of Seljord.

BELOW: the small harbour at Mandal.

mer departures, see www.setesdalsbanen.no; tel: 38 15 64 82), a short way north of the city, and southwest on the way to Mandal, the **Kristiansand Cannon Museum** (Kanonmuseum; tel: 38 08 50 90; www.kanonmuseet.no), the highlight of which is a cannon built by the Germans in World War II to guard the Skagerrak. It is the world's second largest land-based cannon, weighs a whooping 337 tonnes, and its range extends halfway to Denmark.

West to Lindesnes Fyr

About 45km (28 miles) west of Kristiansand is **Mandal ❷**. A busy port long before Christian IV felt the urge to build Kristiansand, it suffered from the competition afterwards. A 1799 traveller remarked that "the houses are jammed together so tightly that a careless pipe-smoker at any open window could spit into his neighbour's parlour." The point known as **Kastellet** is where a wealthy Dane, who once reached into his pocket to make a personal loan to the notoriously empty-pocketed King Frederik IV, installed a cannon to keep pirates away from his estate.

Another 40km (25 miles) west, the lighthouse at **Lindesnes Fyr ❸** (all year; charge to museum) marks the southernmost point of Norway, and in bad weather is buffeted by ferocious winds. The small islands 5km (3 miles) offshore are often mentioned in ancient Norse sagas as a refuge for Viking ships waiting for better weather before turning the corner into or out of the Skagerrak. **Farsund**, a little further west and once a privateer centre, has suffered the misfortune of being destroyed by fire so often that there is hardly a building left pre-dating the 20th century. Nevertheless, the relatively modern houses are painted white and present a pleasing spectacle.

Flekkefjord's Dutch Town

The region is rich in rock carvings and ancient sites including, near **Vanse**, the remains of nine Iron Age homes surrounded by 350 burial mounds. **Lomsanden**, a popular beach on the Lista peninsula, is 10km (6 miles) of white sand. The last town before Vest Agder rises to meet Rogaland is the small port of **Flekkefjord ❹**, known for its Dutch Town (Hollenderbyen), a historic area with Dutch-style white houses lining narrow streets. This is mountainous country which, apart from necessitating the construction of some of Norway's longest railway tunnels (there are 46 between Flekkefjord and Kristiansand), has created several waterfalls, especially around **Kvinesdal**.

East to Grimstad

The principal centres along the coast east from Kristiansand are, in order, Lillesand, Grimstad, Arendal and Risør. **Lillesand ❺**, apart from being a pretty holiday town with a pleasant selection of cafés and restaurants around the harbour, has a special place in Norwegian history as the centre of an 18th-century revolt led by a farmer named Lofthus, a Robin Hood figure who travelled to Copenhagen to confront the crown prince with a long list of grievances. On

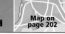

his return he collected a force of 2,000 men and caused panic among the Danish Establishment in the coastal towns. The house where he was arrested still stands. The **Lillesand Town and Maritime Museum** (By og Sjøfart museum; tel: 46 81 75 10; mid-June–mid-Aug Mon–Fri 11am–3pm, Sat 11am–2pm, Sun noon–4pm or by appointment; charge) tells the whole story.

Grimstad ❻ is indelibly associated with the playwright Henrik Ibsen. It was here that he served his apprenticeship to a chemist. Ibsen was an unhappy young man and Grimstad, though a pretty place, must have contributed (together with Skien, where he was born) to his searing exposure of goings-on in small Norwegian towns. His works caused a scandal at the time, but years have healed the wounds and he is commemorated in the **Ibsen House/Grimstad Town Museum** (Bymuseum; tel: 37 04 04 90; late-June–mid-Aug Mon–Sat 11am–5pm, Sun noon–5pm; early June and mid-Aug–Sept weekends only; charge), which holds the largest collection of Ibsen memorabilia in Norway.

Arendal's island setting

Arendal ❼ is full of character, every ounce of which was needed to thwart King Christian's plan to close it down and transfer the inhabitants to his pet project, Kristiansand. Arendal prospered in the 17th and 18th centuries as a conduit for timber shipments abroad, including much of the timber used for the rebuilding of London after the 1666 Great Fire. In 1863, Arendal itself was struck by fire, losing the houses on stilts which had earlier given it the nickname of "Little Venice", but, overflowing onto a number of small islands, it retains its lovely setting.

An unusual addition to its attractions is a museum meticulously created by unpaid volunteers out of the contents of a pottery factory that went out of business some years ago. Located in the Regency-style Kløcker's House (1826), the enthusiasm of the staff at the **Arendal Town Museum** (Kløckershus; tel: 37 02 59 25; Tue–Fri 10am–3pm, Sat 10am–2pm; charge) is infectious. The **Town Hall** (Rådhus), previously the home of a merchant, is said to be one

Henrik Ibsen completed his first play, Catalina, *in 1850, while serving his apprenticeship to a chemist in Grimstad. Soon after, he left behind his provincial existence and headed for Oslo.*

BELOW: images of Grimstad.

of the largest wooden buildings ever constructed in Norway.

Risør, the most easterly town in Aust Agder, was also threatened by the creation of Kristiansand. Its traders were forced to maintain residencies in the new city, but they kept their links with their hometown. Mary Wollstonecraft, an English visitor in 1795, noted an addiction to tobacco. The men never took their pipes out of their mouths and absolutely refused to open a window. The women, she decided, dressed like "sailor girls in Hull or Portsmouth". Many of these women were probably Dutch, since it was fashionable among young seamen to bring wives back from the Netherlands, the main trading partner. In Risør, as in other parts of Sørlandet, children may still be given distinctly Dutch names.

Skien, Ibsen's birthplace

The capital of Telemark is **Skien ❽**, the birthplace, in 1828, of Henrik Ibsen. His home, **Venstøp**, forms part of the **Telemark Museum** (Brekke Park; tel: 35 54 45 00; www.telemark.museum.no; late May–Aug Mon–Fri noon–5pm; Sat–Sun 11am–5pm,; weekends only in early May; charge) and has become a national shrine.

Skien might be better known for its Ibsen connection, but it originally came into existence producing stone projectiles for military slingshots. This was perhaps even stranger than another industry which prospered in the nearby village of Ulefoss until the late 19th century, namely the production of ice. Ice was easily transported along Telemark's natural waterways, which were later rationalised into a canal system, the **Telemarkskanal ❾** (see box, below).

Inland Telemark

Throughout Telemark one senses an older Norway lurking just beneath the surface. The upper districts were, until recently, impenetrable except on skis, travel in winter being easier than in summer. Isolated communities were not inclined to take orders from interfering outsiders, although a lot of water has passed under the bridge since the people were described (in 1580) as "shameless bodies of the Devil whose

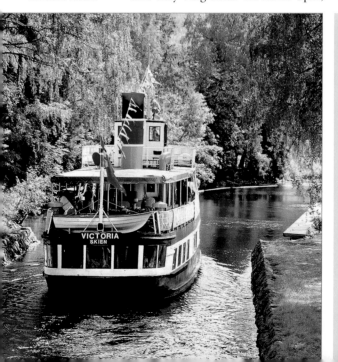

Telemark Canal

The impressive Telemark Canal (Telemarkskanal), completed in 1892, links lakes and waterways between **Skien** and **Dalen** at the foot of Hardangervidda. Eight sets of locks raise boats a total of 72 metres (225ft) up to Flåvatn, which in turn leads into Kviteseidvatn and Bandak, and on to Dalen, where travellers can check in at the historic Dalen Hotel. The canal cuts 105km (65 miles) into the interior and is now used by pleasure boats such as the M/S *Victoria*, M/S *Henrik Ibsen* and M/S *Telemarken*. The voyage from Skien to Dalen takes 10–11 hours (tel: 35 90 00 30; www.telemarkskanalen. no; operational May–Sept). There are many attractions en route, including the old lock-keepers' houses, smithies and sawmills, and the **Vrangfossen** waterfall above Ulefoss, as well as places to stay.

chief delight is to kill bishops, priests, bailiffs and superiors – and who possess a large share of all original sin".

A finger of Telemark reaches out to the sea at Kragerø, not far from the mouth of the Oslofjord, but the province is associated in most minds with the inland terrain, which inspired an eccentric farmer named Sondre Norheim to turn the pedestrian business of plodding about in snow on two planks into the sport of skiing *(see page 98)*. His discovery of the delights that could be achieved with planks that were properly shaped and had heel bindings made him overlook his domestic chores. It is apparently true that, when he ran out of firewood in winter, he simply hacked off another piece of his house and put that to burn on the fire.

Morgedal ❿, where Norheim lived (he later emigrated to America) deserves to be called the cradle of skiing, but it is now only one of dozens of skiing centres in the county. Norheim's statue is a feature of the **Norwegian Skiing Adventure Centre** (Norsk Skieventyr; tel: 35 05 42 50; mid-June– mid-Aug daily 9am–9pm; times vary the rest of the year; charge), near Kviteseidvatn.

Heddal stave church

Visitors with their own transport in Telemark can hardly go wrong: pick any of the winding roads that head inland and the scenery is bound to be breathtaking. For those who do not have a car, the waterways are a wonderful alternative: Skien is a good place to pick up boats going north through Sauherad to Notodden (schedules from Skien tourist office; tel: 35 90 55 20); roads 36 then 360 cover the same route.

West of Notodden, along Road 11, lies **Heddal** ⓫ with its famous **stave church** (Stavkirke; tel: 35 01 39 90; www.heddalstavkirke.no; mid-May–mid-June 10am–5pm; mid-June–mid-Aug 9am–7pm; mid-Aug–mid-Sept 10am– 5pm; charge), the largest and most impressive in Norway. Built between 1147 and 1242, it has a richly carved doorway with animals and human faces. The Telemarkers are masters at expressing nature through art, and

TIP

Notodden Blues Festival takes place every year in August and is one of the most popular music festivals in Norway (www.bluesfest.no).

BELOW: a romantic way to travel.

Inside the silver mine at Saggrenda, 50km (31 miles) east of Heddal on Road E134.

BELOW: Heddal stave church.
RIGHT: *Lindesnes Fyr* (lighthouse) on the southernmost tip of Norway.

nowhere is this more evident than in the rose paintings in the Ramberg room of **Heddal Museum** (Heddal Bygdetun; tel: 35 02 08 40; farmhouses: mid-June–mid-Aug 10am–7pm; charge).

Further on, Road 37 branches off to the north past Lake Tinnsjø towards **Rjukan** ⑫. A breathtaking alternative route is to stay on the E134 to Sauland and turn north, through Tuddal, to drive past Gausta Toppen, one of Norway's landmark peaks. The stretch from Rjukan west to Rauland is also lovely and can be covered by public bus. Keep an eye open for highly decorative wooden houses and double-storey barns, with a ramp leading to the upper floor.

The attraction of Rjukan and nearby Vemork is the heavy-water plant, now the **Norwegian Industrial Workers Museum** (Norsk Industriarbeidermuseum; tel: 35 09 90 00; May–Sept daily 10am–4pm; mid-June–mid-Aug 10am–6pm; Oct–Apr Tue–Fri noon–3pm, Sat–Sun 11am–4pm; charge), but in 1943 the target of a daring sabotage attack by the Norwegian Resistance (*see page 62*).

Rjukan is generally rather gloomy because the sun is nearly always blocked off by surrounding mountains. On top of those mountains, though, another world of vast vistas opens up, and it is said that on a good day it is possible to see one-sixth of Norway. You can take northern Europe's oldest cable car, the **Krossobanen** (tel: 35 09 00 27; late June–late Aug 10am–8pm; times vary rest of the year; charge) from Krosso to the top of Gvepseborg at 860 metres (2,800ft) for just such a view.

Remote Setesdal

An alternative route inland is Road 9 from Kristiansand, which climbs up the Otra valley and runs north along **Byglandsfjorden** to **Setesdal**. Until modern times this area was very remote. The inhabitants sent their timber down to Arendal by pushing it into a river, which plunged 700 metres (2,300ft) over a distance of about 150km (90 miles). They preserved their own almost medieval way of life, including a distinct dialect, dress and cuisine, into the 20th century.

Setesdal is a haven for those in search of rural culture. The most famous dwelling is **Rygnestadtunet**, a 16th-century windowless tower of three storeys with an amazing collection of relics, such as leather hangings depicting St George's battle with the dragon.

The tower was built by Vond-Asmund who, on discovering that his fiancée was about to marry someone else, snatched her away from the wedding procession. From the upper floor of his fortress, he fired off arrows at anyone who approached and in so doing killed at least four people. Rygnestadtunet is part of the **Setesdalmuseet** ⑬ (Heritage Museum; tel: 37 93 63 03; mid-June–Aug daily 11am–5pm; charge), 15km (9 miles) to the south.

You can also visit the Sommarland family park at **Bø** (tel: 35 06 16 00; June–Aug, 10am–7pm most days; charge), Scandinavia's largest waterpark. ❏

ROGALAND

This often overlooked corner of the country contains many delights, from the picturesque fishing harbour of Egersund to an eagle's-eye view over Lysefjord from the top of Pulpit Rock

Many people believe that Norway's fjord country begins at Hardangerfjord and the city of Bergen, and stretches north. If so, they are missing all the southern fjords and islands, where Norway first became a nation. Today this area of Rogaland is centred on Stavanger, the heart of Norway's international oil industry, and contains some of the fjord country's most spectacular natural sights: what a pity to miss **Preikestolen** (Pulpit Rock), a flat slab of rock swooping some 600 metres (2,000ft) up from Lysefjord, which offers a 180-degree view over *fjell* (mountain) and fjord.

Rogaland has the mildest climate in Norway and the beauty of the coast is unsurpassed, but it pays a penalty for its closeness to the sea in unexpected showers and a higher rainfall. In winter, thanks to the Gulf Stream, there is little snow, and the fertile fields of Jæren are green for most of the year.

Starting in the south

By air, the way in is Stavanger's international airport at Sola, or you might come by express boat from Bergen in just under three hours. From the south, the main road is the E39, which crosses into Rogaland north of the old town

of **Egersund ⑭**, now Norway's largest fishing harbour. There is also a coastal route (the scenic Road 44), which hugs the coastline all the way north to Stavanger. At the southern corner of this route, small fjords bite into a rough, rocky coast, which lead to green valleys and a myriad of shining lakes.

The best view of Egersund's sheltered harbour, with its dozens of yachts both big and small, is from the top of the lighthouse. The town itself has a fine **cruciform church** (June–Aug; charge) from 1620 (renovated in the

Main attractions
EGERSUND
HAFRSFJORD BATTLEFIELD
JÆREN
KONGEPARKEN
PULPIT ROCK
KJERAGFJELL
UTSTEIN MONASTERY
KARMØY
UTSIRA

PRECEDING PAGES: Lysefjord enclosed by sheer walls of rock. **LEFT:** taking a boat trip on Lysefjord. **RIGHT:** Egersund's cruciform church.

WHERE

Three huge sculptured swords rise out of the ground to mark the spot where Harald Hårfagre won the Battle of Hafrs-fjord in AD 872. The site is on the edge of Hafrs-fjorden, the circular fjord to the southwest of Stavanger.

late 18th century) and the **Dalane Folk Museum** (tel: 51 46 14 10; June–Aug; charge), which includes the **Egersund Fayance Museum** (displaying painted earthenware crockery, which was once the town's main industry).

Inland is the waterfall **Fotlandfos-sen ⑮**, and further north on the E39 you come to the southern end of **Ørsdalsvatn**. From here, Rogaland's last remaining inland waterway boat, *Ørsdølen*, sails the 20km (13 miles) to Vassbø at the far end of the narrow lake. Near there you can have a simple home-made meal before the boat returns. A few miles further on is Vikeså, where Road 503 to Byrkjedal runs north past **Gloppedalsura**, where the boulders are as big as houses.

Victory on Jæren's fields

Jæren, the flat and fertile country north of Egersund, is Norway's main area for the production of meat, dairy products, poultry and eggs, but it was not always as peaceful as it is today. In AD 872, at Hafrsfjord, it was the scene of the **Battle of Hafrsfjord ⑯**, where King Harald Hårfagre (Fair Hair) won

his most important battle to unite the warring Norwegian kingdoms.

A narrow strip of coast some 70km (43 miles) long, from Raumen Island at the southern end to **Tungenes Fyr ⑰** (lighthouse; June–Aug; charge) northwest of Stavanger, forms a Protected Landscape Area, **Jærstendene landskapsvernområde ⑱**. It includes the scenic Jæren beaches and offshore islands. Raumen itself is one of eight bird sanctuaries where, at different times of the year, you can find turn-stones, ringed plovers and knots taking a brief rest on the long flight to or from southern Europe or Africa; offshore are wintering eider and long-tailed ducks, and the islands provide nesting places for seabirds (often closed to visitors during the breeding season).

In the eight botanical reserves you can find such delights as the spear-leaved fat hen saltbush, and the rare marsh orchid growing in the reserve near **Ogna ⑲**. There are also four geological sites and no less than 150 monuments listed and protected. But this does not mean that Jærstrendene is given over solely to flora and fauna.

BELOW: Gulliver at Kongeparken.

Beaches with white-gold sand are popular picnic spots, and though the water can be chilly, this does not deter swimmers (*see box, page 223*). **Orrestranda** 🐧, which stretches from Vik in the south to Reve in the north, is Norway's longest sand beach, and many come here in summer to watch the sun set below the horizon in the evening.

Sandnes by bicycle

Sandnes on Sandfjord is Norway's "bicycle town", where the famous DBS bicycles are made and where you can hire bikes to explore the surrounding countryside. It is also home to one of Norway's largest shopping centres, Kvadrat (Mon–Fri 10am–8pm, Sat 10am–6pm). A delight for youngsters is **Kongeparken** 🐧 (tel: 81 52 26 73; June–Aug daily 10am–6pm; May and Sept Sat–Sun only 10am–6pm; charge), Norway's biggest amusement park, south of Sandnes at the little town of Ålgård. At 80 metres (260ft) long, Kongeparken's Gulliver is hard to miss. Inside, Gulliver's body is full of unusual playthings. The park has Scandinavia's longest bobsleigh ride.

In many of the mountain areas around the fjords, waterfalls cascade hundreds of metres below. One of the most famous is **Månafoss** 🐧 on the Frafjord, the innermost finger of the Høgsfjord, reached by Road 45 south from Ålgård to Gilja. At Gilja, turn down the steep road to Frafjord, which gives a fantastic view of the water. There are directions to Månafoss in the car park at the foot of the mountain.

Awesome Lysefjord

The **Ryfylke** 🐧 area northeast of Stavanger is true fjord country, one of the least-known parts of Norway despite the drama of its scenery. In the south, due east of Stavanger, Ryfylke starts with **Lysefjord**, under Pulpit Rock, and stretches north past long narrow lakes that once were open fjords, until it reaches **Vindafjord**, **Saudafjord** and **Suldalsvatn**. Although he never saw it, Victor Hugo described Lysefjord in The

Toilers of the Sea as "the most terrible of all the corridor rocks in the sea". Hugo probably meant "awesome", and that the fjord still is. Every visitor to Norway should try to walk out through heather moor and scrubland to stand on the top of **Pulpit Rock** 🐧 (Preikestolen), a rock platform high above the fjord (*see box, below*).

From the village of Forsand at its mouth, Lysefjord is 40km (25 miles) long and, at its innermost end, has one of Europe's most remarkable feats of civil engineering: the road to the hydroelectric power station at **Lysebotn**, which is hidden hundreds of metres inside the mountain. This road, which seems to defy gravity, snakes up and down more than 750 metres (2,500ft), with 27 hairpin bends, and connects Lysebotn to Sirdal and Setesdal to the east along the Lyseveien. If you dare to keep your eyes open as the bus takes its near perpendicular route downwards, the view is magnificent.

Near the end of the fjord on the south side towers **Kjeragfjell** 🐧, an enormous granite mountain around 1,100 metres (3,550ft) high. Lie on

Wedged between two rocks, the famous Kjerragbolten offers a breathtaking vantage point from which to view Lysefjord below.

Preikestolen: the Rock with a View

The most famous mountain formation in the Lysefjord, east of Stavanger, is Pulpit Rock (Preikestolen), which protrudes about 30 metres (98ft) from the precipitous mountain and towers more than 600 metres (1,968ft) over the water below. Preikestolen is, not surprisingly, among the most famous tourist attractions in Norway, visited by some 120,000 people every year.

The trail to the top of Preikestolen, which starts near the stunning new Preikestolen Mountain Lodge *(fjellstue)*, climbs 350 metres (1,148ft) through somewhat uneven terrain, although the hike is accessible to most. On the way, look out for golden eagles, willow grouse, ptarmigan and other birds, as well as reindeer or even an elk if you are lucky. The hike takes two hours each way. Pack sturdy walking boots, warm clothing (the weather can change quickly, so even if you set off in sunny conditions, it might be foggy or windy by the time you reach the top) and some water. There are no railings near the steepest spots, so keep an eye on children, and walk as closely to the mountain wall as possible. The views from the top over the fjord are amazing, so allow enough time there before starting your descent back to the car park.

Sightseeing boats leave from Stavanger for Lysefjord all year round to view Pulpit Rock from below.

TIP

Allow some time to visit Flor og Fjære, where lush exotic gardens and a restaurant surrounded by palm trees await. You'll find Flor og Fjære on the island of Sør Hidle, 20 minutes by boat northeast from Stavanger. Tel: 51 11 00 00; www.florogfjare.no.

your front and look down through the wedge cut out of the mountain plateau to the fjord below. To get there takes about two hours' walking from several spots along the Lyseveien. Lysebotn has become a base for extreme-sports daredevils in recent years, and Kjerag is a favoured spot with both base jumpers and climbers.

Music on Mosterøy

The sheltered bay north of Stavanger, and the outer islands such as Karmøy, protect Ryfylke's inshore islands from the North Sea. Christianity flourished early here under the protection of the bishops of Stavanger, and the islands have many churches.

In summer, the 12th-century **Utstein Monastery** ㉖ (Utstein Kloster; tel: 51 72 00 50; mid-May–mid-Sept Tue–Sat 10am–4pm, Sun noon–5pm; charge) on **Mosterøy** makes a beautiful setting for concerts which are mostly classical. It offers the traveller a refreshing break on the way from Stavanger to Bokna-fjord. The monastery's acoustics and the palpable sense of history give these concerts a very special atmosphere.

The many **lighthouses** are not only landmarks for islanders and seafarers but make excellent bird-watching sites, with the hunched outlines of cormorants and other seabirds on wave-washed rocks below. The waters around these peaceful islands are a sea kingdom for sailors of all kinds, with many yacht harbours. Most of the island grocers provide boat services, and it is easy to hire rowing boats and small craft with outboard engines.

Suldal highlands

Here fjords, lakes and rivers are rich in fish and fine for sailing and canoeing, and all these inland, eastern areas of Rogaland have good cross-country skiing tracks in winter as well as some fine Alpine slopes. Among the best holiday areas is the **Suldal district**, stretching from Sand on the Sandsfjord, along the Suldalslågen River – where the rushing waters have produced huge salmon (the largest so far weighed almost 44kg/97lb) – to the long, narrow Suldalsvatn. At the Sand end of Suldalslågen, **Lakses-tudioet** ㉗ (daily mid-June–mid-Aug 10am–6pm; charge), is an observation

BELOW: preparing for a base jump.

studio, built under a waterfall, where visitors look through two large windows at the salmon resting before their next leap up the fish ladder on the way to their spawning grounds. Where river meets lake is **Kolbeinstveit Museum** (Rural Museum; tel: 52 79 93 04; mid-June–mid-Aug Tue–Sun 11am–5pm; charge), with the old Guggedalsloftet farm which dates back to the 13th century.

From Sand, a bus follows the path of the river to the giant **Kvilldal ㉘** power station, opened in 1982 by King Olav, who chiselled his signature into the mountain side, a popular royal tradition in Scandinavia. On the way to this cavernous power station the bus stops at the **Lakseslottet ㉙** (Salmon Castle) at Lindum, built by Lord Sibthorp in 1885 when the British "salmon lords" looked on a few weeks in Norway as part of the fishing season. River and lake still draw anglers, and the castle is a popular guesthouse.

From Stavanger and Jæren, ferries and express boats reach this fjord country and its islands, and it is easy to combine bus and ferry. Vindafjord,

Saudafjord and Suldalsvatn look up to 1,500-metre (5,000ft) peaks that lead the way to the great mountain plateau of Hardangervidda. In summer you can take the exciting **old mountain road** north from Sauda to Røldal; the new road has tunnels to keep it open all year. At Røldal, where there's a stave church, you pick up the **Discovery Route ㉚** (Opplevelsesrute, E134), which has come over the Haukeli Mountains from Telemark, and you can continue north along it until it becomes Road 13 towards Odda.

Express boat to Karmøy

The sea route north to Bergen is one of the most popular ways to see the northern coast. By taking an express boat (a cross between a catamaran and a hydrofoil) you can drop off at any of the harbour stops and stay a night or a week according to your whim. **Karmøy ㉛**, the island at the south of the outer islands chain, is big enough to merit its own boat service, which goes to **Skudeneshavn** in the south, an idyllic old port with white wooden houses along narrow streets (tours

While on Karmøy, pay a visit to the Fisheries Museum at Vedvågen, with its saltwater aquarium. The building was designed by Norwegian firm of architects Snøhetta, the people behind the National Opera House in Oslo.

BELOW: typical "seahouses" in Skudeneshavn.

Following claims by the Norwegian film critic Pål Bang-Hansen that Marilyn Monroe's father was a Norwegian émigré from Haugesund, the town erected a statue on the quayside to the Hollywood goddess.

BELOW: young buskers in Haugesund during the film festival.
RIGHT: church at Egersund.

from **Mælandsgården Museum**; June–Aug). The north of the island is linked to the mainland just south of Haugesund, the first sizeable coastal town north of Stavanger.

Karmøy's known history dates back to saga times, when it was the "North-way" shipping lane that gave Norway its name. Harald Hårfagre made his home at **Avaldsnes** ❷ after the battle at Hafrsfjord. Also here is **St Olaf's church** (kirke), which was built between 1248 and 1263 by King Håkon Håkonson and restored in 1922 as the parish church. Near its north walls stands **St Mary's Sewing Needle**, a strange 6.5-metre (21ft) high stone pillar leaning towards the church wall. Legend tells that the Day of Judgement will come when the pillar touches the wall; many priests are said to have climbed the pillar in the dead of night to pare away the top to make sure that the day is not yet nigh.

On the west coast at **Ferkingstad** are historic boathouses with walls made of stone blocks 1.5 metres (5ft) thick. Further north on the west coast, outside the town hall at **Åkrehamn**, stand two

stone pillars from the Iron Age. Crossing to the east coast, near the town of **Kopervik** are burial hills and mounds and stone pillars. The largest burial mound, Doøa Hill, was restored in 1978 and, though it has not yet been fully excavated, it dates back to the Bronze Age. Further north, on the mainland side of the bridge to Haugesund, are the **Five Bad Virgins** (Dem Fem Dårlige Jomfruer), stone monuments some 2.5 metres (8ft) high, where excavations in 1901 revealed a Roman bowl dating from AD 300–400.

Haugesund and the islands

Haugesund has long been a centre for fishing, shipping and farming. Today its harbour is filled with pleasure boats. The town has also become a festival and congress centre, and plays host to the Sildajazz Festival and the Norwegian Film Festival (both Aug) and Rockfest in June.

Numerous fjords and lakes cut into the roughly shaped peninsula, ideal for fishing, sailing, rowing, canoeing, diving and walking. A boat trip to the idyllic group of islands of **Røvær** ❸, around 10km (6 miles) to the west, occupies a day and offers shore fishing, interesting flora and fauna and, in summer, a wharf-side café.

For the adventurous, M/S *Utsira* (tel: 91 88 15 65 or 47 88 01 44) provides a daily service to the island of **Utsira** ❹, familiar from European shipping forecasts and Norway's western outpost. The 90-minute voyage makes a wonderful tour for bird-watchers, as does the island itself. Fishing is also excellen, and Norwegian saltwater fishing is free to holders of a national licence *(see pages 107–8)*. Day licences for lakes and rivers are available: contact Haugesund Tourist Office, tel: 52 01 08 30.

To the north, **Espevær** ❺, a fishing village situated at the mouth of Bømlafjorden River, is well endowed with heritage sites. The village itself is one of the best-preserved sites in Norway; there is a maritime and fisheries museum, as well as a bathing house. ❏

STAVANGER

Once the port from which thousands emigrated to the United States, today Stavanger attracts an international crowd – and cuisine – as the centre of Norway's thriving oil industry

Strange though it may seem in a city which has devoted nearly 1,000 years to the sea, the best way to arrive in Stavanger is by overnight train from Oslo. As the dawn arrives, the train slips along the side of the fjord with black mountain peaks outlined on either side, past the huge latticework of oil rigs and drilling towers which have made Stavanger Norway's oil capital. Enormous though they are, somehow they do not intrude on the landscape because the size and grandeur of mountain and fjord dwarfs even these industrial giants.

Stavanger has been lucky because the sea has always been good to the city. As one source of prosperity disappeared, another arose. Shipping, fishing and trading have taken the city's ships and people all over the world, and brought seamen to Stavanger, to give it an easy-going relationship with other nations. Today, Norway's fourth-largest city, which was European Capital of Culture in 2008, is as international as ever: nearly a tenth of its 121,600 inhabitants are foreigners.

International eating

This international community has demanded high standards, and Stavanger has good restaurants, hotels, entertainment and a cosmopolitan atmosphere out of all proportion to its size. As well as **restaurants** specialising in good Norwegian food, there is a choice of Indian, Italian, Greek, Portuguese, Mexican, Chinese and Japanese eateries. The city is also home to Scandinavia's largest food festival, **Gladmat**, which draws thousands of visitors every year in late July, and to the country's only gastronomic institute.

Restaurants, and particularly alcohol, are expensive in Norway, but a great many cafés, bars and pubs have sprung up, sometimes with live music,

Main attractions
GLADMAT FESTIVAL
NORWEGIAN PETROLEUM MUSEUM
ØVRE HOLMEGATE
OLD STAVANGER
NORWEGIAN CANNING MUSEUM
STAVANGER CATHEDRAL
ROGALAND MUSEUM OF FINE ARTS

LEFT: Stavanger's past prosperity was based on sardines. **RIGHT:** Norwegian flags for sale at Stavanger's market.

TIP

See Stavanger Museum's five sites in one day for the price of a single ticket. Stavanger Museum itself, the Canning Museum, the Maritime Museum, the royal residence of Ledaal and the 19th-century manor house Breidablikk are all included.

so going out needn't cost an arm and a leg. In the **fish market** on the quayside, where fresh prawns eaten on the spot are the favourite buy, and at the **fruit and flower market** nearby, you will hear many languages, and in the heart of Stavanger's shopping streets behind the market almost all the assistants speak English.

Apart from the oil prosperity, Stavanger is also the principal town and seat of government of Rogaland.

An American connection

In the 19th and early 20th centuries Stavanger was the exit port for Norway's extensive emigration programme to the United States *(see page 52)* – there are more Americans of Norwegian descent than there are Norwegians. Not surprisingly, therefore, the city is host to the **Norwegian Emigration Centre A** (Det Norske Utvandrersenteret, Strandkaien 31; tel: 51 53 88 60; Mon–Fri 9am–3pm), where Norway's emigration history is documented and commemorated. For a fee, genealogical researchers will even help you to find your Norwegian roots.

The smell of sardines

The *iddis* (the colloquial name, meaning sardine label, for a person from Stavanger) claims to be the oldest true Norwegian, dating from 872 and the Battle of Hafrsfjord, which took place just south of the city, and in which King Harald Hårfagre won his final battle to unite the kingdom.

When work began on Stavanger Cathedral (Domkirken) in 1125, Stavanger was simply a cluster of small wooden houses at the end of the narrow inlet called **Vågen**. It was chosen as the heart of the bishopric, nevertheless, because it was the only recognisable settlement along this southwestern coast. From then on Stavanger was the most important town in the area. It grew slowly; the population was only 2,000 at the start of the 19th century, but had jumped to 30,000 by 1900.

In the 18th and 19th centuries, the city depended on fishing and maritime trade, and faced the world with an unbroken row of wharves and warehouses dedicated to these industries. Around the 1870s, at a time when fishing and shipping were beginning

BELOW: salt cod for sale at the market.

to face decline, the fishermen turned their attention to brisling (small herring), which were cured and canned in the town and sent as Norwegian "sardines" all over the world.

At one time Stavanger had as many as 70 canneries, and nearly three-quarters of the population worked in the industry. In the first half of the 20th century, the smell of oily fish hung over the town, permeating every breath. But Stavanger never doubted the value of that smell. When, on a particularly malodorous day, a cheeky youngster wrinkled a disdainful nose, a mother would say: "Don't scorn it, that's the smell of money." It was, and Stavanger thrived on sardines until, after World War II, that all-pervasive tang began to fade along with the demand for sardines.

Offshore oil

For nearly 20 years, Stavanger knew difficult times. Then, in the late 1960s, came oil – once again the sea had provided. Visit the **Norwegian Petroleum Museum ❸** (Norsk Oljemuseum, Kjeringholmen; tel: 51 93 93 00; June–Aug daily 10am–7pm; Sept–May Mon–Sat 10am–4pm, Sun 10am–6pm; charge) by the harbour for an insight into this valuable source of energy. Here you will learn how petrol and gas were formed millions of years ago, and the history of its discovery in the North Sea in the late 1960s. You will also, with a range of models, films and interactive exhibits and experiments, get an insight into the technology used to harvest this source of energy, and the challenges it represents. You can find out what life on an offshore platform is like, and learn more about the way oil has influenced Norwegian society in the past few decades. This modern, exciting and highly educational museum is one of the best in Norway, and a must-see in Stavanger. The Bolgen & Moi restaurant on the premises is also one of the best in town.

Street of many colours

Round the corner from the Petroleum Museum, **Øvre Holmegate**, Stavanger's most colourful street, where all buildings have been painted in pastel hues, is a great place for a stroll and a bit of shopping. It is home to many

Chemical analysis has confirmed that the copper used to cover New York's Statue of Liberty came from one of the old Visnes copper mines on the island of Karmøy northwest of Stavanger.

BELOW: the Petroleum Museum.

Outdoor Activities

Stavanger is on the doorstep of the **Jærstendene landskapsvernområde**, a Protected Landscape Area which stretches 70km (43 miles) along the southern coast and its offshore islands, with nature reserves (see page 214) and silver-sand beaches, ideal for swimming and picnicking. Sport is good year-round: swimming, sub-aqua diving, sailing, windsurfing and fishing. There is a hiking club, tennis and horse riding in Jærstendene. In winter, the climate remains mild and the fields are rarely covered by snow; yet the good ski slopes are only an hour or so away.

Stavanger also hosts the Sand Volleyball World Cup in late June–early July. The event attracts top beach volleyball players from around the world, who compete for medals, cash and Viking swords on courts set up around the harbour.

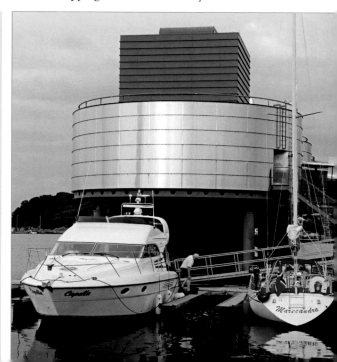

cosy cafés, the most famous of which is probably Sjokoladepiken (The Chocolate Girl) at No. 27 (see Restaurants, page 356), and small boutiques selling anything from funky retro fashion to second-hand books.

Old Stavanger

Many traces remain of these fluctuations in the city's fortunes. **Old Stavanger** ❸ (Gamle Stavanger) is a preserved neighbourhood of more than 180 early 19th-century white wooden buildings looking down towards Vågen, with cobbled streets lit by old-fashioned streetlamps. But this is no museum. There may be a preservation order on the exteriors, and the owners take pride in keeping them in character, but the interiors have every comfort and gadget that modern Norwegians expect, and Gamle Stavanger is one of the most coveted areas in Norway in which to live.

Nor have the canning factories been lost. Many are converted into modern offices, and buildings that once canned sardines may now be the headquarters of an international oil company. One

factory at Øvre Strandgate, in the old part of town near the harbour, has been preserved in its original state as the **Norwegian Canning Museum** ❹ (Norsk Hermetikkmuseet; tel: 51 84 27 00; June–Aug daily 11am–4pm; Sept–May Tue–Sun 11am–4pm; charge). In the big open room with its curing ovens, the guides describe the life of the people who worked long hours at the intricate process of threading the sardines onto long rods, smoking, then packing them, almost all of it being done by hand.

Even nearer the harbour is the **Stavanger Maritime Museum** ❺ (Sjøfartsmuseet; tel: 51 52 59 11; mid-June–Aug daily 11am–4pm; 1 Sept–mid-June Sun only 11am–4pm; charge) in one of the old mercantile houses on Nedre Strandgate, with its warehouses towards the sea. It traces the history of Stavanger's maritime links over the past 200 years. Today, large windows have replaced the warehouse doors, and you turn your head from the history behind you to the modern town outside. On the Nedre Strandgate side of the museum, away from the harbour, is a general store, full of the provisions that it would have held before World War II. Upstairs, where the owner lived, is an office just as it might have been when a crewman called in during the 1930s in search of a berth, or the skipper came to pay his respects. The flat shows the comfortable life of a ship-owner in the late 19th century.

On the other side of the harbour, facing the Maritime Museum, is the site of the original Viking settlement. The **Valberg Tower** ❻ (Valbergtårnet; tel: 51 89 55 01; Mon–Sat all year; charge), built in the early 1850s as a fire lookout, is the best point from which to get a view over the city. There is a small watchmen's museum on the first floor.

Centre of worship

The heart of modern Stavanger is the area around **Breiavatnet**, the small lake in the middle of the city, near the oldest and biggest building, the 12th-

Antony Gormley's Stavanger Figures

Antony Gormley, the British sculptor known for his *Angel of the North* in England, has made his mark on Stavanger with *Broken Column* (2003). Twenty-three cast-iron figures have been strategically placed to give the appearance of an imaginary column stretching from the Rogaland Art Museum to the city's harbour. The figures are based on a casting of the sculptor's own body, and have been placed to reflect a broad perspective of people's life in the city, with the figure standing gazing out to sea on the fish market forming the cardinal point for all the other sculptures. The height of each sculpture (1.95 metres/6ft 5in) is the same as that of the sculptor himself. The first sculpture stands in its own room in Rogaland Art Museum, 41.41 metres (136ft) above sea level. The next sculpture on the line is in Mosvannparken at 39.46 metres (130ft) altitude (ie 41.41 minus 1.95 metres). The column of figures continues in this fashion down through the the city until it reaches the sea. The last sculpture stands partly submerged on a rock beyond Natvigs Minde in Stavanger's harbour.

century **Cathedral** (Domkirken, June–Aug Mon–Sun 11am–7pm; Sept–May Tue–Thur and Sat 11am–4pm; services every Sun at 11am). Construction began in 1125 by Bishop Reinald of Winchester in the Anglo-Norman style. It can claim with justification to be among the best-preserved medieval cathedrals in Europe. Alongside is the **Cathedral School**, built in 1758 on the 12th-century foundations of the Bishop's residence.

Inside, this stone cathedral has a feeling of austere strength in the massive pillars which contrast with the elegant arches of the chancel and a tapestry by Frida Hansen (1927) in the vestibule. Both chancel and vestibule were rebuilt after 1272 in a style similar to the Scottish Gothic of the times, a reminder of Stavanger's international connections even in those early days.

Ullandhaug discovery

Even earlier than the cathedral is **Jernaldergarden**, the Iron Age farm at **Ullandhaug** (tel: 51 83 26 00; late May–late Sept Sun 11am–4pm; late June–mid-Aug Sun–Fri 11am–4pm; charge), about 2km (1¼ miles) or so to the southwest of the centre. Here archaeologists unearthed and then reconstructed part of the farm to show three houses, parts of a cattle track and the original encircling stone wall from AD 350 and 550. This was a golden age in Norway, and the city's **Archaeological Museum** (Arkeologisk Museum, Peder Klows gate 30a; tel: 51 83 26 00; June–Aug Tue–Sun 11am–5pm; Sept–May Tue 11am–8pm, Wed–Sat 11am–3pm, Sun 11am–4pm; charge) is gradually furnishing the houses to show how people lived then.

From Ullandhaug, it is worth visiting the nearby **Botanical Garden** (Botanisk Hage; daily; charge), which has a herb and perennial garden with more than 1,500 species from all over the world. Rogaland is rich in birds and fauna, and the **Stavanger Museum** (June–Aug daily 11am–4pm; Sept–May Tue–Sun 11am–4pm; charge; tel: 51 84

27 00) has an excellent exhibition, not only on Rogaland wildlife, but on cultural history, and the history of fishing (covering the industry and its creatures, including whales and seals).

Lakeside art gallery

Last, but not least, the **Rogaland Museum of Fine Arts** (Kunstmuseum, Henrik Ibsensgate 55; tel: 51 53 09 00; Tue–Sun 11am–4pm; charge), beautifully located in a park surrounding Lake Mosvannet, 3km (2 miles) south of Stavanger centre, has a good collection of Norwegian art ranging from 19th-century to contemporary. Of particular interest is the collection of paintings by Lars Hertervig (1830–1902), who was born near Stavanger and whose haunting landscapes still have as strong an impact as they did when he painted them over a century ago. The museum houses the Halvdan Hafsten Collection, some 200 works by mid-20th century painters, making it a national centre for art from this period. Also to be seen is the first of Antony Gormley's *Broken Column* figures *(see box, opposite)* that spread through town. ❏

Artefacts from Stavanger's canning industry are kept in the Canning Museum (Hermetikkmuseet).

BELOW: the nave of Stavanger Cathedral.

HORDALAND

An inspiration to generations of Norwegian artists, the mighty Hardangerfjord lies at the heart of this region, which mixes wild coasts with sheltered islands, and spring blossoms with fjord waters

Stretching 180km (110 miles) between the North Sea in the west and the reaches of the Hardanger plateau in the east, the Hardangerfjord offers a variety of landscapes, from windswept islands and skerries at the ocean's edge to picturesque villages clinging to the hillsides further inland, not to mention mighty waterfalls in the mountains and majestic glaciers on the horizon.

Nobody knows how many islands lie off the coast of Hordaland. Many of the inner islands around Bergen are linked by bridges and causeways in a pattern of islands and sea that seems all of a piece with the multitude of branched fjords, including the famous Hardangerfjord.

The Hardangerfjord is also known for its orchards – the fruit-growing districts of Ulvik and Ullesvang are among Norway's largest, and Lofthus on Sørfjorden is home to a popular cherry festival.

Early Christianity

The southwest district of **Sunnhordland** has islands, skerries, sounds and straits, good harbours and sheltered bays. Though the North Sea is its neighbour, the climate is surprisingly mild. The main islands are **Bømlo**, **Stord** and **Tysnesøy**, and even though they are close to the sea they have a variety of scenery.

Stord makes a good paddling-off point for sea canoeing, either from island to island, or into the mouth of the Hardanger. It is an "oil island", too, where the gigantic outlines of oil platforms take shape, some rising nearly 380 metres (1,250ft) out of the water.

The sagas tell that in 1024 St Olav first introduced Christianity to Norway in these islands. Today, an annual outdoor performance (late May or early June; tel: 53 42 07 90) of the historical play *Mostraspelet*, held at **Mosterhamn ❶** on Bømlo, dramatises this ancient saga. Nearby is a stone cross erected in 1924 on the 900th anniversary of the arrival of Christianity, and Mosterhamn has the oldest **stone church** in Norway (May–Sept; charge), built around 995–1100. The church bells bear images of St Olav.

Southern Hardangerfjord

The mouth of the Hardangerfjord is as beautiful as anywhere in the fjord itself, but the irony is that Sunnhordaland as a whole tends to be overshadowed by the fame and drama of Hardangerfjord. Too many visitors travel through quickly on their way to other places. The discriminating know it deserves a longer look.

Leirvik on Stord is a good starting point, with short ferry connections to most of the surrounding islands and to the mainland. It is also the location of the **Sunnhordland Museum** (all year; charge), which was established in 1913 as the local history museum.

To the south, the ferry to **Valevåg** puts you on the right track for **Ryvarden Fyr** (lighthouse; every Sun, plus Wed and Sat from July to mid-Aug), sitting at the mouth of Bømlafjord, the home of the innovative composer Fartein Valen (1887–1952), where overnight stays can be arranged. There is also a museum, art gallery and café at nearby Møstrevåg.

To the east, a ferry to Sunde on the mainland brings you to where the cold waters of Hardangerfjord begin to seep into the warmer tides from the west and the lovely 17th-century **Rosendal Barony** (Baroniet Rosendal; May–Sept; charge) in **Rosendal** ❷, the only one of its kind in Norway, which lost its aristocracy largely with the departure of the Danes. The manor house was built in 1665 by Ludvig Rosenkrantz. He is buried in the nearby medieval Kvinnherad Kirke (church), snuggled into the shelter of a rock face and once owned by the barony. The barony today has a peaceful park and a large, carefully tended 300-year-old rose garden, and is held in trust by Oslo University. Throughout the summer there are art exhibitions, lunchtime concerts, and the **Rosendal Music Festival** is staged here during May and June.

Hardangerfjord is part of the Norwegian legend, the fjord that gave its name to Norway's national musical instrument, the eight-stringed Hardanger fiddle, and provided inspiration for the composer Edvard Grieg (1843–1907), the musician Ole Bull (1810–80) and, indirectly, for the 19th-century nationalist movement that eventually led to Norway's independence. Among these mountains and fjords, Grieg and Bull travelled on foot and horse, learning old melodies and dipping into centuries-old cultural traditions and and folk customs.

Poetic odyssey

Tourism came to the Hardanger district back in the 1830s when the poet Henrik Wergeland (1808–45) wrote about "wonderful Hardanger", and foreign as well as Norwegian artists, scientists and other travellers began to arrive; first in a trickle, then in a flood when, 30 years later, the steamers began to run from Bergen or Stavanger. Like the visitors

An upland ridge on the island of Stord reaches nearly 750 metres (2,500ft) high, and the view stretches east to Hardangerfjord and the white sheets of the Folgefonna Glacier.

PRECEDING PAGES: Hardangerfjord. **LEFT:** taking the Norway in a Nutshell trip. **BELOW:** enjoying the water.

Southwest Coast

of today, they came to Hardanger for its waterfalls, the smaller fjords that lead almost to the Hardanger plateau, and for glaciers and mountains that rarely lose their snowcaps, contrasted with orchards lining the fjord side. Nearly half a million fruit trees grow here, including plum, cherry, apple and pear, turning the fjord pink and white in spring as the blossom reflects in the deep, still water. At this time the waterfalls are in full spate, shooting over the sides of the mountains, and the Hardanger has two of Norway's highest and best known: **Skykkjedalsfossen**, which falls 300 metres (1,000ft), and **Vøringfossen**, lower but famous for its beauty.

Northern Hardangerfjord

Crossing by ferry to the north shore, Road 49 runs along the sunny side of the Hardangerfjord towards the fjord villages of **Norheimsund** and **Øystese** ❸. Alternatively, they can be reached through day or longer excursions from Bergen either by boat or road (E16 and then Road 11). Both of these villages offer excellent trips for exploring the fjords by car and ferry, and marked paths here and at **Kvamskogen** further inland make for safe walking. Take time out to visit the **Ingebrigt Vik Museum**, part of **Kunsthuset Kabuso** (year round; charge) at Øystese, one of Norway's most distinctive museums, containing virtually all the works by the sculptor of that name (1867–1927).

Not to be passed by is the **Hardanger Ship Conservation Centre** (Hardanger Fartøyvernsenter; all year) at Norheimsund, where conservationists are patiently restoring the wooden craft that made Norwegian boatbuilding famous. They range from small rowing boats to the centre's most prestigious restoration, the M/S *Mathilde*, a 22 metre (73ft) Hardanger yacht launched in 1884. This superb yacht has regained her former splendour under the guidance of Kristian Djupevåg (who also restored Roald Amundsen's polar vessel, *Gjøa*), and it has the world's largest authentic yacht rigging. The *Mathilde* sleeps 25 passengers in bunks or hammocks and is available for cruises and day excursions, when she can take 50

Edvard Grieg used to visit a small hytte poised on the edge of Hardangerfjord near the village of Ullensvang where, with piano and writing desk at hand, he would compose surrounded by the beauty of the Norwegian fjords.

BELOW: the old fjord village of Utne.

Trolls are fearsome creatures from Norse mythology. The fairy tale of the Three Billy Goats Gruff, *featuring a troll, is of Scandinavian origin.*

BELOW: taking a ski lift at Folgefonna.
BELOW RIGHT: local folk costume.

people to sail fjord and sea as they might have in bygone days.

Across to Jondal

Ferries make the crossing from Tør-vikbygd to **Jondal ❹**, on the south side of the fjord, and the entrance to the **Folgefonna Glacier** and **Folge-fonna Summer Ski-Centre**. The safe but exciting 19km (12-mile) toll road to the new ski centre is clear from May to September. With snow at the centre for almost all of the year, there are three mobile ski lifts, Alpine and cross-country skiing tracks (you can hire all the equipment), a cafeteria and guided walks on the glacier.

Jondal itself has a country museum in the old **Sheriff's House** (Lens-mannshuset; May–Sept; charge), and **Hardanger Cathedral** (mid-June–mid-Aug 10am–8pm). It was built in 1888 and is the largest church in the Hardanger region. Concerts are held in the church on Wednesdays in July at 11.30am.

About 13km (8 miles) northeast at **Herand** you will find Bronze Age rock carvings and, at Herandsholmen,

Hardanger's first guesthouse, which opened in 1754.

By now into the inner fjords, the road suddenly turns sharply southeast towards Utne village, part of Ullens-vang *kommune*, which also includes both sides of Sørfjorden. When the fjords were west Norway's main "roads", **Utne ❺** was an important junction between east and west and had the first post and telegraph offices in Hardan-ger, in 1836 and 1876 respectively.

Two establishments in Utne which sum up Hardanger life over the past centuries are the **Hardanger Folk Museum** (Folkemuseum; daily, closed winter weekends; charge, for details *see below*), and the **Utne Hotel** (tel: 53 66 64 00), founded in 1722, the oldest hotel in Norway still in oper-ation. Since 1787, five generations of the same family have owned the hotel. It first became famous internation-ally during the time of Torbjørg Utne (1812–1903), known with affection as Mor (Mother) Utne. Her picture hangs on the sitting-room wall. The family is represented today by her great grand-daughter, Hildegun Aga Blokhus. It has always been a favourite spot for artists, who have donated many paintings, and the hotel also holds exhibitions of national costumes and embroidery.

Since it opened in 1911, the Hardanger Folkemuseum has collected old houses and farm buildings and has created a "cluster farm" as it would have been before the Norwegian agricultural reforms in the middle of the 19th century. Along the shore are old boathouses and a merchant's shop, which was in use in Utne not all that long ago, and an orchard preserves many old varieties of fruit which have now disappeared from other parts of the Hardangerfjord. Inside, the museum has a modern exhibition, rooms showing traditional crafts, local folk costumes and folk art and the famous Hardanger fiddle along with a resident fiddle maker, and changing exhibitions on fjord themes.

Around Sørfjord

Past Utne, the fjord-side road turns due south into the **Sørfjord**. Once you are used to the narrow road and would like to enjoy the magnificent view, you should stop at **Agatunet ❻** (mid-May–mid-Aug; charge), the farm of a 13th-century local sheriff. From the Middle Ages to the recent past, Agatunet grew into a nine-family village with a hamlet of some 30 buildings. Today, the families no longer live there but the buildings have been preserved.

On the eastern side of Sørfjord, a short ferry ride away, is an amusement park, **Mikkelparken** (mid-June–mid-Aug daily; late May–mid-June and late Aug Sat–Sun only) at **Kinsarvik ❼**. A favourite with children, it has a water chute, trampoline, a miniature zoo, a boating lake, and lends out surfboards, water mopeds and water skis. Kinsarvik was also part of the main east–west route, and its marketplace attracted merchants from both sides of Hardangervidda to exchange bog iron and furs for sea salt. The **stone church** is said to have been constructed by Scottish builders around 1160, and has a 17th-century pulpit painted by Peter Reimers. Until Utne church (kirke) was consecrated in 1896, Kinsarvik had for centuries drawn its congregation from all around the fjords, and many worshippers arrived in church boats.

Dramatic Eidfjord

Heading northeast from Kinsarvik on the E13 and then Road 7, you will find one of the area's most beautiful stretches of water, **Eidfjord ❽**. It cuts far into the dramatic landscape, which includes the **Hardangerjøkulen** and, below it, **Skykkjedalsfossen ❾**, Norway's highest waterfall, and **Vøringfossen ❿**, which falls 180 metres (590ft) down into the wilds of Måbødalen. There is a path at the top overlooking the fall which is not for vertigo sufferers. Alternatively, you can walk down to view this great outpouring from below, and fitness fanatics might welcome the challenge of the age-old packhorse track up Måbøfjell, with 1,500 steps and 125 bends. Look out for signs to the **Måbødalen Agricultural Landscape Museum** (Kulturlandskapsmuseum; all year; guided tours available),

BELOW: snowman outside Voss Church.

TIP

The Hardangervidda Nature Centre in Eidfjord is a good place to learn about the flora and fauna of Europe's largest mountainous plateau (tel: 53 67 41 00; www. hardangervidda.org).

which provides a network of trails, all signposted and with information boards. The public barbecue areas make fabulous picnic stops.

Above tiny Simadalsfjord is a mountain farm, **Kjeåsen** ⓫, which claims to be the world's most isolated settlement. It lies like an eagle's nest 620 metres (2,000ft) on near-vertical rock above the distant waters of the fjord. Those feeling strong and brave can tackle the old path to the top and marvel that this was how the villagers struggled up with their every need. For frailer spirits it is possible to reach Kjeåsen by car through a magnificent new tunnel. Inside the mountain is the **Sima Kraftverk** (Hydroelectric Power Station; daily mid-June–mid-Aug; charge), which arranges guided tours three times a day.

Crossing Eidfjorden at Brimnes you enter a farming and forestry district. Instead of taking the E13, take a right turn onto Road 572, which will bring you to **Ulvik** ⓬. Artists and other visitors have been coming here for longer than almost any other place in Hardanger, and the village has perma-

nent exhibitions by artists such as Tit Mohr (born 1917) and Sigurd Undeland (1903–83). No one should miss the fine examples of **rose painting** in Ulvik's 19th-century church, painted in 1923 by Lars Osa (1860–1958).

Sporting Voss

Continuing on in a loop back to the E13 you come to **Voss** ⓭, which lies next to a lake, **Vangsvatnet**, in the middle of rich farmland. The Voss *kommune* (district) makes full use of its surroundings to attract visitors. In summer they come for touring, fjord excursions, mountain walking, parachuting, hang-gliding and paragliding from **Hangurfjell**, and fishing and water sports on Vangsvatnet. In winter, everything changes and Voss becomes one of the best centres for Alpine and cross-country skiing of the more energetic touring variety.

Voss is also a good place for mountain touring and sport fishing in the 500 or so lakes and innumerable mountain rivers and streams, with the Vosso River famous for the size of its salmon. Even in summer the high

BELOW: traditional wedding at Voss led by a fiddler and toastmaster.

mountains call for boots or very strong shoes and plenty of extra clothes – temperatures drop quickly; this applies in all upland areas.

The top station of the **cable car** up Hangurfjell gives one of the best prospects of Voss in its bowl-shaped valley. As the ground drops away below, the two gondolas, "Dinglo" and "Danglo", take only four minutes or so to lift you 570 metres (2,000ft). On a sunny day, a coffee on the platform outside the cafeteria is magnificent, with the occasional excitement of a paraglider soaring into the sun and over Vagnsvatnet, spread out below.

At the beginning of World War II, Voss was badly damaged by German bombing, and not much remains of the old town centre except the church, **Vangskyrkja** (June–Aug daily), which dates back to 1277. The inside is certainly worth seeing, with a colourfully painted ceiling liberally adorned with flying angels. Outside, a stone cross stands in a field south of the church which, according to legend, was raised two centuries before the church was built by the proselytising King Olav Haraldson. The church walls are 2 metres (7ft) thick, and the wooden octagonal steeple is unique in Norway.

Below Hangurfjell, about half an hour's walk above the town, is **Voss Museum** (Folkemuseum; all year; tel: 56 51 15 11), a collection of 16 old wooden buildings standing in traditional form around a central courtyard. The houses date from 1500 to 1870 and contain implements and furniture in use until 1927, incredible though it may seem. Yet somehow, despite the heavy farm work and meagre evening light, farm people like these managed to produce some beautiful embroidery, wood and other craft work.

Artistic tradition

Voss has long been a centre for artists and musicians, and their monuments are scattered around. The 1957 Sivle monument marks the centenary of the birth of the author and poet Per

Sivle (1857–1904), who grew up on the mountain farm of Sivle, in the great Stalheim Skleive (gorge); the monument behind Voss church commemorates three Bergslien artist brothers, Brynjulf, Nils and Knut; near Voss Fine Arts Society is a memorial to actor Lars Tvinde, born and bred on the farm of Tvinde, which lies below the Tvindefossen (a waterfall to the north of Voss); and on the same road the 1958 Sjur Helgeland Memorial commemorates another local fiddler and composer.

This artistic tradition continues, and Voss is one of the best places to hear the Hardanger fiddle and see the old dances performed in beautiful costumes. On the main street is a shop where you can see, or buy, the ornate silver belts and jewellery that go with the traditional Norwegian costume (*bunad*). An international jazz festival is held in the town every April.

Around Bergen and north

From Voss the E16 is the quickest way to Bergen. After an hour's drive to the long narrow island of **Sotra** ⑭, which shelters the city from the North Sea,

Apart from its artistic associations, the village of Ulvik has the unlikely privilege of being where the first potatoes were grown in Norway, back in 1765.

BELOW:
at Voss Folk Museum.

Post office sign.

BELOW: Kjosfossen waterfall. **RIGHT:** Gudvangen in Aurland, on the Norway in a Nutshell route.

there is no doubt that this is a different world. Sotra is a good base for sea canoeing in and out of its small offshore islands and rocks and, in good weather, as far as the open sea to combine canoeing with ocean fishing. In any case, shelter is never far away.

North of Bergen is a second island district, **Nordhordland**, that stretches as far north as Sognefjorden and includes the islands of Holsnøy, Radøy and Sandøy. At weekends, it is a favourite area for Bergensere who go sailing, swimming and fishing.

In Nordhordland the sea can be at its wildest, smashing against the western coast, yet the area has been inhabited for some 8,000 years. Håkon den Gode (the Good) is buried at **Seim** **⑮**, near Knarvik (half an hour from Bergen by express boat). Another rare reminder of the Vikings is a beech wood, also at Seim, 1,000 years old and the northernmost beech wood in Europe.

Today, fish-farming is important to Nordhordland, which exports vast quantities of salmon and trout all round the world, and the fish-farmers are also attempting to rear cod, halibut and other species. Some fish farms are open to the public. There is good sea fishing for cod and coalfish, and special rosy-coloured trout inhabit many of the lakes. Diving and sub-aqua fishing, as well as treasure-hunting, are easy in these transparent waters. Oil is a modern, though not conflicting industry in this widespread area, with the night gleam of the light from Mongstad one of the few reminders of this large refinery.

Picnic on Fedje

Most remote of all, and a target for both sailing picnics and holidays, is the island of **Fedje** **⑯**, an important navigation point for many centuries with two 19th-century lighthouses still in use today. In these ever-changing waters, Norwegian sea laws insist that all ships must carry a Norwegian pilot, and tankers destined for Mongstad refinery are navigated from here through the unreliable waters. Stay overnight on Fedje in one of the guesthouses in Kræmmerholmen or in the Pensjonat or lighthouse there and enjoy this idyllic bird and flower habitat. ❑

Norway in a Nutshell

If you have only a day to spare in this region, this tour which, but for the lack of an island or two, might well be called "Hordaland in a Nutshell", covers many of the sights. It runs throughout the year and combines bus, ferry and train *(see page 344)*.

The tour starts with a train journey from either Oslo or Bergen to Myrdal and can be done in a day in the summer months (in winter an overnight stop is necessary). From Myrdal it sets off on one of the steepest train journeys in the world, the 50-minute panoramic trip down 850 metres (2,800ft) of mountain gorge to the pretty village of Flåm, stopping – thanks to one of the five separate sets of brakes – to photograph the torrent of Kjosfossen and to pick up passengers at one or two of the tiny stations.

The next leg is by ferry, which travels through Aurlandsfjord and Norway's narrowest fjord, Nærøyfjord, its rocky sides twice as high as the water is wide and now included on Unesco's World Heritage list. From here the journey continues on by bus to Voss, skirting around Oppheim Lake.

In summer the bus makes the hairpin ascent to the Stalheim Hotel. The hotel parapet looks down over the depths of the Stalheimskleive (gorge). A tortuous descent leads to the fjord.

BERGEN

With its relaxed atmosphere, stunning setting and vibrant cultural life, Bergen is an appealing mix of the cosmopolitan and the outdoors, with easy access to the western fjords

There's always a sense of symmetry and order about a city built on hills. If it also stands on a peninsula and has a harbour at its heart, it is bound to be beautiful. Bergen, the capital of west Norway, has all these things. Built on seven hills, the city grew outwards from the coast and harbour in the quaintly named Puddefjord and spread across the steep slopes and over the bridges that link islands and headlands.

Too many people make the mistake of allowing only a day or even half a day for Bergen at the start and end of a visit to the western fjords, which doesn't give the city a chance. It makes an ideal base for a fjord holiday, combining the cosmopolitan delights of the city with the splendid scenery of the fjords. Bergen has plenty to do and see, or you can simply spend some time just soaking up the atmosphere down by the busy harbour. But take an umbrella: Bergen may be one of the prettiest towns in Norway, but it is also the wettest – on average it rains 220 days a year.

A view from the top

The best place to get a feel of the city's natural location is to take the funicular, **Fløibanen** Ⓐ (www.floibanen.no;

daily every 15–30 minutes, early Apr–Aug 7.30am–midnight; Sept–early Apr until 11pm; charge), that climbs more than 300 metres (1,000ft) in just eight minutes from the centre to **Fløyen**, high above Bergen. On the downward journey, you seem to be tipping head-first into the city.

At the top is the lovely old-fashioned building that houses Fløyen Restaurant, built in 1925, and the start of eight marked walking routes, the longest no more than around 4km (2½ miles), though this does not mean they do not

PRECEDING PAGES: storm clouds over Bergen. **LEFT:** café life, Bryggen.
RIGHT: Bergen's funicular railway on its way up to Fløyen.

Bergen

| 0 | 250 m |
| 0 | 250 yds |

N

Fana, Milde

contain steep hills through woods and open moor. There are several huts for shelter along the way.

A leisurely coffee or lunch on the veranda of the restaurant gives a chance also to drink in the superb view over hundreds of islands, many with small *hytter* (wooden cabins) and a couple of boats tied to a landing stage that sums up a Norwegian's ideal summer. All around are the mountains and hills that cradle the city – Fløifjellet, Damsgårdfjellet, Løvstakken, Sandviksfjellet, Rundemånnen, Blåmannen, and the highest of them all, **Ulriken** at around 640 metres (2,100ft) and reached by a cable car (tel: 53 64 36 43; daily May–Sept 9am–9pm; Oct–Apr 9am–5pm; the cable car might not operate on very windy days; charge). The Ulriken mountain café is open when the cable car is running. There is a double-decker bus connection (peak season only) with the cable car from Torget, the site of the famous Bergen fish market.

A long tradition of international trade has made this city the most outgoing in Norway and given the Bergensere a jauntiness in their walk that hints at generations of sailors, quick wits, worldliness and a sense of their own worth. Bergensere are certain they are the best, secure in the knowledge that, although Olso may now be the capital, it is historically a mere toddler compared with Bergen.

Olav Kyrre's city

King Olav Kyrre is credited with founding Bergen in 1070 at Torget. But it would be naive to believe that, long before, the perfect natural harbour and sheltered fjords were not a home for people who depended on the sea. During the 13th century, Bergen became the first capital of a united Norway, and a great ecclesiastical centre, with a cathedral, 20 churches and chapels, five monasteries and two hospitals for the poor. Bergen lost its capital status to Oslo during the Middle Ages, but still dwarfed the new capital. In medi-

eval times, it was the biggest city in the Nordic countries and, until 1830, the largest in Norway. Today, with a population of around 256,000, it is roughly half the size of Oslo.

Much of this early size and success came when Bergen was chosen as the hub of the medieval German Hanseatic League in the north. Their trading base on the north side of **Vågen** became the powerhouse of all trade on the northwest Norwegian coast. But the Hansa began to grow too powerful all over Scandinavia and, at last, Norway broke the tie that kept the west in thraldom.

The perils of fire and war

As in all wooden cities, fire has swept through Bergen on many occasions, often devastating it. The result is that the oldest surviving buildings are noticeably built of stone, and the present streets, following the last fire in 1916 when a gale fanned the flames to an inferno, are wide and designed as fire breaks.

During World War II, Bergen was a centre of the Resistance movement, and many young people from the town

Serving as the starting point for numerous tours and cruises, Bergen is known as the "gateway to the fjords".

BELOW:
Bergen's harbour.

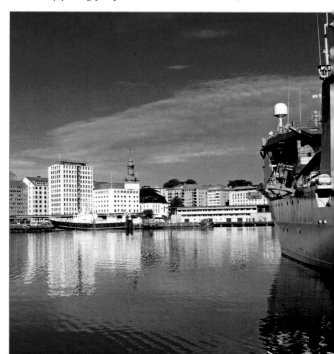

Bergen Cathedral (Domkirke), a short walk from Bryggen, started life as a small stone church around 1150. At the time of the Reformation in the 16th century, it became the seat of the Lutheran bishop. Look out for a cannon ball in the west wall, lodged there in a battle in 1665.

BELOW:
the Hanseatic
Museum illustrates
Bergen's history.

took the perilous route out through the islands to Shetland. One group, with members aged 19–22, escaped to Scotland and returned with radio equipment to establish contact with exiled Norwegian authorities in England. The actions of the movement are commemorated by the **Theta Museum** in Bryggen (tel: 55 55 20 80; June–Aug Tue, Sat, Sun 2–4pm; charge). Yet the major disaster of this unhappy period came not directly from war but through accident caused by war. In 1944 a Dutch ammunition ship in the harbour blew up, damaging many of the oldest buildings on the northern promontory, including Håkonshallen and Rosenkrantztårnet. Anti-German feelings ran high at that time. The famous Tyskebryggen (quay named after Hansa merchants) has been tactfully renamed **Bryggen**.

Starting with the past

The earliest archaeological remains are in **Bryggens Museum** B (tel: 55 58 80 10; mid-May–Aug daily 10am–4pm; Sept–mid-May Mon–Fri 11am–3pm, Sat noon–3pm, Sun noon–4pm;

charge), past the Hansa houses on the north side of the harbour. The museum contains the medieval remains uncovered during archaeological digs between 1955 and 1972. There are also many artefacts and re-creations of medieval rooms. Together it gives a picture of the time when Bergen was a small fishing and sailing community that clung to the shallow slopes above the shore.

Nearby is the oldest building still in use, **St Mary's Church** (Mariakirken; tel: 55 31 59 60; mid-June–mid-Aug Mon–Fri 9.30am–11am and 1pm–4pm,;0pm; charge in summer), built in the early years of the 12th century and justly proud of its rich Baroque pulpit. The only other medieval churches to survive periodic fires are the present **Bergen Cathedral** C (Domkirke; tel: 55 31 58 75; mid-June–mid-Aug Mon–Fri 11am–4pm; Sept–May Tue–Fri 11am–12.30pm), once dedicated to St Olav – the church has been rebuilt five times owing to fire, and the **Church of the Holy Cross** D (Korskirken; Mon–Sat 11am–3pm), most of it now in the Renaissance style of the 17th century.

Leprosy in Bergen

In many parts of the world leprosy is known as Hansen's disease, named after the Norwegian physician Armauer Hansen who discovered the leprosy bacillus in Bergen in 1873. At that time Bergen was an international centre for leprosy, with the largest concentration of patients in Europe. They were cared for in three hospitals in the city, the oldest of which, St George's, is now both a monument to thousands of personal tragedies, and an important arena for the dissemination of Norwegian work and research on leprosy. The last patient at St George's Hospital to suffer from this stigmatising illness died in 1946.

The **Leprosy Museum** (Lepramuseet), St George's Hospital, Kong Oscars gate 59; tel: 55 96 11 55; late May–late Aug daily 11am–3pm; charge.

The last two are relatively close to the harbour, and all three merit a visit.

Medieval Håkonshallen

Holmen was the site of **Bergenhus**, the old timber-built royal palace used when Bergen first became a capital. At a time of much building in the 13th century, it was converted to a fortified stronghold of stone, and the restored remains are close to where the original cathedral and bishop's residence stood. There are two particularly notable buildings: **Håkonshallen** ❸ (tel: 55 31 60 67; mid-May–Aug daily 10am–4pm; Sept–mid-May daily noon–3pm, Thur 3–6pm; charge), built by King Håkon Håkonsson between 1247 and 1261, which was used for the wedding of King Magnus Lagabøte (the Lawmaker), who was Håkon's son and co-ruler; and **Rosenkrantztårnet** ❼ (tower; tel: 55 31 43 80; mid-May–Aug daily 10am–4pm; Sept–mid-May Sun only noon–3pm; charge), which was the work of a Danish governor of Bergenhus, Erik Rosenkrantz, who grafted it onto Håkon's original "Keep of the Sea" in the 1560s. It is possible to buy a discounted joint ticket for Håkonshallen and the tower, and guided tours in English and Norwegian start every half-hour.

Håkonshallen is the largest secular medieval building still standing in Norway. When both it and Rosenkrantztårnet were badly damaged in the 1944 explosion, Norwegian historians took the opportunity to reconstruct them as closely to the originals as possible. Today, Håkonshallen makes a magnificent concert hall. Rosenkrantztårnet is now a museum, with both permanent and special exhibitions.

Bryggen's Hansa houses

In summer, guides from Bryggens Museum also conduct tours through the row of Hansa houses that line **Bryggen**. These Hansa homes and warehouses were all built after the great fire of 1702, which destroyed many buildings, and they are on the Unesco World Heritage list. One key to understanding the Hansa way of life is a visit to the **Hanseatic Museum** ❸ (Hanseatiske Museum; tel: 55 54 46 90; mid-May–mid-Sept 9am–5pm; mid-

BELOW: Bryggen on the quayside.

TIP

Buy a *Bergen Kortet*
(card), valid for 24 or 48
hours, and enjoy free
admission to many
museums, free travel on
city buses and on the
funicular to Mount
Fløyen, plus numerous
discounts. Available
from the Tourist
Information Office
and hotels.

BELOW: Bryggen's
characteristic
wooden houses and
carvings.

Sept–mid-May Tue–Sat 11am–2pm, Sun 11am–4pm; charge), furnished in the style of the time when the merchant had his accounting room within the main office on the first floor. This small room enabled him to keep an eye on the liquor room next door. The adjoining room, decorated with a "royal cod", distinguished by a bump on its head and said to bring luck, served as dining and sitting room for merchants and apprentices. On the floor above are the apprentices' tiny box beds, one above the other. The sleeping quarters were tiny, but importantly retained heat. Although apprentices were merchants' sons, sent to learn their business with a colleague, they were locked into their "prisons" at night.

As a fire precaution – all too often in vain – no heating was allowed in these Hansa houses, and the Germans must have suffered torments of cold in the biting damp of a Bergen winter. No wonder that **Schøtstuene** ⓗ (mid-May–mid-Sept daily 10am–5pm; mid-Sept–mid-May Sun 11am–2pm; charge; tel: 55 54 46 90), the assembly rooms nearby, were so popular dur-

ing winter when trade was slack and few ships were in the harbour. The long central table held both beer jugs and the Bible, exemplifying the two religions of the Hansa. In a drawer was the cane used to discipline the apprentices who had their schooling there. The "rules of the club" adorn one wall, written in Low German (old northern dialect).

Old Bergen

At Elsesro, further out along the coast road, past Bergenshus and the North Sea quay, is **Old Bergen** (Gamle Bergen; tel: 55 39 43 00; early May–Sept 10am–4pm, guided tours only, every hour; charge), the obligatory open-air museum beloved of Scandinavia. Here there is a collection of 40 wooden buildings from the 18th and 19th centuries, the interiors decorated to show different styles. Along the cobbled streets, guides in traditional red calf-length costumes and black shawls lead tours, which range from the French Empire splendour of the official's drawing room to the tiny house where the seamstress plied her diligent needle in the 1860s. Nearby is the popular **Sandvik Sjøbad** (bathing area), which looks out over Byfjorden to the city.

Ships, sharks and more

Back along Vågen, a short ferry trip from below Rosenkrantztårnet to the Nordnes peninsula gives a good opportunity to view the beautiful lines of the sailing ship *Lehmkuhl*, which trains youngsters in sailing techniques and gleams with polished brass. A short walk towards Nordnes point reveals another castle, **Fredriksberg** (no visitors), and further north is **Nordnes sjøbad**, which includes a heated outdoor pool.

Here, too, you will find **Bergen Aquarium ❶** (Akvariet; tel: 55 55 71 71; www.akvariet.no; May–Aug daily 9am–7pm; Sept–Apr 10am–6pm; penguins' feeding times at 11am and 5pm, seal show at noon, 3pm and 6pm all year; charge). The aquarium might be showing its age a bit (it is celebrating its 50th anniversary in 2010), but it is one of the main attractions in Bergen, and is particularly popular with

children. The penguins and the seals always steal the show, but here you will also find the largest collection of crocodiles in Norway, plus snakes, reptiles and fish aplenty, as well as a new shark tunnel, where you can see sharks swim right over your head.

Fish market spectacle

Early each weekday morning, **Torget ❶** is the site of Bergen's fish, fruit and flower market. Customers engage the fishermen in serious conversation about the day's catch, watched by an interested circle, and the stalls sell *gravlaks* (cured salmon), lobster and *klippfisk* (dried cod). This busy scene is the heart of Bergen, where there is always something going on and where people linger to watch the transactions or peer into the boats tied up at the quay after a night's fishing.

Just south of the fish market is another square where people like to linger, **Torgalmenningen**, housing many of the city's best shops and departments stores, the most striking of which is **Sundt**, built in the Scandinavian Funkis style, popular in the late

When strolling round Bergen remember to look up to catch all the architectural details.

BELOW LEFT: souvenirs for sale at Bergen harbour. **BELOW:** at the fish market.

The Sailors' Monument at Bergen harbour.

BELOW: view from the top of Fløyen.

1920s and 30s in Norway (the building dates from 1938). The square also holds the **Sailors' Monument**. Carved figures march round the base of this memorial dedicated to all Norwegian sailors who lost their lives at sea.

Just up the hill from the fish market, in another historic quarter of the city, is the **Old Town Hall** (Gamle Rådhuset). Originally built as a private house in 1558, it was presented to the town in 1562 and served the city for several centuries until, in 1974, the city administration moved to an inelegant high-rise modern block.

Museum cluster

Bergen is a good walking city and, if you fix your eye on the tall steeple of **St John's Church Ⓚ** (Johanneskirken; mid-June–mid-Aug Tue–Fri 11am–2pm; rest of the year until 12.30pm), a short walk up Vest Torggate from Torgalmenningen takes you to the top of **Sydneshaugen**, near the university area and the site of a clutch of museums: the **Natural History Museum Ⓛ** (Naturhistorisk Museum; tel: 55 58 29 20; June–Aug

Tue–Fri 10am–4pm, Sat–Sun 11am–4pm; Sept–May Tue–Fri 10am–3pm, Sat–Sun 11am–4pm; charge) standing in the fine **Botanisk Hage** (Botanic Garden), with its tropical greenhouse; the **Cultural History Museum Ⓜ** (Historisk Museum; same opening times as the Natural History Museum above), where you can learn more about stave churches and religion in Norway, among other things; and the **Maritime Museum Ⓝ** (Sjøfartsmuseum; tel: 55 54 96 00; daily 11am–3pm; charge), which traces the history of this seafaring area from the Old Norse period to the present day.

The university area consists of beautiful merchants' villas from the turn of the 20th century, and is where the Arctic explorer Fridtjof Nansen spent the early years of his career. It was also a base for the father of weather forecasting, Vilhelm Bjerknes.

Famous names

It is not surprising that this lively city, with its close European links, should have been the birthplace of many famous people. It was also a strong base for 19th-century nationalism which culminated in 1905 in Norway gaining its independence from Sweden. The prime minister at the time was Christian Michelsen, whose home **Gamlehaugen** (tel: 55 11 29 00; June–Aug Tue–Sun noon–3pm, English tour at noon; gardens all year; charge) at Fjøsanger is now the residence of the king when he is in Bergen.

Drama and music

Nationalism had strong roots in the 19th-century revival of Norwegian culture, led by the playwright Henrik Ibsen, the violinist Ole Bull, the composer Edvard Grieg and writers such as Bjørnstjerne Bjørnson. Though Ibsen and Bjørnson were not natives of west Norway, Bjørnson was for a time director of Bergen's **National Theatre** ⓞ (Den Nationale Scene) founded by Ole Bull in 1850, and Bjørnson's statue stands on the steps in front.

The virtuoso violinist Ole Bull's contribution to Norwegian culture came through his wanderings in the villages of west Norway and the great Jotunheim mountain plateau east of the fjord country. Here he collected many old folk melodies which were played on the Hardanger fiddle, the area's traditional instrument. Later, Grieg transcribed some of these folk tunes for piano, saving them from being lost. He also founded Norway's National Theatre and hired a young Henrik Ibsen as a writer.

Grieg's summer retreat

Every year, thousands of visitors come to look round Grieg's summer home at **Troldhaugen** (tel: 55 92 29 92; May–Sept daily 9am–6pm; Oct–Apr daily 10am–4pm; closed mid-Dec–early Jan; charge) some 8km (5 miles) south of Bergen, where Grieg found the peace to compose in his *hytte* (holiday lodge).

The house is just as Grieg left it; his manuscripts are scattered around and even his piano is in working order in the comfortable drawing room. In the past, this room was the venue for many musical evenings; today, if you are lucky, the curator will play some of Grieg's music for you. The size of the room inevitably limited the size of the audience, and in 1985 Troldhaugen

The composer Edvard Grieg (1843–1907).

BELOW LEFT: statue of Ole Bull. **BELOW:** the National Theatre.

opened a special **Chamber Music Hall** seating 200, with a turf roof and built into the hillside so that it is barely visible among the tall trees. The floor-to-ceiling windows behind the stage provide the audience with a lovely view of the composer's *hytte* and Lake Nordås. The latest addition is the **Edvard Grieg Museum** close to the concert hall and villa.

Troldhaugen is a wonderful setting for a concert and a continuation of the summer evening tradition when Grieg and his wife, Nina Hagerup, a Danish singer, would entertain their friends in the quiet garden outside the drawing room. Any bus for the Fana district goes to Hopsbroen, then a 15-minute walk leads to Troldhaugen; many city excursions also include Troldhaugen.

Ole Bull's island

Ole Bull built his home on the island of **Lysøen** (tel: 56 30 90 77; mid-May–Aug Mon–Sat noon–4pm, Sun 11–5pm; Sept Sun only noon–4pm; charge) in 1873, when his fame had long spread throughout and beyond Norway. Bull turned the island into

a park with woodland and walking routes, and the house itself is unlike any other in the country. Made of traditional Norwegian wood, the decorated and screened balcony and the pointed arches of the windows on the front of the building have an almost Moorish flavour, and the tower topped by a minaret is reminiscent of St Basil's in Moscow's Red Square.

To reach Lysøen, take the bus marked "Lysefjordruta" (No. 566/567) from bus station gate 19 or 20. The ride takes 50 minutes and stops at Buena Kai. Then take the Ole Bull ferry, which leaves at noon, 1pm, 2pm and 3pm. By car, take road 553 and head south in the direction of Fana.

It's a good idea to combine your visit to Lysøen with a stop on the way at **Lysekloster**, where the ruins of a 12th-century Cistercian abbey, a daughter monastery of Fountains Abbey in Yorkshire, England, can be seen.

Composer's home

Dedicated music-lovers could also check out **Siljustøl** (tel: 55 13 60 00; late June–Sept Sun only noon–4pm; charge), the home of Harald Sæverud, at Rådal on the way to the airport. Sæverud (1897–1992) was the most important Norwegian composer of the 20th century, and he designed part of the interior of his unusual home, built in wood and natural stone, himself.

Grieghallen concert hall

Whether as a result of the fame of people such as Bull and Grieg, Bergen has a lively artistic and cultural life – hence it was honoured as one of the European Cities of Culture 2000. The **Bergen International Festival** (Festspillene; www.fib.no), held each year in late May–early June, attracts international artists and thousands of visitors. At the end of the 1970s, the festival led to the building of a new concert hall, **Grieghallen** ❷, with marvellous acoustics. The outside of the building looks remarkably like that of a concert grand piano, perhaps as a tribute to the

BELOW: in Ole Bull's home on Lysøen.

composer whose name it bears. This is the heart of the 12-day festival, but the whole city is involved, with events in Håkonshallen, Troldhaugen, Lysøen and Mariakirken.

Artistic enclave

Bergen also has several strong art collections, mostly centred on **Lille Lungegårdsvann**, the octagonal lake in the middle of the park, not far from the statues of Edvard Grieg and of Ole Bull playing his violin, and near Grieghallen. Here you will find the **Bergen Art Museum Q** (Bergen Kunstmuseum; tel: 55 56 80 00; June–Aug daily 11am–5pm; Sept–May closed Mon; charge), with a large collection of Norwegian paintings from the Renaissance to the present day. It is one of the largest art museums in Scandinavia.

The museum collections are spread over three sites, all within easy walking distance of each other; the Lysverket, housed in a stunning white Funkis building, presents a general introduction to Norwegian art, and is the natural place to start; **The Rasmus Meyers Collection** focuses on the golden years

of Norwegian art, and includes many paintings by Edvard Munch; and the **Stenersens Samling** features works by international artists such as Picasso and Klee, as well as temporary exhibitions. Bergen is also strong in private galleries, many of which specialise in modern painting.

Design and craft

If you are interested in design, check out the **West Norway Museum of Decorative Arts Q** (Vestlandske Kunstindustrimuseum; tel: 55 33 66 33; mid-May–mid-Sept daily 11am–5pm;mid-Sept–mid-May noon–4pm; closed Mon; charge), which has a permanent collection featuring furniture, textiles, ceramics, glass and silver, as well as contemporary objects, and Norway's largest collection of Chinese art. The museum also stages new temporary exhibitions every year.

Shops often offer opportunities to see traditional crafts. Best known is **Husfliden** (on Vågsalm), which has richly decorated traditional Norwegian costumes (*bunader*), textiles and woodwork, including the famous *rosemaling*

BELOW:
Bergen Art Museum.

Science in Action

Bergen is a big university town, and knowledge is at the centre of much of what's going on here. Another museum worth mentioning, therefore, is **Vilvite**, the Bergen Science Centre, which opened in 2007 south of Nygårdsparken.

The name Vilivite means "Want to know", and the centre, which contains 75 interactive displays, installations and experiments, aims to make science and technology fun, encouraging visitors to be curious about their environment, and how things around them work. It is popular with children of all ages.

A free shuttle bus departs every 10 minutes Mon–Fri from the main tourist office on Torget, and the journey takes about eight minutes (Thormøhlensgate 51; tel: 55 59 45 00; Tue–Fri 9am–3pm, Sat–Sun 10am–5pm, closed Mon; charge).

Damsgård Hovedgård in Laksevåg, about 4km (2½ miles) west of Bergen centre, was built in 1770 and is Europe's best-preserved wooden rococo building, with original interiors and a period herb garden (Alleen 29, Laksevåg; tel: 55 94 08 70; June–Aug daily 11am–4pm; charge).

BELOW: the harbour at Bergen.
BELOW RIGHT: Bergen glass.
RIGHT: old houses in the maze of narrow lanes behind Bryggen.

(rose painting). For Norwegian glass, try Bergen's **Glasmagasin** at Torgallmenningen 8.

Open-air performances

During the summer (mid-June to late August) the open-air stages at Lille Lungegårdsvann and Torgalmenningen are used almost daily for music and dance performances. Folk dancing and music from rural Norway are particularly popular with the Bergensere and visitors alike. Nearest to the real thing is Bergen Folklore (tel: 55 55 20 06), a small group of Norwegian folk musicians and dancers who perform at Schøtstuene, a historic and intimate venue in Bryggen. Shows take place every Tuesday from mid-June to late August at 9pm (charge, tickets sold at the tourist office).

Outdoor city

The most popular pastime is sailing. Not far behind are sea fishing and swimming. Or you could simply take a fjord cruise. The *White Lady* departs daily from the fish market, and offers both one-hour Bergen harbour tours

and half-day (four hours) boat trips in the nearby fjords (tel: 55 25 90 00; May–Sept; charge). The hills above Bergen, just 10 minutes away from the centre, are ideal for walking, and **Sandviken Ridesenter**, not far from the Gamle Bergen Museum, organises horse-riding tours.

For something different, try a racing evening at **Travpark** (Thur from 5.30pm; tel: 55 39 68 00) at Åsane, around 16km (10 miles) from the city (bus 285). This is a peculiarly Scandinavian sport. The atmosphere is electric as the "trotting" horses and their drivers race round the track.

Apart from the gardens at Troldhaugen and Lysøen, the Norwegian Arboretum at **Milde** (tel: 55 98 72 50; daily; free), founded in 1971, has with gusto planted up shrubs and trees from many parts of the world, and this pretty area along the shore has rocky gorges, hills and a small lake. The nearby Fanafjord also provides good swimming. It is about 23km (14 miles) south of Bergen. To get there take bus 525 to Mildevågen, and then a 15-minute walk to the arboretum. ❑

THE MOST BEAUTIFUL VOYAGE

This is one of the great sea journeys of the world: from Bergen to the end of Norway and back again, the vessels plying the Hurtigruten route are mail boats, freight ships and passenger liners in one

The ship slips out of **Bergen**'s hill-ringed harbour at 10.30pm, day in, day out, all year round. In winter, it has been dark for hours, and passengers linger no longer than to wave goodbye to the lights of the city before scuttling below to the warmth of saloon and cabin. In summer, it is a different matter: the deck is crowded as the ship sweeps out towards the fjord, leaving behind the small houses where the Hansa merchants once lived.

The coastal express heads north through Byfjord and Hjeltefjord, past the islands of **Askøy** and **Holsnøy** for the open sea, at the start of a trip of 1,250 nautical miles round North Cape (Nordkapp) and then to Kirkenes near the Russian border, crossing the Arctic Circle en route.

Nowadays, this coastal voyage has become one of the most popular journeys for visitors, but it is much more to the Norwegians themselves. From earliest times, this long and beautiful coast has been the main link in Norway for communication and trade, connecting communities hundreds of kilometres apart; the western and northern Norwegians once regarded Scotland and Iceland as being easier to reach than the region around present-day Oslo. In winter, it was the only way to travel because the Gulf Stream kept, and still keeps, the seaways open all year round.

The swift route

The first steamship, the *Prinds Gustav*, set out from Trondheim to Tromsø in 1838. In time, other steamers began to journey between the coastal towns, and in 1893 a local steamship company, Vesteraalens Dampskibsselskab, opened the Hurtigruten (literally "swift route") between Trondheim and Hammerfest, in the far northwest. As the line extended to Bergen and Kirkenes,

PRECEDING PAGES: Hurtigruten ship at Molde. **LEFT:** the dramatic Lofoten Islands. **RIGHT:** taking the Hurtigruten.

NORWEGIAN SEA

Vardø
Berlevåg
Mehamn
Båtsfjord
Kjøllefjord
Vadsø
Nordkapp ❻
Nordkapp ❼
Honningsvåg
Kirkenes
Havøysund

RUSSIA

Hammerfest

Øksfjord

Skjervøy

FINLAND

Tromsø ❺

Finnsnes

Risøyhamn
Vesterålen
Sortland
Harstad
Stokmarknes
Stamsund
Svolvær
Lofoten ❹
Kjerringøy

Bodø
Ørnes

Gulf of Bothnia

Arctic Circle (Polarsirkel) ❸

Nesna

Sandnessjøen

SWEDEN

Brønnøysund

Rørvik

Trondheim ❷

Kristiansund

Molde

Ålesund ❶
Torvik

NORWAY

Måløy

Floro

Oslo

NORTH SEA

Bergen

Skagerrak

The Hurtigruten

0   100 km
0   100 miles

Stavanger
Kristiansand

- - - route of the Hurtigruten

DENMARK

several shipowners became involved. Following various mergers, the last two companies running the fleet merged to form Hurtigruten Group in 2006. Today the group operates 14 ships, with 11 plying the Hurtigruten route (the Norwegian Coastal Voyage) at any time, as well as cruise ships in the Antarctic, Spitsbergen, Greenland and the Baltic. It also owns several fast-ferry routes in Norway, and other travel-related products. A round trip from Bergen to Kirkenes on its modern ship takes 11 days. Shorter trips are available, and many people only take one leg of the journey.

The Hurtigruten makes 34 ports of call along this ever-changing coast, some at places no bigger than a handful of houses around the harbour, with local people waiting on the quayside to collect a car or a container or to greet friends who have hopped a short distance between small towns where the alternative is a long, difficult drive.

From October to May the first stop for going ashore is **Ålesund ❶**. It has all the natural design of a town built round a harbour and, because of a disastrous fire in 1904, it was rebuilt all of a piece, with the wooden houses in an Art Nouveau style, carefully preserved and painted in brilliant colours. From June to September, the vessel heads north to **Molde** instead of Ålesund, and between April and September the ship takes a detour via Geirangerfjord.

The next main stop is **Trondheim ❷**, further north along a magnificent coast with 87 peaks, snow-capped for much of the year. When it was the ancient capital of Norway, Trondheim was called Nidaros, and **Nidarosdomen** (cathedral) is a national shrine; it contains a memorial to King Olav Haraldsson, who became St Olav after his death at the Battle of Stiklestad. The Trondheim stop is long enough for a morning tour of this historic city, with its busy harbours and bays, and wide streets lined with small wooden houses and old warehouses. From May to September, the tour also visits the Museum of Musical History at Ringve.

Early next morning, as the ship steams north again, it crosses the **Arctic Circle ❸** (Polarsirkel) and sails into "the land of the midnight sun". From April to September passengers can board a smaller vessel at Grønøy to navigate the narrow Hollandsfjord inland. The tour then alights at the foot of the spectacular Svartisen, Norway's second-largest glacier. At the Arctic Circle crossing, "King Neptune" joins the celebrations on board to award Arctic Circle certificates.

Hamsun's Nordland

On its way to the **Lofoten Islands ❹**, the ship enters Nordland, the territory of one of Norway's most famous writers, Knut Hamsun. Hamsun named the old trading centre of **Kjerringøy** "Sirilund" in his novels, which describe the surprisingly outward-looking lives of these northern fishing and trading families around the early 1900s

On deck, as the ship weaves in and out of the islands, bird-watchers find it difficult to go below even to eat or sleep in case they miss one of the numerous seabird colonies, the congregations of colourful exotic ducks in winter harbours and, particularly, the comical little puffins in their hundreds of thousands.

Between **Svolvær** and **Stokmarknes**, the ship makes a brief detour (weather permitting) into **Trollfjord**, something no big cruise liner could do because the sheer faces of rock and scree press close in this narrow fjord. In winter, ice makes entry impossible, but instead there is the endless fascination of the **aurora borealis** (northern lights) – sometimes white spears, at other times a blue-green or multicoloured aura that seems to dance across the sky. The high mountains of the fjord country have disappeared by now but, during the brief light of a winter day, the low slanting sun picks out the white cones of snow-covered hills.

Watching the seasons go by

In spring and autumn, the 11-day journey feels like a voyage through the seasons. Leave Bergen in May, when the fjord valleys are brilliant with blossom,

TIP

A novel by Knut Hamsun, particularly *The Wayfarers*, is a good accompaniment to a voyage that illuminates his characters and their thinking, and gives an insight into life in these northern lands today.

BELOW LEFT: the harbour at Ålesund.
BELOW: many snow-capped peaks can be seen from Molde.

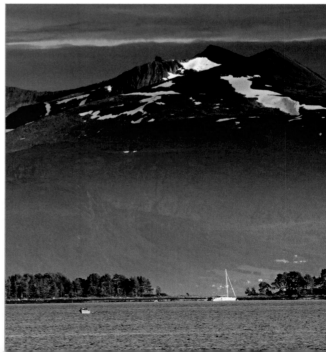

BELOW: commemorative plaques at the North Cape. **RIGHT**: late evening during the midnight sun, north of Bodø.

and the hills and mountains of the north will still be white as snow flurries scurry across the fjords and mountains. The return journey is the reverse: just as the north is beginning to slip out of its winter grip, the swift Norwegian summer marches north and will have already reached Bergen and the mountains around it, and it could be warm enough to lie out in a sheltered corner of the deck.

The northern city of **Tromsø** ❺, set on an island in a rugged landscape, has a relaxed cosmopolitan atmosphere that fits with its nickname "Paris of the North", and can be enjoyed in its numerous restaurants and street cafés. It has the most bars per capita in Norway, with a bustling nightlife. Among the stops are **Tromsø Museum** and the **Arctic Cathedral** (Ishavskatedralen), which has the largest stained-glass window in Europe.

Into Finnmark the ship sails past a coast of scoured hills and watercourses with forests along the valleys, to **Hammerfest**, Norway's most northerly town. In summer, the ship makes a concession here and slips through

the Margerøy Sound to Honningsvåg and the start of an excursion by bus to **North Cape** ❻ (Nordkapp) – a highlight of any visit to Norway.

North Cape also marks a change of direction to the east across the very top of Norway on the way to **Kirkenes** ❼, 5km (3 miles) from the **Russian border**, a coast where the place names begin to show Sami and Finnish origins. Kirkenes itself is a mining town in a strange no man's land between east and west, which is also influenced by the local Sami culture. Here you can join a king-crab safari in summer, where donning a survival suit you will jump (and float) in the Barents Sea to watch the day's catch being hauled on board – before sampling the crabs' delicious flesh at a specially prepared meal; or opt to go dog-sledging or snowmobiling in winter instead.

Nowhere missed

Heading south, after visiting Tromsø, the vessel takes in a brief sightseeing tour at Harstad before moving on to **Trondenes Church**, the world's northernmost medieval church and, at 750 years old, the historical centrepiece of Trondenes. After a visit to Trondheim, passengers take in a short tour of the beautiful coastal fishing town of Kristiansund, then arrive at Molde to experience the panoramic views of the Romsdal fjord and the Romsdal Alps. On the way south, the ship stops by day at the places it visited when northbound passengers were fast asleep below decks, so nowhere is missed. Nor is it generally a rough voyage: the Hurtigruten hugs the coast or weaves in and out of islands that shelter the ship from the excesses of the Atlantic Ocean and the Norwegian Sea.

With the ever-increasing tourist traffic, the emphasis on delivering supplies to distant traders is changing, and Hurtigruten is now offering cruise-orientated packages and even side trips into the Geirangerfjord. For booking information visit www.hurtigruten.com or tel: 76 96 76 00/810 30 000. ❏

FROM SOGN TO NORDFJORD

The presence of the last Ice Age is felt strongly here, in the shape of the great Jostedal Glacier, and Norway's deepest fjord; but humans have also left their mark, most impressively in the form of a plethora of stave churches

From a seat in one of the small planes that somehow contrive to land on the narrow strips along the fjords or the tiny green patches between the mountains, it looks an impossible territory. Yet the land that runs from Sognefjord in the south to Nordfjord to the north has all the features that made the country famous: Norway's longest and deepest fjord, mainland Europe's largest glacier and Jotunheimen, Scandinavia's greatest mountain massif.

The large *fylke* (county) of Sogn og Fjordane lies between a zigzag coastline drawn by the waters of the North Sea and the start of Jotunheimen's heights. Narrow fingers of water push inland from the main fjords to reach far into the mountains, and waterfalls tumble hundreds of metres into the fjord below. The force of all this water feeds powerful hydroelectric power stations tucked away inside the mountains. Aluminium plants also make use of the spouting waterfalls to generate power and, among other things, produce the road barriers for many of Europe's mountain roads.

In the past, fjord, mountain and valley could be near impassable in winter. Today, though journeys often take longer than elsewhere, travel is made easier thanks to the network of ferries, tunnels and bridges. From Bergen, an express boat (a catamaran with water-jet engines) reaches deep inland as far as Sogndal on Sognefjord, almost half-way to Sweden.

Deepest Sognefjord

At 205km (120 miles) long and 1,300 metres (4,260ft) deep, **Sognefjord** ⑰ is unmatched anywhere in the world. After British visitors discovered it in the 19th century, royalty too endorsed the fjord's delights. As crown prince, Edward VII came over from Britain in 1898, and Kaiser Wilhelm II was on

Main attractions
BALESTRAND
JOSTEDAL GLACIER
NORWEGIAN GLACIER MUSEUM
URNES STAVE CHURCH
NÆRØYFJORD
ASTRUPTUNET
BRIKSDAL GLACIER
NORDFJORD FOLK MUSEUM
STRYN

LEFT: fjord scene. **RIGHT:** watching a cruise go by on Sognefjord.

TIP

In summer, guides from the Jostedalsbreen National Park Centre, 20km (12 miles) east of Stryn, lead tours and glacier explorations to different offshoots of the great Jostedal (tel: 57 87 68 00; www.jostedal.com).

holiday in Sogn when he learned of the assassination of the Archduke at Sarajevo which triggered World War I.

In spring, the fjord's scenery is pink and white when this apparently ungrateful soil puts up umbrellas of fruit blossom in orchards and gardens. In the warm summer days, far above the fjord, cattle and sheep cling to the small grass plateaux around the mountain farms or *seter* where once women and young girls spent the summer making cheese. The majority of the 106,000 people in the county still make their living by farming or fishing, forestry or fruit-growing.

On both sides of the fjord small villages cling to every square metre of land, each with its own atmosphere. **Balestrand** ⓲ has been a favourite since the 19th century and has an English church, St Olav's, founded by one of those fearless Victorian Englishwomen who travelled the world. The Kvikne's Hotel was built in the 19th century too, and is one of Norway's largest family-run hotels (it's been in the family since 1877). German artists from the Düsseldorf Academy were also quick to appreciate the beauty of Sognefjord, and built Swiss-style houses, decorated with dragon heads in deference to their hosts' Viking past, to add to the charm of this picturesque village. The area is renowned for having a mild climate and lush vegetation; across a small neck of water at **Dragsvik**, a pastor-botanist planted exotic trees which thrive in the sheltered bay.

Jostedal ice spectacle

A narrow side-fjord leads to the little community of **Fjærland** (road connections here were not completed until 1986. Mind the hefty road toll!), a dairy-farming centre near the two southernmost offshoots of the great **Jostedal Glacier** ⓳ (Jostedalsbreen), mainland Europe's largest glacier. Nestling at its base on a large, flat esker deposited thousands of years ago is the **Norwegian Glacier Museum** ⓴ (Norsk Bremuseum; tel: 57 69 32 88; June–Aug 9am–7pm; Apr–May and Sept–Oct 10am–4pm; charge). In 2007 the museum added a new wing devoted to natural and artificial climate change. Tourists come to Fjærland every year to

BELOW: Balestrand.
BELOW RIGHT: detail of a chair in Kvikne's Hotel.

climb (or merely gaze at) the awesome glacier. From a distance, the concrete-and-glass building designed by Norwegian architect Sverre Fehn looks like part of the glacier itself. The museum includes a cinema for viewing panoramic shots of Norwegian glaciers.

Bokbyen, also in Fjærland, has miles of shelves in a string of second-hand bookshops, most of them housed in quaint little sheds along the picturesque fjord. They sell books in many languages, and this is a great place to browse and while away a couple of hours. Open from May to September (daily 10am–6pm).

Ferry to Vangsnes

The ferry from Dragsvik runs to **Vangsnes** on the south side. From there, it is only a few kilometres to **Vik ㉑** and the 12th-century **Hopperstad stave church** (Stavkirke; May–Sept; charge), with dragon heads on the outside and rich decorations within. Vik also has a stone church, **Hove Kirke** (mid-June–July Wed–Sun 10am–4pm; charge), only 20 years younger than Hopperstad. On the way back, stop at the statue of the heroic Norwegian Viking figure Fritjof den Frøkne (Fritjof the Courageous), in Vangsnes, a gift from Kaiser Wilhelm II in 1913.

Head of the fjord

Going east from Balestrand, a short crossing takes you to **Hella ㉒** and past the glistening arc of **Kvinnafoss** (Lady's Waterfall) close to the main road. At the head of the fjord, **Sogndal** is the centre for trade and administration in an area of forestry and farming. The pretty little town swells during term time because it is also a centre for education, with university colleges and Norway's oldest folk high school. To the north, farms are dotted along Sognadalen's narrow lake. This is a popular spot for walking in summer and skiing in winter. Sogndal's airport is located at Haukåsen, next to Kaupanger.

Kaupanger Stavkirke (June–Aug; charge), a little further along Road 5,

was built in the 12th century; its plain dark-wood exterior has been restored, and it is a lovely place to listen to the organist's summer recitals. **Sogn Folk Museum ㉓** (Folkemuseum; tel: 57 67 82 06; June–Aug 10am–5pm, May and Sept 10am–3pm; charge) was set up in 1909 as a living museum with animals, including 35 houses and farm buildings, to show how people lived in Sogn from around 1500 up to the present. The museum is used as a setting for folk music and dancing.

Standing tall beside the fjord at **Nordnes** is a stone to mark the Battle of Fimreite in June 1184. That was when King Sverre and his peasant Birkebeiner (so called because of their birch-bark footwear) defeated King Magnus Erlingsson and the nobility, a turning point in Norwegian history.

Urnes stave church

In **Luster ㉔**, to the northeast of Sogndal, is **Urnes stave church** (Stavkirke, and Unesco World Heritage Site; tel: 57 67 88 40; www.sognefjord.no; late May–mid-Sept daily 10.30am–5.30pm and by appointment; charge), thought to

The replica Viking knarr (freighter) Saga Siglar in Sognefjord before leaving for a two-year round-the-world voyage.

BELOW:
inside the
Jostedal Glacier.

Taking a break on the Flåm to Myrdal mountain railway.

be the oldest stave church in Norway and linked with the coming of Christianity. It reopened in May 2010 after a two-year-long facelift.

Also within easy reach is yet another icy tongue from Jostedal Glacier, called **Nigardsbreen**, where one of the delights is a boat trip over the ice-cold, green waters of a glacier lake.

South of Sogndal, Sognefjord ends in the two most easterly fjords leading to Årdal and Lærdalsøyri, lovely valleys with mountain farms, plenty of opportunities for walking, climbing, or fishing in upland lakes and streams. The **Norwegian Wild Salmon Centre** (Norsk Villakssenter; tel: 57 66 67 71; May–Sept, hours vary; late in July until 10pm; charge) at **Lærdalsøyri ㉕** provides an observation pool for wild salmon. Lærdal's one-time importance as an east–west trading route is evident in Old (Gamle) Lærdalsøyri, an area of beautifully restored 18th- and 19th-century listed buildings.

BELOW: Urnes stave church. **BELOW RIGHT:** the Lærdal Tunnel.

Aurlandvangen, Flåm and Gudvangen lie along the innermost recesses of the fjord, which stretch south from the main fjord like an upside-down "Y". **Nærøyf-**

jord ㉖ to the west is the narrowest in Europe and another World Heritage Site. Both provide the most dramatic fjord cruise in west Norway, the mountains pressing so close that you wonder if the boat will squeeze through.

Nærøyfjord is also popular with kayakers, and gliding on the fjord's surface, halfway between the lush mountain sides and the green waters, is quite an experience indeed.

Mountain climb by rail

Not to be missed either is the **mountain railway ㉗** from Flåm to Myrdal, which spirals up the steep mountain gorge *(see page 236)*. A masterpiece of Norwegian engineering, the 20km (12-mile) -long railway stretch, which is among the world's steepest, runs from Myrdal all the way down to the Aurlandsfjord some 800 metres (2,620ft) below, clinging to the mountainside at a vertiginous angle, and passing through no fewer than 20 tunnels on the way. Magnificent scenery awaits round every bend, and a trip on the Flåm railway is a must for anyone visiting the region.

North to Førde

If from Balestrand instead of heading inland you turn northwest, along Road 5-13 towards Førde and the coast, you come to one of the region's many lakes – **Jølstravatnet** – that penetrate the foothills of the high tops in the east and feed into the fjords in the west.

On the south side lies the farm **Astruptunet** ㉘ (tel: 57 72 67 82; May–Sept; charge), home of the artist Nikolai Astrup (1880–1928), who found themes for his art in his own surroundings. Astruptunet is just as it was during the painter's life, though the barn has been replaced by a new art gallery with a permanent exhibition.

After leaving Jølstravatnet, the Jølstra, said to be one of the best salmon rivers in the area, drops hundreds of metres by the time it reaches **Førde** ㉙ on Førdefjord. Here you find the main **Sunnfjord Museum** (tel: 57 72 12 20; July–mid-Aug Mon–Fri 10am–6pm, Sat–Sun noon–5pm; June and mid-Aug–late Aug Mon–Fri 10am–4pm; rest of the year Mon–Fri 10am–3pm; charge), a collection of 25 restored buildings, 17 of which are reconstructed as a farmstead dating from around 1850.

Along the coast

The best view of Sunnfjord's hundreds of islands is from the high peaks in the east, though the coast itself is by no means flat. **Bleia** rises straight from the north side of Førdefjord to more than 1,300 metres (4,300ft), the summit of the Sunnfjord Alps, and many of the islands have high peaks. These islands stretch the length of the coast, from Fensfjord and the island of Sandøy, north to Vestkapp (West Cape) where the Hurtigruten turns northeast to its next stop at Ålesund.

It's an odd thought that **Florø**, the only community in this large county big enough to be called a town, should lie on the remote edge of the sea, but not so strange when you remember that Norway has always depended on the sea for food, trade and transport. The **Sogn og Fjordane Coastal Museum** (Kystmuseet; tel: 57 74 22 33; mid-June–mid-Aug Mon–Fri 11am–6pm, Sat–Sun noon–4pm; rest of the year Mon–Fri 10am–3pm, Sat–

TIP

The Lærdal Tunnel, which links the villages of Aurland and Lærdal in the county of Sogn og Fjordaney, is the world's longest road tunnel – it is 24.5km (15 miles) long. The old road, which winds its way up the flank of the mountain, offers much better views of the stunning Aurlandsfjord though. The Stegastein platform is located here (see page 127).

BELOW:
Nærøyfjord.

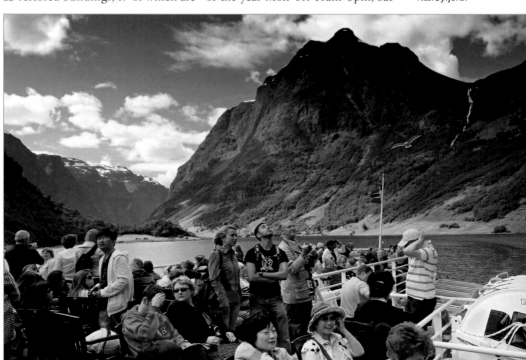

Sun noon–3pm; charge) in Florø has a fine collection of old boats displayed in three modern buildings. This most westerly town had its birth in the herring industry, which flourished in the middle of the 19th century. Today, it still depends on the sea for fish, while oil- and gas fields away to the west have turned Florø into an oil centre.

Offshore sights

There are many places to see: rock carvings at **Ausevik**, southeast of Florø; the nearby island of **Svanøy** with the ancient stone cross of St Olav, covered in runic inscriptions, a manor with an old garden and magnificent trees; a Romanesque medieval church on **Kinnøy**, where the Kinna play *Songen ved det store djup (The Song of the Great Deep)*, is performed by the county theatre grup and local people, and draws thousands to the island each June.

To the north of Fløro, at the mouth of Nordfjord, is the island of **Bremangerlandet ③** with its **Vingen carvings**, which are even older than Ausevik's and show the lives of the fishing-settlers of Nordfjord. Further

north, the village of **Måløy** on **Vågsøy** is one of Norway's largest fishing and trading ports, and at Raudeberg fish of all kinds are salted and dried. But size is relative, and industry does nothing to detract from the rural quietness of this hilly island. Måløy features the Allied Monument, a 6-metre (20ft) high granite obelisk raised in memory of 52 Allied soldiers who died during the Måløy raid in 1941.

North of Vågsøy and Raudeberg is **Silda**, a tiny island for sea-anglers, divers and bird-watchers. It has fewer than 30 permanent inhabitants, no cars and, on an islet in the middle of the harbour, a restored fish-salting works serves a feast of seafoods. On the nearby island of **Selje ③** are the medieval ruins of **St Sunneva Monastery** (Kloster). On the northernmost tip is **Vestkapp**, where winds blow fiercely. Its closest neigbouring land is the Shetland Isles off the north of Scotland.

Inland along Nordfjord

Nordfjord is 100km (60 miles) shorter than Sognefjord. With so many sidefjords, lakes and valleys, it is easy to get into the mountains or make the journey along Oldedalen up to **Briksdal Glacier ③** (Briksdalsbreen), where a great cascade of ice hangs above the ice floes and the green waters of the glacier lake. Even better is that you can climb up to the base of the glacier in the two-wheeled farm carriages *(stolkjærrer)*, pulled by small, sturdy, cream-coloured fjord horses *(fjording*; for details, contact Briksdalsbreen Tourist Information, tel: 57 87 68 00).

The traditional home of the *fjording* is the Eid district, centred around **Nordfjordeid**, where Nordfjord proper has already divided itself into Eidsfjord and Isefjord. **Eid ③**, which is also connected to the coast by Road 15, is famous for **Firdariket**, the seat of the last Viking chief, and the town has traditional white-painted buildings. The church, which dates from 1824, is decorated with beautiful **rose paintings**.

To the south of Eid, Road 1 crosses Utfjord and then runs along Gloppen-fjord, which ends at **Sandane ㉞**, the main town of Gloppen, the biggest farming district in the county and also a large fur-breeding centre. The **Nordfjord Folk Museum** (Folkemuseum; tel: 57 88 45 40; July–mid-Aug Mon–Fri 11am–4pm, Sun 1am–4pm; mid-Aug–June Mon–Fri 11am–3pm; free) started in 1920 with five turf-roofed houses and now has more than 40 historic buildings, including a mountain *seter*. At the fjord side is a 100-year-old **sailing barge**, *Holvikjekta*, the last of the traditional freighters that served coast and fjord. There is also a fine adventure centre, **Glopen Camping og Fritidssenter** (tel: 57 86 62 14), which offers a variety of activities, including riding, canoeing, rafting, mountain- and glacier-walking, mountain cycling and sightseeing to various beauty spots.

Continuing east along Road 15 from Eid you come to Hornindalsvatnet, which leads to Grodås, sited where the ground begins to climb. Hornindal valley has traditions in handicrafts and folk music, and musicians wear the black breeches, or the long black skirt and green bodice of the area. The most famous artist here was Anders Svor (1864–1929), first a woodcarver and then, after a time at the Copenhagen Academy of Art, a sculptor. The **Anders Svor Museum** (May–Sept, times vary; charge; tel: 57 87 97 76) contains more than 400 sculptures.

Fjord end

Further east you reach the Inner Nordfjord, where the fjord system ends at **Stryn ㉟**, **Loen** and **Olden**, the start of three spectacular valleys stretching up to the northwest edges of the Jostedalsbreen. Nowadays, three tunnels out of the Stryn valley cut right through the mountain to the renowned Geirangerfjord to the north. Stryn is famous for summer skiing on the northeast of Strynsvatn (www.strynefjellet.com), where the ground rises to Tystigbreen. There are eight prepared slopes on the glacier, a snowboard park, a skiing school and a ski rental shop. Cross-country skiing is another possibility, and the area also attracts many off-piste enthusiasts (guides are available).   ❑

Hornindalsvatnet is Europe's deepest freshwater lake. Following the melting of the ice at the end of the last Ice Age, the Hornindal valley flooded to a depth of 514 metres (1,686ft).

BELOW: Briksdal Glacier, part of the great Jostedalsbreen.

MØRE OG ROMSDAL

The county of Møre og Romsdal has a bit of
everything: a jewel of a fjord, Geirangerfjord; the
Art Nouveau Ålesund; the peaks of Trollheimen,
Home of the Trolls; and delightful islands to spare

For nearly a century the coastal steamers of the Hurtigruten have called at Ålesund, Molde and Kristiansund along the sea route that leads to Trondheim and the north. This part of Norway's jagged coastline is 6,000km (3,730 miles) long; more than 10 percent of the county's population lives on islands. It's scarcely surprising then to learn that, even today, the sea is still the great provider for Møre og Romsdal, with North Sea oil and gas becoming more significant.

Looking at the jumble of coastline, islands and fjord mouths on a map, it is sometimes hard to distinguish where sea and islands end and fjord and mainland begin. Yet move inland and half the area lies above 600 metres (2,000ft). In the southeast, the highest peaks reach more than 1,800 metres (6,000ft). The county is divided into three municipalities: **Sunnmøre**, **Romsdal** and **Nordmøre**, of which the main centres are Ålesund, Molde and Kristiansund.

Sea trade has always been important and, from the Middle Ages, the accolade for a settlement was to be given *kaupang* (market) status. At that time there were just two: Borgundkaupangen, 5km (3 miles) east of Ålesund, in Sunnmøre; and Veøykaupangen, in Romsdal. Both were centres for north–south and east–west trade routes on sea and land. Today, the **Sunnmøre Museum** at Borgundkaupangen (tel: 70 17 40 00; all year; mid-June–mid-Aug Mon–Sat 11am–5pm, Sun noon–5pm; hours vary at other times; charge), a lovely open-air museum with over 50 buildings and 40 boats, retells the region's history.

Art Nouveau Ålesund

Ålesund ❶ is Norway's largest fishing town but is best known for its Art Nouveau architecture, built in 1904 after a

PRECEDING PAGES: Geirangerfjord. **LEFT:** Seven Sisters Waterfall, Geirangerfjord.
RIGHT: Art Nouveau detail in Ålesund.

great fire which destroyed the centre and which gave rise to the Norwegian saying: "I've never heard anything like it since Ålesund burned down."

First to the rescue came the Norvegophile Kaiser Wilhelm II of Germany, who sent four ships laden with supplies and building materials (the stained-glass windows in the gable end of the **church** were an inauguration gift from the emperor) and German architecture students. With help and donations from all over Europe, the people of Ålesund and the students completed the rebuilding of the town by 1907 in the now carefully preserved Art Nouveau style. **Ålesund Museum** (all year; charge; tel: 70 12 31 70) features exhibitions on the 1904 fire and subsequent rebuilding.

Towers, turrets and medieval-romantic frontages, often with more than a trace of Nordic mythology, give the town a harmony which extends to the painted wooden warehouses along **Brosundet**, the deep inlet of the inner harbour. Until the 1950s, Ålesund was a veritable gold mine for fish, fishermen and their boats, and *klippfisk*

(traditional Norwegian split, dried cod). But as fishing changed so did Ålesund, which added fish processing and fish farming. Many former warehouses are now offices and restaurants, pleasant places to try out one of the more unlikely local specialities. These include *bacalao*, a dish created in Portugal from Kristiansund's export of *klippfisk*, and the more traditional *brennsnute*, a potato and meat stew.

Life on the sea

From the top of the 418 steps up **Aksla** hill in the centre of the town – if the climb doesn't leave you breathless, the view certainly will – you can see over several islands, now all linked by 12km (8 miles) of underground tunnels.

Every book and brochure that describes the county's thousands of islands shows similar happy pictures of people in, on or under the sea, and anglers with magnificent catches. There are sea caves, tunnels and bird cliffs, little harbours, campsites, clean, white beaches and *hytter* (holiday lodges) to rent. Some have relics of the Vikings; many have summer festivals.

What these sea islands have to offer is almost unlimited: the difficulty is which to choose. For an introduction to the marine fauna of the area, visit the **Atlantic Sea Park** (Atlanterhavsparken; tel: 70 10 70 60; daily, times vary; charge) at Tueneset (a few minutes' drive from Ålesund town centre), one of the largest saltwater aquariums in Scandinavia.

Bird island of Runde

The island of **Runde ❷**, 67km (42 miles) southwest of Ålesund, is not to be missed. Runde attracts professional and amateur naturalists from all over the world. More than 200 bird species have been recorded, but this small island is best known for breeding birds, which line the cliffs in their hundreds of thousands. When they fly, it looks as if a gigantic swarm of insects has darkened the sky. As a bonus, in the waters round the island are interesting wrecks; not so long ago divers found a cache of gold from a Dutch ship, *Ackerendam*. The island can be reached by road or organised boat tours (tourist information, tel: 90 18 34 55; May–Sept).

Secretive Geirangerfjord

South from Ålesund between Vartdalsfjord and Hjørundfjord, the **Sunnmøre Mountains ❸** plunge straight into the fjord near Ørsta, one of the early targets for the many British climbers who first made Norway's mountains known to the world.

Ålesund is also the main entrance to **Storfjord**, where the cruise ships turn in to reach their goal of **Geirangerfjord ❹**, claimed by many to be Norway's most beautiful fjord. One road (No. 60) to Geiranger goes through Stranda, main town of inner Storfjord, another (No. 655) via Ørsta, both ending at **Hellesylt**. From there you can travel to the inner end of Geirangerfjord by boat or, in summer, there is a path along the fjord's high southern wall.

In this most secret of fjords far from the sea, great waterfalls tumble in such delicate cascades that they are given feminine names – **De Syv Søstre** (The Seven Sisters) and the **Brudesløret** (Bridal Veil). Lofty mountains are reflected in the mirror-still water and, in some places, farms cling to unlikely

With great practicality, the builders used the rock from the tunnels they carved around Ålesund to extend the airport on the nearby island of Vigra.

BELOW:
looking down on Geirangerfjord.

TIP

For keen walkers, instead of taking the road down Trollstigen to Åndalsnes it is now possible to follow the well-marked Kløvstien, the old mountain track that was the only way through the mountains before the road.

pockets of green. The spectacle is much too beautiful to miss, and everyone stays on deck until the boat reaches **Geiranger** ❺, which huddles under the half-circle of mountains.

Halfway up the winding road behind the village is the appropriately named Hotel Utsikten, which has one of the best views in Norway, and further on the road passes by **Dalsnibba**, the highest peak in Sunnmøre. To reach the wild valley of **Norangsdalen**, drive from Hellesylt to **Øye**, where you'll find the classic wooden Hotell Union Øye, a car ferry over the fjord and more stunning views.

Along the Troll Road

Heading north once more (along Road 63) towards Åndalsnes, the first stretch to Eidsdal on the Norddalsfjord is known as the **Ørneveien** ❻ (Eagle's Road), and it is not difficult to see why as it winds ahead to **Ørnesvingen**, another vantage point. Over the fjord is the start of an even more spectacular road across the **Gudbrandsjuvet** gorge. Mountains rise into the distance to the west, until you reach the top of

the **Trolls' Ladder** or **Trolls' Causeway** ❼ (**Trollstigen**). This is the heart of inner Romsdal. To the east is Trolltindane, around 1,800 metres (6,000ft), and this fascinating mountain range can be admired before or after the journey on Trollstigen. From vast amounts of snow up here (even in July) it is only a short but exciting 15-minute journey down through 11 gigantic bends hewn out of solid rock into the green valley towards Åndalsnes.

Åndalsnes is known as "the village between *fjell* (mountain) and fjord". It sits on a promontory in a circle of fjord and mountain, looking up to tops that challenge climbers of every nationality. They arrive by the score to tackle the **Trolls' Wall** (Trollveggen), part of craggy **Trolltindane** ❽, which rises almost vertically from Romsdalen in the east, to its summit bowl of permanent snow. Trollveggen itself has more than 1,000 metres (3,300ft) of vertical and overhanging rock, first climbed in 1965. New routes are still being discovered. By less hazardous paths, the climb up Trolltindane takes four hours and requires boots and strong clothing.

Åndalsnes is the terminus for the Raumabanen through **Romsdalen** ❾ to Trondheim, which brings enough visitors by train each year to double or treble the population. A 19th-century British traveller, Lady Beauclerk, described Romsdalen as "precipitous, grey rocks ending in points apparently as sharp as needles... emerging into the sunniest, and the most lovely little spot... sheltered from every wind by the snow-capped mountains that surrounded it, while a most tempting river ran through the dale". It is as true today as it was then.

Famous climbers

The pleasant valley was the base camp for early climbers such as William Slingsby and Johannes Vigdal who, in 1881, made the first ascent of **Store Vengetind**. In the same year, another early Danish pioneer, Carl Hall, made the second ascent with two local climb-

BELOW: Trolls' Causeway.

ers to the sharp point of **Romdalshornet**. It had first been conquered in 1828 by two local farmers, Cristian Smed and Hans Bjermeland. In later years Arne Randers Heen made a name for himself by ascending Romdalshornet no fewer than 233 times – he is said to have built the shelter at the top of the summit, and to have waved the Norwegian flag there during World War II (something forbidden under the German occupation).

Rafting and canoeing are also good possibilities on the Rauma River, one of Norway's best-known fishing rivers, which runs through the valley. But it is not necessary to be a rock climber to get high into these mountains. Most have easy alternative routes, and roads reach more than 850 metres (2,800ft).

The rose town of Molde

Proceeding back towards the coast and Molde along Road 64, it is worth taking a detour into Langfjord until you reach **Nesset ⑩** on Eresfjord, deep in the mountains. Norway's prominent 19th-century writer and patriot Bjørnstjerne Bjørnson, who had a summer home in the area, described the Nesset Mountains: "some standing white, others standing blue, with jagged, competing, agitating peaks, some marching along in ranking row".

The view today from the ferry along the **Eikesdalsvatnet ⑪** shows you what he meant. The mountain peaks rise abruptly out of the fjord sides, and you get a glimpse of **Mardalsfossen**, northern Europe's highest waterfall at over 650 metres (2,000ft) high. In the 1970s, hundreds of people chained themselves together near the waterfall, to prevent the building of a hydroelectric power station. It became a hot political issue and, though they did not win the final battle, the protesters ensured that the summer falls still exist.

Molde ⑫ is part of an archipelago sheltered from the Norwegian Sea; its mild climate, green vegetation and rose gardens earn it the title "Town of Roses". The statue of the Little Rose Seller stands in the marketplace. Stalls sell everything from fruit and vegetables to clothes and, of course, roses. This modern and easygoing town was almost entirely rebuilt after

The Rauma Line (Raumabanen), the 114km (71-mile) long stretch of railway between Dombås and Åndalsnes, is one of the most spectacular in Norway.

BELOW:
Mardalsfossen.

The First Tourist Hotel

To cater for all the early mountaineers and sightseers to Romsdal in the 19th century, a local police sergeant, Anders Landmark, opened a simple wooden inn at **Aak** in 1850, which is regarded as Norway's first tourist hotel. Many of Europe's mountain addicts have stayed here to take advantage of the beautiful surroundings, with the Troll Wall (Trollveggen) and Romsdalshornet close by.

Situated some 5km (3 miles) into the Romsdal valley from Åndalsnes on the E136, Aak is now both a modern hotel with excellent restaurant (mid-June–Aug; book in advance), and a mountain sports centre, offering summer courses in climbing and scrambling and, in winter, instruction in ice climbing and mountain (or Telemark) skiing (tel: 71 22 71 71; www.hotelaak.no).

When rough weather comes in from the west, the coastal Atlanterhavsveien (Atlantic Road) lives up to its name.

German bombing in World War II. It is an excellent base for touring the fjords by boat or car. From **Varden**, Molde's best vantage point, you look over fjord and island to the snowcaps of the Sunnmøre Mountains, the famous **Molde Panorama** – townspeople claim you can see 222 peaks – and half an hour away to the north are small fishing villages which brave the west winds.

Fishery and folk art

Molde has its outdoor museum, the **Romsdalsmuseet** (mid-June–mid-Aug, hours vary; charge; tel: 71 20 24 60), which includes the Hjertøya Fishery Museum – in a beautiful spot where the timber houses, national costumes and folk dancing seem to fit in with the landscape. The museum's collection of *bunader* (national costumes), showing the fine details of shawl, headdress, bodice, jewellery and embroidered purse, is one of the most appealing. The Fishery Museum, 10 minutes by boat from the marketplace, is in the form of a small fishing village from the 1850s.

Yet there is little that is traditional about Molde's entertainment. The modern stadium is well used, with an all-year football ground located, spectacularly, by the sea, and the streets are often full of musicians, particularly during the famous **Molde International Jazz Festival** (tel: 71 20 31 50; www.moldejazz.no; mid-July), one of Norway's main festivals.

Another fine route is to take roads 64 and 664 from Molde to the 16th-century village of **Bud**, right on the west coast. Here a boat trip goes to the old fishing station of **Bjørnsund**, now only inhabited in the summer. Between Molde and Bud, a walk from Road 64 reveals the **Troll Church** ⓭ (Trollkirka) – a cave, some 70 metres (230ft) long, divided into three sections, with a great waterfall tumbling down from the upper opening into a white marble basin in the mountains.

The Atlantic Road

From Bud a small coastal road leads back to Road 64 and the **Atlantic Road** (Atlanterhavsveien) to Kristiansund, over **Averøya** ⓮, the biggest island in the area. As this road heads north across the rim of the ocean, it's a bit like driving on the sea itself. Averøya deserves more than the view from a car window.

Archaeologists believe that this was one of the first places to be settled after the last Ice Age, and their finds in 1909 are remnants of the early **Fosna Culture** that existed around 7000 BC during the Stone Age. ("Fosna" was the original name of Kristiansund.) One of the best ways to get around is a 50km (30-mile) tour which varies from seaward skerries and small islands linked by bridge or causeway to hills around 500 metres (1,600ft) high.

Near **Bremsnes** ⓰, on the northeastern tip of Averøya, is the Viking **Stone of Horg** (Horgsteinen), where the victor of Hafrsfjord, Harald Hårfagre, had his famous hair cut and washed, having fulfilled his vow not to touch it until Norway was united. It is 15 minutes by ferry from Bremsnes to Kristiansund.

Klippfisk at Kristiansund

Unlike Ålesund and Molde, **Kristiansund** ⓰ has little protection from the worst the North Atlantic can do. It is right on the coast, with weather-beaten rocks pounded by the sea, yet not far inland are grassy areas and small woods. This is the *klippfisk* town, for long the biggest exporter of Norwegian dried cod. There are only 17,000 inhabitants but, because of the centuries-old links with other countries thanks to its sailors and fishermen, and the foreign merchants who settled here, the atmosphere is quite cosmopolitan.

Like most Norwegian towns with "Kristian" in their title, Kristiansund was named after a Danish king, Christian VI, who gave it town status in 1742. A good introduction is by *sundbåtene*, the harbour boats which for more than 100 years have linked the town's islands. **Mellemverftet,** part of the Nordmøre Museum (*see below*; tel: 71 58 70 00; mid-June–early Aug Tue–Fri noon–4pm), once one of four shipyards in **Vågen**, is working again as a centre for preserving the craft of shipbuilding, carefully restoring the beautiful lines of traditional Norwegian boats.

Kristiansund consists of three islands. One of them is **Innlandet,** the oldest preserved part of the town with

While on Averøya, don't miss the fine stave church at Kvernes (July–Aug 10am–5pm; charge). Built in 1300, it has an unusually richly decorated mid-17th century interior in homage to shipping. Next door, the local museum features a collection of buildings from the area.

BELOW:
Kristiansund.

A Country Afloat

Sailing is second nature to Norwegians, a third of whom spend their holidays on the water, while others compete worldwide

To the world, Norway and seafaring are synonymous; the very word Viking means "Men of the Bays". From the age of sail until after World War II, the Norwegian merchant fleet was one of the world's largest, and Norwegian could be heard in ports worldwide.

Among the country's most popular museums by far are the Maritime Museum (Sjøfartsmuseum) on the Bygdøy peninsula in Oslo, along with the Viking Ship Museum (Vikingskipshuset), with magnificently preserved longships unearthed from various sites and burial mounds around Norway, the Kon-Tiki Museum, with the rafts used by ethnographic explorer Thor Heyerdahl, and the Fram Museum (Frammuseet), built around the sturdy vessel that carried Fridtjof Nansen and Roald Amundsen on their heroic polar explorations.

Norwegians seem happiest when they are in, on or around the sea. Each year, over a third of the population spend their summer holidays partly or completely in craft that range from small dinghies to large motor launches and ocean-going yachts. Even the most conservative estimates place the number of pleasure craft in Norway at 650,000, about one for every seven Norwegians. The sea is a natural part of life.

Geography and topography are the deciding factors. There are thousands upon thousands of islands, and the fjords and coastal archipelagos are a paradise for competitive and recreational sailors, king and commoner alike. Rocky shores and fjord meadows are dotted with colourful holiday huts and a boat of some form moored nearby.

King Olav V, the father of the present King Harald, was, in his day, the country's foremost sailor in more than name only. He won a gold medal in sailing in the 1928 Olympics, making him the world's only Olympic medallist monarch. He also won medals in the Sailing World Championships in 1971 and 1976.

In founding its first sailing club in 1868 in Tønsberg, then a major merchant fleet port, Norway triggered a long latent urge. In 1883 the Royal Norwegian Sailing Association was formed in the capital, and in 1900 sailing became an Olympic sport. Norwegians were a major force in Olympic and championship sailing worldwide.

By chance, Norway's leading position in international sailing coincides approximately with the country's yacht production. In the days of wooden yachts, Norwegian shipyards and naval architects were among the world's best, and one in particular stands out: born in the port of Larvik, Colin Archer (1832–1921) grew up with boats and at an early age started building craft to his own design. Among his best known are the stable, sturdy rescue schooners that bear his name and the three-masted Arctic exploration vessel *Fram*, built in 1892. The tradition of boatbuilding, like that of ski-making, continues to this day, albeit somewhat altered: fibreglass hulls and masts changed the picture completely. Nowadays, Norway exports motor cruisers and imports yachts.

Wherever there's water, there are all manner of motor and sailing craft. Small boat harbours in and near major cities, particularly Oslo, Kristiansund, Ålesund, Stavanger and Bergen, never fail to impress visitors by the number and types of crafts lying there.

From windsurfing in fjords to major regattas, Norwegians love being on the water.   ❏

LEFT: sailing is second nature to Norwegians.

its first customs house (1660–1748), hospital, school and other buildings which are being restored. Walk to the **Sjursvika** on the east side for a look at the old warehouses. These interesting parts of the harbour are being amalgamated into a coastal culture centre, to tell the history of the maritime people, alongside the harbour life of today.

The **Nordmøre Museum** (tel: 71 58 70 00; mid-June–early Aug daily noon–5pm; charge) includes archaeological finds from the Fosna culture and the history of *klippfisk* processing. But the town's oddest monuments are the tall pointed natural stones, tributes to town dignitaries: Bäckstrøm, who built the reservoirs, Brinchman, the provider of the water supply, Bræin, the musical founder of a musical family, which gave birth to an annual Opera Festival, and Hanson, the polar explorer.

Kristiansund's main church was destroyed by bombing in 1940. The architect responsible for its replacement named his creation "Rock Crystal in Roses", and whether you love it or loathe it, you cannot ignore this stark white building. Inside the **Atlantic Ocean Cathedral** (Atlanterhavskatedralen; all year), the choir wall is a 30-metre (100ft) sweep of 320 stained-glass panels, which at the foot symbolise the heavy, dark colours of the earth soaring up to eternal light.

Miracle at Grip

An entirely different church stands on the island of **Grip**, northwest from Kristiansund. The island has a long and eventful history of flood and storm, and the islanders often took refuge in the small church. In 1796, a nor'wester tore down and washed away 100 houses and, when the same thing happened seven years later, the pastor recorded the piteous prayer: "Almighty God, spare us further destruction and misery." Whether it was that plea or not, the ancient little red stave church survived, only 8 metres (25ft) above the sea. Once 400 souls lived on Grip, scraping a living from fish: today people live there

only in summer when it metamorphoses into a holiday island and makes a popular excursion from the town. A wedding in the 15th-century church is a very special occasion.

Kuli inscription

To the north and northeast of Kristiansund, the last big island is **Smøla** ⑰, at the mouth of the Trondheimfjord, where the county ends in a gaggle of islands which retain something of the life of the old farmer-fishermen.

Sanden is one of several buildings that form Smøla's scattered museum, with the main 18th-century building, warehouses, barn and a storehouse on wooden pillars, just as it was when the last owners left a few years ago.

A number of these old fishing grounds where cod was split, salted and dried on the rocks are now marinas providing simple accommodation, seafood menus, and the atmosphere of earlier days.

The idyllic island of **Kuli** off Smøla is rich in relics, the most famous being the **Kuli Stone**. On this stone the name Norway is mentioned for the first time

Kvernes stave church dates from the 14th century (see margin on page 279).

BELOW: altar of Kvernes stave church.

Sailing in Trollheimen.

BELOW: waterfall, Trollstigen Pass.
RIGHT: De Syv Søstre (Seven Sisters), Geirangerfjord.

in an inscription which dates to the first years after the coming of Christianity to these parts.

Land of the trolls

Inland, the northern part of the county ends in a crisscross of fjords eating into the islands and peninsulas which lead to **Trollheimen**, the "Home of the Trolls", where the mountains reach nearly 1,600 metres (5,000ft). This haunt of climbers and skiers is bounded by two important valleys, **Surnadalen** and **Sunndalen**, with between them the tiny **Todalfjord**. Beside the last is the surprise of the **Svinvik Arboretum** ⑱ (Svinviks Arboret; early May–mid-Aug; charge; tel: 71 66 35 80), beautiful gardens with thousands of plants, including rhododendrons and conifers. Despite the northern latitude, plants from all over the world grow at Svinvik.

On the way to Sunndalen along Road 70 from Kristiansund, you come to **Tingvoll** ⑲, which has Nordmøre's oldest church, popularly known as the **Nordmøre Cathedral** (Nordmøresdomen; June–Aug; charge), in an area with a large selection of historic churches. The Tingvoll church is believed to date from the 12th century; it's a well-preserved granite-and-brick structure surrounded by a stone wall with an arched entrance way.

Sunndalen is deep in the Nordmøre wilderness, with narrow valleys between the mountain ranges forming sheltered farming country which supplies grain for most of the county. At the end of the fjord lies the industrial town of Sunndalsøra, once a mecca for the British "salmon lords": the **Sunndal Museum and Leikvin Heritage Park** (tel: 71 69 61 80; mid-June–mid-Aug Tue–Sun noon–5pm; charge) at Grøa records their privileged position in society up to the end of the 19th century. The Driva River debouches into the fjord and the surrounding mountains are of breathtaking beauty – a magnificent area for walking and skiing as well as fishing.

Road 70 follows the course of the valley to Oppdal on the third side of Trollheimen. On foot, there are more energetic routes over the mountains, with a mountain centre in Innerdalen and ski lifts as well. The **Driva River** is one of the most famous in a country of good salmon and trout rivers. Between the head of Sunndalen and Grødalen, next door at Åmotan, a spectacular gorge, **Jenstadjuvet** ⑳, is the place where five valleys and their watercourses meet in two furious waterfalls. Grødalen has an oddity in **Alfheim**, a small hunting lodge from 1876 built in Scottish Highland style by a Scot, Lady Arbuthnott, who became something of the "laird" of the valley. It is possible to visit her old farm at **Elverhøy**.

To the north, Surnadal has another good salmon river, the **Surna**; side valleys lead up to the heart of Trollheimen, and to signposted trails from mountain hut to mountain hut, in what seems like the top of the world. At valley level, the road through Surnadal is the inland route out of west Norway, straight on to the city of Trondheim, the gateway to the north. ❏

TRONDHEIM

Although the city has lost its political role, to many Norwegians it remains the country's historical, cultural and religious capital, and is host to the annual celebrations of its patron saint, St Olav

A thousand years ago, Trondheim, then Nidaros, was the capital of Norway, and the resting place of King Olav Haraldson. Founded in 997 by King Olav Tryggvason, a reminder of Trondheim's early days and of the old harbour is provided by the **wharves** and the narrow streets *(veitene)* that run between the wooden buildings. Though they date back only to the 18th century, these coloured warehouses echo the architecture of medieval times, and it is not too difficult to feel what the atmosphere must have been like around that busy harbour when fish and timber dominated the city.

Centre of scientific research

Today, Trondheim is the home of SIN-TEF, Scandinavia's largest foundation for scientific and industrial research, and is at the forefront of Norwegian education and Church affairs. Situated near SINTEF is the Norwegian University of Science and Technology (NTNU), the country's second-largest university. The city has been a scientific centre since the 18th century – the **University Museum**, from 1760, is Norway's oldest scientific institution – and today both SINTEF and the university attract high-tech businesses

PRECEDING PAGES: west facade of Nidaros Cathedral, which dates back to the 12th century. **LEFT:** Olav Tryggvason monument. **RIGHT:** Church of our Lady.

to Trondheim, with the advantage of being able to turn to the research establishments for help.

City charm

Modern though it may be, Trondheim has retained much of the charm of the past, with the heart of the Old City lying on what is virtually an island between the **Nidelva River** and **Trondheims-fjord**, joined only by a narrow neck of land to the west, once the western fort. One building that unites past and present is the **National Museum**

Main attractions
NIDAROS CATHEDRAL
ARCHBISHOP'S PALACE
STIFTSGÅRDEN
MUNKHOLMEN
TRØNDELAG FOLK MUSEUM
ROCKHEIM
RINGVE MUSEUM
STIKLESTAD

of **Applied Art** (Nordenfjeldske
Kunstindustrimuseum; all year; charge;
tel: 73 80 89 50) on Munkegata.

Nidaros Cathedral

Though King Olav Tryggvason had
attempted to introduce Christianity to
Norway in the late 10th century, many
Norwegians still clung to their pagan
gods, and it was only after the death
of his successor, Olav Haraldson, at the
Battle of Stiklestad some 30 years later
(*see page 293*) that Christianity acquired
a focal point in Norway. Olav's men
buried him in sandy ground near the
river, but when miracles began to hap-
pen he was moved to the town's only
church. Then, according to the sagas,
a spring began to flow near his first
grave and "men were healed of their ills
by the waters". The king was declared a
saint and martyr in 1164.

Olav's nephew, Olav Kyrre, built
a great stone church over the place
where the saint's body had lain,
which is now **Nidaros Cathedral** ❻
(Nidarosdomen; to book tours tel: 73
89 08 00; www.nidarosdomen.no; all year;
mid-June–mid-Aug Mon–Fri 9am–

5.30pm, Sat 9am–2pm, Sun 1pm–4pm;
mid-Aug–mid-June times vary; charge,
includes entrance to Archbishop's Palace), Trondheim's finest building. Once
again, the saint's body was moved and
the cathedral became a place of pilgrimage. For centuries, pilgrims came
from the south of Norway, from Sweden and Finland, and from Iceland, the
Faroe Islands and Greenland to pay
homage to St Olav. When the Reformation came to Norway in 1537, the cult
of the ancient relic was abolished and
pilgrimages ceased. From mid-June to
mid-August, a special musical evening
mass is held for visitors.

Royal tradition

Until the Reformation, Nidaros Cathedral was the seat of the archbishop, and
the setting for the coronation of Norwegian monarchs, a tradition revived
after 1814, when Norway shrugged off
its 400 years of Danish rule and united
with Sweden. In 1991 King Harald V
was crowned in Nidaros Cathedral.
The **crown jewels** are on display in a
side chapel (mid-June–mid-Aug Mon–
Fri 9am–5.30pm, Sat 10am–3pm, Sun

noon–4pm; mid-Aug–mid-June times vary; charge).

The **great arched nave** is in a Gothic style and, looking back to the west end, the most striking feature is the brilliant stained-glass **rose window** above the main entrance, the work of Gabriel Kjelland in 1930. Both inside and out there are many statues of saints and monarchs; but the beautiful interior lines of the cathedral, built in a green-grey soapstone, are its finest feature.

Next door to the cathedral is Scandinavia's oldest secular building, once the **Archbishop's Palace** ❶ (Erkebispe-gården; mid-June–mid-Aug Mon–Fri 9am–5.30pm, Sat 10am–3pm, Sun noon–4pm; mid-Aug–mid-June times vary; charge). In 1222, Archbishop Guttorm was empowered by King Håkon Håkonsson to mint and circulate coins, a privilege which his successors exercised until 1537 and the Reformation. Their mint was uncovered in the 1990s when the museum was rebuilt after fire and is a highlight. The Crown Regalia Exhibition also features royal crowns, sceptres and details of the monarchy. The building was at one time a military establishment, and the **Rustkammeret** (Army Museum; mid-May–mid-Sept Mon–Sat 10am–4pm, Sun noon–4pm; charge) includes exhibits on World War II and the Resistance movement. Nearby is **Waisenhuset**, a beautiful timber building dating from 1772, originally an orphanage.

All around the original medieval city are the remains of fortifications, which were reinforced or built in the late 17th century by a military architect from Luxembourg, General Johan Caspar de Cicignon, after the great fire of 1681 devastated most of medieval Trondheim.

From the cathedral area it is just a short walk to the **Old Town Bridge** ❺ (Gamle Bybrua), also erected after 1681 when de Cicignon was constructing **Kristiansten Fort** ❻ (Kristiansten Festning) on a hill to the east, at that time outside the city proper. The first bridge had a sentry box and excise house at either end and the western building still remains, now used as a kindergarten. The present bridge and gates were built in 1861. The local tourist office (tel: 73 80 76 60) organises guided tours to these sites.

View from Kristiansten Fort

Kristiansten Fort, now part of the city, provides one of the best views of Trondheim. From here you can see the old stone walls of the 13th-century **Church of Our Lady** ❼ (Vår Frues Kirke; 24 hours a day) and **Stiftsgården** ❽ (June–mid-Aug Mon–Sat 10am–5pm, Sun noon–5pm; charge), Scandinavia's largest timber mansion, on **Munkegata**. Stiftsgården was built as a private house in the 1770s and today serves as the official residence of the Norwegian royal family when visiting the city.

Northeast from the bustling harbour of the **Ravnkloa** ❶ at the northern end of Munkegata, and past the ornate railway station, is **Fosenkaia**, where sightseeing and other boats tie up. At midday, the Hurtigruten coastal express (*see page 257*) will be lying at one of

Old Town Bridge (Gamle Bybrua) offers good views of the warehouses along Kjøpmannsgate.

BELOW: Church of Our Lady.

Trondheim is the site of the world's first bicycle lift, "Trampe", built on Brubakken hill in 1995. It operates like a ski tow. Cyclists pay using keycards at the bottom and are pulled 130 metres (430ft) to the top.

the two main quays, with a half-day to spend in Trondheim before it heads north. Returning south on a summer evening, the ship is outlined against the light as its passengers make an excursion to see the midnight sun from the summit of **Mount Storsteinen**.

The remains of Trondheim's old defences, **Skansen**, lie to the west where the city gate once stood. Skansen is now a park. Also near the harbour is a curious warehouse built out on iron stilts over the sea; its shape is explained by the fact that it was a World War II U-boat bunker when German forces occupied the city.

Well out into the fjord is the islet of **Munkholmen** ❶ (hourly ferry from Ravnkloa; late May–early Sept; charge), where Benedictine monks built a monastery very early in the 11th century. This was one of the first two monasteries in Norway. Before the arrival of the Benedictine monks, the site had been Trondheim's execution ground and in 1658 it became a prison fort. You can take a tour of the fort, and the island also offers good sea bathing as well as a restaurant.

The Home of Rock

Norwegian pop and rock is showcased at **Rockheim** (Brattørkaia 14; tel: 73 60 50 70; www.rockheim.no), a new museum housed in an eye-catching modern building just north of Trondheim's central train station (Rockheim means literally "the home of rock"). The permanent exhibition at Rockheim presents Norway's pop and rock heritage with a journey through contemporary Norwegian popular music and culture from the 1950s to today. It includes a mix of sounds, images and videos, as well as artefacts from the various periods represented. Additional temporary exhibitions focus on aspects of music history and contemporary culture, taken from the local, national and international scene.

Visitors will also have the opportunity to get involved, by, for example, learning how to play the guitar with TNT guitarist Ronniie Le Tekro, mixing hip-hop tracks using professional equipment, and experiencing the kick of standing on a stage in front of thousands of fans. The *mediatheque*, which is central to the project, gives the public access to a wealth of rock literature and original footage from the museum's extensive music and video archives. There is a professional stage featuring the latest technology and equipment, and an auditorium accommodating up to 350 people. Check out the latest programme of concerts, as well as seminars and tutorials. There is also a restaurant and shop on site.

Walking in the Old Town

Trondheim is an easy walking city. Two places best toured on foot are **Hospitalsløkka** ❸, the area around the old Trondheim Hospital, and **Bakklandet** ❹, on the eastern side of the Nidelva, not far from the Old Town Bridge and opposite the riverside warehouses.

In the grounds of the hospital, which was founded in 1277 and is Scandinavia's oldest surviving hospital, lies the first **octagonal timber church** (1705) to be built in Norway. The surrounding area *(løkka)* is full of old timber houses, lovingly restored by their present owners. Bakklandet is another area of old wooden houses, and was originally the working-class quarter. It and the Mollenberg and Rosenborg districts have been restored to form complete communities of houses and shops.

Looking into the past

For an understanding of the past of this ancient area of Trøndelag, two museums are invaluable. At the **Museum of Natural History and Archaeology** ❿ (Vitenskapsmuseet; July–Aug daily 11am–5pm; Sept–June Tue–Fri 10am–4pm, Sat–Sun noon–4pm; charge), celebrating 250 years in 2010, the main exhibits trace the history of the area up to the Middle Ages, and the development of church furnishings from the 13th to the 18th century. There is also a display covering Trøndelag flora and fauna. The **Maritime Museum** ⓝ (Sjøfartsmuseet; mid-May–mid-Aug daily noon–4pm; Sept–May Sat–Sun noon–4pm; charge), situated in an old penitentiary from 1725, covers shipping, fishing and whaling.

Trøndelag Folk Museum (Folkemuseet; bus 8 or 9 from Dronningensgate; June–Aug daily 11am–6pm; Sept–May Mon–Fri 11am–3pm, Sat–Sun noon–4pm; charge) in Sverresborg, on the west side of the city, looks at life in days gone by. Here, more than 60 reconstructed buildings from the Trondheim area are centred round a market square, including a post office and dentist's surgery. There is a stave church dating from 1170 and an exhibit of *passementerie* (the making of trimmings and lace for women's Sunday best). Within the museum are the remains of King Sverre's palace, **Zion**, from around 1180, and the 18th-century tavern has a good restaurant. There is also a Sami Museum.

Drama and music-making

Trondheim also has Norway's oldest theatre building, **Trøndelag Teater**, in the centre of the Old Town, as well as **Teaterhuset Avant Garden**. Other arts are represented by galleries and institutions such as the **Academy of Art ⓞ** (Trondhjems Kunstforening; tel: 73 52 66 71; noon–4pm), showing and selling contemporary paintings.

Of great interest is the **Ringve Museum of Musical History ⓟ** (buses 3 and 4 from Munkegaten; tel: 73 87 02 80; www.ringve.no; daily 11am–5pm mid-June–mid-Aug; opening hours vary rest of the year; charge). The museum is in an ancient manor. A permanent exhibition opened in 1999 in the former barn. Here, light and sound guides you through various historic stations, such as "the invention of the piano" or "pop and rock".

Since the late 19th century, the house belonged to the Bachke family. In 1946, the last representative, Christian Anker Bachke, died and his widow, Russian-born "Madame Victoria", worked steadily to build up the couple's collection of musical instruments from all over the world. Her persuasiveness in prising relics from many countries is legendary, and when the museum opened in 1952 the collection had grown magnificently. A selection of the instruments are played by the music-student guides during the tour. In addition to the more formal, classical instruments, there are examples of music boxes, old folk instruments such as the *langeleik* – a sort of Norwegian zither – and clay flutes shaped like birds and soldiers.

Just before her death in 1962, Madame Victoria opened the museum's concert hall; it was built into the old cowsheds and is used for formal musical occasions. After the museum, stroll around the **Botanic Gardens** (Ringve Botaniske Hage; daily, free) next door,

The Ravnkloa clock by the fish market.

BELOW: Trondheim is a major stop for the Hurtigruten coastal express.

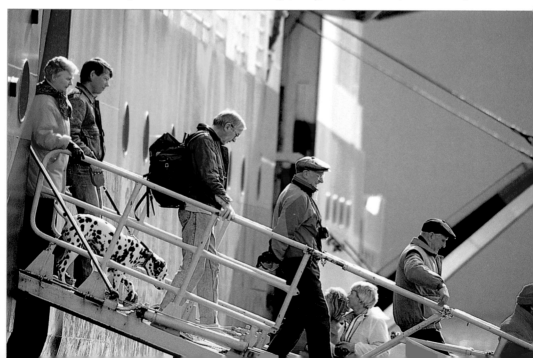

TIP

For a bird's-eye view of the city from the 124-metre (406ft) telecommunications tower, Tyholttårnet (all year; charge) take buses 20 or 60. The tower also houses Norway's only revolving restaurant.

one of the most northerly botanical gardens in the world.

Families with children might also want to check out the **Science Centre ⓠ** (Vitensenteret, Kongens gate 1; 73 59 61 23; www.viten.ntnu.no; mid-June–mid-Aug Mon–Fri 10am–5pm, Sat–Sun 11am–5pm; rest of year Mon–Fri 10am–4pm, Sat–Sun 11am–5pm; charge), a popular science adventure centre with some 150 interactive experiments designed to bring the fun back into science.

Outdoor life

Trondheim's back garden is **Bymarka** to the west, where Gråkallen (Old Man) at some 520 metres (1,700ft) is the city's favourite skiing area. In summer, it is a good spot for walking. Its counterpart to the east is **Estenstadmarka**. Fishing is good in the Nidelva River, which is renowned for the size of its salmon. The Gaula to the south is another fine fishing river, while the fjord itself is ideal for sea fishing.

As well as the hourly boats to Munksholmen, in summer the tourist office runs 1½-hour tours of Trondheim

from the sea, which leave from Ravnkloa (July–late Aug Tue–Sun noon and 2.30pm; late May–early June and late Aug–early Sept Wed and Sun 1.30pm). There is also a two-hour tour of Trondheim, which takes in a number of sites and museums, departing daily at 11am (late May–early Sept) next to the tourist information office. You can also visit the ancient manor of **Austråtborgen** (May–Aug; charge) at Ørland on Trondheimsfjord. Another idea is to take a short leg of the Hurtigruten and return by bus or train. Alternatively, you can travel southeast to the **Knitting Museum** (Strikkemuseum; all year; charge) at Selbu, which shows the history of the famous Selbu knitwear from 1853. Road 705 to Selbu features a particularly scenic route marketed as **Ferieveien** ("holiday road").

For most people Trondheim means history and culture. Like the pilgrims of old, visitors come to see the cathedral, the Archbishop's Palace and de Cicignon's 17th-century city, and for historical events such as the annual 10-day **St Olav Festival** at the end of July (*see opposite page*). ❑

BELOW: an old view of Stiklestad by Johannes Flintoe for an 1839 edition of the *Norse Sagas*.

Stiklestad

Thousands of pilgrims flock to Sticklestad every summer to commemorate the battle at which the venerable King Olav died

Stiklestad is a name that is revered by Norwegians. A momentous battle on this site in 1030, at which King Olav Haraldson died at the hands of King Canute, was a turning point in Norwegian history. For Stiklestad, 100km (60 miles) north of Trondheim, saw the foundation of Norwegian national unity and the adoption of the Christian faith. A church marks the spot where Olav died.

In the 11th century Norway was a country constantly disrupted by disputes between rival chieftains, and Olav's ambition was a united Norway. He also aimed to create a Christian country with Christian laws and churches and clergy.

He was not the first to attempt this. In the previous century Olav Tryggvason (a descendant of Harald Hårfagre) had been converted to Christianity in England and confirmed by the Bishop of Winchester. He returned to his native land in 995 with the express purpose of crushing the chieftains and imposing his new-found faith. But Olav Tryggvason's conversion had not swept away all his Viking instincts, and in his religious zeal he used great cruelty in his attempt to convert the populace. As a result, he fell in the Battle of Svolder in the year 1000, due to the defection of some disenchanted Norwegian chieftains.

Olav Haraldson was also a descendant of Harald Hårfagre and he ascended the throne in 1015. But, like his predecessor, Olav foolishly made too great a use of the sword to establish Christianity. The result was the same: with his eye on the Norwegian throne, King Canute of Denmark and England gave support to discontented factions within the country and in 1028 invaded Norway, forcing King Olav to flee to Russia.

Undaunted, King Olav returned with a few followers, but whatever loyalty he had once inspired had been lost through his ruthless methods. He died on 29 July 1030 at the Battle of Stiklestad. Olav's corpse was taken to the then capital, Nidaros

(the Trondheim of today) and buried on the banks of the Nidelva River. When the body was disinterred a year later by the bishop, it showed no signs of decay: his face was unchanged and his nails and hair had grown. At that time this was taken as a sign of sanctity.

Following this revelation, Olav was proclaimed a saint and his body placed in a silver shrine in Nidaros Cathedral. Faith in the holiness of King Olav – or St Olav as he now was – spread and, until the Reformation, his shrine became a goal of Christian pilgrims.

Canute's triumph at the Battle of Stiklestad was brief. He ceded the reins of power to his son Sweyn but, as the rumours of Olav's sanctity grew, support for Canute evaporated and Sweyn was exiled to Denmark in 1035.

All the while, St Olav's son, Magnus, had also been in exile – he had been living in Russia. Norway now invited Magnus to return and accept the crown.

Stiklestad has been a place of pilgrimage ever since. People still come at the end of July for a festival to commemorate the battle. There is a beautiful open-air theatre here, and on the anniversary of the battle, a cast of more than 300 actors, choristers, dancers and musicians re-enact the events of July 1030 (for more details, see www.stiklestad.no/international/english). ❏

RIGHT: King Olav (1016–28) became St Olav, patron saint of Norway.

INTO THE ARCTIC

North of Trondheim lies a beautiful but often harsh landscape, caught between the warm sea and the mountains inland, and cutting across it an imaginary border into the vast expanse of the Arctic

Main attractions
STIKLESTAD
SVARTISEN GLACIER
ARCTIC CIRCLE
SALTSTRAUMEN
TORGHATTEN

The city of Trondheim is the gateway to the north. But anyone who looks for an immediate change in scenery will be disappointed. The first county north of Trondheim, Nord Trøndelag, has wide areas of rich agricultural land with prosperous-looking farms. Running right up the middle of the county is Norway's north–south jugular, the E6 highway, which lures drivers ever further north. But this is also rail country, and the Nordland railway follows much the same route. Just north of Trondheim, a branch line (with a companion road) reaches over the border into Sweden. It veers off at the small village of **Hell**, whose station must be one of the most photographed in the country and whose tickets are collectors' items. In September, Hell hosts an annual Blues Festival, which attracts international stars to this otherwise quiet settlement.

From a motorist's point of view, there is not a great deal of interest along this section of the E6 and the inclination is to keep going north; but make time for **Værnes** ❶, which has an interesting church from the Middle Ages with a fine Baroque pulpit. Adjoining that is the **Stjørdal Museum** (tel: 74 82 70 21; mid-June–mid-Aug Mon–Wed and Fri 11am–4pm, Sun noon–4pm; charge). The **Frostatinghaugen rock carvings** at Frosta are the site of the first Norwegian legislative assembly (AD 600–1000), with rock carvings going back a further 3,500 years.

Some 6km (4 miles) east of Stjørdalshalsen on the E14 is the **Falstad Museum** (tel: 74 02 80 40; Jan–Nov; charge) at Levanger. Located in the main building of Norway's second-largest SS prison camp during World War II, the memorial includes two execution sites and a cenotaph in the Falstad forest.

About 4km (2½ miles) further on lies **Hegra Fort** (Hegra Festning; June–Aug 11am–5pm; charge). Built following independence, it was the site of several battles during World War II as well as a 25-day German siege. The fort has been restored and includes a Resistance Museum.

St Olav's battleground

Just north of Verdalsøra is the road to **Stiklestad ❷**, the battleground where King Olav Haraldson was killed in 1030, and revered by Norwegians as the birthplace of Norwegian national unity *(see page 293)*. The **National Cultural Centre** (Nasjonale Kultursenter; tel: 74 04 42 00; all year; charge) in Verdal produces an annual open-air play about St Olav (end of July), a spectacular dramatisation of the battle and Olav's death. The centre also has exhibitions about local natural and cultural history, and includes a Resistance Museum, a Folk Museum with 30 buildings and Stiklestad church from 1180.

The first town of any size north of Trondheim is **Steinkjer**, which has been a centre of commerce for more than 1,000 years. Like so many northern Norwegian towns, Steinkjer was destroyed in World War II. After the German invasion in 1940, the king and government moved north, eventually to Tromsø, before they left to continue the government in exile from London. This meant that these sparsely populated northern areas suffered dreadful destruction through the bombing which followed the German invasion.

Nowadays Steinkjer is home to a hard-rock festival in June, and a popular traditional market in August. One of Norway's foremost contemporary artists, Jakob Weidemann (1923–2001), who was a local resident, decorated Steinkjer's church with murals and a beautiful stained-glass window.

Reindeer rock carving

North of Steinkjer it is worth branching off the E6 onto Road 763, which runs along the eastern side of Snåsavatnet (lake), to take a look at the impressive rock carvings near **Bøla ❸** (May–Oct). Of these, the best is the 6,000-year-old Bøla reindeer. The scenery around the lake is remarkably soft and gentle for a latitude between 63 and 64 degrees north, and at its northern end is **Snåsa**, the centre of south Sami (Lapp) culture. It has a Sami cultural centre at Saemien Sijte,

The Bøla reindeer.

PRECEDING PAGES: Svartisen Glacier. **FAR LEFT:** a popular village to photograph. **BELOW LEFT:** orchids grow in the woods around Snåsa. **BELOW:** a rock festival is held in Steinkjer every June.

Into the Arctic

0   20 km
0   20 miles

which includes a museum (tel: 74 13 80 00; June–Aug Mon–Sat 11am–5pm, Sun noon–5pm; Mon–Fri 9am–3pm rest of the year; call to see if someone can show you around; charge).

To the east, about 50km (30 miles) away and close to the border with Sweden, the **Gressåmoen National Park** ❹ (Nasjonalpark) contains an area of typically thick Trøndelag forest and mountain landscape.

Dotted throughout Norway – and particularly in the north – are small towns or villages which are essentially crossroads for many forms of transport. Typical is Grong, where the E6 runs north to south and the road and railway to Namsos, on the coast, goes off to the west, while just south of the town the secondary road, No. 74, runs east through wild countryside to the Swedish frontier at Gäddede. It is also the junction of two rivers, the Namsen and the Sanddøla, both popular with anglers. Each river has an impressive waterfall not far from Grong: to the north, **Fiskumfossen** ❺ on the Namsen and to the south, **Formofossen** on the Sandøla. You can learn all there is to know about salmon at the **Namsen Salmon Aquarium** (Laksakvarium; tel: 74 31 27 00; June–mid-Aug 10am–5pm, until 6pm in July; charge) at Fiskumfossen. Namsos is also home to the **Nord Trøndelag Art Gallery** (Fylkesgalleri; tel: 74 21 73 30; Mon–Fri 11am–4pm, Sat 11am–2pm), whose collection includes works by Norwegian and international artists.

Touched by the Gulf Stream

This is the beginning of the long valley of **Namdalen**, while to the northeast is **Røyrvik**, a huge mountainous area which stretches to the Swedish frontier. Half this region is above the tree line and there are three major lakes: Tunnsjøen, Limingen and Store Namsvatnet. The first has an island peak soaring to 812 metres (2,660ft), and was once a Sami place of sacrifice.

Here the contrast between the east and west of Nord Trøndelag is very marked. The frontier mountains to the east, which bulge into Sweden, have a harsh beauty, but much of the land is desolate and empty. To the west, the coastal scenery is a pleasant surprise, green and fertile. All year round, the Gulf Stream warms the western coast to the very north of Norway, making the climate much gentler at the same latitude than it is further inland, and allowing the Hurtigruten to continue working even in the depths of winter.

Nordland's coast and caves

The north end of Namdalen valley marks the border with the county of **Nordland**, the beginning of the real north. This border is straddled by the **Børgefjell National Park ❻**, a district of high mountains, lakes and numerous watercourses – a backpacker's idyll for walking and to see nature.

Nordland stretches 500km (300 miles) north to Narvik. The Arctic Circle (Polarsirkel) runs through the middle, and the county includes the long, narrow islands of Vesterålen and the grey peaks of the Lofoten Islands (*see pages 311–28*). Nordland has immense

variety. If you take in all the fjords and islands, it contains a quarter of Norway's coastline, as well as mountains more than 1,900 metres (6,200ft) high, countless islands and skerries, the second-largest glacier in Norway, Svartisen, and the largest inland lake, Røssvatnet.

Near the Helgeland coast is **Bindalen** (valley), green with forests. At one time, the discovery of gold turned it into a mini-Klondike. Today, it has gone back to sleep. Close to Bindal is the mountain massif of **Tosenfjellet**, a favourite haunt of potholers and cavers. The biggest cave is **Etasjegrotten ❼**, which is 1,400 metres (4,600ft) long, where cavers have discovered an underground lake.

Between Trofors and Mosjøen on the E6 is the wide but shallow **Laksfossen** (waterfall), which has a 16-metre (50ft) drop. At **Mosjøen ❽**, an industrial town where a splendid location fights for domination with a large aluminium works, there is **Dolstad** church, built in 1735 and the oldest octagonal church in north Norway. Look closely at the traces of the old ornamental decor and

TIP

The best time to see Norwegian waterfalls is in late May, or even June this far north, when summer creeps northwards, melting the snow and ice to swell the rivers.

BELOW: Vesterålen.

Flowers growing in front of Svartisen Glacier.

BELOW: the edge of Svartisen Glacier.

at a wooden angel in the ceiling, which is lowered for use as a baptismal font. Near the church is the **Vefsn Open-Air Museum** (tel: 75 11 01 22; late June–mid-Aug Mon–Sat 10am–3pm, Sun 11am–3pm; charge). Founded in 1909, it brings together 12 buildings from the surrounding district and a collection of some 5,000 objects from the old days of farming, fishing, hunting and domestic life.

Last stop before the Arctic

Beyond Mosjøen the scenery changes as farmland gives way to bare mountains (*Fjell*). There are camping sites with tents and cabins on both sides of the road north to cater for the outdoor holidaymakers who especially love these northern regions. **Mo i Rana** is also on a fjord and, like Mosjøen, is dominated by industry – in this case, the former steelworks of Norsk Jernverk, now privatised. These industries in small remote towns may displease the casual visitor, but they illustrate a Norwegian determination to minimise the pull of the more populated south and to help people to find work locally.

Though Mo i Rana itself may be too modern for a visitor's taste, it is within reasonable distance of several "must sees" – caves, a glacier and the Arctic Circle (Polarsirkel).

The **Grønnligrotten** ❾ (caves; tel: 75 13 92 00; June–Aug, guided tours throughout the day; charge) lie about 20km (12 miles) north of the town, and guides shepherd parties 40 minutes through a glittering underground world of stalactite-hung caverns. At **Setergrotta** the cave calls for care and is more suitable for enthusiasts, with unexplored caves, crevices and passages, and interiors of marble and limestone. Guided tours can be arranged (tel: 95 97 44 97).

From Mo i Rana, it is easy to reach Norway's second-largest glacier, **Svartisen** ❿ (Black Ice), which covers 370 sq km (140 sq miles) over two separate glaciers, east and west side. It is also one of the lowest-lying glaciers on the European mainland, reaching down to within 170 metres (560ft) of sea level. The route lies off the E6, 32km (20 miles) north of Mo i Rana, which heads northwest to Svartis Lake. You then cross the water by boat, and walk about 3km (2 miles) to the glacier.

Crossing into the Arctic

Many try but few have managed to explain why it is so exciting to cross a line you cannot see. But most people experience an inexplicable thrill and sense of achievement as they cross the **Arctic Circle ⓫** (Polarsirkel). It seems to mark the end of modern comforts and the beginning of the wild north, and nowhere is that sense of entering the unknown stronger than on highway E6 on its long trek north.

From Mo i Rana, the road makes its way through the temperate landscape of Dunderlandsdalen, past Storsforshei iron-ore mine. Then, beyond Krokstrand, the scenery begins to change as the road approaches **Saltfjellet**, a wild and majestic valley flanked by bare, brooding mountains. Apart from the road, railway line and river, there is nothing else until you come to the monuments that mark the Arctic Circle. Alongside the official markers are numerous small stone cairns erected by visitors who felt a common

need to mark the event. A short visit to the architecturally pleasing **Arctic Circle Centre** (Polarsirkelsenteret; tel: 75 12 96 96; mid-July–mid-Aug 8am–10pm; June–mid-July and late Aug 9am–8pm; May and early–mid-Sept 10am–6pm) is a good way of celebrating the moment. The centre provides information on the local flora and fauna, the climate and Sami culture – and also sells souvenirs.

There is a darker side to this area, which dates back to World War II when thousands of prisoners-of-war, mainly Yugoslavs and Russians, were used to build the railway. Many perished in the bitter winter conditions, and their memorial stands in the wild mountains where they worked and died.

The summit of the Saltfjell road, at **Stødi**, is 700 metres (2,300ft) high; these mountains mark the limit for most temperate flora and fauna. As the road begins to descend, first the trees reappear at Lønsdal and then, as it races down towards sea level at Rognan, the vegetation becomes lush and abundant but flanked by impressive mountains on either side. About halfway down, a

The winter colours of the Arctic fox stand out against the summer landscape.

BELOW:
reindeer in the North Cape.

The area around Fauske provides the unique reddish marble known as Norwegian Rose, which has been used to decorate major buildings all over the world, including the United Nations building in New York.

BELOW: inside Blood Road Museum.

detour to the right and a steep climb to **Junkerdalen** takes you to the "silver road", a historic route from Skellefteå, on the Gulf of Bothnia in Sweden, to Bodø. This dramatic mountain scenery also leads to a remarkable botanical phenomenon. A bedrock of mica, which provides exceptional growing conditions, has led to a profusion of rare plants such as cyclamens, usually found only in lowland or more temperate regions. Nowhere else can you find similar growth at this height and nearly 67 degrees north.

At **Rognan** ⓬, the **Saltdal Museum** (mid-June–Aug daily 11am–5pm; charge) includes the ominously named **Blodveimuseet** (Blood Road Museum; tel: 75 69 06 60; mid-June–Aug daily 11am–5pm), the only museum in Norway dedicated to prisoners-of-war. The 1,657 Yugoslav, Russian and Polish prisoners who died here in World War II are buried in a cemetery a little further north at **Botn**. Though these prisoners slaved to build a road and not a railway, the result was the same and the stretch between Rognan to Fauske earned the name of the "blood road".

In another cemetery nearby 2,700 German soldiers are buried, and a plaque commemorates the 1,932 who died on the battle cruiser *Scharnhorst*, sunk off Nordkapp (North Cape) in 1943.

Copper, silver and gold

Fauske, on the Skjerstadfjord, is another crossroads town. The ever-present E6 goes north to south, while another road (No. 830) disappears east towards the mountains. It stops at **Sulitjelma** ⓭, which owes its existence to the discovery of copper by a Sami in 1858. The mines go down to 400 metres (1,300ft) and produced half a million tonnes of ore a year. Copper pyrites, sphalerite and iron pyrites were extracted from the ore, plus a useful haul of silver and gold.

For many years, a railway was the only link between Sulitjelma and the outside world, but when that closed the road was built over the former track-bed. The wild and desolate mountain scenery of this remote area is dominated by the **Sulitjelma Glacier**. Scenery like this and the Sulitjelma Mining Museum (tel: 75 50 35 18; mid-June–mid-Aug

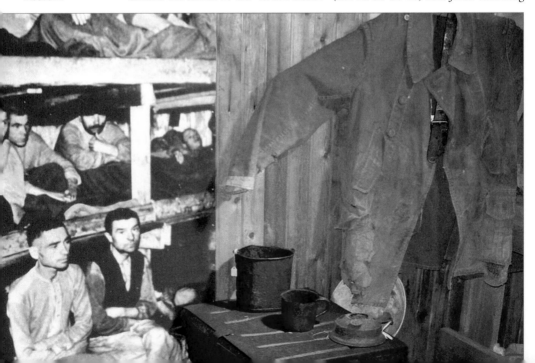

daily 11am–5pm; rest of the year Mon–Fri 9am–3pm; charge) at Sulitjelma make a detour worthwhile, and there is tourist accommodation and a camping site.

In this narrow part of Norway – and even more so as the road heads north – you are never far from either the sea or the Swedish border. At Fauske, midway between both, Road 80 and the railway turn west and run along the north of the fjord to Bodø, on the west coast.

End of the line at Bodø

Bodø ⓮ is another marker along the way to the far north. Like many of the coastal towns, it began as a small community, a safe place for boats and fishermen, and stayed small until the 1860s, when three changes brought prosperity: the herring fisheries developed fast, the Sulitjelma mines started production, and the first coastal steamer service began to link the towns of the west coast.

Bodø, too, was largely laid waste in attacks by German forces in May 1940; and today it is a spacious modern town with a population of around 45,000. It is the commercial and administrative centre of the area. It is also a staging post for summer visitors, the end of the Nordland railway line, where the backpackers alight and continue north by coastal express or bus.

The midnight sun can be seen in Bodø from 2 June to 10 July. The town is home to the **Norwegian Aviation Museum** (Norsk Luftfartsmuseum; tel: 75 50 78 50; daily all year; charge), which includes U2s, Spitfires, Mosquitos, a flight simulator and even an old traffic control tower.

Some 40km (25 miles) to the north on the coast is the old trading centre at **Kjerringøy** (late May–Aug; charge). Long overtaken by Bodø, Kjerringøy was one of the richest trading settlements in northern Norway in the 19th century. It has 15 preserved buildings, all with their furnishings, and some typical Nordland boats.

South, away from the E6

If you are travelling north on the E6, largely an inland route, when you reach Bodø again on your return journey, take another route south even

Aeroplanes on display at Bodø's Norsk Luftfartsmuseum (Norwegian Aviation Museum).

BELOW: Bodø lit by the midnight sun.

though it takes in innumerable ferry crossings. Road 17 starts by bridging the **Saltstraumen** ⑮, where the combination of powerful currents and a narrow channel twice a day creates a vast rush of water, and violent "kettles" or whirlpools. This is the most powerful maelstrom in Scandinavia: some 370 million cubic metres (480 million cubic yards) of water pour through the sound, which is less than 15 metres (50ft) wide, at a rate of up to 28 knots. Saltstraumen is a joy to anglers and seabirds alike, as the current brings an abundance of fish.

The road follows coast and fjord on its way south, and passes **Våg** on the island of Sandhornøy, and **Blixgård** (manor house; June–Aug; charge), which has a memorial to the Norwegian poet Elias Blix.

At **Glomfjord** ⑯ a chairlift gives wonderful views and you can also reach an arm of the Svartisen Glacier (Norway's second-largest, *see page 300*). However, it is better to keep to Road 17, which goes through a major tunnel under the outer edge of the glacier and comes out alongside Nordfjord, cross

the Holandsfjord and then walk to the base of the glacier.

Alstahaug's parson-poet

Four ferries later, the road reaches **Sandnessjøen**, on the northern tip of the island of **Alsten**, a trading centre for more than 300 years. **Alstahaug** ⑰ on the southern point has a 12th-century church and memorial stone to the parson-poet Petter Dass, who lived there from 1689 until his death in 1707. Dass was so well known that, after his death, most Norwegian ships carried a black patch on their sails as a badge of mourning, a practice that continued for more than 100 years. Today, his life and work are commemorated by a biennial event organised by the striking **Petter Dass Museum** (tel: 75 11 01 50; June–mid-Aug daily 10am–7pm; rest of the year Tue–Fri 10am–3.30pm, Sat–Sun 11am–5pm; charge) at Alstahaug.

A short ferry crossing takes you to the island of **Dønna**, where **Dønna Manor** has been an estate from saga times until the present day. The 13th-century stone church has secret passages cut into the walls which revealed a hoard of coins, some dating back to the time of King Håkon Håkonsson (1204–63).

On the eastern side of Alsten is a mountain range with seven peaks known as **The Seven Sisters** (De Syv Søstre). South of Sandnessjøen is **Tjøtta** which was the home of Hårek, one of the chieftains who killed King Olav at Stiklestad. This area is full of burial mounds and monoliths. There is a cemetery for 7,500 Russian prisoners-of-war and equally heart-rending is the **Riegel Cemetery**, which has the graves of 1,000 of nearly 3,000 Russians, Germans, Poles, Czechs and Norwegians who died when *Riegel* was sunk in 1945 outside Tjøtta, destroyed by Allied aircraft unaware of its human cargo.

The legend of Torghatten

Further south near Brønnøysund, and after two more ferry crossings, is another strange natural phenomenon. The hat-shaped peak of **Torghatten** ⓲ is pierced 160 metres (520ft) up by a great hole more than 40 metres (130ft) high. Legend has it that the hole was made by a horseman, thwarted in love,

who shot an arrow at his lady, the Maid of Leka. Just in time, the mountain king of Sømnafjellet saw what was happening and threw his hat in the air to intercept the arrow.

At that very moment the sun rose and all were transformed into stone. The Maid of Leka stands petrified on the island of **Leka**; Torghatten has its hole; and to the north is the island of **Hestmona** to represent the horseman. A more prosaic explanation lies in the action of frost and sea towards the end of the last Ice Age, when the island was lower than it is today. A small road takes you to Torghatten, from where it is a 30-minute scramble up to the hole.

The Brønnøysund area has some of the most fertile land in northern Norway. The island museum of Leka has many curiosities, including boats and fishing equipment. South of Leka is **Vikna**, linked to the mainland by a bridge over the Nærøysund, which, so the old legends relate, was the battleground of giants and trolls. After one more ferry, Road 17 moves inland through Namsos until it joins the E6 just north of Steinkjer.   ❏

A sea eagle spotted on a bird-watching safari.

BELOW LEFT: at Alstahaug market. **BELOW:** Brønnøysund.

LAND OF THE MIDNIGHT SUN

Some of Norway's most stunning natural wonders lie above the Arctic Circle and are a prime target for tourists visiting the north in summer

The phrase "land of the midnight sun" was originally coined by the French American explorer Paul Belloni Du Chaillu (*c.*1831–1903), who published a travelogue by the same title in 1881 after travelling extensively in northern Europe. The name caught on: more than 100 years later, tourists still flock to the North Cape every summer to experience this natural spectacle.

The phenomenon of the midnight sun is due to the inclination of the Earth's axis, and to the fact that the axis points in the same direction during the whole period of the Earth's yearly revolution around the sun. It may be witnessed at any point on the Arctic Circle on 21 June or on the Antarctic Circle on 21 December. Within these circles the length of time the sun is in the sky without setting gradually increases, being 76 days at latitude 70° and 134 days at latitude 80°. For six months, the sun never sets at the poles.

Winter Darkness

Of course, the downside to the phenomenon is that during the winter the sun never appears above the horizon and thus all regions above the polar circles are plunged into darkness as they experience a long polar night. In Tromsø this period of darkness lasts from 26 November to 15 January, while the midnight sun can be seen from 20 May to 22 July. For the people of the north, the midnight sun is not so much a phenomenon as a way of life.

ABOVE: enjoying the midnight sun – when the sun remains above the horizon at midnight – in Trømso.

BELOW: near the Arctic Circle the sun stays above the horizon all night from around 21 May to 21 July.

LEFT: the winter sun is a popular draw to the north.

THE NORTHERN LIGHTS

The northern lights, or aurora borealis *(above)*, are a huge natural light show, filling the winter sky with patterns of light and colour.

In medieval Europe this remarkable phenomenon was thought to be reflections of heavenly warriors; we now know that it originates from electric particles sent out into space by the sun. These are drawn into the Earth's magnetic field where they collide with other particles in our atmosphere. The resulting electric charges give rise to the greenish patterns of light which dance across the night sky.

The sun has a number of holes in its corona from which high-energy particles stream out. These particles are ejected into the solar system as solar wind that meets the Earth's magnetosphere, compressing it on the daylight side, while drawing out the tail at night.

The solar wind particles accelerate to Earth along the open magnetic fields of the polar regions. When the particles collide with air molecules their energy is transferred into light. These processes occurring simultaneously result in the northern lights.

ABOVE: glacier-walking on Briksdal Glacier, an arm of Jostedal.

ABOVE: kayaking is popular among hardy adventurous types in the fjord region.

THE FAR NORTH

For many, the aim of travelling this far north
is to visit Nordkapp, Norway's northernmost tip;
along the way you can go island-hopping in
the Lofotens or cross the great expanse
of the Finnmarksvidda

V iewed from the mainland across
the broad expanse of Vestfjord,
the **Lofoten Islands** present an
imposing wall of jagged peaks rising
up sheer from the sea. On the west
these mountains form a mighty break-
water from the onslaught of the Arctic
Ocean, a 112km (70-mile) archipelago
which stretches from the tiny island
of Røst in the south to the waters of
the narrow Raftsundet in the north. In
winter the coast is one of the stormiest
in Europe, while the unsurpassed summer beauty of the islands makes them
one of Norway's major tourist attractions. The midnight sun is visible from
27 May until 17 July.

Between the mountains, which are
composed of some of the oldest rocks
in the world, are stretches of fertile
farmland, fjords and deep ravines,
while the coastline is sprinkled with
white sandy beaches, fishing villages
and one or two small towns.

A phenomenon peculiar to the Lofotens is the annual cod fishing, which in
the past involved up to 6,000 boats and
30,000 fishermen. Between January
and March these migrant fishermen
lived in simple waterside wooden cabins called *rorbuer*. By 1947 the number
of fishermen was declining, and today
it is down to 2,000, and this seasonal

event has been replaced by a year-
round fishing fleet. In the summer, the
cod is left to dry on traditional wooden
racks by the harbour.

Around the Lofotens

Svolvær ❶, the main town on the
island of Austvågøy, has been a trading centre since the 17th century. Surrounded by water, and confusing to the
visitor on that account, it is flanked
by sharp, pointed rocky peaks. Some
of these rise almost straight up from
the gardens, and the town has its own

Main attractions
THE LOFOTEN ISLANDS
WHALE SAFARIS
HAMSUN CENTRE
TROMSØ
HJEMMELUFT ROCK CARVINGS
KAUTOKEINO (SAMI CULTURE)
HAMMERFEST
NORTH CAPE
KARASJOK
KIRKENES

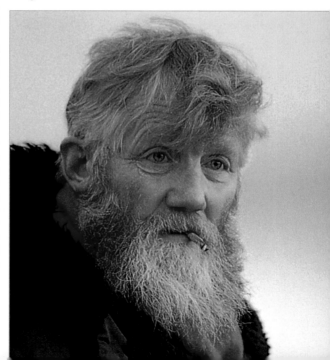

PRECEDING PAGES: Røst in the Lofoten
Islands. **LEFT:** small boats and *rorbuer*
(old fishing cottages) in Stamsund.
RIGHT: island fisherman.

Many of the old rorbuer on the Lofotens have been restored and fitted with modern conveniences and are rented out to summer visitors.

special mountain, the Svolværgeita ("Svolvær goat"). Svolvær is connected to the mainland by ferry to Skutvik, and by boat (including the coastal express) and air to Bodø. It, like the Lofotens as a whole, has attracted many artists and craftsmen, and is now the site of the **North Norwegian Artists' Centre** (Nordnorsk Kunstnersenter; tel: 76 06 67 70; all year; charge). Scenes like those described above are captured on canvas by local artist Dagfinn Bakke who owns and runs a gallery here (May–Aug), while at **Kabelvåg ➋** there is an art school and an impressive wooden church which looks old but was in fact built in 1898.

Payment in fish

On the outskirts of Kabelvåg is the **Lofoten Museum** (Lofotmuseet; tel: 76 06 97 90; June–Aug daily 10am– 7pm; times vary rest of the year; charge), sited where Vågar, the first town north of the Arctic Circle, existed in the Middle Ages. In the 14th century, 80 percent of Norway's national export was stockfish, allowing Vågar a broad market and cultural exchange

with Europe. The main museum building was originally in the centre of the thriving fishing community, and one room is furnished as a fish station owner's office from the 1880s. He would own all the *rorbuer*, and the fishermen who rented them would pay in fish from their catches. There is a typical *rorbu* from 1797, with its primitive and crowded living conditions, and a boathouse with three traditional boats of various sizes. Another building is devoted to the development of the Lofoten fishing industry, which in its modernised form plays a vital role in the economy of the islands.

Kabelvåg is also home to the **Lofoten Aquarium** (Lofotakvariet; tel: 76 07 86 65; Feb–Nov daily 10am–7pm June–Aug; charge), which is designed as a small fishing village, and includes both salt- and freshwater fish and a seal tank as well.

Island-hopping, Norwegian-style

To journey south on the E10 means going from island to island, all of which, bar one, have been linked by

The Far North

impressive bridges. This route must rank as one of the most outstanding in Norway. At every turn the traveller is confronted with another seemingly haphazard series of jagged peaks possessing a stark beauty which contrasts with the green scenery at sea level.

On the southern tip of Austvågøy is **Henningsvær**, one of numerous Lofoten fishing villages and home to the Karl Erik Harr Gallery. The imposing bridge over Gimsøystraumen, 840 metres (2,760ft) long, provides access to the small island of Gimsøya. From here a second bridge takes the road across Sundklakkstraumen to Vestvågøy. **Stamsund**, on a secondary road, is a coastal village and a port of call for the Hurtigruten.

The **Lofotr Viking Museum** in Borg (tel: 76 08 49 00; open daily 10am–7pm in summer; charge) includes a reconstruction of an 83-metre (272ft) long Viking chieftain's house (the largest of its kind found in Norway), a smithy and three Viking ships. Guides in period dress demonstrate old crafts, and various activities take place in summer (you can help row the Viking

ship, for example). **Leknes** is the main centre of population on the island and a typical small Norwegian town with a long straggling main street.

Flakstadøya heritage site

A few kilometres south of Leknes at Lilleeidet there was once a ferry to **Flakstadøya**, which was replaced by a tunnel that goes 50 metres (165ft) below the surface of Nappstraumen.

The west coast of Flakstadøya provides the surprise of wide **sandy beaches**. On a sunny summer's day, the sight of children paddling belies the fact that it is in the Arctic. The hamlet of **Flakstad ❸** has a pretty 18th-century church with an onion dome, while nearby are monuments to those who died in World War II and fishermen whose lives were lost at sea.

Nusfjord ❹ and Sund are two other fishing villages on the island. The former is on Unesco's list of preservation-worthy environments because of its unique wooden structures (Nusfjord is considered the best-preserved fishing village in the whole of Norway), while Sund has a small fisheries museum and

The Varanger peninsula in eastern Finnmark is one of the best places in Norway for bird-watching.

The Sortland Bridge, one of the many stunning bridges between islands in the Lofoten and Vesterålen archipelagos.

BELOW: a statue looks out to sea from Leknes on the Lofoten island of Vestvågøy.

smithy, famed for its stylishly crafted steel cormorants (June–Aug; charge). Also on the island is **Storbåthallaren**, the oldest known Stone Age settlement in northern Norway, populated 6,000 years ago.

The last bridge takes the road across to the island of Moskenesøya. This also has its quota of fishing villages, of which the most picturesque is **Reine**. Here you can hire a kayak or a bike to explore the area, or visit the excellent Gallery Eva Harr.

Ending at Å

The E10 finally runs out at Å ➎ – aptly named, as "Å" is the last letter of the Norwegian alphabet – which marks the end of the line of peaks that make up the **Lofotenveggen** (Lofoten "wall"). It has one of the few trading posts to be preserved in its original condition. There is the small **Norwegian Fishing Village Museum** (Norsk Fiskeværsmuseum; tel: 76 09 14 88; all year; closed weekends Sept–June; charge) in a 19th-century barn, and a café opposite offers coffee and homemade cakes. Beyond the tip of Moske-

nesøya is the **Moskenesstraumen** ➏, a maelstrom which may not match the Saltstraumen near Bodø but which was once greatly feared by sailors. Even in calm weather it seethes and boils, and was made famous through the works of Jules Verne, in *20,000 Leagues Under the Sea*, and Edgar Allan Poe.

The maelstrom separates Moskenesøya from the small island of **Værøy**, beyond which is the even smaller island of **Røst** ➐. These are the "bird islands", which attract thousands of different species including puffin, auk, eider, guillemot, kittiwake and cormorant. Both islands have small airfields with flights to Bodø, obviating a sea trip which, because of the rapidly changing sea conditions, can be unpleasant. Thanks to the Gulf Stream, Røst and Værøy do not have severe winters, and sheep can graze on the meadows.

Vesterålen: home of the Hurtigruten

North of Svolvær the views may be splendid but they do not quite measure up to those in the south. The road keeps close to the Austnesfjord, beyond

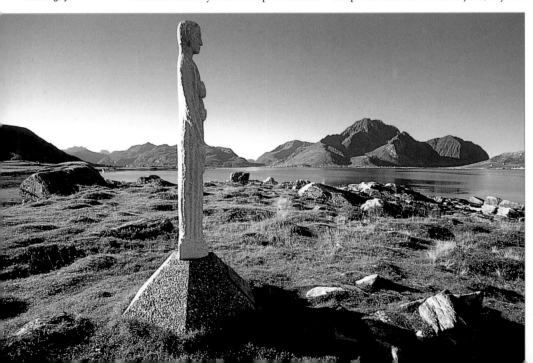

which, to the northeast, is Raftsundet and the narrow **Trollfjord**, which is used by the coastal steamer in summer. At Fiskebøl the ferry takes the visitor away from the Lofotens to **Melbu** on the first of the Vesterålen Islands, **Hadseløya**. As if to emphasise that you have left the Lofotens behind, Melbu has the **Vesterålen Museum** (all year; charge; tel: 76 15 75 56), housed in an Empire-style manor house.

Between Melbu and Stokmarknes on the northern side of the island is **Hadsel Kirke** (church; 1824), distinctive in style and with an altarpiece from 1520. **Stokmarknes** is the headquarters of the Vesteraalen Steamship Company, founded by Richard With, sometimes called the father of the coastal steamer. At the **Hurtigruten Museum** (Hurtigrutemuseet; tel: 76 11 81 90; mid-June–mid-Aug daily 10am–6pm; times vary the rest of the year; charge), you may buy special Hurtigruten tickets for return trips to Svolvær.

The Hadsel Bridge carries the main road to the island of **Langøya**. Here the principal town is **Sortland**, a commercial centre with a fishing harbour

that has a busy and pleasant atmosphere. The western side of the island has imposing mountains, the most unusual being the sway-backed **Reka** at 620 metres (2,000ft), which is popular with climbers.

Whale safaris

The **Sortland Bridge** ❽, 950 metres (3,150ft) long, is the link to **Hinnøya**, mainland Norway's largest island, which hosts a popular festival every June in Harstad. Away to the northwest is the long island of **Andøya**, which is also connected by bridge and, unlike most other Vesterålen islands, is flat. Much of the land is peat, renowned for its cloudberries.

Andenes ❾, at the northwestern extremity, is a large fishing village with the **Polar Museum** (Polarmuseet; tel: 76 11 54 32; daily late June–mid-Aug; charge). It was a fishing village in the Middle Ages and then a Dutch whaling base in the 17th century. Today it is one of the starting points of the famous **whale safaris** *(see margin)*.

Hinnøya's varied scenery includes farmland along the coastal fringe,

TIP

Whale safaris are very popular, so it is worth booking in advance. Trips leave from Andenes, Stø and Nyksund and last 3–5 hours. If you don't spot a whale first time around, repeat the journey for free. Details from the tourist information office in Svolvær, tel: 76 06 98 00; www.whalesafari.no.

BELOW: morning service at Hadsel Kirke (church), Vesterålen.

Salami for sale in the Lofotens.

BELOW: the Lofotens.

green valleys, rugged mountains and fjords. Following the E10 southeast from the Sortland Bridge you come to Lødingen on the eastern coast, with a ferry service to **Bognes** on the mainland and the E6. A little further to the north is **Trondenes** , which has a 13th-century stone church (all year). In the bay below there are Viking burial mounds. Also here are the **Adolf Cannons** (Adolfkanonen; June–Aug), massive long-range guns installed by the Germans during World War II to protect the approaches to Narvik.

A final lengthy bridge carries the E10 over **Tjeldsundet** and onto the mainland, with the road skirting Ofotfjord, which provides deep-water access to Narvik.

Taking the E6 north

If the Lofoten and Vesterålen islands are ignored, the only alternative way north is by the E6. From Fauske it clings to the side of fjords, going through a succession of tunnels, with the **Rago National Park** away to the east. This is a vast mountainous area with no roads, judged to be the most magnificent but least accessible of all Norway's national parks.

A superb section of highway has been built from Sommarset, where formerly there was a ferry, which cuts across exciting mountainous country. There are several tunnels, the longest being below the Sildhopfjell.

North of Kråkmo, at **Sagelv**, there are 5,000-year-old rock carvings of reindeer. At Ulvsvåg a road goes off west to **Skutvik** for the ferry to Svolvær. The road continues onto Engeløya island, which was a seat of power many centuries ago, and there are numerous graves and burial mounds, the biggest being at **Sigarshaugen**. At Presteid on the island of Hamarøy you will find the new **Hamsun Centre** , dedicated to Norway's most famous novelist (*see box, below*).

Back on the E6, a little north of **Bognes**, are more rock carvings depicting 40 different subjects. To the east of Tysfjord is a mountainous section popular with climbers, especially **Stetind**, 1,392 metres (4,567ft) high, which is called the "world's greatest obelisk". There are many caves for those who

Hamsun Centre

The Hamsun Centre (Hamsunsenteret; tel: 75 50 35 00; www.hamsunsenteret.no; mid-June to mid-Aug daily 11am–6pm; rest of the year Tue–Fri 10am–3.30pm, Sat–Sun 11am–5pm; charge), located in Presteid on Hamarøy, west of Narvik, was opened in 2009 to mark the 150th anniversary of the birth of Knut Hamsun (1859–1952), Norway's most famous novelist, considered by many as the father of the modern novel. Hamsun, who received the Nobel Prize for Literature in 1920, was a controversial figure in his homeland, as famous for his writings as for his Nazi sympathies. He was a fervent supporter of the Nazi regime both before and after World War II, and famously mailed his Nobel medal to Joseph Goebbels. His best-known works include *Growth of the Soil, Hunger* and *Mysteries*.

prefer to go down rather than up, the best known being **Råggejavie**, 620 metres (2,000ft) deep.

Narvik

The deep, ice-free waters of the Ofotfjord allowed **Narvik** ⓬ to become a major centre for exporting iron ore mined in northern Sweden. A railway was completed from the mining town of Kiruna to the port in 1883. Narvik is now the end of the Ofotbanen line, the Norwegian railway connecting with the northern Swedish line. In World War II Narvik was the scene of bitter fighting, and German forces occupied it for over five years – portrayed in the **War Museum** (Krigsminnemuseum; tel: 76 94 44 26; all year, times vary; charge). For an overview of Narvik take the cable car (in summer) 650 metres (2,132ft) to the top of Fagernes. At ground level Narvik is uninteresting, which is maybe why the local tourist office sells tickets for the "tourist train" (June–Aug), a three-hour guided tour between Narvik and the Swedish border, with photo opportunities and a chance to buy Sami souvenirs.

Troms, a county of contrasts

North of Narvik the E6 crosses Rombakfjord over another major bridge, passes the junction with the road to Sweden, and joins with the E10 at Bjerkvik. Then it follows a climb up Gratangseidet county boundary into Troms. Troms has widely contrasting scenery, all typically north Norwegian: rugged mountains with sharp peaks, countless islands and skerries, a softer landscape at sea level and fast-flowing rivers and numerous lakes. The county is split up by a number of major fjords and is also notable for its extensively forested valleys.

Setermoen, just north of Narvik, lies in the heart of a military area and has a large garrison. The military presence is also apparent further north at Bardufoss, with its major airbase. From Bardufoss the E6 follows the Målselv

River until it turns abruptly east past Takvatnet, where a new turn-off provides some stunning views of distant mountains. Near **Balsfjord church** (kirke), about 10km (6 miles) from Storsteinnes, are rock carvings which are 2,500 to 4,000 years old. The area around Balsfjord has some of the richest farming land in Troms, and goat-farming is a major activity.

Predators at Øvre NP

Alternatively, before you get to Bardufoss turn eastwards at Elverum onto Road 857, from which you can reach **Målselvfossen** ⓭ (waterfall). It may only have a drop of 15 metres (50ft), but it extends over 600 metres (2,000ft). There are salmon ladders, and the Målselv River, which is renowned for its salmon, was discovered by English anglers in the 1840s. At Rundhaug a secondary road follows the Målselv River to Øverbygd, then continues along **Tamokdalen** until it rejoins the E6 near Øvergård.

To the south, adjacent to the border with Sweden, lies the **Øvre Dividal National Park** ⓮, where all four of

TIP

The rock carvings near Balsfjord church (Kirke) are part of the Tennes Heritage Trail, which is one of the many trails included in *Fotefar mot Nord (Trails to the North)* available from tourist offices.

BELOW: *rallar* (railwayman) statue in Narvik.

Norway's major predators – bear, wolf, lynx and wolverine – have their habitat.

Tromsø, city of the Arctic

Tromsø ⓰ occupies most of the island of Tromsøya and overflows onto the adjoining island of Kvaløya. With a population of 67,300 it is the largest city in northern Norway and, until the opening of the first bridge, in 1960, everything had to be ferried across from the mainland.

Today there is a second bridge and an amazing network of road tunnels under the city, including subterranean car parks and roundabouts that appear to be formed around giant stalactites. The tunnel system links the city centre with Tromsø Langnes International Airport: if you arrive by air and take a taxi the driver will gladly take you via the tunnel system (at the extra cost of the toll). The town has variously been called the Gateway to the Arctic, the Arctic Ocean City and even the Paris of the North.

Archaeological finds indicate settlements dating back 9,000 years. Tromsø became an ecclesiastical centre in 1252,

and much of the subsequent development from 1300 to the 1700s was influenced by the Hanseatic League. Trade restrictions led to strong dependence on Bergen throughout the Middle Ages. In 1794, the town was granted market town (*kaupang*) privileges and the right to independent trade, and became a focal point for the Pomor trade, with Russian ships bringing timber, rape, flour and other items from the White Sea in exchange for fish and goods brought north by the Hanseatic traders.

In the early 19th century Tromsø was the natural starting point for trapping expeditions to the pack ice both to the north and east to Svalbard (Spitsbergen). It has also been the site of a number of sea battles, including the sinking of the German battleship *Tirpitz*, pride of the German fleet, which was destroyed by British bombers while guarding the entrance to Tromsø in 1944.

Tromsø has one of the greatest amounts of northern-light activity in the world, but in midsummer the skies are too light for this phenomenon.

BELOW: Tromsø.
BELOW RIGHT: racks of drying fish have their own "guards" to deter hungry birds.

Polar art and worship

Though fishing (for shrimps, herring and other fish) is of prime importance, Tromsø University and a regional teaching hospital are also major employers here. **Tromsø University Museum** (tel: 77 64 50 00; daily 9am–6pm June–Aug; times vary rest of the year; charge) focuses on the cultural and natural history of the north and the Sami, and contains a reconstructed Viking longhouse. Polar explorers are the centre of attention at the **Polar Museum** (Polarmuseet; tel: 77 60 66 30; mid-June–mid-Aug daily 10am–7pm; times vary rest of the year; charge) in the historic harbour area. Housed in a distinctive building a bit further south on the waterfront, **Polaria** (tel: 77 75 01 00; mid-May–mid-Aug daily 10am–7pm; rest of year noon–5pm; charge) is another stop for anyone interested in the Arctic, and includes a museum, an aquarium and a 3D cinema.

The **Art Museum of Northern Norway** (Nordnorsk Kunstmuseum; tel: 77 64 70 20; all year Tue–Fri 10am–5pm, Sat–Sun noon–5pm; free) has a good collection of Sami and northern Norwegian art. In the centre of the town is the **Cathedral** (Domkirke; June–Aug, Tue–Sun) dating from 1861, one of the country's largest wooden churches.

Situated on the mainland is the striking **Arctic Cathedral** (Ishavskatedralen; June–mid-Aug Mon–Sat 9am–7pm, Sun from 1pm; times vary rest of the year; charge), designed by Jan Inge Hovig and completed in 1965. The cathedral features a huge stained-glass window by Victor Sparre covering the entire east wall, 23 metres (75ft) high, depicting the Second Coming. Nearby is the cable car to the top of the **Storsteinen** (420 metres/1,380ft), from where there are magnificent views over the town and the surrounding area. Tromsø also contains botanical gardens, and Europe's northernmost brewery, Mack, established in 1877 and famous for its Arctic Ale. The brewery is a short walk from the centre, and there is a beer hall on the premises.

Where glacier and sea meet

To the northwest of Tromsø a number of islands stand guard where the lengthy Ullsfjord and **Lyngenfjord**

Tromsø is situated right in the centre of the northern lights zone, and is one of the best places on Earth to observe the phenomenon. The sky must be dark and clear (without clouds) for the lights to be visible, which is why you will never see them in summer.

BELOW: the Arctic Cathedral (Ishavskatedralen) in Tromsø represents the shape of a Sami tent and the iciness of a glacier.

reach the sea. Between these is a long, wide peninsula. On its eastern side lie the range of mountains known as the **Lyngen Alps** (Lyngsalpene). The full majesty of these snow-capped peaks and glaciers is best seen from the eastern side of Lyngenfjord. There is a short cut that avoids the main road and affords fine views of the mountains. Take Road 91 just south of Tromsø through the Breivik valley, a ferry across Ullsfjord to Svensby, then drive to Lyngseidet and a second ferry across Lyngenfjord to Olderdalen and the E6.

The more obvious route is south along the E8 to where it joins the E6 at Nordkjosbotn and then northeast through Skibotn, keeping along the shore of the Lyngenfjord with its views of the mountains across the water. After continuing east along the side of the Rotsundet, opposite the island of Uløya, the road swings inland before meeting Reisafjord. There are fine views to the west, which are even better after climbing over the summit of **Kvænangsfjellet**. There is an impressive panorama of islands and moun-

tains before descending to Burfjord. Just past Alteidet, a minor road goes north to the Jøkelfjord where the **Øksfjordjøkelen** (glacier) calves into the sea, the only one in Norway to do so. To the east is the boundary into Norway's most remote county, Finnmark.

Finnmark

Noone describes Finnmark without a combination of superlatives and impressive statistics. It is Norway's most northerly county and the largest, covering 48,000 sq km (18,500 sq miles), equal to 15 percent of the entire country, and yet it has only just over 72,000 inhabitants, less than 2 percent of the population.

Finnmark lies along the same latitude as Alaska, but the Gulf Stream ensures that the harbours do not freeze even in the depths of winter. Inland, the temperature can drop to a chilling –50°C (–70°F), while during the short summer it may hit 32°C (90°F). Between mid-May and the end of July the sun never sets – you can read a newspaper outside at midnight – while in winter the sun stays snug below the

BELOW: the Hurtigruten at Ullsfjord.

Scorched Earth

World War II was a particular nightmare for Finnmark. When Soviet liberators crossed Norway's northern border in the autumn of 1944, the German occupation forces began a "scorched earth" policy as they retreated south, burning towns and villages and even individual farms as they went. Whatever fields or forests they encountered were not spared either, and local transportation and communication infrastructure suffered as a result.

The result of this widespread devastation can be seen in **Alta**, the first town across the county border from Troms and the biggest in Finnmark, where some of the architecture is undistinguished. This is often the case in the towns of northern Norway, which had to rebuild rapidly after the war came to an end.

horizon from the end of November to the end of January.

The scenery is spectacular, with the highest areas in the northwest and a vast mountain plateau, the **Finnmarks-vidda**, to the south and southeast. The bare grey rocks of the coast take the full force of the winter storms. It is the vastness of the uninhabited areas that makes the greatest impression: ranges of mountains and *fjell* stretch away to the horizon, seemingly without end, silent and awe-inspiring.

Much of this wonderful county is now easily accessible by car or public transport on well-surfaced main roads, while there is an extensive network of air services which land at tiny airports dotted all over the area, and the Hurti-gruten serves towns and villages along the coast.

The people of Finnmark are greatly attached to their part of Norway, which has been inhabited for 10,000 years. They include not only Norwegians and Sami (Lapps) but also many Finns. The Norwegians settled the coast in the 14th century, but major changes in the 18th and 19th centuries brought in

people from the south of the country. At the same time came a large migra-tion from Finland and Sweden.

Ancient rock carvings

On the southern outskirts of **Alta** is an outstanding collection of prehis-toric rock carvings at **Hjemmeluft** ⓲ (signs from Alta; tel: 78 45 63 30; all year, times vary; charge). Discovered in 1972 and on Unesco's World Heritage list, there are about 5,000 carvings on four different sites. The biggest concen-tration is at Hjemmeluft itself. These "stories in pictures" are about 2,500 to 6,000 years old and depict people, animals (particularly reindeer), boats and weapons. Traces of these early inhabitants, the Komsa people, were discovered in 1925 on Komsafjell, on Altafjord. The dwelling sites go back some 10,000 years – a sobering reminder of how long humans have lived in this inhospitable region.

Sami culture

Finnmark has few roads, so it's easy to find your way. Going south from Alta is Road 93 to **Kautokeino** ⓳ and the

One of the prehistoric carvings at Hjemmeluft.

BELOW LEFT: an early print of a Sami woman and child. **BELOW:** near the Finnmark coast.

*The Sami language is
related to, yet very
different from,
Finnish, Estonian
and Hungarian.
There are many
dialects, of which
North Sami is the
most widely spoken.*

Finnish frontier. Kautokeino is the largest Sami community in the country, the centre of Sami education with a reindeer-herding school, and possibly the coldest town in Norway. The **Kulturhuset** has the only Sami theatre in Norway, and the **Samisk Museum** (all year; charge) has exhibits showing life in Old Kautokeino.

Northwards from Leirbotnvatn (around the fjord from Alta) to the village of **Skaidi** are 45km (28 miles) of sheer emptiness. The E6 takes a lonely course through the wild countryside. Almost the only building is the small **Sami chapel**, dwarfed by its surroundings. The only signs of life away from the road are the herds of reindeer. You are constantly aware of how little human activity has impinged on the grandeur of these great empty spaces.

History of disasters

Skaidi is a popular base for anglers, hunters and winter-sports enthusiasts. It is also the junction of the E6 and Road 94 to **Hammerfest ⍉**, 56km (35 miles) away on the bare, rocky island of Kvaløya. Hammerfest is the world's most northerly town. Founded in 1789, for centuries it was the best ice-free harbour in northern waters, although storms and hurricanes plus many man-made disasters have repeatedly wrought havoc on the town. In 1825, a hurricane destroyed houses and boats, and an even more ferocious storm in 1882 moved the German kaiser, Queen Victoria and the tsar of Russia to donate money to repair the considerable damage.

In 1890, the town had ambitious plans for a hydroelectric power station, but only a month after work started, fire again destroyed two-thirds of the town. In the following year, nevertheless, Hammerfest became the first European town to have electric lighting when it purchased a generator from Thomas Edison in 1891.

The harbour has always been of importance both commercially and strategically, and ships have long called there. For more than 100 years it was also the principal Norwegian base for hunting and fishing. When Norway was invaded in 1940, it was a growing and flourishing community. The

BELOW:
Hammerfest.

retreating Germans burned down the entire town, and by 10 February 1945 it had been wiped out except for the **chapel** in the graveyard. Today, Hammerfest is Norway's main trawler port and an increasingly important base for offshore oil and gas activity tied to the Snow White field.

Measuring the planet

Hammerfest clings to the shoreline, which is backed by a steep escarpment. Its most notable monument is the **Meridian Column** (Meridianstøtta), which was erected by King Oskar II in the late 19th century to mark the first international measurement of the Earth (1815–52), a joint enterprise by Russia, Norway and Sweden.

On the highest point of a walk from the town up the escarpment is the Midday Pole, topped by a cannonball. When the shadow from the pole points directly to the Meridian Column, the time is 12 noon precisely.

In 1809, after Norway entered the Napoleonic Wars, two British warships attacked Hammerfest. The town fell and the British stayed for a week of plunder and destruction. The cannonball placed on top of the Midday Pole is the permanent reminder of this unhappy event.

To prevent further attack the military built a redoubt or **Skansen** in 1810 with eight guns, which, Hammerfest folk are happy to report, never fired in anger. This walk also passes a beacon built by the town's young people in 1882–3 "as they had no other amusements".

More noticeable today is the circular **Polar Bear Hall** (Isbjørnhallen), used for sporting events and exhibitions. At the other end of town is the equally striking **church** (June–Aug), its form inspired by traditional fish-drying racks. Its altarpiece, a glass mosaic dating from 1632, comes from the town's first church.

In a shrewd move in 1963, Hammerfest created the **Royal and Ancient Polar Bear Society** (Isbjørnklubben), which offers one of the more attractive souvenirs of its kind. To get a certificate of membership, you must apply in person to the society's **museum** (tel: 78 41 31 00; June–Aug daily 9am–5pm; Sept–

Watch out for elk crossing.

BELOW: North Cape (Nordkapp)

June daily 10.30am–1.30pm; charge) in the town hall.

On top of Europe

From Skaidi the E6 goes northeast across wild, uninhabited territory before the road descends to the sea at Olderfjord. Here most visitors turn north for **North Cape** ㉑ (Nordkapp), Europe's northernmost point. This is for many the end of their pilgrimage by car, motor home, motorbike, bus or even bicycle. The alternative is to fly to Honningsvåg or sail there by Hurtigruten or cruise liner.

The road hugs the edge of Porsangenfjord, with rugged country to the landward side, and ends at Kåfjord, where a ferry and tunnel connect to **Honningsvåg** on the island of Magerøya (toll). Between Honningsvåg and Nordkapp lie 35km (21 miles) of the only genuine Arctic scenery in Europe. It may be bare and treeless, but there is an unusual beauty about the island which, on a sunny day, is emphasised by the clarity of the atmosphere; too often, alas, it is misty. The coastal steamers have provided the biggest

impetus to tourist traffic, and by 1920, the wild grandeur of the headland had learned to live with the incongruity of its first building. The road from Honningsvåg opened in 1956, as did a centre with the usual souvenir shop, cafeteria and post office.

In 1989, this earlier building gave way to the **North Cape Hall** (Nordkapphallen; tel: 78 47 68 60; all year, times vary; charge), with its circular Compass Restaurant and, below, the Supervideograph, a 225-degree screen with wraparound sound which brings the four seasons of Finnmark to the visitor, whatever the time of year. It also has a chapel for marriage ceremonies. Nordkapp illustrates the seasonal extremes in this area: 24-hour darkness occurs from November to the end of January, while the midnight sun lasts from mid-May to the end of July.

An underground tunnel leads from the new hall and champagne bar, which is like an amphitheatre cut out of the rock and overlooks the Arctic Ocean. Even if you suffer from vertigo, look briefly from the balcony, which provides a spectacular view straight

A New Route to China

The name North Cape was given to the imposing headland by an Englishman, Captain Richard Chancellor. In 1553, as master of the *Edward Bonaventure*, he was seeking a new route to China when he rounded Europe's most dramatic northern point; but it was not until the 19th century that Nordkapp began to attract visitors.

In 1845, passengers from the *Prinds Gustav* were rowed ashore and then had to struggle up 300 metres (1,000ft) to the plateau at the top. After a visit by the intrepid King Oskar II in 1873, Thomas Cook arranged the first organised tour for 24 Englishmen in 1875. By 1880, a path with primitive railings from Horn Bay to the top had appeared and you can still see the remains of the quay by taking the 11km (7-mile) walk from the plateau.

down to the sea far below. Along the tunnel are tableaux depicting historical events at Nordkapp. On what is in danger of becoming a crowded plateau are seven circular, wheel-like sculptures. They are monuments to the children of the world, sculpted in 1988 by seven children from seven lands to celebrate "joy, friendship and working together".

"Haddock" English

Apart from the main road to Nordkapp itself, there is only one other road on the island, which leads to the village of **Gjesvær** on the west coast. On the eastern side of Magerøya is the little fishing community of Skarsvåg. **Honningsvåg**, where the ferry arrives, has been a fishing harbour for many years and an important pilot station. In the old days, trawlers were the most frequent visitors, and up to 4,000 called each year. Most were British and, through their visits, Honningsvåg developed "haddock English", a mixture of sign language and occasional English words. Like other centres in the north, Honningsvåg was burned down during World War II, and by the

end of the war, the 1884 church was the only building left standing. There is a small local museum, the **North Cape Museum** (Nordkappmuseet; tel: 78 47 72 00; June–mid-Aug Mon–Sat 10am–7pm, Sun noon–7pm; mid-Aug–June Mon–Fri noon–4pm; charge).

Most villages and towns in Finnmark sit along the coast, but the two main Sami communities are the exception: Kautokeino and **Karasjok** ㉒ are deep inland. Returning from Nordkapp, continue south through Lakselv at the end of Porsangenfjord to get to Karasjok. The town's 1807 **Gamle Kirke** is the oldest church in Finnmark, having survived the war, and the **Sami Museum and Library** (De Samiske Samlinger; all year, times vary; charge) has a notable collection of Sami literature. Karasjok is the seat of the Sami parliament and Samiland's capital.

Sápmi, the Sami theme park (tel: 78 46 88 00; mid-June–mid-Aug 9am–7pm; rest of year times vary; charge), depicts Sami culture and history through dwellings, food, colourful costumes and handicrafts. At Karasjok the E6 makes a massive U-turn and heads

The comical puffin can be found all along the northern coasts.

BELOW: a good catch: Atlantic salmon at Honningsvåg.

BELOW:
on safari at
Kirkenes.

north again, keeping company with the **Tana River** through its every twist and turn, all the way to **Tana Bru** ㉓, which is at the first bridge across the river and is the meeting place of four roads. One is the alternative route east from Lakselv (Road 888), which veers away from the E6 at the head of Porsangerfjord. This long road has few communities but an abundance of beautiful scenery, and it rolls ahead across two magnificent inland stretches – from **Børselv** to **Laksefjord** and across the **Ifjord-fjellet**.

At Ifjord the road pushes further north to the Nordkyn peninsula and **Kjøllefjord** ㉔, Mehamn and Gamvik, across the very top of the country. About 15km (9 miles) from Kjøllefjord, including a 30-minute ramble along a well-prepared trail, are the remains of the **Oksevåg whaling station**, which was used from 1864–1905. Further walks are marked through the **Slettnes Nature and Heritage Reserve** at Gamvik (all year).

Over the bridge at Tana Bru, the road divides; the E6 winds a long route east towards **Kirkenes**, only 5km (3

miles) from the Russian border, while Road 890 heads north to **Berlevåg** and **Båtsfjord**, crossing the highest pass in Finnmark, the **Oarddojokke** at 400 metres (1,300ft) above sea level. Berlevåg and Båtsfjord are fishing villages, both on the far coast of the Varanger peninsula. Places of interest include the **Løkvika Fishing Cabin and Partisan Cave** (Fiskehytte og Partisanhule; all year), where locals fought off the Germans in World War II.

Varangerfjord

Continuing east on the E6, you come to **Varangerbotn** ㉕. In this part of Norway, where the fjords bite deep into the land, you are rarely far from water. Varangerbotn has a small but interesting Sami Museum, the **Samiske Museum** (tel: 78 95 99 20; mid-June–mid-Aug daily 10am–6pm; mid-Aug–mid-June Mon–Fri 10am–3pm; charge), and it is worth making a detour along the north coast of the Varangerfjord on Road 98 to **Vadsø** ㉖, the administrative centre of Finnmark. At **Nesseby** you will find a wooden church (1858) and Varanger's oldest log cabin (1700).

This remote area is rich in archaeological finds, indicating human occupation as early as 9000 BC.

Finnish migration

A monument in Vadsø explains why many inhabitants are of Finnish origin and Finnish-speaking (Kvens), and the local **Ruija Kven Museum** (tel: 78 94 28 90; mid-June–mid-Aug, times vary; charge) is housed in two buildings, one a Finnish-style dwelling, Tuomaingården, and the other, Esbensengården, a patrician house from 1840. Vadsø's **church**, built in 1958, is of striking appearance. In front, the King Stone bears the signatures of King Olav V of Norway, President Kekkonen of Finland and King Carl Gustav of Sweden, who all visited the town in 1977 to unveil the **Immigrant Monument** (Innvandrermonumentet) to the Finns who came to find food and work in Finnmark in the 1800s. Another landmark is the **mooring mast** (*luftskipsmasta*) used by Amundsen's airship, *Norge*, in 1926 and Nobile's airship *Italia*, two years later.

Beyond Vadsø there is only the town of **Vardø ㉗**, Norway's easternmost town and the only one situated in the Arctic climate zone. There have been fortifications at Vardø since around 1300, but the present octagonal star-shaped redoubt was built in 1738. The only remnant of the original fortress is a beam which bears the signature of King Christian IV and is dated 1599, while later monarchs have added their names: King Oskar II (in 1873), King Håkon VII (in 1907) and King Olav V (in 1959); the beam is in the **Vardøhus Fortress** (Festning; tel: 90 92 28 13; mid-Apr–mid-Sept daily 10am–9pm;until 6pm rest of the year; charge).

Along the coast west of Vardø is the abandoned fishing village of **Hamningberg** with its old architecture and church – one of the few not destroyed in World War II. As you return south again, you come to **Ekkerøya**, Finnmark's only bird rock accessible by car. Beyond Varangerbotn, the E6 follows the coast through another huge uninhabited area to the southeast and some beautiful views across the waters of Varangerfjord. **Bugøynes** is an old fishing village on the coast, which, like Hamningberg, escaped destruction in

After two months of winter darkness, Vardø celebrates the return of the sun, usually around 20 January, with a gun salute on the first day that the entire disc is visible above the horizon.

BELOW: the harbour at Vadsø.

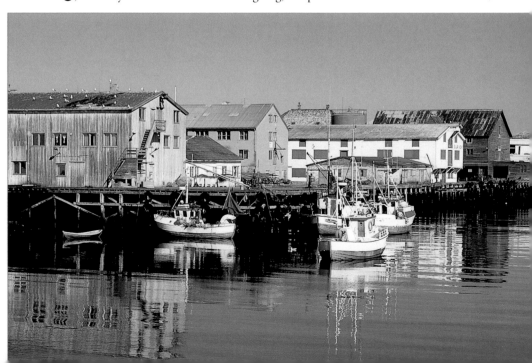

The Kirkenes Snow Hotel is built from scratch every year. Tel: 78 97 05 40; www.kirkenessnow hotel.com.

the war. Further east, **Bugøyfjord** is an old trading centre and birthplace of the Sami artist John Savio.

Only 8km (5 miles) from the Finnish border to the southwest, the little town of **Neiden** has the only Greek Orthodox church in Norway, where the Skollé Lapps worship. Each year since 1965, the church has held a service to bless the waters of the Neiden River to ensure that their reputed healing powers continue. The restored Labahå farm at Neiden, built by Finnish immigrants, is part of the **Sør-Varanger Museum** (all year daily 10am–3.30pm; charge) at Svanvik.

This easternmost wedge of Norwegian territory became important with the discovery of iron ore, at Bjørnevatn, which from 1906 until 1996 was mined and shipped from the port of **Kirkenes ㉘**. The region is also a centre for fishing, farming, forestry and reindeer husbandry. Kirkenes is dominated by the deserted installations of the Sydvaranger Iron Ore Company. Although it has acquired a brand-new hotel, the Thon Hotel Kirkenes, which opened in May 2010, the town's somewhat rough-

and-ready appearance is explained and easily forgiven when you learn that the 20th century brought no less than four wars fought in or near it. Apart from Malta, Kirkenes acquired the unsolicited honour of being the most bombed centre in Europe in World War II. It was liberated by the Russians in 1944, which engendered a rare lack of nervousness of, and sympathy for, the "Russian Bear". Subterranean tunnels used to shelter residents during the war can be visited. Kirkenes is the final point of call for the Hurtigruten coastal express before it returns south to Bergen.

Unusual border post

The extreme eastern tip of Norway, at **Grense Jakobselv**, has a chapel built on the order of King Oskar II in 1869 as an unusual means of protecting Norwegian interests. The idea of a chapel rather than a fort at this strategic location came about when the Norwegians noticed that the Russians attended their own Orthodox church not far over the border. Faced with a Protestant church, the argument ran, the Russians would realise they had strayed into Norwegian territory. This unusual approach to maintaining the frontier was highly successful.

In the extreme north of Finnmark, Norway is sometimes only a kilometre or two wide between the border and the sea, and a long pocket of the country hangs south between Russia and Finland. Here the **Øvre Pasvik National Park ㉙** (Nasjonalpark) includes the largest virgin forest in the country. This comparatively flat area has pine forests, bare rock, swamps, and two watercourses that are tributaries of the Pasvik River (the official boundary between Norway and Russia). Wildlife in the park includes elk, reindeer, bear and wolverine; there are whooper swans, great grey owls, bean geese, sea eagles, gyr falcons, spotted redshanks and cranes; the whole area is protected from development and pollution to form a peaceful border, 122km (76 miles) long between east and west. ❑

RIGHT: winter in Kautokeino.
BELOW: postboxes brighten up the winter landscape.

SVALBARD

Nearly as close to the North Pole as to Norway, the Svalbard Archipelago (with its main island of Spitsbergen) teems with bird, mammal and plant life in the short Arctic summer

NORWAY

rom Tromsø in the north of Norway, the big airliner drones almost due north for an hour and a half. Far below is a seemingly empty sea, hidden here and there by banks of clouds. Suddenly the traveller becomes aware that through the clouds, stark, jagged mountain peaks project like huge fangs, and that the clouds in between are in reality great snow-covered glaciers. This is Svalbard, the land of the pointed mountains.

The Svalbard Archipelago lies 640km (400 miles) north of the mainland of Norway and has two main islands, Spitsbergen and Nordaustlandet, with numerous smaller islands dotted around in the seas nearby. In winter, the pack ice of the Arctic is all around and only some 950km (600 miles) separate the islands from the North Pole. Only three islands are populated: Spitsbergen, Bjørnøya and Hopen.

Longyearbyen

The smooth asphalt runway lies on the narrow coastal plain between the mountains of Spitsbergen and the sea of Isfjord. With a minimum of formality, you are through customs and onto a land where the forces of nature are still in control. On the landward side, the mountain slopes darkly up into the

clouds, traversed by a row of pylons; now disused, they carried coal from the mines down to the loading jetties. The Svalbard coal mines are rare in that the mine shafts do not go down into the ground but are driven horizontally into the mountains. The township of **Longyearbyen ❶** was built solely to accommodate the people who came north, mainly from Norway, to work at the hard and dangerous job of mining coal from the inside of the mountains.

Coal was first discovered in the early 17th century, but for many years it

Main attractions
LONGYEARBYEN
SPITSBERGEN AIRSHIP MUSEUM
MINE VISITS
NORTHERN LIGHTS
BIRD COLONIES
SKIING AND DOG-SLEDGING TRIPS
BOAT TRIPS AND WALKING
POLAR BEARS

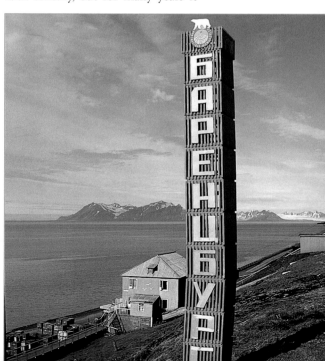

PRECEDING PAGES: freezing-cold swimming at Svalbard. **LEFT:** polar bears roam the Arctic. **RIGHT:** the Russian mining settlement of Barentsburg.

was used only as a source of fuel for trappers. Only since around 1900 have serious attempts been made to exploit this resource, and the first to claim mining rights was a Norwegian skipper from Tromsø called Zakariasen. He was followed by others, including John Longyear, an American after whom the village is named.

Over 2,000 people live in Longyearbyen, mainly in modern, well-insulated houses, served by facilities such as shops, a bank, restaurants and bars, a café, a library, and a sports centre with a swimming pool. The population is much younger than on the mainland, probably because the climate is not particularly kind to the elderly, and there are three kindergartens and one school in Longyearbyen. There is also an interesting little **museum** which, as well as stuffed examples of typical Spitsbergen birds and mammals, displays many artefacts from the days when the only people to live in these Arctic islands were a few hunters and trappers; an art gallery with permanent and changing exhibitions; and since November 2008 the **Spitsbergen**

Airship Museum, a museum focusing on the history of three airships with particular ties to the Arctic.

As if to remind you that summer, if sweet, is short: in front of most houses you will see a parked skidoo, a motor scooter with rubber tracks and steering "skis", which is the only means of transport in the long winter months when snow lies thick on the ground.

Mineral rights

After World War I, Norway was granted sovereignty over the archipelago, though the various countries which agreed to the treaty reserved the right to exploit minerals. Today, Russia is the only one of the original signatories to the Svalbard Treaty to retain an interest in coal mining, and has a substantial operation at **Barentsburg ❷**, only a few miles further down the fjord from Longyearbyen. Around 500 people, mostly Ukrainians, live in a coal-dusty village on the steep fjordside which, nevertheless, has an indoor farm of dairy cattle and chicken sheds. Kittiwakes scream from their nests on the window ledges and, on an esplanade

BELOW: hiking in Svalbard.

Svalbard

below, well-dressed fur-hatted groups sell cheap Russian souvenirs and, now and then, a family "treasure" to cruise-ship passenger.

Nature in the raw

Svalbard should not, and is unlikely ever to become, a place for mass tourism: the islands cannot support it and, in any case, the appeal is to people who like to find their own wildlife and explore nature in the raw. However, the cruise ships are beginning to threaten the peace. Longyearbyen has two hotels, several guesthouses and even a campsite, and hardly a day goes by in summer without a luxury cruise ship depositing its passengers on the shore for a barbecue or a short trip around the area. For safety reasons, visitors are normally accompanied by men with loaded guns and may not leave the pre-set routes. Thus, the polar bear takes care that mass tourism never spoils the environment and only a few well-equipped campers go further afield.

The area around Longyearbyen is a pleasant place during the summer, the stark mountains offset by a valley which has meadows spangled with flowers. Here you will find the tiny bells of cassiope mixed with purple saxifrage and, perhaps, a patch of boreal Jacob's ladder, *Polemonium boreale*, an Arctic rarity with beautiful flowers. Near the shores where the glaucous gulls congregate, look for the fleshy-leafed *Mertensia maritima*, or oyster plant.

The polar winter is a different matter. The sun does not rise above the horizon and everything is locked in darkness, lit only by the moon and the multicoloured rays of the **aurora borealis** (northern lights, *see page 307*). When the sun reappears and gathers strength, the ice pack retreats north, speeded by the warming influence of the Gulf Stream. This warm current flows up the west coast of Spitsbergen and ensures that, in summer, ships can have an ice-free passage. The sun's return is cause for a week-long Sunfestival in March, with concerts and outdoor events.

Spitsbergen is mountainous and glaciated, with around 60 percent covered in permanent ice. The high-

The small yellow blooms of the Svalbard mohn.

BELOW: a coal train in Ny-Ålesund.

est mountain, **Newtontoppen**, reaches over 1,700 metres (5,500ft). Further from the influence of the Gulf Stream, the second-largest island, **Nordaustlandet**, is almost completely covered in ice.

Unknown and unexplored

According to the old Icelandic annals, in 1194 land was found to lie "four days sailing from Langanes, at the northern end of the sea". They called it Svalbard, but then the islands were forgotten for several hundred years. The next mention was in the journals of the great Dutch explorer, Willem Barents, in 1596. Barents, with two ships under his command, was trying to find a northern route to China when he sighted an island which, from the shape of its mountains, he named Spitsbergen (Dutch for "jagged mountains"). The two ships parted, one to carry news of fjords filled with whales and walrus back to the Netherlands, while the other ship with Barents on board continued eastwards, only to become trapped in the pack ice and forced to spend the winter there, during which Barents and many of his crew died.

BELOW: taking a really close look at an Arctic skua.

Story of the whales

By 1612 hunting expeditions had begun to arrive around the coast of Spitsbergen. News of the numbers of whales spread, and soon the Dutch whalers were joined by English, French, Basques and Danes. Inevitably, trouble flared as they disputed rights and fought pitched battles when warships came north to defend the claims of their whalers.

The English and Dutch at last agreed on a division of hunting territories and some peace was restored. The Dutch set up a shore base on **Amsterdam Island**, which grew to be almost a town, with a fort, church and whale-oil refinery, and a summer population of a couple of thousand. They called it **Smeerenburg ❸**, the "blubber town", and you can still find the outlines of stone buildings and the furnaces built to render the whale blubber into oil. The large numbers of bleached whale bones testify to the growing demands for whale oil, and in some places there is further mute testimony in the graves of men who died, either in battles or from natural causes. Under the pressure of all the killing, it was inevitable that the whale stock would decline, and by around 1720 whaling ceased.

This intensive whaling was purely a summer activity. In winter the islands were deserted except by accident. In 1630, an English ship was wrecked and the crew managed to cling to life throughout the winter. In 1633, some Dutchmen wintered at Smeerenburg, but the following year those who attempted to stay on all died of scurvy. The English had intended to colonise the archipelago, but even prisoners under sentence of death refused to face the prospect of the Arctic night.

Tough life of the trapper

The Russians were made of sterner stuff, however, and in the early part of the 18th century a number of hunting parties built houses on Svalbard and continued to hunt bear, fox, walrus and seals throughout the winter dark-

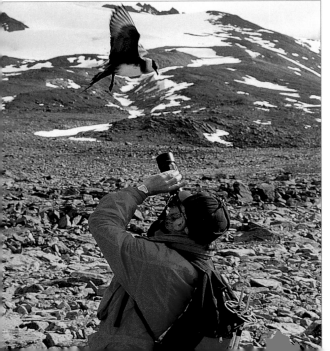

ness. Not until the late 18th century did Norwegian hunters first arrive. They too overwintered, and today their cabins still lie along the shores of many fjords. They are mainly deserted, yet scientists and explorers often make use of them, and many are kept in a good state of repair.

A trapper led a tough and rigorous life. He had to set his traps, mainly for Arctic fox whose beautiful pelts were most valuable in winter, in a hunting territory that covered many square kilometres. He also shot or caught polar bears in baited "fell traps" and hunted seals, not just for food and skins, but for the oil which he extracted from the blubber.

Ever since its discovery, Svalbard has attracted scientific expeditions. The first on record was in 1773 and included no less a personage than Horatio Nelson, then a midshipman. In 1827, the first Norwegian geological expedition took place under Professor B.M. Keilhau, and this was soon followed by expeditions from many nations. Today, the **Norsk Polarinstitut** is the clearing house for all expeditions to this Arctic outpost.

Natural laboratory

Svalbard offers a splendid environment for the study of ecology and natural history by scientist and amateur alike. Almost every visitor who makes the long journey north has more than a passing interest in wildlife in general and birds in particular, and Svalbard's short Arctic summer offers a rich feast. For though the archipelago can seem desperately inhospitable, in the 24-hour days of summer the tundra slopes between the mountains and near the sea offer enough thin soil to encourage and support a surprising number of plants. These, in turn, support other wildlife such as insects, 36 bird species and a few mammals. The surrounding seas, although cold, are rich in fish and invertebrates, which attract seabirds and sea mammals which use the shores and cliffs for breeding and resting.

Kittiwakes, and glaucous and ivory gulls push north as soon as daylight allows and are soon followed by Arctic terns, all the way from the southern hemisphere. The kittiwake is essentially an ocean bird which feeds almost exclusively at sea. At nesting time they set up huge, noisy colonies on suitable cliffs, or even on window ledges in some places. Another ocean wanderer is the fulmar. Most of the Svalbard fulmars are in the "dark-grey phase" of development and therefore largely confined to Arctic waters, which at first puzzles some bird-watchers from further south. Four species of auks breed in Svalbard: Brünnich's guillemot, the little auk, puffin and black guillemot. While Brünnich's guillemot nests on open but inaccessible ledges, the others seek the safety of crevices or burrows, where predators such as Arctic fox and glaucous gulls have less chance of getting at their eggs or young. There are also some waders.

The large expanses of barren mountains do not offer much in the way of food for land birds, but try the slopes and valleys which are often carpeted

TIP

Svalbard offers a wide range of activities for the outdoor enthusiast, including dog-sledging and skiing, camping expeditions, walks with packhorses and boat trips. See www.svalbard. net for details.

BELOW: Svalbard reindeer are much shorter than other species.

Map on page 334

The seal-hunters who once flocked to Svalbard in the summer months used to refer to ringed seals as "floe rats".

in dwarf birch and polar willow, and you will find snow buntings foraging for seeds and singing from the rocks. The Svalbard ptarmigan also uses this habitat, and it is the only bird to stay through the winter. Three kinds of geese breed on Svalbard – pink-footed, Brent and barnacle – and the many naturalists who have studied the barnacle geese now realise that the entire Svalbard population travels to Scotland each year, to spend the winter in the Solway area in the southwest, then return in spring to breed. When you spot the plentiful flocks of common eider along the shores, look closely because you may be lucky enough to find a few king eiders showing off their plumage, superior to that of their less flashy kin.

Arctic monarch

There is only one kind of grazing mammal on the islands, and that is the hardy Svalbard reindeer. Smaller than its Samiland counterpart, the Svalbard reindeer is quite tame, living a spartan life off plants and lichens in the valley bottoms. They live in groups. The

RIGHT: visiting a glacier in Svalbard.

only other land mammals are the Arctic fox and the bear. The Arctic fox is a very attractive-looking little animal, with a coat of varying shades of white and grey in summer and pure white in winter. Though it was hunted heavily in the past, it is still remarkably tolerant and curious about humans, and is not too difficult to find on the seabird cliffs in summer, where it digs out nests or picks up any young birds that have fallen from the ledges.

The undoubted king of the Arctic, however, is the polar bear. Adult males especially lead a nomadic life on the pack ice for much of the year and live mainly on seals, while young males and females with cubs tend to spend the summer on the island feeding largely on a vegetarian diet. Though they were formerly hunted for their skins, polar bears are now protected and can be killed only if they threaten human life. They are not uncommon, especially on favourite breeding islands, such as **Barentsøya** and **Edgeøya**. But climate change is threatening their habitat and hunting grounds – today the polar bear is listed as a threatened species.

The fjords of Svalbard may no longer be "filled with whales and walrus", as they were said to be in the 15th century, but you will certainly find sea mammals around the islands. Though it is now rare to see any of the great whales, species such as the lesser rorqual or minke whales come into the fjord quite often. The beluga or white whale is easiest to identify with its white body and lack of dorsal fin. You might be lucky enough to sight the remarkable narwhal, with its spear-like tusk projecting out in front.

The immense herds of walrus which in days past thronged places like **Moffen Island** have never fully recovered from over-hunting, but sometimes small groups appear at Moffen or on the south of Edgeøya, where they feast on the clam beds or rest on the shore: a hopeful sign in an age when Svalbard is visited for its stark natural beauty and summer wildlife. ❏

Svalbard Seed Bank

In February 2008 the Norwegian government opened a seed bank, effectively a "Noah's ark" for the world's most important plant varieties. The Svalbard Global Seed Vault (nicknamed Doomsday Seed Vault by some) serves as a repository for crucial seeds in the event of global catastrophe, be it nuclear war, natural disasters or gene pollution from genetic modification.

The bank, which is located just outside Longyearbyen, has been carved into the permafrost and rock of the remote Svalbard Archipelago. Its location ensures the vault will remain below freezing point, and the seeds are further protected by metre-thick walls of reinforced concrete, two airlocks and high-security blast-proof doors.

The Svalbard seed bank will be of global importance; local seed banks rely on artificial refrigeration and are prone to local problems – dozens of unique crops were lost during the wars in Iraq and Afghanistan.

Construction of the seed vault, which cost NOK 45 million (US$9 million), was funded entirely by the Norwegian government, and storage of seeds in the vault is free of charge. In March 2010, the seed count at the Svalbard Global Seed Vault passed half a million samples. Each sample can contain up to 500 seeds, which means that the total number of seeds currently being stored is about 250 million individual seeds.

⚛ INSIGHT GUIDES TRAVEL TIPS
NORWAY

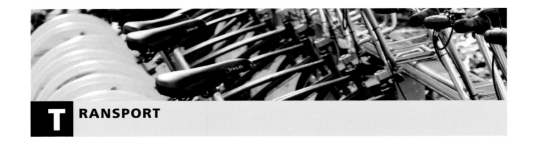

T RANSPORT

GETTING THERE
AND GETTING AROUND

By Air

Scandinavia's flagship carrier, **SAS** (Scandinavian Airline System), runs a wide range of flights between Oslo Gardermoen Airport and other world capitals (usually involving a feeder service to and from one of the main European hubs – London, Copenhagen or Frankfurt), with some direct services to Bergen, Oslo, Stavanger, Tromsø and Trondheim. **British Airways**, **Lufthansa**, **Air France** and **KLM** also connect Norway's cities with daily flights to Europe.

Approximate flying times to Oslo are: London, 2 hours; Frankfurt, 1 hour 50 minutes; Paris, 2 hours; Budapest, 3 hours 35 minutes; and Warsaw, 3 hours 25 minutes.

SAS offers several daily flights from Heathrow to Oslo and two to Stavanger; there are also flights in and out of Manchester. **BA** operates from Heathrow and Manchester to Oslo. **Ryanair** offers low-cost flights from London Stansted, Edinburgh, Liverpool and Glasgow Prestwick to Oslo Torp, near Sandefjord (in fact 130km/80 miles south of the capital) and from London Stansted and Newcastle to Moss Rygge Airport, 66km (41 miles) southeast of Oslo.

Oslo Gardermoen Airport

The main terminal building at Oslo Gardermoen Airport, completed in 1998, is the largest laminated wood structure in the world.

Widerøe flies to 36 destinations within Norway and has flights from Aberdeen, Edinburgh, Newcastle, Copenhagen and Gothenburg. It is based at Oslo Torp Airport in Sandefjord, 130km (80 miles) south of Oslo. **Norwegian Air Shuttle** is a low-cost airline operating from 15 airports in Norway; flights go to Oslo from London Gatwick and Edinburgh, and from London Stansted to Trondheim.

SAS
In UK
Tel: 0906 294 2772
www.flysas.com
In North America
Tel: 1-800 221 2350
In Norway
Tel (reservations): 05400

British Airways
In UK
Tel: 0844 493 0787
www.ba.com
In Norway
Tel: 8153 3142

Norwegian Air Shuttle
In UK
Tel: 020 8099 7254
Tel: +47 21 49 00 15
In Norway
Tel: 81 52 18 15
www.norwegian.no

Widerøe
In Norway
Tel: 75 11 11 11 (info)
or 81 00 12 00 (bookings)
www.wideroe.no

Ryanair
In UK
Tel: 0871 246 0000

Oslo: Cruise Destination

Oslo has over recent years become an important port of call for cruise ships heading to both the Baltic and the Norwegian west coast. In 2009, 153 ships called into Oslo, bringing with them 269,500 passengers from 134 countries. This is a 12.5 percent increase on 2008, and almost five times as many passengers as in 1993. The main cruising market comes from Germany, the UK, the US and Norway, which together account for 66 percent of cruise passengers visiting the Norwegian capital.

In Norway
Tel: 82 00 40 02
www.ryanair.com

By Sea

There is currently no ferry service between the UK and Norway. **Color Line** is the main ferry service linking Oslo to the Continent, with big new cruise-ferries sailing to Kiel in Germany, and services to the northern tip of Denmark (Hirtshals) from Kristiansand and Larvik.
Color Line
PO Box 1422, Vika
N-0115 Oslo
Tel: 22 94 42 00
www.colorline.com

By Rail

Numerous rail services link Norway with the rest of Scandinavia and Europe. From the Continent, express trains operate to Copenhagen, where inter-Scandinavian trains connect to Oslo. There are train connections in Oslo to other cities in Norway. First- and second-class coaches are available on these express trains, plus sleeper coaches on all of the overnight expresses.

Seat reservations are required on all night and long-distance day trains, as well as on express and high-speed "Signatur" services.

The Norwegian State Railway (NSB) is part of the InterRail, Eurailpass and Eurail Youthpass system, which offers various discount tickets (including to students). InterRail: www.interrailnet.com, Eurail: www.eurail.com.

There are frequent connections from Copenhagen, Stockholm and Gothenburg to Oslo.

You can also get to northern Norway from Stockholm, with Trondheim and Narvik the principal destinations, again usually twice daily (the line in Norway terminates at Bodø).

International arrivals and departures are located at Sentralstasjon (Oslo S). Flytoget, the high-speed rail link to/from Oslo Gardermoen Airport, has a terminal at Oslo S, and trains also run to/from Asker via Nationaltheatret station. NSB provides train information and also operates as a travel bureau across Norway:

Norwegian State Railways
NSB Reisesenter
PO Box 673, N-5001 Bergen, Norway
Tel: 81 50 08 88
www.nsb.no
Flytoget
Tel: 81 50 07 77
www.flytoget.no

By Road

Most major shipping lines to Norway allow passengers to bring cars. But coming by car increases sea travel costs, and petrol is expensive in Norway.
Norges Automobil Forbund
(NAF or Norwegian Automobile Federation)
Østensjøveien 14, 0609 Oslo
Tel: 22 34 14 00
Emergency tel: 810 00 505
www.naf.no
Kongelig Norsk Automobilklub
(KNA or Royal Norwegian Automobile Club)
Cort Adelersgt. 16, Oslo
In Norway
Tel: 08505
In UK
Tel: +47 92 60 85 05
Emergency tel: 22 30 30 50
(members only)

GETTING AROUND

Public Transport

There is an excellent network of domestic transport services – a necessity in a country so large and often impassable by land. You may have to use more than one means (for example, train and bus or plane and bus), but if you're travelling beyond Oslo you'll find these services indispensable.

Although covering great distances can be expensive, Norway offers transport bargains through special tourist cards such as the Fjord Pass, plus some of the pan-European programmes like InterRail and Eurail. Within larger cities, tourist passes cover urban transport and give free entry to many museums.

From the Airport

Gardermoen Airport is 50km (30 miles) north of Oslo. It is served by the Airport Express Train/Flytoget to Oslo S (the Central Station) every 10–20 minutes and takes 30 minutes. Details at www.flytoget.no. Regional and local trains also connect Oslo and the airport, and are cheaper – they take about 45 minutes; there is normally a train at least every hour. Note that rail passes are not valid on the Flytoget. See also www.nsb.no.

The airport bus departs six times an hour to and from the Radisson SAS Scandinavia Hotel via Stortinget (Parliament), Oslo Busterminal, Helsfyr and Furuset. It takes 40 minutes. Tel: 177 or 22 80 49 71; www.flybussen.no.

Nor-Way Flybusekspress. No. F1 also links Majorstuen in west Oslo to

BELOW: Bergen Airport.

Tickets and Info

For tickets, routes, times and all other queries about public transport, **Trafikanten** in Oslo offers an information and booking service. Its office is at Jernbanetorvet 1, by Oslo Sentralstasjon (at the bottom of the glass tower at the front of the station). Office: Mon–Fri 7am–8pm, Sat–Sun 8am–6pm (May–Sept until 8pm). Tel: 81 50 01 76 (lines: Mon–Fri 7am–11pm, Sat–Sun 8am–11pm). Info line: 177; www.trafikanten.no.

There is an additional Trafikanten at Gardermoen Airport.

Gardermoen with frequent departures throughout the day. Tel: 81 54 44 44; www.flybussekspressen.no.

If you arrive from London Stansted at **Torp Airport** at Sandefjord on the southwest side of the fjord, buses and trains will take up to 2½ hours to reach the capital, depending on traffic conditions.

Bergen Airport is at Flesland, 19km (12 miles) south of the city. The airport bus goes to the Radisson SAS Royal Hotel at Bryggen, via Radisson SAS Hotel Norge and the bus station. For details, tel: 177; www.flybussen.no.

All other major city airports are serviced by buses and taxis.

By Air

Considering its size, Norway is exceptionally well served by domestic airlines, with about 50 airports and airfields throughout the country.

The main domestic airlines are SAS, Widerøe and Norwegian Air Shuttle. Each offers discount travel passes.

Norway in a Nutshell

One of the most pleasurable ways of seeing Norway is to take a **Norway in a Nutshell** journey (see page 236). The trip uses various forms of public transport and takes you from Myrdal to Flåm, Gudvangen and Voss, through some of the country's most beautiful scenery. A selection of packages is on offer. Tel: 81 56 82 22; www.fjord-tours.no.

The railway line from Myrdal to Flåm is a masterpiece of engineering. When you have made the 850-metre (2,800ft) descent you are at the head of one of the longest fjords in the world, Sognefjord, and on the brink of another scenic high

through Aurlandsfjord and narrow Nærøyfjord.

The trips can be made in either direction and from any of the stations between Oslo and Bergen. **Norway in a Nutshell round trip:** train from Oslo to Myrdal/Flåm, boat to Gudvangen, bus to Voss, train to Oslo.

Norway in a Nutshell one way: train from Oslo to Myrdal/Flåm, boat to Gudvangen, bus to Voss, train to Bergen.

Tickets are sold at the railway stations in Oslo and Bergen or from travel agencies. See www.norwaynutshell.com for more details.

SAS Scandinavian Airlines
Tel: 05400
Widerøe's Flyveselskap ASA
Tel: 75 11 11 11 (info) or 81 00 12 00 (bookings)
Norwegian Air Shuttle
Tel: 81 52 18 15

By Rail

Rail services are far more comprehensive in the south than in the north, and tend to fan out from Oslo, so you will have to supplement your trip with ferries and buses, unless you are travelling strictly in the south or to the major towns.

Oslo S (Oslo Sentralstasjon) is Norway's busiest railway station, located in central Oslo at the eastern end of Karl Johansgate on Jernbanetorget. Long-distance, express and local suburban trains arrive and depart here. It is also the terminal for the Oslo Gardermoen Airport high-speed rail link, Flytoget (some trains continue under the city

to Asker via Nationaltheatret station). The end of the line in Norway is at Bodø, but the most northerly railway station is at Narvik, which is reached through Sweden by train or by bus from Fauske. Most of Norwegian State Railways' (NSB) lines run through tourist country, presenting continuous panoramas of unspoilet scenic beauty. The Oslo–Bergen line, which celebrated its 100th year in 2009, is hailed as one of the world's most spectacular railway journeys for its scenery.

Most trains are modern and efficient, but the older rolling stock has a touch of nostalgic luxury. New inter-city express (ICE) trains offer one class only. There is a wide range of special offers that can make your holiday better value for money.

National rail passes from NSB are valid for 3–8 travel days in any month. The rail pass is sold under the name of Norway Rail Pass (or Eurail Norway Pass) in the US, while in Europe the offer is called Interrail

Norway (see www.nsb.no). Visit www.interrailnet.com or www.raileurope.com for more information.

If you plan to take special fast trains, you must book ahead. Ticket sales are from the main hall of the train station (tickets for ordinary trains may also be bought on board). Watch out for minipris tickets on the Norwegian State Railways' website (www.nsb.no) – if you're flexible with dates, and book well in advance, you could snap up a single ticket to any destination in Norway for as little as NOK 199.

For information about timetables, ticket prices and bookings, contact Trafikanten, Jernbanetorvet 1, by Oslo S; tel: 177.

By Bus/Coach

Where the rail network stops, the bus goes further: you can get to practically anywhere you want by bus on an ever-growing number of bus lines. Time Express is a popular one (see www.nettbuss.no). Usually it is not necessary to book in advance; just pay the driver on boarding. NOR-WAY Bussekspress (bus pass) guarantees a seat for all passengers. On sale only outside Norway through the company's agents, the pass offers unlimited travel within 7 or 14 consecutive days. Children up to the age of 4 travel free, 4 to 16 years pay 75 percent of the adult price. **NOR-WAY Bussekspress AS**, Karl Johans gt. 2, NO-0154 Oslo; tel: 81 54 44 44; www.nor-way.no.

Water Transport

Ferries

You are never very far from the sea in Norway. Ferries are an invaluable means of transport that allow short cuts across fjords to eliminate long

Fjord Tours

Whether you are planning a short break or a long holiday, many companies offer tours of the fjord, coastal and mountain scenery. Two of the main ones are:
Fjord Tours
Strømgt 4
5015 Bergen
Tel: 81 56 82 22
www.fjordtours.com
Fjord Travel Norway
Østre Nesttunvei 4–6
5221 Nesttun, Bergen
Tel: 55 13 13 10
www.fjordtravel.no

BELOW: the Hurtigruten is the best way to see the Norwegian coastline.

road journeys; in built-up areas they are crucial to commuters, like the Horten–Moss ferry across Oslofjord between Vestfold and Østfold. Ferries to the fjord islands around Oslo leave from the Vippetangen quay near Akershus Castle.

Almost all town marinas have places for guest boats. A mooring fee is required.

The following company operates the ferries that run between the centre of Oslo and the Bygdøy Ppeninsula, where many of the main museums are located.

Bygdøfærgene Skibs
Rådhusbrygge 3
Tel: 23 35 68 90
www.boatsightseeing.com

Long-Distance Ships

Hurtigruten, the Norwegian Coastal Express service, is a vital means of water transport for Norwegians, but also a superb way for visitors to see Norway's dramatic coast. In summer, boats leave daily, travelling between Bergen and Kirkenes and back in 11 days and putting in at 35 ports (see page 257).

The ships take cars, and should be booked well in advance. You can travel on shorter stretches too, and special packages are available year-round. Either contact your local travel agent or:

Hurtigruten
Tel: 81 00 30 30
www.hurtigruten.com
Kystopplevelser (Coastal Experiences)
Tel: 76 96 76 00 or 81 03 00 00
www.kystopplevelser.no

Buses and Trams

Oslo's bus and tram system is comprehensive and punctual; there are detailed timetables at every stop. Trafikanten (see Tickets and Info box on page 343) can suggest bus or tram routes to get you where you wish to go. There are night buses on some routes and very early morning buses (starting at 4am), so that public transport is available virtually around the clock. Bergen and Trondheim also have tram systems.

Underground

Oslo's underground is called the T-bane (see map on page 385) and is simple to use. There are five lines that converge under the centre of Oslo. A circle line linking the station of Storo with Carl Berners plass was completed in 2006. You can catch

any train to any of the far-flung suburbs from any of the stations between Tøyen and Majorstuen. Station entrances are marked with a "T". Trafikanten (see box on page 343) has route maps. The most scenic route must be T-bane 1 up to Frognerseteren. From there enjoy panoramic views back down to Oslo.
Økernveien 9, Tøyen
Tel: 22 08 42 40
www.tbane.no

Taxis

Taxis are widely available, even in many suburban and rural areas, so you need never risk drink-driving (for which penalties are severe).

No matter where you are in Oslo, telephone 023 23 and you will be transferred to the nearest taxi rank. Minibuses and taxis (for up to 16 people) can also be booked on 22 38 80 70. Otherwise, you can take a taxi from one of the many taxi ranks scattered around the city.

In Oslo, taxis are more expensive at night or if ordered by phone. At night there are two things to watch out for: when everyone leaves the bars and restaurants late, long queues build up at taxi ranks. This can be extremely uncomfortable in the winter if you are not dressed correctly. The problem has given rise to a second difficulty: "pirate" taxis. These either cruise

Travel Passes

The Oslo Pass, issued for one, two and three days, with half-price for children, is your ticket to unlimited public transport (including city ferries), free parking, free guided tours, free entry to over 30 museums and many other discounts. If you want a card for travel only, there are all kinds of passes, including a Minikort (four rides at a discount) and Flexikort (eight rides at a discount), plus other passes appropriate for longer stays.

The Oslo Pass may be purchased at the Central Railway Station (Oslo S), Trafikanten (see box on page 343), as well as all Narvesen kiosks and hotels, campsites and tourist offices.

Other cities offer similar tourist travel cards: for example, the Bergen Card, a 24-hour or 48-hour pass available from tourist information offices, the railway station, hotels, campsites and the Hurtigruten terminal.

ABOVE: Oslo tram.

up out of the blue or a "dummy" comes and asks you if you want a taxi without queuing. Pirate taxis are a risk, but if you do use one, make sure you agree a price beforehand. They tend to gather at Stortorget, opposite GlassMagasin.

Private Transport

By Car

Norway's roads are good, particularly in view of the treacherous weather conditions encountered in winter. Be prepared for tunnels, though, as some routes have long lengths of road underground, most notably in the fjords.

EU driving licences are valid in Norway, but drivers from some countries must carry an international driving licence. Drive on the right.

Traffic regulations are strictly enforced (see Rules of the Road, page 346).

Winter Driving

With Norway's winters, you should never assume that all roads are passable.

Small roads in the north and in mountainous areas are often closed so the authorities can put all manpower into keeping main roads safe, and even the E6 highway from Oslo to Trondheim has been known to close.

If you intend to travel on minor roads, seek a local's advice and go prepared for anything. Your car must be equipped with winter tyres.

Snow-Tyre Hire

If you are driving in Norway in winter you can hire the appropriate tyres and snow chains by the week. Ask in any petrol station. In the UK contact:

Snowchains Europroducts
Tel: 01732 884408
www.snowchains.co.uk

Breakdown and Accidents

The AA and RAC are affiliated to the AIT (Alliance Internationale de Tourisme), so members receive free assistance (with journey planning as well as backup in case of breakdown or accident) from Norway's NAF (Norges Automobilforbund). More comprehensive repairs can be carried out at NAF-contracted garages (for which you will have to pay). NAF also patrol Norway's main roads and mountain passes from mid-June to mid-August. They have emergency phones along the mountain passes.
NAF, Storgaten 2, N-0155 Oslo
In Norway
Tel: 08505
In UK
Tel: +47 92 60 85 05
www.naf.no

If you are involved in an accident where there are no injuries, telephone

Viking Redningstjeneste AS on 06000 or 22 08 60 00. Their offices provide a 24-hour service for all Norway.

In an emergency you can contact **Norsk Luftambulanse** (Air Ambulance), tel: 64 90 44 44; www. norskluftambulanse.no.

It is not necessary to call the police for minor accidents, but drivers must exchange names and addresses; leaving the scene without doing so is a crime.

Only call the **police** (on **112**) or an **ambulance** (on **113**) if it's a real emergency.

Rules of the Road

It is essential for visitors to Norway to be aware of Norwegian driving regulations, some of which vary significantly from those in the UK and on the Continent. Here are a few tips to help you drive safely, but for further guidance it's worth getting a copy of *Velkommen på norske veier (Welcome to Norwegian Roads)*, which includes

an English section and is available at tourist offices.

Speed Limits The maximum speed limit is usually 80 kph (50 mph), though 100 kph (62 mph) is permitted on some roads (mainly motorways). The limit is reduced to 40 kph (24 mph) in built-up areas, and even 30 kph (18 mph) on certain residential roads. On-the-spot fines are given for drivers found speeding (this may be as much as NOK 3,500). Speed cameras and radar traps are both used.

Giving Way This can be very confusing to the visitor. Roads marked at intervals by yellow diamond signs indicate that you have priority. On all other roads you are required to give way to traffic entering from the right. This is further confused by the fact that some roads have a series of white triangles painted across them at junctions, which mean stop and give way, though as you can imagine these easily become obliterated by snow and ice in the winter.

On roundabouts, priority is from the left. Always give way to trams, buses and taxis. Many roads have a right-hand lane exclusively for buses and taxis.

Drinking and Driving You are strongly advised not to drink at all if you anticipate driving within at least eight hours. The current permissible limit is 0.02 per ml, and penalties are severe (imprisonment, a high fine and loss of licence are automatic).

Documentation and Equipment You must always have the following with you in your car: driving licence, car registration documents, European accident statement form, insurance policy and a reflective warning triangle. A snow shovel and tow-rope are also useful in winter. For regularly updated information in the UK, the AA runs a very good fact line for just a small charge on tel: 0870 600 0371; www.theaa.com.

Lights It is obligatory to drive with dipped headlights on during the daytime, even on the brightest summer day. This rule applies to all vehicles, including motorcycles and mopeds. We recommend you carry spare bulbs. Do not forget that right-hand-drive cars require black adhesive triangles (often supplied by ferry companies), or clip-on beam deflectors, so you don't dazzle oncoming drivers.

Seat Belts These must be worn, both front and back (again, there are on-the-spot fines for failing to comply). Motorcycle and moped drivers and their passengers must wear helmets.

Toll Roads

Road	Toll Area	Price (in NOK)
E6	Trondheim–Stjørdal	25
E6	Øsfold	20
E10	Nappstraumen Tunnel (Nordland)	65
E18	Vestfold	20
E18	Eidangerhalvøya (Telemark)	15
E18	Aust-Agder	20
E18	Kristiansand (Vest-Agder)	10
E39	Rennesøy (Rogaland)	90
E39	Trekantsambandet (Hordaland)	85
E39	Nordhordaland Bridge (Hordaland)	45
E39	Øysand–Thamshamn (Sør-Trøndelag)	15
E39/ Str.70	Kristiansund Mainland connection (Møre og Romsdal)	70
E134	Åkrafjord (Hordaland)	40
E69	Kåfjord–Honningsvåg (Finnmark)	145
Str.4	Oppland (Gjøvik-Raufoss)	15
Str.5	Sogndal–Fjærland (Sogn og Fjordane)	180
Str.5	Naustdalstunnel (Sogn og Fjordane)	45
17	Helgeland Bridge (Nordland)	85
Str.23	Oslofjordtunnel (Akershus)	55
Str.64	Skålavegen (Møre og Romsdal)	55
Fv64	Atlanterhavstunnelen	85
Str.207	Bjorøy (Hordaland)	120
Fv519	Finnøytunnelen (Rogaland)	200
Fv544	Halsnøysambandet (Hordaland)	100
562	Askøy Bridge (Hordaland)	70
Str.566	Osterøy Bridge (Hordaland)	62
Str.658	Ålesund–Ellingsøy–Giske/Vigra (Møre og Romsdal)	55
Str.714	Hitra–Frøya, Dolmøy (Sør-Trøndelag)	75
Str.714	Hitra–Festland, Sandstad (Sør-Trøndelag)	75
Str.714	Hitra–Fjellværøy, Ansnes (Sør-Trøndelag)	60
755	Skarnsund Bridge	65
Str.769	Namdalsprojeckt (Nord-Trøndelag)	15
Oslo Toll Road		26
Stavanger Toll Road Work days 6am–6pm		
Bergen Toll Road		15
Trondheim Toll Road		15

Toll prices are for a private car (with trailer of maximum weight 3,500 kg/7,700 lb). They are subject to change without notice and credit cards are not accepted, so Norwegians tend to keep a stash of change handy in the car.

Road Information

Vegmeldingssentralen (The Road User Information Centre) is an office of the *Statens Vegvesen* (Public Roads Administration). Its main function is to monitor and provide information about roads and road conditions. You may also get information about distances and ferry timetables. 24 hours all year, tel: 175 or 81 54 89 91.

Tyres It is obligatory to use winter tyres from October to April. These are either tyres with studs *(piggdekk)* or specially designed tyres for use in ice and snow. Studded tyres are preferred, but these may soon be prohibited in urban areas for environmental reasons, and in many places (including Oslo) a fee is levied on cars using them.

Caravanning
For information contact:
PO Box 104, 1921 Sørumsand
Tel: 63 82 99 90
www.caravanklubben.no

Car Hire
Hiring a car in Norway can be expensive, but may be worthwhile if shared between several people. Otherwise, watch for special weekend and summer prices.
Avis Bilutleie-Liva Bil AS
PO Box 154, N-1361 Billingstad (near Oslo)
Tel: 66 77 11 00
Booking tel: 81 53 30 44
www.avis.no
Europcar
Grini Næringspark 10, PO Box 173, 1332 Østerås
Tel: 67 16 58 00
Booking tel: 67 16 58 20/800 41 400
www.europcar.no
Hertz Bilutleie
PO Box 331, N-1324 Lysaker/Oslo
Tel: 67 16 80 80
Booking tel: 67 16 80 00
www.hertz.no

Cycling

Cycling in Norway is safe, as there is so little traffic on many minor roads. But you must ride with caution as, though there are a few cycle routes, it is not an integrated system. Cyclists are not allowed to go through the larger tunnels, for example (because of car fumes). Out in the countryside you'll find surfaced cycle paths. Cycling is a good way of exploring

ABOVE: in Oslo bikes are available for hire at bike stations.

outside Oslo: bicycles are allowed on most trains and buses for a small charge.

Special cycle trains are laid on during the summer. Pick up a copy of *Oslo Guide* (download or order free from www.visitoslo.com) and you'll find suggestions for a *Nordmarka* (Oslo's forest land) route. Tourist offices have details of mountain cycle tours.

The Cycling Association (**Syklistenes Landsforening**) can help plan tours and cycling holidays: Storg. 23C Pb. 8883 Youngstorget, 0028 Oslo. Tel: 22 47 30 30; www.slf.no

To organise cycle routes and transport for bicycles, contact Skiforeningen, Kongeveien 5, 0787 Oslo. Tel: 22 92 32 00; www.skiforeningen.no/english

Cycle Rental
In Oslo and Bergen bikes can be hired from hotels, campsites, local tourist offices or sports shops, as well as small cycle-hire shops.
A/S Skiservice, dept. bike, Tomm Murstadbakken 2, 0791 Oslo
Tel: 22 13 95 00
www.skiservice.no
White Water AS
Grensen 3, Oslo
Tel: 23 10 40 50
www.whitewater.no
White Water AS deals in extreme-sports gear. Off-road and mountain bikes are available for hire.

On Foot

There is almost nowhere in Norway you can't go happily on foot; it is a nation of devout walkers, and walking is one of the most popular outdoor activities at weekends.

The law of access to the natural environment, known as

allemannsretten or "everyman's right", allows you to walk wherever you want in the wilderness such as seashore, forests, mountains and in other non-cultivated regions. This should be done with consideration. Use paths and roads when walking in agricultural and populated areas.

It is preferable to make use of campsites if you are staying overnight outdoors. If you pitch a tent in the wilderness, it should be situated at least 150 metres (160 yards) from the nearest house or hut. Open fires are prohibited from 15 April to 15 September.

Detailed maps are available from the Norwegian Trekking Association (DNT). Membership allows you to use the association's huts. The map and guidebook selection is excellent; there is a charge for survey maps of Norway, but sketch maps are free.

The Norwegian Tourist Board publishes a handbook, *Mountain Hiking in Norway*, which gives suggested itineraries for mountain walks and details of chalets and where to stay.
Visit Norway
(Norwegian Tourist Board)
PO Box 448 Sentrum, 0158 Oslo
Tel: 22 00 25 00
www.visitnorway.com
Den Norske Turistforening
(Norwegian Trekking Association)
Storgate 7, Oslo
Tel: 22 82 28 22 (tour info)
or 40 00 18 68 (general info)
www.turistforeningen.no

Hitchhiking

Hitching is not as common in Norway as elsewhere in Europe; but it is not impossible. You'll have the best chance on busier coastal roads. Using a sign is recommended.

A CCOMMODATION

HOTELS, YOUTH HOSTELS, BED & BREAKFAST

Norwegian hotels can be expensive, but, in common with the rest of Scandinavia, they reduce their rates during the outdoor summer holiday period when business decreases. Weekends are also usually cheaper. Normal weekday rates outside summer are geared towards business occupants, but are generally in line with hotels elsewhere in Europe or the US.

When it comes to places to stay, Norway has something to suit every requirement. The range covers hotels from the luxurious to the simple, to more modest guesthouses, campsites, cosy self-catering cottages, and youth and family hostels. Facilities and service are of international standard. A lot of hotels provide luxury facilities like fitness centres and secretarial services, and newer, larger Norwegian hotels are very business conference-oriented.

The British-style bed and breakfast is developing in Norway, and country or farm holidays offer an opportunity

BELOW: fjord breakfast.

to experience day-to-day farm life at close quarters.

Full-board terms are available to guests staying at the same establishment for at least three to five days. Children often go for free, provided the child stays in the parents' room. Guesthouses (*pensjonat* or *gjestehus*) offer lower rates and are generally good, although may have shared baths (the bathroom may be down the hall).

The state-run visitors' site, www.visitnorway.com, can be a good starting point for tracking down hotels. *See also Tourist Information, page 370.*

Hotel Chains

Some of the major hotel chains are well represented in Norway's larger cities, but many are not, or they operate through a local brand.

Several local chains, meanwhile, offer passes and discount schemes to help reduce the cost of accommodation. These passes, available for sale at participating hotels, usually involve a modest one-time fee (around NOK 100) and then entitle the holder to discounted rates, mostly in the summer and at weekends. Some passes also offer a free night of accommodation after the pass holder has logged several nights on the programme. The one that covers the most hotels is Fjord Pass®; www.fjord-pass.com

Among the hotel chains in Norway:
Best Western Hotels
Tel: 22 94 40 60
Toll-free (bookings): 800 11 624
www.bestwestern.no
Choice Hotels AS
Tel: 22 40 13 00
www.choicehotels.no

Norlandia Hotels
Tel: 22 98 97 00
www.norlandia.no (Norwegian only)
Radisson Blu Hotels
Tel: 800 160 91
www.radisson.com
Rica Hotels
Tel: 66 85 45 60
www.rica-hotels.com
Scandic Hotels
Tel: 23 15 50 00
www.scandichotels.com
Thon Hotels
Tel: 815 52 441
www.thonhotels.no

Hotels

The hotels are listed geographically, and given a price category. There is a separate box on page 349 with information on booking rooms at some of Norway's historic hotels, many of which are a destination in themselves.

Breakfast Included

Norwegian hotels almost always offer a breakfast buffet that is included in the room rate. All hotel taxes are also included in the quoted rates, so there are rarely any nasty surprises upon checkout (unless you have used the phone in your room to make external calls, or made liberal use of the minibar).

Booking in Oslo/Bergen

In Oslo, the tourist information centres at Fridtjof Nansens Plass 5 (Mon–Sat 9am–5pm) and at the Central Station (daily 8am–11pm; *see page 370 for more information*) will book accommodation in the capital for those requesting it in person. This service covers private rooms, pensions and hotels.

The tourist office in Bergen offers a similar service, and has hotels in Bergen and the surrounding area. It is located at Vågsallmenningen 1 (tel: 55 55 20 00; www.visitbergen.com).

Oslo City Packages

Oslo has some packages that offer great value for money, and include accommodation with breakfast (there are 40 hotels to choose from), the Oslo Pass (which includes free entrance to many attractions, free inner-city transport and numerous discounts), and tickets to a show, a festival or a sporting event. The packages must be booked through the tourist information office.

Chalets (Hytter)

There are abundant holiday *hytter* (cabins or chalets) available for rent. These usually house four to six people. If you want to spend just one night in a chalet and then move on, you can stay in one on a campsite without booking ahead. See accommodation guides at www.visitnorway.com, or try the Cultural Heritage Association's website at www.olavsrosa.no/en.

Fishermen's Cabins (Rorbuer)

In the Lofoten Islands in northern Norway, and at numerous places elsewhere along the coast, you can rent a traditional former fisherman's cabin, called a *rorbu*. The fishermen used to come to Lofoten from other parts of the coast for the winter cod-fishing season from January to April, and would make these cabins their

temporary homes. Most of them have been modernised, and some have their own shower and toilet, but the main appeal is their character.
Lofoten Tourist Office
Tel: 76 06 98 00
www.lofoten.info
Also www.lofoten.com

Camping

Norway has more than 1,000 campsites, classified by 1–5 stars, depending on the standard and facilities available. The fixed charge per plot is usually NOK 80–160, with additional charges per person.

With the Scandinavia Camping Card, you receive a faster checking-in service along with special discount deals. The card is available from participating campsites in Norway, but also Sweden, Finland and Denmark, and can be used in those countries too. It can also be ordered online. Many campsites have cabins that may be booked in advance. Some are small and basic, but others are large and well equipped with a sitting room, one to two bedrooms, kitchen, shower and toilet.

For further information, log on to www.camping.no.

B&Bs

British-style B&Bs are catching on in Norway, and they are all of a high standard. You can book at local tourist offices or at Oslo's Central Railway Station.

Alternatively look out for signs for *Rom* or *Husrom* outside houses as you drive. A guidebook, *Bed & Breakfast in Norway*, with listings throughout the country, is available from bookshops in Norway or from www.amazon.co.uk. The following website may also be useful: www.bbnorway.com.

ABOVE: camping in Oppland.

Youth and Family Hostels

There are 75 youth hostels in Norway, all of a relatively high standard, and more are opening up and down the country – 10 in 2010 alone, including one at Gardermoen Airport. The plan is to have 100 youth hostels throughout Norway by the end of 2012.

A night's accommodation in a dorm costs NOK 200–300, and breakfast is usually included. Many hostels also have double or family rooms for hire, usually at a good price. Further information can be obtained by contacting Hostelling International Norway, or your local yha office.

Reserving space during the high season is essential, as hostel accommodation is the cheapest way to travel and everyone knows it. Bear in mind too that only one-third of youth hostels in Norway are open year round, the others only open during the summer season, so check beforehand.
Norske Vandrerhjem
(Hostelling International Norway)
Tel: 23 12 45 10
www.vandrerhjem.no

Norway's Historic Hotels

Tradition runs strong in Norway, and Norwegians are known for preserving their heritage. Massive investment in historic properties has made it possible for visitors to stay in a wide range of them, while enjoying every modern convenience and gourmet meals as well.

A few hotel organisations have been formed during the past decade to keep Norway's historic hotels alive and up-to-date, while maintaining their character and charm. Some of these fairytale-like structures are in towns and cities, but many

are in the mountains, along fjords and frankly in relatively obscure but often beautiful locations, making them a destination in themselves. All of the properties are unique, and most include dinner and breakfast as part of the room rate. Overnight accommodation for two including dinner and breakfast generally runs to around NOK 2,000, plus drinks. A couple worth trying:
De Historiske
Tel: 55 31 67 60
www.dehistoriske.no
This is a group of around 40 historic

hotels, manor houses or timbered lodges and a dozen selected restaurants around Norway, catering to visitors keen on style and good food.
The Great Life Company
Tel: 24 12 62 10
www.thegreatlifecompany.com
Controlled by a shipowning Oslo family who have made a business out of restoring gracious old lodging establishments. The group consists of around 14 mostly historic inns and restaurants, with a few modern surprises.

ACCOMMODATION LISTINGS

OSLO

ABOVE: the Grand Hotel.

Best Western Karl Johan Hotel
Karl Johans Gate 33
Tel: 23 16 17 00
www.norlandia.no/karljohan
Now part of the Best Western chain, this stately old hotel is a cut above most of its sister properties and the location can't be beaten, right in the heart of Oslo's downtown. **$–$$**

Hotel Bristol
Kristian IV's Gate 7
Tel: 22 82 60 00
www.thonhotels.no/bristol
Now part of the Thon Hotels chain, Bristol remains a classy place to stay in the heart of downtown. Known for its "Bibliotek (Library) Bar" and its Bristol Grill restaurant, the hotel is a popular meeting place for local celebrities. **$$$**

Coch's Pensjonat
Parkveien 25
Tel: 23 33 24 00
www.cochspensjonat.no
A friendly low-price alternative with a loyal following, a block from the park around the Royal Palace. Not all rooms have private baths. **$**

Hotel Continental
Stortingsgate 24–26
Tel: 22 82 40 00
www.hotel-continental.no
This classy five-star family-run hotel is famed for its classic Theater Café, a Viennese-style café that's the place to see and be seen in Oslo. The hotel was refurbished in 2008. **$$$**

First Hotel Grims Grenka
Kongens Gate 5
Tel: 23 10 72 00
www.firsthotels.com
Oslo's first design hotel attracts a hip and trendy crowd. The 50 rooms and suites are functional and stylish, and there is a rooftop lounge. **$$$**

Hotel Folketeateret
Storgaten 21–23
Tel: 22 00 57 00
www.choicehotels.no
A new luxury hotel in the old Opera premises, near Youngstorget. There's funky art on the walls, a hip bar and restaurant, and a theatre. Part of the Clarion Collection of hotels. **$$$**

Gabelshus Hotel
Gabels Gate 16
Tel: 23 27 65 00
www.gabelshus.no
This ivy-clad hotel in a quiet residential neighbourhood near downtown opened in 1912. It's a favourite of travellers to Oslo, who return for the good service, well-kept rooms and complimentary dinner. **$$**

Grand Hotel
Karl Johans Gate 31
Tel: 23 21 20 00
www.grand.no
This is where the Nobel Banquet is held. Close to the Norwegian parliament, its venerable Grand Café was a favourite haunt of Henrik Ibsen. **$$$**

Holmenkollen Park Hotel
Kongeveien 26
Tel: 22 92 20 00
www.holmenkollenparkhotel.no
This magnificent wooden

hotel is perched high above Oslo in the hills adjacent to the Holmenkollen ski jump, and with hiking and skiing trails out the front door. Rooms are located in a modern annexe. **$$**

Perminalen Hotel
Øvre Slottsgate 2
Tel: 24 00 55 00
www.perminalen.no
A basic hotel near the Parliament that appeals to young people on a tight budget. Simple rooms with bath, where it's possible to pay just for a bed in a four-bunk room. **$**

Thon Hotel Panorama
Rådhusgaten 7B
Tel: 23 31 08 00
www.thonhotels.com
A lovely new hotel, originally designed as a block of flats, in the Kvadraturen neighbourhood near Akershus Fortress. **$–$$**

AROUND OSLO AND ITS FJORD

Oscarsborg Festning
1443 Oscarsborg
Tel: 815 51 900
www.nasjonalefestningsverk.no/oscarsborg
Here you can stay in a fortress on an island off picturesque Drøbak in Oslo-

fjord; good value for money and open all year. **$**

Quality Hotel Fredrikstad
Nygata 2–6, 1607 Fredrikstad
Tel: 69 39 30 00
www.qualityinn.com
Fredrikstad's best hotel, conveniently located on the main pedestrian street, only a short walk from the bars and restaurants on the riverside. **$$–$$$**

Radisson Blu Airport Hotel
Oslo Gardermoen Airport
Tel: 63 93 30 00
www.radissonblu.com
You can't beat this for

convenience; you can walk from baggage claim to this elegant and comfortable hotel in minutes. **$$**

Hotell Refsnesgods
Godset 5, 1518 Moss
Tel: 69 27 83 00
www.refsnesgods.no
On the island of Jeløy, about an hour south of Oslo, this is an elegant getaway spot known for its gourmet food and art collection. Munch used to be a regular. **$$$**

Thon Hotel Halden
Langbrygga 1, 1767 Halden
Tel: 69 21 33 00

www.thonhotels.com
Halden's newest hotel enjoys a great location right by the harbour, and views of the famous Fredriksten Fortress. There's alfresco eating in summer. **$–$$**

KRISTIANSAND

1-2-3 Hotel
Østre Strandgate 25,
4610 Kristiansand
Tel: 38 70 15 66
www.123-hotel.no
Basic, modern budget
accommodation enjoying a
superb location along the
sea front, only 100 metres/
yds from the marina. **$**

Hotel Norge
Dronningensgate 5,
4666 Kristiansand
Tel: 38 17 40 00
www.hotel-norge.no
Stately old hotel, now part
of the Rica chain, in the

heart of town, and a short
walk to the scenic harbour
area. On-site spa offers
thalassotherapy. **$–$$**

**Radisson Blu Caledonien
Hotel**
Vestre Strandgate 7,
4663 Kristiansand
Tel: 38 11 21 00
www.radissonblu.com
Large hotel in a central
location near the ferry
terminal and bus and train
stations; all 205 rooms are
modern and comfortable,
with views of the sea. **$$$**

Rica Dyreparken

Kardemommeby, 4609 Kristiansand
Tel: 38 14 64 00
www.ricadyreparkenhotel.no
A super fun hotel for
kids of all ages, right by
Kristiansand's famous
zoo. Designed like a
Noah's ark, with animal
prints throughout, this
safari-themed hotel is very
popular, so book well in
advance. There is a big
playroom for children. **$$**

Scandic Kristiansand
Markensgate 39, 4612 Kristiansand
Tel: 21 61 42 00
www.scandic-hotels.com/kristiansand

Though somewhat lacking
in character, this hotel is
very conveniently located in
the main shopping area of
town, and a 10-minute walk
from the station. **$–$$**

STAVANGER AND ENVIRONS

Myhregaarden Hotel
Nygaten 24
Tel: 51 86 80 00
www.myhregaardenhotel.no
One of the latest hotels
to have opened, it offers
modern, comfortable rooms
(each with its own fireplace)
in a red-brick building halfway between the Petroleum
Museum and the cathedral.
Free evening food during the
week. **$$–$$$**

**Radisson Blu Atlantic
Hotel**
Olav V's Gate 3
Tel: 51 76 10 00
www.radissonblu.com
High-rise business
hotel overlooking Lake
Breiavatnet. Five-minute
walk to the harbour and all
its restaurants and bars,
with discounted room rates
in the summer. **$$–$$$**

Radisson Blu Royal Hotel
Løkkeveien 26
Tel: 51 76 60 00

www.radissonblu.com
Located behind its sister
property, Atlantic, this is a
mid-rise luxury hotel most
memorable for its themed
floors. Pool and spa on site.
$$–$$$

**Rogalandsheimen
Gjestegiveri**
Musegate 18
Tel: 51 52 01 88
www.rogalandsheimen.no
A lovely guesthouse that
is over 100 years old
and offers a charming
alternative to big modern
hotels. Only a short walk
from the city centre. Free
parking and bike rental. A
huge breakfast is included
in the price. **$**

Skagen Brygge Hotell
Skagenkaien 30
Tel: 51 85 00 00
www.skagenbryggehotell.no
A Stavanger classic, whose
white facade has been
dominating the harbour for

years, and within walking
distance of all the sights.
Well-equipped rooms and
friendly, competent staff.
Ask for a room with a view of
the water. **$$**

Victoria Hotel
Skansegate 1
Tel: 51 86 70 00
www.victoria-hotel.no
Established in 1990,
this first-class family-run
hotel on the harbour is in
the heart of the bar and
restaurant district yet quietly
removed. **$$**

Environs

Sola Strand Hotel
Nordsjøvegen, 4050 Sola
Tel: 51 94 30 00
www.sola-strandhotel.no
"Strand" means "beach" in
Norwegian, and this hotel is
located on one of the many
windswept beaches along
the North Sea, a 20-minute

drive from downtown
Stavanger. A classic,
traditional hotel with plenty
of space to unwind. There is
a spa on site. **$$**

Utstein Kloster Hotel
Mosterøyveien 661, 4156 Mosterøy
Tel: 51 72 01 00
www.utsteinklosterhotell.no
Another waterfront hotel,
this one is on an island
north of Stavanger near
the Utstein Monastery. It is
connected to the mainland
by an underwater tunnel.
Excellent area for cycling
and seeing historic sites. **$$**

BERGEN

**Best Western Hotel
Hordaheimen**
C. Sundtsgate 18, 5004 Bergen
Tel: 55 33 50 00
www.hordaheimen.no
Established over 90 years,
this recently refurbished
hotel has 88 rooms and a
new conference section.
The hotel's "Kaffistove"

restaurant serves
traditional fare in pleasant
surroundings. **$–$$**

Clarion Admiral
C. Sundtsgate 9, 5004 Bergen
Tel: 55 23 64 00
www.clarionadmiral.no
One of Bergen's finest
hotels, the Admiral has 210
rooms, many of which have

views over the harbour to
Bryggen. The restaurant has
excellent cuisine. **$$$**

**Clarion Collection Hotel
Havnekontoret**
Slottsgaten 1, Bryggen,
5003 Bergen
Tel: 55 60 11 00
www.choicehotels.no
Right on Bryggen, this stylish

ABOVE: sunset over Bergen harbour.

new hotel, opened in 2006, is a welcome addition to the Bergen hotel scene. Housed in converted warehouses dating back to the 1920s, the hotel successfully blends period features with modern conveniences and comfort, making it a popular choice with travellers. **$$$**

Det Hanseatiske Hotel
Finnegårdsgaten 2A, 5003 Bergen
Tel: 55 30 48 00
www.dethanseatiskehotell.no
Located in Finnegaarden, right next to the Hanseatic Museum on Bryggen, this small upmarket hotel, in one of the city's oldest buildings, offers 16 rooms in a very atmospheric setting. The rooms are individually decorated and have their own features, and all come with big bathrooms. **$$$**

Hotel Park Pension
Harald Hårfagresgt 35, 5007 Bergen
Tel: 55 54 44 00
http://hotelpark.no
This family-operated hotel with 40 rooms has its own unique flavour and character, due to the owner's taste for original antiques. It is located in the university quarter. **$**

Radisson Blu Hotel Norge
Nedre Ole Bulls Plass 4, 5012 Bergen
Tel: 55 57 30 00
www.radissonblu.com
One of Bergen's best-loved hotels and meeting places, right in the centre, with 350 rooms and suites of the highest standard. Four restaurants, including the gourmet Ole Bull. Winter garden, swimming pool, nightclub. **$$$**

Scandic Bergen City
Håkonsgaten 2, 5015 Bergen
Tel: 55 30 90 80
www.scandichotels.com
The modern Scandic is Bergen's largest business hotel, conveniently located in the centre of town, close to the sights and museums. The 254 rooms are all comfortable and spacious, and as with all Scandic hotels, kids stay for free in their parents' room. **$$**

Strand Hotel
Strandkaien 2–4, 5013 Bergen
Tel: 55 59 33 00
www.strandhotel.no
Superb harbour views make for a pleasant stay. Family-run hotel with a cosy breakfast room and one of Norway's top bars (serving Varg Veum's favourite drink, Simmers Taffel aquavit – the famous Bergen private investigator in Gunnar Staalesen's popular crime novels had his office at this address). **$–$$**

Thon Hotel Rosenkrantz
Rosenkrantz 7, 5003 Bergen
Tel: 55 30 14 00
www.thonhotels.com/rosenkrantz
Comfortable, early 20th-century hotel located in the street behind Bryggen in the heart of the Old Town; well modernised in light, airy colours. The best rooms have a view of the harbour, but book up fast. There's a restaurant and piano bar. Hotel nightclub entrance is next door. **$$**

FROM SOGN TO NORDFJORD

Sognefjord

Kvikne's Hotel
Kviknevegen 8, 6898 Balestrand
Tel: 57 69 42 00
www.kviknes.no
Owned by the Kvikne family since 1877, this Swiss-style hotel is in a lovely setting on the edge of Sognefjord – most of the rooms have delightful views looking out over the water. The hotel makes a good base for walking, mountain hiking and glacier trips. **$$**

BELOW: interior of Kvikne's Hotel.

Lavik Fjord Hotell
6947 Lavik
Tel: 57 71 40 40
www.lavikfjordhotell.no
This family-run hotel on the Sognefjord offers fantastic views. From here you can fish, swim, row, sail, paddle, cycle or go rock climbing and mountain walking. It can be easily reached by car or bus, or express boat from Bergen. Only 15 rooms. **$**

Midtnes Pensjonat
6898 Balestrand
Tel: 57 69 11 33
www.midtnes.no
A pretty, characterful guesthouse overlooking Sognefjord, with its own pier, bathing-place and rowing boat. Bike hire can be arranged through the tourist office. **$**

Along the coast

Quality Hotel Florø
Hamnegata 7, 6900 Florø
Tel: 57 75 75 75
www.choice.no
Sitting on the waterfront with a view of the fjord, mountains, islands and the sea, this hotel has 79 maritime-style bedrooms and a first-class restaurant. It's not far from the shopping centre and walking trails. **$**

Nordfjord

Innvik Fjordhotell Misjonsheimen
6793 Innvik, Stryn
Tel: 57 87 49 90
www.innvikfjordhotell.no

This locally owned hotel sits in the heart of the fjord area in Nordfjord, with some rooms overlooking the fjord, and others the mountainside. The kitchen uses fresh local produce when in season. There is a sauna, solarium, and fitness room. 34 rooms. **$**

PRICE CATEGORIES

Price categories are per night for two people in a double room with breakfast in high season.
$$$ = More than NOK 2,000
$$ = NOK 1,200–2,000
$ = Less than NOK 1,200

MØRE OG ROMSDAL

Hotel Brosundet
Apotekergata 5, 6004 Ålesund
Tel: 70 11 45 00
www.brosundet.no
Alesund's only boutique hotel, and its most stunning, housed in an Art Nouveau building right by the water. No two rooms are alike, but all blend historical surroundings with modern comfort. Part of the De Historiske chain. **$$$**

Juvet Landscape Hotel
Alstad, 6210 Valldal
Tel: 95 03 20 10
www.juvet.com
This new hotel, opened in 2009, consists of several wood units, each containing one hotel room. All the rooms have huge glass walls, letting the surrounding nature come

right in, hence the name. Summer only. **$$$**

Molde Rical Seilet Hotel
Gideonvegen 2, 6412 Molde
Tel: 71 11 40 00
www.rica-hotels.com
This striking hotel, whose huge glass panels are designed to look like a sail glimmering in the sunset, is the region's largest conference hotel, but is equally popular with leisure travellers. **$$**

Scandic Ålesund
Moloveien 6, 6004 Ålesund
Tel: 21 61 45 00
www.scandichotels.com
Also by the water, the hotel has 150 comfortable rooms. Big buffet breakfast, and no supplement for kids staying in the room with their parents. **$–$$**

Hotel Union Geiranger
6216 Geiranger
Tel: 70 26 83 00
www.hotel-union.no
A family-run historic hotel with postcard-pretty views of Geirangerfjord, 197 spacious rooms, a new spa and restaurants, make this hotel a popular choice. **$$**

BELOW: the extraordinary Juvet Landscape Hotel.

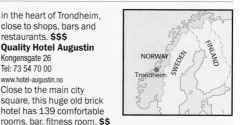

TRONDHEIM

Britannia Hotel
Dronningensgate 5
Tel: 73 80 08 00
www.britannia.no
Trondheim's grande dame, and the city's first luxury hotel, might be showing her age in places, but it is still one of the most stylish places to stay in town. A new spa opened in 2009. **$$$**

Comfort Hotel Park
Prinsensgate 4A
Tel: 73 83 39 00
www.choicehotels.no
Popular hotel offering comfortable rooms in the centre of town, with a few

extras seldom found in this price category, such as a sauna and outdoor hot tub, and free waffles and coffee in the afternoon. **$–$$**

Elgeseter Hotel
Tormodsgate 3
Tel: 73 82 03 30
www.elgeseter-hotell.no
A 10-minute walk from the city centre, this hotel has 23 basic but clean rooms at very reasonable prices. **$**

Grand Olav Clarion Hotel
Kjøpmannsgaten 48
Tel: 73 80 80 80
www.choicehotels.no
Top-class hotel situated

in the heart of Trondheim, close to shops, bars and restaurants. **$$$**

Quality Hotel Augustin
Kongensgate 26
Tel: 73 54 70 00
www.hotel-augustin.no
Close to the main city square, this huge old brick hotel has 139 comfortable rooms, bar, fitness room. **$$**

Radisson Blu Royal Garden Hotel
Kjøpmannsgate 73
Tel: 73 80 30 00
www.radissonblu.com
With 298 well-appointed rooms, plus solarium,

indoor pool, gymnasium, sauna, good restaurants, and a great location right by Nidelva River, this is one of the best hotels in Trondheim. Runs an airport bus. **$$–$$$**

TROMSØ

AMI Hotel Tromsø
Skolegata 24
Tel: 77 62 10 00
http://amihotel.no
Centrally located B&B offering 17 simple but clean rooms. Pay a token NOK 20 for the evening buffet (a bargain) or use the kitchen facilities on site to cook your own dinner. Free internet connection and coffee throughout the day. **$**

Clarion Collection Hotel With
Sjøgata 35–37
Tel: 77 66 42 00
www.choicehotels.no
A first-class hotel on the waterfront, it offers a beautiful view to the famous Arctic Cathedral, and has a maritime atmosphere. **$$**

Grand Nordic
Storgata 44
Tel: 77 75 37 77

www.nordic.no
Close to the centre, and 4km (2½ miles) from the airport, this hotel, part of the Rica chain, offers full conference facilities and well-appointed rooms. **$$**

Rica Ishavshotel
Fr. Langesgate 2
Tel: 77 66 64 00
www.rica.no/ishavshotel
First-rate luxury hotel close to the centre, with 180

tastefully decorated rooms overlooking the fjord. **$$$**

E ATING OUT

RECOMMENDED RESTAURANTS, CAFÉS AND BARS

What to Eat

Norwegians eat hearty breakfasts, but light lunches; the size of the evening meal (middag) depends on the day of the week and the occasion.

With the abundant supply of seafood and what can be gleaned from forest and field, the Norwegian diet has traditionally been healthy and appetising. For example, white bread is rarely purchased as most Norwegians prefer brown bread or dry crackers for breakfast. However, the younger generation tends to eat frozen pizzas and ready-meals.

The hunting season (early autumn) offers some irresistible temptations: pheasant, grouse, elk and reindeer steaks served with peppercorns, berry preserves and coulis, and rich wild mushroom sauces. It is also a good time of year to make the most of

Coffee

Coffee is the national stimulant and served whenever people meet. But the real difficulty is coping with the mounds of pastry often served with the coffee; if you must refuse, do so politely, especially if you are turning down home-made pastries.

seafood (with cod considered best in months with an R in them).

Outside main meals there are many coffee breaks, often served with bolle (raisin buns) and wienerbrød (lighter pastries with fruit or nuts).

Frokost (breakfast) is more or less a variation of the lunch Kaldtbord, a spread including breads (try grovbrød and knekkebrød), sausage, cheese (try the piquant Gudbrandsost, a delicious burned goats' milk cheese

with a dark golden colour), ham, eggs, and coffee and tea. Norwegians seldom eat a warm meal for lunch. Instead, many take a packed lunch (matpakke) to work, often consisting of a couple of slices of bread with any of the toppings above. Smørbrød (from the Danish "butter and bread") is an open-faced sandwich sold in cafés around lunchtime. Popular toppings include ham, smoked salmon, shrimps and karbonade, or a small minced-meat patty.

Dinner in a city restaurant can be anything you wish. In someone's home you might eat mutton stew or a fish ragout. Boiled potatoes, sometimes with parsley, usually accompany a hot main course. When dining in more remote places, the menus will invariably be limited by availability. Norwegians usually eat their dinner early when at home (4pm

Norwegian Specialities

Norway is not famed abroad for its cuisine, but there are many excellent specialities to try out, particularly around Christmas time, so if you're travelling to Norway in December do make sure you give them a go. They include:

Pinnekjøtt: Salted, dried and sometimes smoked mutton or lamb ribs which are rehydrated and then steamed, usually over birch twigs (pinne), hence the name.

Ribbe: Roasted pork belly, usually served with sauerkraut and boiled potatoes, Christmas sausage, meatballs and gravy. Easy to prepare, cheap, and therefore very popular.

Lutefisk: Cod treated in lye and served with bacon bits, green peas,

butter sauce and again, boiled potatoes. The fish acquires a jelly-like texture (the more pronounced the longer you cook it), so some find the appearance rather off-putting, although many locals love it. You decide.

Other non-Christmas-related specialities include, fårikål, rakfisk and smalahove.

Fårikål: One of Norway's most popular dishes, traditionally eaten in the last week of September, fårikål literally means "sheep in cabbage", although some Norwegians use lamb instead. Because the cabbage and the meat simmer for hours in the pot, both end up being so soft they melt in the mouth.

Rakfisk: A speciality from Valdres, in eastern Norway, rakfisk is made of fish (usually trout or char) that has been left to ferment in brine for two to three months before being eaten raw, usually on a slice of flat bread with onions, sour cream and boiled potatoes. It's pungent stuff, but it is not without its adepts – there is even a Rakfisk Festival, which takes place every year in November, that attracts thousands of rakfisk-lovers.

Smalahove: Not for the squeamish: half a head of sheep is salted and smoked, then boiled for a few hours before serving. It makes up with taste what it lacks in looks – although not many tourists can pluck up the courage to try it.

is not unusual in winter), and may also take a little snack later in the evening (called *aftens*), usually of bread or crackers with butter, cheese and salami or ham.

For dessert, ice cream is a favourite, as is apple pie. In summer there are all kinds of puddings based on the fresh berries that grow in the Norwegian woods. Waffles are also extremely popular, and are usually served with sour cream and strawberry or raspberry jam.

Where to Eat

There has been a significant increase in what's on offer when you choose to eat out in Norway. Pizza is very popular, and the main chains are Peppes and Dolly Dimple's, both of which serve large, American-style pizzas to share. Asian food has also become a local favourite, although many restaurants tend to tone down the spices to suit the Norwegian palate. Continental European dishes have always played a role in Norwegian cuisine (such as Viennese-

Drinking Notes

No one talks about a trip to Norway without complaining of the high cost of alcohol. For those who can afford the prices, serving hours are long; in Oslo you can drink spirits until midnight and wine or beer until 3am.

Outside Oslo, times are less predictable; a conservative Lutheran culture holds sway in many west-coast areas, rendering some counties virtually dry. But there are exceptions to this: in Oslo, for example, there are some no-alcohol hotel/restaurants, and in the "dry" counties it is always possible to find

and French-style dishes), but pride in native foods and an interest in "new Scandinavian" cuisine is prevalent.

At lunchtime many restaurants offer special fixed-price menus. More casual meals can be had from establishments such as *stovas*, *kros*, *bistros*, *kafés*, *kafeterias* and *gjæstgiveris*, and may sell alcohol as

a hotel/restaurant that serves some form of alcohol. The Vinmonopolet (state off-licences/liquor stores) in cities are open Mon–Fri 10am–6pm and Sat 9am–2pm; they are closed on election days, holidays and the preceding day of a holiday.

Most Norwegians drink beer and/or wine. Traditional *Akevitt*, similar in taste to Schnapps, is derived from potato and caraway seeds, and is also a favourite. It can be sipped neat in small glasses at room temperature, or served cold with beer to accompany salty, spicy or pungent dishes.

well as coffee and soft drinks. For an even more casual meal, buy a hot dog (*pølse*) or kebab from a kiosk.

Restaurants

Restaurants are grouped by area starting with Oslo. They are listed alphabetically.

RESTAURANT LISTINGS

OSLO

Norwegian

Bølgen & Moi Tjuvholmen
Tjuvholmen allé 5
Tel: 22 44 10 20
The latest restaurant in the successful Bølgen & Moi stable, located in the new Tjuvholmen development, on the Oslo waterfront. Top-notch brasserie-style food served in funky, colourful surroundings. **$$**

De Fem Stuer
Holmenkollen Park Hotel
Tel: 22 92 27 34
Elegant dining inside the historic timbered salons of this fairytale-like hotel overlooking the city and fjord. **$$$**

Det Gamle Raadhus
Nedre Slotts Gate 1
Tel: 22 42 01 07
Housed in the capital's old city hall from the 1600s, now best known for its *lutefisk* in the months leading up to Christmas. **$$**

DS Louise
Stranden 3
Tel: 22 83 00 60
This was one of the first restaurants to open at the waterfront complex Aker Brygge. Nostalgic maritime decor and a wide range of traditional dishes. **$$**

Ekeberg Restaurant
Kongsveien 15
Tel: 23 24 23 00
Take the No. 18/19 tram to Sjømannsskolen and walk up the hill to this recently restored gem. Knockout view over the city and fjord; large outdoor terrace. **$$**

Grand Café
Karl Johans Gate 31
Tel: 23 21 20 00
Henrik Ibsen's former haunt, known for its murals and stylish surroundings near the Parliament. **$$**

Kaffistova
Rosenkrantz Gate 8
Tel: 23 21 42 10
Cafeteria-style place

dishing up authentic rural Norwegian food. Fast and filling. **$**

Posthallen
Prinsensgate 8
Tel: 22 41 17 30
Striking restaurant in what used to be Oslo's main post office. Excellent food and a sexy vibe that makes Posthallen a great place to start a night out in town. **$$**

Solsiden
Sondre Akershus Kai 34
Tel: 22 33 36 30
One of the best seafood restaurants in Oslo, situated right on the harbour under the historic Akershus Fortress. Summer only. **$$**

Sult
Th. Meyers Gate 26
Tel: 22 87 04 67
Named after Knut Hamsun's novel *Hunger*, this restaurant in the newly revitalised Grünerløkka district serves simple, fresh food dubbed

"neo-Norsk". **$$**

Theatercafeen
Stortings Gate 24–26
Tel: 22 82 40 50
Vienna-style café; classic dishes served with flair, live violin music. The place to see and be seen. **$$**

Continental/International

Alex Sushi
Cort Adelers Gate 2
Tel: 22 43 99 99
The *New York Times* lavished praise on this

PRICE CATEGORIES

Price categories are based on a three-course evening meal per head, excluding wine. Expect to pay a little bit more in Oslo and Bergen, a little bit less in less touristy places.
$ = Less than NOK 250
$$ = NOK 250–500
$$$ = More than NOK 500

TRANSPORT

ACCOMMODATION

EATING OUT

ACTIVITIES

A – Z

LANGUAGE

neighbourhood sushi place. Book well in advance. **$$**

Baltazar Ristorante & Enoteca
Dronningens Gate 27
Tel: 23 35 70 60
Oslo's best Italian restaurant, offering authentic cuisine in convivial surroundings. It is located in the arches behind the cathedral – with alfresco eating in summer. Casual *enoteca* downstairs and a more formal restaurant on the first floor. **$$–$$$**

Bambus
Kirkeveien 57
Tel: 22 85 07 00
Blend of Thai, Vietnamese and Japanese food in a stylish setting in Oslo's trendy Majorstuen district. **$**

Beach Club
Bryggetorget 14
Tel: 22 83 83 82
There is no shortage of places to eat in Aker Brygge, but this laid-back café is a great place to enjoy a substantial burger and a milkshake while watching

life go by. There is a huge outdoor terrace for hot summer days. **$**

Brasserie France
Øvre Slottsgate 16
Tel: 23 10 01 65
You'll think you're in Paris, but the quality of the shellfish is definitely Norwegian. **$$**

Dinner
Stortingsgate 22
Tel: 23 10 04 66
This upmarket Chinese restaurant serves spicy Szechuan cuisine, hailed by Chinese aficionados. **$$**

Hells Kitchen
Møllergata 23
Tel: 22 11 20 00
A good address by Youngstorget, serving excellent pizzas, including several meat-free options for vegetarians, in a somewhat tired, but ever so popular diner. **$**

Nighthawk Diner
Seilduksgata 15B
Tel: 96 62 73 27
This is the restaurant *du jour*, in trendy Løkka (Grünerløkka), inspired

by Tom Waits's album *Nighthawks at the Diner*. You might have to wait for your order to reach your table, and your waiter might forget part of it, but this American diner makes up with attitude and chrome what it lacks in expertise or originality. **$–$$**

Oro Restaurant and Bar
Tordenskiolds Gate 6A
Tel: 23 01 02 40
Choose between elegant dining in the main gourmet restaurant, or tapas in the adjacent bar/café. **$$–$$$**

Restaurant Eik
Universitetsgata 11
Tel: 22 36 07 10
Arguably the best of Oslo's "menu-based" restaurants, where you select how many courses you want from a carefully planned multi-course meal. Excellent value for money. **$$**

San Leandro Tapas
Haakon VIIs Gate 10
Tel: 22 83 34 44
Tapas are increasingly popular in Oslo, and there are many outlets to choose

from. This informal place situated in Vika serves tasty titbits from early afternoon to late at night. It makes a good choice for a pre- or post-theatre dinner. There are two other branches in Oslo, one in Majorstuen, and another in Grünerløkka. **$**

Statholdergaarden
Rådhus Gate 11
Tel: 22 41 88 00
Danish chef Bent Stiansen is host in the elegant restaurant upstairs and the bar downstairs, in an urban home dating back to the 1700s. **$$$**

Villa Paradiso
Olaf Ryes Plass 8
Tel: 22 35 40 60
Arguably serving the best pizzas in Oslo, this family-friendly pizzeria in Grünerløkka also has a good choice of antipasti and desserts. Grab a table outside overlooking the little park and enjoy a meal and a glass of wine while the children run free in the playroom downstairs. **$**

STAVANGER

Charlottenlund
Kongsgaten 45
Tel: 51 91 76 00
Norwegian- and French-inspired cuisine served in a mansion on the lake in the heart of town. **$$–$$$**

Hall Toll
Skansegaten 2
Tel: 51 51 72 32
Housed in a former customs hall on the waterfront, this relatively new restaurant is cavernous, with an

innovative menu and chic clientele. Open kitchen. **$$**

Naree Thai
Breigata 22
Tel: 51 89 05 10
This small restaurant, a stone's throw from the Norwegian Petroleum Museum, serves cheap and very decent Thai food. **$**

N.B. Sørensens Dampskibsexpedition
Skagen 26
Tel: 51 84 38 20

One of the most traditional restaurants in Stavanger, decorated in nautical style to match its location by the waterfront at Vågen. The menu features international dishes using fresh Norwegian ingredients. **$$**

Sjokoladepiken (The Chocolate Girl)
Øvre Holmegate 27
Tel: 47 20 19 84
Not a restaurant as such, but this gorgeous café

has become a bit of an institution. Great coffee, ice cream, cakes and of course chocolate, declined in all its glorious forms. **$**

Tango Bar & Kjøkken
Nedre Strandgate 25
Tel: 51 50 12 30
Hailed by many locals as one of the best restaurants in Stavanger. The menu features the best ingredients prepared with imagination and care. **$$$**

BERGEN

Bølgen & Moi
Rasmus Meyers Allé 9
Tel: 55 59 77 00
A great choice for anyone visiting the art galleries on Rasmus Meyers Allé, this is the Bergen outlet of the popular franchise. Modern fare, with good-value lunch menus. **$$**

Bryggen Tracteursted
Bryggen 6
Tel: 55 33 69 99
Traditional Norwegian fare and great fish dishes in historical surrounds. **$$**

Dickens
King Olav Vs Plass
Tel: 55 36 31 30
This informal setting is

popular and relaxed, serving good meals, light snacks or just drinks. **$$**

Fløien Folkerestaurant
Top of Fløien funicular
Tel: 55 32 18 75
Good, reasonably priced food with intoxicating view. Work up an appetite by walking there. **$$**

Holbergstuen
Torgallmenningen 6
Tel: 55 55 20 55
In the heart of the town. Good traditional dishes. **$$**

Lucullus
Valkendorfsgaten 8
Tel: 55 30 68 00
This award-winning, classic gourmet French

ABOVE: the freshest seafood.

restaurant in the Neptun Hotel has been hailed as one of the best in Norway. Expertly prepared dishes, professional service and an extensive wine list. **$$$**

Mago Café
Neumanns Gate 5
Tel: 55 96 29 80
Eco-friendly restaurant that

claims to be good for your digestion as well as tasty. Organic vegetables and free-range meat and fish. **$**

Peppes
Finnegården, Bryggen
Tel: 22 22 55 55
This popular pizza chain has several outlets in Bergen, the best one of which is

this one, located just a few metres from the fish market and Bryggen. Expect the usual fare of American-style pizzas, with a couple of more exotic options. **$**

Potetkjelleren
Kong Oscars Gate 1
Tel: 55 32 00 70
Don't be fooled by the unpromising name – the "potato cellar" is one of Bergen's best restaurants, and an obvious choice for a romantic dinner, with its vaulted ceilings and candlelit dining room. The food is excellent, and influences from around the world can be seen on the menu. Dinner only. **$$–$$$**

Stragiotti Bar & Ristorante
Vestre Torggate 3
Tel: 55 90 31 00
This family restaurant

makes a change from Norwegian staples; it's located in pleasant surroundings and offers authentic Italian food with good service. **$$**

To Kokker (Two Chefs)
Bryggen 29
Tel: 55 30 69 55
Located on Bryggen in Bergen, this well-known restaurant serves Norwegian and French dishes. Specialities of the house include game, fish and seafood. **$$$**

Wesselstuen
Øvre Ole Bulls Plass 6
Tel: 55 55 49 49
Traditional Norwegian fish and meat dishes, including the much-praised Bergen fish soup, are served in pleasant, rustic surroundings. **$$**

TRONDHEIM

Big Horn Steakhouse
Munkegate 14, Ravnkloa
Tel: 73 50 94 90
Chain restaurant specialising in tasty spare ribs and juicy steaks. **$$**

Bryggen Asian Cooking
Øvre Bakklandet 66
Tel: 40 61 88 07
One of the most elegant restaurants in Trondheim, enjoying a great location right by the Nidelva River. Serves a range of Asian dishes, including sushi. **$$$**

Chablis Brasserie and Bar
Øvre Bakklandet 66
Tel: 73 87 42 50
Chablis is an informal French restaurant under the same roof as Bryggen Restaurant. Carefully sourced ingredients prepared with skill. **$$$**

Credo Restaurant and Bar
Ørjaveita 4A
Tel: 73 53 03 88
International-style restaurant acclaimed for its highly original, and perfectly

executed, food. No fixed menu. The wine cellar is one of Norway's best. **$$$**

Grenaderen
Kongsgårdsgata 1e
Tel: 73 51 66 80
A traditional menu, including fish and reindeer, is served in a 16th-century forge. **$$–$$$**

Havfruen
Kjøpmannsgata 7
Tel: 73 87 40 70
Some of Norway's finest fish and seafood dishes,

although meat is also available. Trendy bar. **$$**

Jadab Indian Restaurant
Brattørgata 5
Tel: 73 52 46 00
Indian restaurants are not so common in Norway, but this place offers very decent food at a good price. **$**

Trondheim Mikkrobryggeri
Prinsensgate 39
Tel: 73 51 75 15
Affordable pub-style fare served in a former brewery, with a choice of beers. **$**

TROMSØ

Compagniet
Sjøgata 12
Tel: 77 66 42 22
Gourmet fare in historical surroundings. The small selection of dishes changes with the seasons, but always features the best of local raw ingredients. **$$$**

Emmas Drømmekjøkken (Emma's Dream Kitchen)
Kirkegata 8
Tel: 77 63 77 30
A restaurant that's been getting rave reviews since opening more than 10 years ago. Romantic setting and

top-notch food make this an excellent choice for that special evening. **$$$**

Store Norske Fiskekompani
Storgata 73
Tel: 77 68 76 00
Just fish served here, to the highest quality and taken straight from the harbour. Styles vary from traditional to "New Scandinavian". **$$$**

Studenthuset Driv
Søndre Tollbugate 3b
Tel: 77 60 07 76
Simple, student-style restaurant with reasonably

priced pizzas, said to be the best in town, and pastas. Outdoor sitting in summer. **$**

Thai House Restaurant
Storgata 22
Tel: 77 67 05 26
Small, cosy restaurant offering a good selection of authentic Thai dishes at reasonable prices. **$**

Vertshuset Skarven
Strandtorget 1
Tel: 77 60 07 20
This popular, informal restaurant serves the likes of seal lasagne, seaweed and shellfish soup, fresh

mussels and reindeer stew. The *biffhus* in the same building specialises in steaks, while Arctandria is a seafood restaurant. **$$**

TRANSPORT

ACCOMMODATION

EATING OUT

ACTIVITIES

A – Z

LANGUAGE

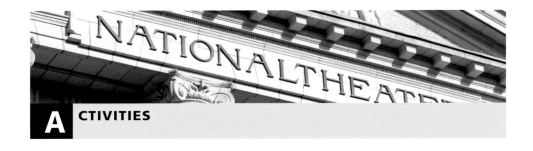

ACTIVITIES

THE ARTS, NIGHTLIFE, FESTIVALS, SHOPPING, OUTDOOR ACTIVITIES AND CHILDREN

THE ARTS

Music and Opera

In summer the arts take to the outdoors in Norway, and classical music and opera are no exception. For Oslo dates, pick up the *What's On in Oslo* guide. The very active Oslo Philharmonic, founded by Edvard Grieg and based at the Oslo Concert House (Konserthuset) in Vika, has frequent visits by acclaimed guest conductors and soloists. Den Norske Opera (National Opera), which relocated in 2008 to new premises on the waterfront in Bjørvika, stages big productions such as *La Bohème* and *Don Giovanni* during the year.

Akershus Fortress and the Henie Onstad Art Centre (in Høvikodden) are two other fine settings for summer concerts, and there are several outdoor rock and pop festivals from June to August *(see Festivals, below)*.

Whether the performers are Norwegian or foreign, the season winter or summer, Norway has a rich and varied musical and operatic life (consult area guides for festival schedules). This may be your chance to listen to some of the conductors and performers you had previously only heard on Deutsche Gramophone CDs, or a first opportunity to see Grieg performed by Norwegian musicians.

Theatre and Dance

Theatre is booming in Norway, with small, contemporary theatres springing up everywhere; but performances are in Norwegian. Some plays are held in English during the Ibsen Theatre Festival in August in Oslo. Dance has also come into its own. Classical ballet is performed at the Oslo Opera House. Traditional folk dances can be seen in many towns on National Day (17 May), and at Oslo's Konserthus.

Cinema

The Norwegians love films, hence the vast number of cinemas; Oslo has around 40 screens, including the impressive wide-screen cinema at Colosseum in Frogner. First-run and repertory films are always shown in the original language, with Norwegian subtitles. Kiosks, newspapers and local city guides have listings. Book ahead for Fridays and Saturdays.

NIGHTLIFE

Oslo, once considered a big yawn at night, is now vying with Stockholm and Copenhagen to be Scandinavia's nightlife capital. Loads of new bars, pubs and clubs have come onto the scene, but many can't recoup their investments quickly enough and go out of business. So check locally for up-to-date venue listings, or see the official *Oslo Guide* on the website www.visitoslo.com. DJs from around the world regularly come to Oslo, and there are often live concerts, especially at weekends. International rock, folk and jazz musicians often include Oslo on European tours. The city also has a well-established jazz scene. All towns and cities have nightlife guides.

Please note that all restaurants, bars and nightclubs in Norway are smoke-free. Many have outdoor tables for smokers (with heaters and blankets provided in winter).

Bergen, Stavanger, Trondheim and Tromsø also have good nightlife, although on a smaller scale. In minor towns most large hotels have nightclubs and bars, but little else.

There are only two things you need to be warned about before a night out: the high cost of drinking, and age restrictions: some clubs have minimum ages as high as 26 (21 and 23 are more common).

FESTIVALS

January

Geilo: Ice Music Festival, where all the musical instruments have been carved from a block of ice.
Tromsø: International Film Festival.

February

Kristiansund: Opera Festival. Two or three opera productions plus church music, ballet and other concerts.
Longyearbyen, Svalbard: Polar Jazz. The world's nothernmost jazz festival, 645km (400 miles) from the North Pole. First held in 1998, this festival is still going strong.
Rorosmartnan: The Roros Fair has been an annual tradition since 1854. Markets, concerts, exhibitions.
Tromsø: Northern (De)lights Festival. Music ranging from Baroque to contemporary, from jazz to classical.

March

Alta: Northern Lights Winter Festival, with music, theatre, markets, ski and

Bergen Festival

Bergen's International Festival (*Festspillene i Bergen*) in late May/early June is one of Scandinavia's largest cultural events, covering music, drama, ballet, opera, jazz and folk arts.

For a festival brochure and further details contact: Bergen International Festival, PO Box 183, 5804 Bergen, tel: 55 21 06 30; www.fib.no.

snowmobile competitions and plenty of fun in the snow.
Narvik: Winter Festival. Church music, jazz, classical music, markets, carnival and sports events.
Lillehammer: Blues Festival. International and Norwegian musicians.
Voss: Vossajazz. Three days and nights of jazz and folk music with international and Norwegian performers.
Oslo: Church Music Festival. Concerts in Oslo Cathedral and other churches in the city. Oslo: Inferno Festival, heavy metal.
Kautokeino: Sami Easter Festival, with concerts, art exhibits, reindeer races and snowmobile rallies.

April

Trondheim: Nidaros Blues Festival.
Bergen: Music Festival, including blues, country & western, cajun and rock. Norwegian and international artists perform throughout the city.

May

Constitution Day (17 May). Celebrations and parades all over Norway.
Stavanger: International Jazz Festival.
Bergen: International Festival. One of Norway's artistic highlights. World-class music, dance and theatre in a beautiful setting. Also Nattjazz – an international jazz festival.
Ål: Norwegian Folk Music Week with concerts, song and dance. Competition between the best fiddlers and dancers in the region.
Bergen: Dragon Boat Festival in the harbour.
Stavanger: Maijazz. Traditional jazz festival. Both international and Norwegian artists perform in more than 30 concerts.
Hardanger: Music and culture from the Hardanger fjord area, with chamber, church and folk music.

June

Oslo: Norwegian Wood. Rock music festival with Norwegian and international artists.
Kopervik: Viking Festival, with plays, storytelling, market and Viking camp.
Harstad: North Norway Festival, with music, theatre, dance and art exhibitions.

June/July

Grimstad. Norwegian Short Film Festival. With around 80 short and documentary films.
Vestfold: Arts festival – Norwegian and international artists perform in locations all over the county.

July

Kristiansand. Quart International rock festival. Performers from the US and Europe.
Forde: Norway's largest folk music festival, with more than 250 performers from all over the world.
Molde: International Jazz Festival. Norway's largest jazz festival, with more than 400 performers, many of them world-famous.
Bø: Telemark Festival with traditional folk, blues and jazz music.
Stavanger: Gladmat, the country's largest food festival, taking place around the harbour.
Lofthus: Cherry Festival.
Åndalnes: Norway's Mountain Festival.

July/August

Vinstra: Peer Gynt Festival. Art exhibits, music, processions with national costumes, open-air theatre. Performance of Henrik Ibsen's *Peer Gynt* and Edvard Grieg's music.

BELOW: one of Oslo's many outdoor festivals.

Trondheim: St Olav's Festival. Various cultural events commemorating the death of St Olav at the Battle of Stiklestad in 1030.

August

Oslo: Jazz Festival. Over 60 concerts in six days. Øya Music Festival, rock music festival.
Bodø: Nordland Music Festival. Classical, jazz, rock and folk music – with national and international artists. Also church concerts, music theatre, art exhibitions.
Stavanger: International Chamber Music Festival. Renowned soloists and new talents perform chamber music in various ensembles.
Hammerfest: Music and Theatre Festival focusing on culture in northern Norway.
Haugesund: Norwegian International Film Festival. Also Sildajazz, international jazz festival.
Risør: Wooden Boat Festival.
Notodden: Notodden International Blues Festival.
Ålesund: Food Festival (Den Norske Matfestivalen).

September

Oslo: Ultima Contemporary Music Festival. Norway's largest.

October

Lillehammer: Jazz Festival. Mainly Norwegian performers.
Stavanger: Norwegian Youth Chamber Music Festival.

November

Fagernes. Rakfisk Festival: a festival celebrating this local speciality, which consists of salt-cured trout left to ferment in brine for several months, and then eaten uncooked. You can sample this local favourite on the first weekend of the month.

December

Oslo: Parade past the Grand Hotel to honour the winner of the Nobel Peace Prize, plus a Nobel concert in the Oslo Spektrum. Christmas Market at City Hall Square.

SHOPPING

What to Buy

Popular souvenirs from Norway include knitted jumpers, cardigans, gloves and mittens, pewter, silver jewellery and cutlery, hand-painted wooden objects (like bowls with rose designs), trolls and fjord horses carved out of wood, goat and reindeer skin, enamel jewellery, woven wall designs, furs, handicrafts, glassware and pottery (see Tax-free Shopping, below, on how to reclaim tax).

The major department stores have a good selection of most of these items. If you want speciality stores in Oslo, there is a Where to Shop guide, as well as a detailed "Shopping" section in the Oslo Guide (see www.visitoslo.com). Karl Johans gate, Grensen and Bogstadveien are all major shopping streets. With the exception of Oslo, most towns are so compact that your best bet is to window-shop and go into the places that look most appealing.

There are several bookshops in Oslo with English-language sections, including: **Tanum Karl Johan** at Karl Johans gate 37/41, tel: 22 41 11 00, and **Norli**, Storgata 17, 0162 Oslo,

tel: 22 00 43 91.

Anyone interested in buying Norwegian art will have ample prospects – from south to north, Norway abounds in galleries. Get a local recommendation.

If you are food shopping, fruit and vegetable prices vary considerably throughout the year. Look out for lavpris (low-price) shops offering discounts. The first Saturday of each month is "Super Saturday", when shops in Oslo open longer and offer special discounts. Most bottles (whether plastic or glass) have a returnable deposit of NOK 1 (pant).

Glasmagasinet, Stortorvet 9, and Steen & Strøm, Kongensgate 23, are Oslo's largest department stores. Oslo City and By Porten, next to Oslo main train station, and Aker Brygge on the waterfront are three major malls. The largest shopping centre of all, indeed the biggest in Scandinavia, with 190 shops over eight floors, is located a few kilometres west of the city centre at Sandvika.

Tax-Free Shopping

If you are a resident of a country other than Norway, Sweden, Denmark or Finland, you are entitled to tax-free shopping on purchases in excess of NOK 315 at any of the 3,000 stores connected to the scheme.

The store issues you with a tax-free voucher for the amount of VAT paid. When you leave Norway, a refund of 11–18 percent (depending on the sale price) will be refunded on presentation of the goods, the tax-free voucher and your passport, on condition that the item has not been used while in Norway. Global Refund has its own representatives at a total of 100 refund places, including airports, international ferry terminals

Shopping Hours

Weekdays Generally 9am–5pm, with late Thursday opening for many stores until 7 or 8pm. Stores may close earlier in summer, especially on Fridays.
Saturday Usually 9am–1, 2 or 3pm.
Shopping centres such as Aker Brygge, Palléet and Oslo City in Oslo, Galleriet in Bergen and City Syd in Trondheim are open until 8 or 9pm on week nights.
Kiosks tend not to close until 10pm or even 11pm, and are usually open all weekend.
Supermarkets Most stay open until 8pm.
Petrol stations are usually open until at least 11pm.

and at the main border crossings. Check opening times, as they are not open 24 hours, and make sure there is a refund desk if you are using a small border crossing. Customs officials cannot refund VAT.

For details, contact Global Refund Norge, PO Box 48 N-1332 Østerås; tel: 67 15 60 10; www.globalrefund.com.

OUTDOOR ACTIVITIES

If Norwegians can contrive a sport as an excuse to be outdoors, they'll do it. That's why there are such great facilities here; all Norwegians love sport. For a full listing of sports and sports facilities in the Oslo region, see the Outdoor Activities pages of the Oslo Guide; www.visitoslo.com.

Boating

Foreign visitors are always welcome in boating circles, and there are hundreds of sailing and boating clubs and associations throughout Norway. The national organisation for recreational and competitive motor-boating is: Kongelig Norsk Båtforbund, Vågebyveien 23, 0569 Oslo; tel: 22 35 68 00; www.knbf.no.

The most popular volumes of the six-volume Den Norske Los (Norwegian Pilot), the meticulously detailed manual of all navigable waters, is available with Norwegian and English texts. Volume 3 covers the southwest coast from south of Stavanger to north of Bergen, volume 2 Oslofjord and the south coast. If you are planning a sailing holiday, obtain a copy of Guest Harbours in

BELOW: you're never too young to start fishing.

Norway (available from tourist offices, see page 370), which provides valuable information, including place descriptions, sketch maps and details of the coastguard escort service. Cruising in Norwegian Waters is another useful boating book.

Canoeing

Numerous rivers and lakes in Norway offer canoeing and kayaking. Some of the best include the Femund area, Østfold, Aust and Vest Agder, Telemark and suburban Oslo. Contact the local tourist office for details, or **Norges Padleforbund** (Norwegian Canoe Association), Service Boks 1, Ullevaal Stadion, 0840 Oslo; tel: 21 02 98 35; www.padling.no.

Cycling

As a particularly popular method of transport in Norway, cycling is considered relatively safe. Special routes exist during summer, and special cycle paths can be found in rural areas. For details on planning a cycling holiday and renting bicycles, see Getting Around, page 347.

Fishing

With a coastline of 21,465km (13,330 miles), as well as countless fjords, lakes and rivers, Norway is a fisherman's paradise. In summer there are many boat cruises, and in some fjord towns groups can charter boats for fishing or pleasure.

The fishing is excellent in Norway, whether you're at sea or on a fjord, lake or river; enquire locally about short-term permits. To fish char,

Wildlife Safaris

Wildlife safaris are a popular way of getting up close and personal with local fauna. Many different safaris are organised up and down the country, whether it's whale-watching off the Lofoten Islands, king-crab fishing in the Barents Sea, swimming with wild salmon near Stavanger, or elk-spotting in the vast expanses of forest in eastern Norway. Several operators also arrange bird-watching safaris, and many cater for photo-enthusiasts, even renting equipment if required. For more information, contact the tourist office (see page 370), which will point you in the right direction, depending on your interest.

Night Skies

Midnight sun Above the Arctic Circle the sun does not sink below the horizon for several weeks in the summer. The best time to see the midnight sun is mid-May to late July. The further north one goes, the longer the midnight sun lasts. Longyearbyen on Svalbard has the longest period of midnight suns, from about 20 April to 20 August.

Aurora borealis The northern lights, or aurora borealis, are most likely to occur from November to February. Again, you need to go north of the Arctic Circle, which cuts through Norway just south of Bodø on the Nordland coast. As with all natural phenomena, however, there is no guarantee they will occur during your stay.

salmon, sea trout or inland fish, you must be over 16. A fee is payable. See Angling in Norway (available from tourist offices, see page 370) for full details. Fishing at sea does not require a licence.

Golf

This popular sport has only recently caught on in Norway, and many landowners, be they farmers or municipal authorities, have turned over land to developing golf links. The few Norwegian golf courses are by and large difficult and challenging. Many of them require either a Green Card or a handicap under 20. Green fees are more expensive than at other European golf courses.

In the Oslo region professional competitions are held at Bogstad, Larvik, Borre and Vestfold golf clubs, but by far the most beautifully situated is the Tyrifjord golf links. For information and club details, contact: **Norges Golfforbund**, 0840 Oslo Tel: 21 02 91 50 www.golfforbundet.no

Hiking

One of the country's favourite pastimes, hiking can be done anywhere and combines well with other activities such as berry-gathering or swimming in a lake. The country's mountain ranges and high plains make ideal walking terrain. The most popular areas include the Jotunheim mountain range; the Rondane and Dovrefjell Mountains; the Hardangervidda plateau; and the Finnmarksvidda plain. Mountain cabins are open from the end of June until mid-September, and at Easter.

The Norwegian Trekking Association (DNT) runs guided hikes of varying difficulty during the summer, and glacier walks in winter. It also has a wealth of information on hiking and maps for the whole of Norway and can recommend cabin-to-cabin hiking holidays. Foreigners can write

requesting membership, which gives you certain free publications and hut access (there are 440 in the network). **Den Norske Turistforening** (The Norwegian Trekking Association) Youngstorget 1, 0181 Oslo Tel: 22 82 28 22 www.turistforeningen.no/english

Glacier-Hiking

Not for the lily-livered, glacier-hiking is an exhilarating and exciting experience – which should only be attempted with an experienced local guide. Several Norwegian tour companies offer guided glacier (bre) walks, most particularly in the following areas:
Fjords: Hardangerjøkulen, Folgefonna, Buarbre, Bondhusbre, Smørstabbre, Fannaråkbre and Nigardsbre.
Oppland: Styggebre.
Norland: Svartisen and Engenbreen.
Alternatively, you could contact one of the **Glacier Information Centres** in western Norway at Oppstryn (tel: 57 87 72 00), Fjærland (tel: 57 69 32 88/33) and Josterdalen (tel: 57 68 32 50).

Horse Riding

The Norwegian fjord horse is one of the world's oldest horse breeds. Norway offers a wide range of opportunities for the rider, whether you wish to hire a pony for trekking or take lessons. Enquire at the local tourist office or at your hotel or camp-site for further information, or contact the Norwegian Equestrian Federation at www.rytter.no.

Skiing

Along with hiking, this is the primary participant sport in Norway. Even in the summer Norwegians take to the slopes in the country's mid-north (as a rule from June to September), and the sight of people swooping down the slopes wearing bikinis or trunks

TRANSPORT
ACCOMMODATION
EATING OUT
ACTIVITIES
A – Z
LANGUAGE

Walking in the National Parks

The Ministry of Environment has set up 40 national parks (33 on mainland Norway, seven on Svalbard) to protect the country's distinctive characteristics. Here are the highlights:

Børgefjell 1,107 sq km (427 sq miles), on the border between Nord-Trøndelag and Nordland. Fishing and hunting (licences required) for hare and grouse are available. The western part of the park has high peaks with cirque glaciers and steep-walled ravines. Many birds inhabit the wetland areas, while Arctic foxes and wolverines live in the park.

Dovre 256 sq km (100 sq miles), in central Norway. The western part of the park is dominated by precipitous slopes, with Snøhetta rising to 2,286 metres (7,500ft). The east has calcareous bedrock; this is northern Europe's richest mountain in terms of plant life. Wild reindeer and a few musk oxen, introduced to Norway from Greenland, inhabit the area.

Femundsmarka 390 sq km (150 sq miles), between Hedmark and Sør-Trøndelag. Lakes and streams make Femundsmarka a dream for anglers, with big trout abounding in the many streams and lakes.

Gressåmoen 182 sq km (70 sq miles), in Nord-Trøndelag. This was established to protect ancient and almost undisturbed spruce forest. The park has lakes abounding in trout and burbot. Wading birds, with the whimbrels as a characteristic species, thrive in the wetland areas.

Gutulia 19 sq km (7 sq miles) south of Femundsmarka, bordering with Sweden. The undisturbed forest supports numerous species of birds. Here, 250-year-old spruce trees and 350-year-old pine trees can be found.

Hardangervidda 3,422 sq km (1,320 sq miles), covering parts of the Hordaland, Telemark and Buskerud regions in southern central Norway. The park is the home of the largest herd of wild reindeer in Europe, and also the southern limit of many Arctic plants and animals, such as the Arctic fox and snowy owl. The largest mountain plateau in northern Europe.

Jostedalsbreen 1,230 sq km (475 sq miles), situated between the Sognefjord and the Nordfjord, is the largest glacier in mainland Europe, being 80km (50 miles) long. Many wild reindeer inhabit the western part of the park, whereas

domesticated reindeer can be found in the Lom-Vågå district.

Jotunheimen 1,145 sq km (442 sq miles), extends over parts of Oppland and Sogn and Fjordane. Jotunheimen features Norway's highest mountains.

Ormtjernkampen 9 sq km (3 sq miles), just northwest of Lille-hammer, in the county of Oppland. Ormtjernkampen is Norway's smallest national park. It represents a typical eastern Norwegian old-growth spruce forest undisturbed by logging activities.

Rago 167 sq km (65 sq miles), approximately 25km (15 miles) north of Fauske in Nordland. Rago is dominated by a wild mountain landscape with deep ravines. The unique watercourse landscape is characterised by waterfalls and rivers flowing over polished rock.

Reisa 803 sq km (310 sq miles), in Nordreisa in Troms, about 60km (37 miles) from Finnmark. Consists of narrow valleys and ravines, mighty waterfalls, river gorges and potholes. The national park is dominated by Reisadalen – a canyon in northern Troms formed by the cutting action of the Reisaelva River into the mountain plateau.

Rondane 580 sq km (225 sq miles), just south of Dovrefjell Park, in Oppland. Known as the last outpost of the vulnerable wild reindeer. The vegetation is sparse because of altitude and climate. Most of the area is characterised by impressive, barren mountains, narrow gorges and deep cirques. Among the animal species which can survive the climate are wild reindeer, stray wolverines, snow bunting and rock ptarmigan.

Saltfjellet – Svartisen 1,840 sq km (710 sq miles). Svartisen Glacier (370 sq km/140 sq miles) is the largest ice sheet in northern Scandinavia. Glomdalen offers polished marble, caves and underground rivers. Stormdalen's mountain-birch forest has an unusually high plant production.

Stabbursdalen 98 sq km (38 sq miles), south of Porsanger peninsula in Finnmark. The world's northernmost pine forest. The Stabburselva, which runs through the entire length of the park, is a famous salmon river.

Øvre Anarjåkka 1,399 sq km (540 sq miles), in the south of Finnmark. This remote area is characterised by

an ancient rolling landscape of birch forest, sparse pine, bogs and lakes.

Øvre Dividal 743 sq km (287 sq miles), in the region of Troms, bordering Sweden. The park has a rich mountain flora, with square-stemmed heather and Arctic rhododendron growing abundantly. A large number of domesticated reindeer graze in the park. Norway's four large animals of prey – brown bear, wolverine, wolf and lynx – are found in the area.

Øvre Pasvik 67 sq km (26 sq miles), the easternmost corner of Norway in Finnmark, bordering Finland and Russia. The largest area of primeval forest in the north. The area has a brown bear population. The watercourses are rich in fish, especially pike and perch.

Ånderdalen 69 sq km (27 sq miles), on the island of Senja in Troms. Undisturbed mountain-birch forests and wetlands dominate the park, but some coastal pine forests can be found. Stunted and contorted pine trees lend an air of wilderness.

On Svalbard

Nord-vest Spitsbergen 3,560 sq km (1,375 sq miles), covers the northwestern corner of Spitsbergen. Large colonies of seabirds, reindeer and walrus, plus areas of cultural and historical interest. The park includes the Moffen nature reserve and areas such as Danskøya and Amsterdamøya, where archaeological excavations have brought to light several whaling stations and graveyards from the 17th century.

Forlandet 640 sq km (247 sq miles), a long, thin island with flat beaches, high mountain peaks and small glaciers. The warming effect of the Gulf Stream makes this the nesting place of many bird species.

Sør Spitsbergen National Park 5,300 sq km (2,046 sq miles), covers the southern parts of Spits-bergen. Glaciers and permanent snow and ice cover 65 percent of the total area. The Arctic landscape is varied. There is a rich bird life, including several seabird colonies and important breeding sites for eider ducks and barnacle geese.

For more information

Contact regional tourist boards or the Directorate for Nature Manage-ment, N-7485 Trondheim. Tel: 73 58 05 00; www.dirnat.no.

is something to behold. There is both downhill and cross-country skiing available. The main ski resorts are at Lillehammer, Trysil, Geilo, Hemsedal, Norefjell (the nearest to Oslo) and Voss, but there are many more; all tourist offices can advise on local ski facilities for crosscountry and slalom.

Ask the Norwegian Tourist Board for a copy of the *Winter Travel Planner* for details of ski operators and resorts, or see www.skiinfo.no.

Swimming

Temperatures at beaches along the coast and inland reach 24°C (68°F), and even in the north it can be warm enough to swim. Most larger hotels have pools, and there are numerous leisure centres throughout Norway.

Water Sports

There are several possibilities for water-skiing and windsurfing along the coast, as well as on Norway's numerous lakes. Kite-surfing is also gaining popularity.

White-water rafting is available on the following rivers: Sjoaelva in Oppland, Trysilelva in Hedmark and Driva in Sør-Trøndelag.

The Norwegian coast offers very good conditions for diving. Cave and wreck diving are popular and there are many dive centres in the north, such as in Narvik and Lofoten, where the water visibility is extremely high. There are several diving centres along the west coast, particularly in the counties of Møre and Romsdal.

Spectator Sports

Annual skiing competitions, such as the Holmenkollen Ski Festival *(see*

Glaciers

One of the highlights of Norway is seeing the glaciers, but every year there are fatalities, when tourists are careless. Glaciers are in motion, so crevasses several metres wide and 30–40 metres (100–130ft) deep occur, often covered with snow. Never climb or venture onto or under a glacier without a guide.

Glacier Information Centres at the following places show films and exhibitions about the glaciers, and offer tours:

Oppstryn (tel: 57 87 72 00)
Fjærland (tel: 57 69 32 88/33)
Jostedalen (tel: 57 68 32 50)

ABOVE: glacier-walking on Briksdalsbreen.

page 105) are the primary spectator sport in Norway. Check local guides.

There are several horse-trotting and race tracks in Norway.

Other popular spectator sports include athletics (Bislett Games), marathon running, football (soccer), ice hockey and boat races. Again, check the *Oslo Guide* (www.visitoslo.com) or a local area guide or tourist office for further details.

Sporting Events

January

Tromsø: Polar Night Half-Marathon.
Geilo: World Kickslegding Championships.

February

Oslo: Holmenkollen Ski Marathon. Cross-country 42km (26 miles) through Nordmarka, Oslo's vast outdoor park. Biathlon World Cup.

March

Oslo: Holmenkollen: Ski Festival with World Cups in cross-country skiing, Nordic combined and ski jumping.
Lillehammer: World Cup Alpine Skiing Finals. Downhill, slalom, giant slalom and super G at the Kvitfjell and Hafjell.
Hemsedal: Winter Golf Tournament. Norway's only winter golf tournament on snow ("whites" instead of "greens").
Oslo: Holmenkollen: the world's largest ski competition for children 4 to 12 years old. Including cross-country races and family games.
Svolvær, Lofoten: World Cod Fishing Championships. Up to 300 competitors from near and far.
Lillehammer/Rena: Birkebeineren. International cross-country ski race with historical roots, covering the distance between Lillehammer and Rena, a 53km (33-mile) trek.

April

Svalbard Ski Marathon, the world's northernmost ski race, Spitsbergen.

May

Oslo: Holmenkollstafetten Street relay race.

June

Oslo: Bislett Games. International track and field competition with some of the best athletes in the world.
Trondheim: Midnight Golf Tournament over 18 holes. Every night until 2am.
Spitsbergen Marathon. The world's northernmost marathon. Also half-marathon and 10Ks.
Tromsø: Midnight Sun Marathon. Marathon and other competitions at midnight. Concerts and other entertainment.
Trondheim: The Great Challenge. Bicycle race from Trondheim to Oslo (540km). Also shorter distances: Lillehammer–Oslo and Eidsvoll–Oslo.
Bergen: Bergen Horse Show.

July

Lofthus: Fédération Aéronautique

BELOW: taking on the rapids, Sørlandet.

ABOVE: Hunderfossen Familiepark.

Internationale Paragliding Competition.
Stavanger: World Tour Beach Volleyball. One of the world's largest beach-volleyball tournaments.
Voss: Extremsport Veko: extreme sports festival.

August

Oslo: Norway Cup, the world's largest international football tournament for children.
Rena/Lillehammer: International bicycling race, Rena to Lillehammer.

September

Oslo: Marathon.
Suldalslågen: International salmon-fishing competition.

October

Oslo: Horse show. Competition and Grand Prix.

Winter Norway

Norway is often dubbed the "Cradle of Skiing". What we today know as a sport is the way Norwegians used to get around, and Norway is said to be responsible for the invention of ski waxing and the laminated ski.

Skiing is just one of Norway's winter attractions. There are snowmobile trips to the North Cape, reindeer safaris and dog-sled races over the plain of Finnmarksvidda. You can go on horse-drawn sleigh rides, or try your hand at sledding, ice fishing, snow boarding or ice skating.

For details, see *Specialist Tour Operators* on page 371. Or contact the Norwegian Tourist Board, which has a list of holiday agents offering winter packages.

December

Lillehammer: Ski Festival. Opening of the World Cup Season.

CHILDREN

Norway is a welcoming and safe place for children; this is one reason why you will see them out on their own here at a young age. Many outdoor activities, from skiing to kayaking, are geared up for youngsters, and it is easy to rent equipment for them too. Train rides are also popular. The Flåm railway is the most spectacular, but the Rauma and Bergen lines are other good options. You can usually get child rates for travel and accommodation.

In and Around Oslo

Horse riding, minigolf and Minizoo Ekeberg near Ekeberghallen at Ekebergveien 103; tel: 22 68 26 69.
International Children's Art Museum (Barnekunstmuseet), Lille Frøens vei 4; tel: 22 46 85 73; www. barnekunst.no (all year; charge). Exhibits and workshops.
Norwegian Museum of Technology (Norsk Teknisk Museum), Kjelsåsveien 143; tel: 22 79 60 00; www.tekniskmuseum.no. Interactive exhibits for children of all ages (all year, charge).
Puppet Theatre Frognerveien 67; tel: 22 34 86 80 (May–Sept).
Tusenfryd Amusement Park, Ås, Akershus; tel: 64 97 64 97; www. tusenfryd.no. Transport by bus 541 from Oslo S or Rådhuset. Attractions include: roller coaster, Spaceshot, flume ride, carousel, magic carpet, climbing wall and so on. Height restrictions apply on some rides (Apr–Sept; charge).

Around Norway

Aquarium (Akvariet), Bergen; tel: 55 55 71 71; www.akvariet.no. Shark tunnel, penguin-feeding and seal show (all year, charge).
Atlantic Sea Park (Atlanterhavsparken) near Ålesund; tel: 70 10 70 60; www.atlanterhavsparken.no. One of the largest saltwater aquariums in Scandinavia (daily; charge).
Hunderfossen Family Park near Lillehammer; tel: 61 27 55 30; www. hunderfossen.no. Attractions include: river rafting, fairytale castle, the world's largest troll, fairytale cave, Supervideograph, Photo Adventure, Energy Centre (exhibition centre

for oil and gas), Wax Museum, Experience Centre for Ice Cream, plus outdoor entertainment (May–Sept; charge).
Kongeparken near Stavanger; tel: 81 52 26 73; www.kongeparken.no. Over 40 attractions, including life-sized model of the Giant Gulliver (85 x 7.5 metres/280 x 25ft), riding tracks, bob track, farm, car track, Wild West City, funfair (Apr–Sept; charge).
Kristiansand Dyrepark tel: 38 04 97 00; www. dyreparken.com. Norway's largest wildlife park, with an amusement park, water park, show and entertainment park, leisure park and Kardemomme by, a tiny village from a well-known children's book by the Norwegian author Thorbjørn Egner (all year; charge).
Mikkelparken, Kinsarvik; tel: 53 67 13 13; www.mikkelparken.no). Theme park (May–Aug, charge).
Telemark Sommarland at Bø, Telemark; tel: 35 06 16 00; www. sommarland.no. Norway's biggest water park with various wet and dry attractions, including waterslides, a 26-metre/80ft high water chute, surf wave and a floating river. Plus live entertainment, pony rides, Wild West City and children's playground (June–Aug; charge).
Vilvite, Bergen; tel: 55 59 45 00; www. vilvite.no. Interactive science centre (closed Mon; charge).
Vitensenteret, Trondheim; tel: 73 59 61 23; www.viten.ntnu.no. Popular science adventure centre; interactive experiments (daily; charge).
Youth Information in Oslo provides information on all subjects for young people:
Møllergata 3, Oslo; tel: 24 14 98 20; www.unginfo.oslo.no. Mon–Fri 11am–5pm (July–Aug Mon–Fri 9am–6pm, Tue 11am–6pm).

BELOW: Holmenkollen.

TRANSPORT

A – Z

A HANDY SUMMARY OF PRACTICAL INFORMATION, ARRANGED ALPHABETICALLY

A dmission Charges

You can expect to pay between NOK 30 and NOK 80 for admission to a museum or gallery, and over NOK 100 for admission to some of the most popular attractions. Several museums and galleries in Oslo are free, and many museums have a day when they don't charge admission; check individual venues for more information. Family tickets are usually good value for money, so opt for these if you are travelling with children. Bear in mind also that most places have discounts for students and OAPs. The Olso Pass and Bergen Card offer free entrance to museums and attractions together with free public transport and parking *(see page 345)*.

B udgeting for Your Trip

Norway has a reputation for being expensive, and certainly this is true in some respects: the price of a cup of coffee in a smart city café can be exorbitant, and even the smallest of items like toiletries can be double the amount they are elsewhere in Europe. Look out for *lavpris* shops, which offer

lower prices. It is true that the cost of alcohol is enough to make even heavy drinkers think twice about another bottle of wine; beer is a cheaper alternative and can be bought from supermarkets at good prices. Discount cards on accommodation *(page 348)* and public transport *(page 345)* are available, plus Norway offers tourists tax-free shopping *(page 360)*. The Oslo Youth Information Centre *(see Children, page 364)* publishes a budget guide, *Streetwise*, available from tourist offices.

When it comes to budgeting for a stay in Oslo, there are a number of ways to save your kroner. Norwegian hotel breakfasts usually offer a large buffet, so if you can have a hearty breakfast as your main meal of the day, and avoid eating a large evening meal in a restaurant, you'll manage to keep to a reasonable budget. The most common street snack is the *pølse* – a long, skinny hot dog served either with *brød* (bread) or rolled in a *lompe* (potato pancake). But there are now a lot of cafés, brasseries and pizzerias where you can get small to medium-sized meals that won't break the bank. Full meals can be

reasonable, too, as long as you don't order any alcohol, which is notoriously expensive.

In summer, hotel rates are deeply discounted to make up for the lack of business and conference traffic. In winter, you can sometimes do fairly well with weekend rates, but watch out for school and ski-holiday weeks when hotels are crowded and rates higher again. Pensions and youth hostels are usually reasonably priced. Camping is another option in summer: the site at Ekebergsletta, a hilly park suburb with wonderful views over Oslo and the fjord, is 3km (2 miles) from town.

A beer: NOK 70
A glass of house wine: NOK 70
A main course in a budget restaurant: NOK 100
A main course in a moderate restaurant: NOK 250
A main course in an expensive restaurant: NOK 350
A double room in a cheap hotel: NOK 800
A double room in a moderate hotel: NOK 1,200
A double room in a de luxe hotel: NOK 2,000

ACCOMMODATION

EATING OUT

ACTIVITIES

A – Z

LANGUAGE

A taxi journey from Gardermoen to Oslo centre: NOK 600
A single bus/metro ticket: NOK 26
A one-day travel pass: NOK 70
The Oslo Pass: NOK 230 for 24 hours, NOK 340 for 48 hours and NOK 430 for 72 hours (children and seniors pay less than half-price).

Business Travellers

Norwegians have all the props when it comes to doing business. Don't be caught out without possessing a firm handshake, mobile phone, business card and, if possible, a laptop.

Like all Scandinavians, Norwegians take their summer holiday very seriously as a time for retreating to a fjord or mountain *hytte* (usually a log cabin). During the common holiday in July, offices and factories empty, and it is virtually impossible to arrange an appointment or do any business.

People take work seriously, but also know how to maintain a pleasantly relaxed business atmosphere. Norwegians dress for business much as they do elsewhere, although in summer dress codes are relaxed slightly.

Norwegians are rarely deceitful. They may well mention the bad points of something first, to get them out of the way; then it's on to the sell. In other words, you won't be drowned in a sea of hype, and the honesty can be a little hard to get used to. Ultimately you'll appreciate not having to figure out the pitfalls for yourself.

If you are looking up someone's number in a phone book, you'll find his or her profession listed next to the name; not only is this a matter of professional pride, but a real help in a country with a limited number of surnames. Amazingly, you can also find a person's yearly taxable income, the details of which are freely available on government internet sites. Norwegians take freedom of

information quite literally. So much for generalisations; there will always be exceptions. The only really important things to remember are that liquid lunches are unusual, and the work day often ends at 3.30 or 4pm (even an hour earlier in summer).

Most Norwegian consulates and embassies have commercial attachés.

C limate

In Oslo the January average daytime high is −2°C (28°F) and the night-time low is −7°C (19°F); Bergen is less cold (high 3°C/37°F, low −1°C/30°F). Further north sub-zero temperatures can last for months, and a good number of roads shut over winter due to long-term snow, although right on the coast it is usually a little milder. February and March are the best skiing months. March and April and sometimes even early May are the wet spring months when skies are grey, and roads are buckled due to thaws and refreezes; during this time the daily high temperature slowly lifts from about 4°C (39°F) to 16°C (61°F).

Come summertime and the season of the midnight sun, Oslo can enjoy daily temperatures averaging 20–25°C (68–77°F), while the sunlight-bathed north has a perfect hiking temperature, hovering around 17°C (63°F). October sees temperatures dip below 10°C (50°F), then continue their slide towards zero. The first snow can be expected any time from mid-October to early December, depending on the location.

Independent travel during the winter months of November to February should be treated with caution, especially away from coastal cities to inland, colder regions.

The summer months are the most popular with visitors, but May and September are good times to visit

CLIMATE CHART

Oslo

Maximum temperature
Minimum temperature
Rainfall

too. The Easter ski break is a time of mass exodus from schools and jobs to the slopes and trails. Otherwise, Norwegians mainly holiday from mid-June to early August. The traditional common holiday is in July *(ferietide)*, when some businesses shut down.

What to Bring/Wear

You're in for a pleasant surprise if travelling to Norway in summer. As it is protected by the Gulf Stream it can get even warmer than some of its southern neighbours. In the south, temperatures above 25°C (77°F) are not unusual. The average temperature for the country as a whole in July, including the far north, is about 16°C (60°F), 22°C (71°F) in Oslo. Bring swimming gear, as the water in most fjords, except northern Norway, is 20°C+ (68°F+) in midsummer.

Pack the clothes you would normally wear in northern Europe, including jumpers and a raincoat, and bring some strong walking shoes.

The mountains can be cold, so bring some warmer garments. You are not usually required to dress formally for dinner at Norwegian resort hotels. Spring and autumn are rainy (an umbrella is always useful), and nights can be chilly. It is rainy year-round on the west coast.

In winter bring very warm clothing and dress in layers (cotton against the skin and then wool). Woollen mittens or gloves and hats (covering the ears) are strongly advised (and face cover and goggles, if you are skiing). In the far north, temperatures drop to below −20°C (−4°F). In January, the average daytime temperature in Oslo is −2°C (28°F) and −7°C (19°F) at night. Inland areas are generally colder than the coast.

A first-aid kit is recommended for those who plan to make any trips to remoter parts. And be sure to include

BELOW: beautiful Norway in winter.

medicines for preventing and treating mosquito bites, as from midsummer into early autumn biting insects are rife, especially in Finnmark.

Crime and Safety

The streets of Oslo are relatively safe compared with the bigger cities of Europe and North America, even though the tabloids report an abundance of muggings, stabbings and other crimes of violence, as they do everywhere.

Crime against tourists is rare, however. Take the same precautions here as anywhere: park safely and hide valuables out of sight. The same applies when out on the town. Simply stick with the happy crowds and avoid the sleazy joints.

Norwegian cities late at night are usually full of young people, many of them drunk: this is mainly because of the lengthy opening hours and the Nordic drinking culture (a Norwegian often drinks to get drunk).

Most bars have good bouncers, so alert them if you're having trouble. Police patrols are now outnumbered by private-sector security personnel and *Nattravene* (Night Ravens, a Guardian Angel-type patrol).

Another potential threat can be drug abusers. However, they are usually placid and in Oslo generally gather around Jernbanetorget (Central Station). There is no strict rule here; a no-go area today could be tomorrow's in place.

Customs Regulations

The following can be brought into Norway by visitors:
Money Notes and coins (Norwegian and foreign) up to NOK 25,000 or equivalent. If you intend to import more, you must fill in a form (available at all entry and exit points) for the Customs Office.
Alcohol Permitted imports for people aged 20 and over include 1 litre of spirits (up to 60 percent vol.), plus 1 litre of fortified wine (up to 22 percent vol.) or 3 litres of wine (if no spirits) and 2 litres of beer; or 5 litres of beer.
Tobacco European residents over the age of 18 may bring 200 cigarettes or 250g of other tobacco goods.
Meat and dairy products Meat, meat products, cheese and foodstuffs except dog and cat food, totalling 10kg (22lb) altogether from EEA (European Economic Area) countries. From countries outside the EEA, it is prohibited to bring meat, meat

products, milk and milk products with you in your luggage.
Sundries Other goods (excluding articles for personal use) may be brought in duty-free up to a value of NOK 6,000.
Prohibited goods Narcotics, medicines (except for personal use), spirits over 60 percent volume, endangered animal and plant species, poisons, firearms, ammunition and explosives. Note: the mild narcotic leaf *khat* is illegal in Norway.
Agricultural produce This comes under strict surveillance. If it concerns you, get specific details beforehand.

D isabled Travellers

Visitors in need of assistance should contact **Norges handikapforbund**, Schweigaardsgt. 12, 0185 Oslo; tel: 24 10 24 00; www.nhf.no.

Norway, like the other Scandinavian countries, compares favourably when it comes to accessible travel, and as a result it is a popular destination for travellers with special needs.

Hotel listings in accommodation guides have symbols designating disabled access and toilets. In the *Oslo Guide* (see www.visitoslo.com) under "Oslo for All" you'll find some listings that specially mention capacity for disabled visitors. Most hotels adapt their furnishings to the needs of

people with physical disabilities. These hotels are indicated in *Accommodation in Norway* (available from the Norwegian Tourist Board).

The Norwegian State Railways (NSB) have carriages specially furnished for the disabled, and the new Coastal Express ships have lifts and cabins for disabled people. The **Euro Terra Nova AS**, at Grensen 8, 0159 Oslo, offers brochures on coach tours around Norway for wheelchair-users. They also provide hotel bookings and hire cars; tel: 22 94 13 50; www.euroterranova.no. Guidebooks for Nordland county (north Norway) can be ordered free of charge from Nordland Reiseliv *(see page 371)*.

The Society for Accessible Travel and Hospitality (SATH) provides information and advice for travellers with disabilities; www.sath.org.

E lectricity

220 volts AC, 50 cycles. Plugs have two small round pins, so you may need an adaptor for appliances you bring with you.

Embassies and Consulates

Australia (in Denmark)
Dampfærgevej 26, Copenhagen
Tel: +45 70 26 36 76
Fax: + 45 70 26 36 86

Etiquette – Visiting a Norwegian Home

Norwegians usually eat dinner around 5 or 6pm, but dinner parties generally start later, at around 7.30pm. An invitation for any other time of the day usually means coffee and cake (if in doubt call the host and make certain).

Let's say you've been invited to dinner and you want to make a good impression. Norway is not a "drop-in" society, so you can expect the food to be well planned and of high quality. You could do far worse than taking note of the following protocol:
• Norwegians are very punctual and expect others to be. Guests usually arrive exactly on time, jokingly called *Norsk time*, sometimes even early. Make sure you dress correctly for the occasion (again, if in doubt ask the host in advance).
• When entering a room, shake hands with everybody present, unless a large function makes that impossible. Introduce yourself to those you have not met before; give

a friendly greeting to those you do know, but still shake hands.
• If it's your first visit to someone's home it is customary to take a small gift along (usually flowers, a plant or chocolates).
• Dinner parties in Norwegian homes follow a fixed pattern and include short speeches even on family occasions. After tapping his glass, the host will always give a welcome speech and then propose a *skål*. It would be discourteous to touch the wine *before* this initial toast (but expect a liberal helping of *skåls!*).
• Second helpings *(annen servering)* are so much the rule in Norwegian homes that the host will specifically point out if the dish is only to be passed round once. The secret is not to take too much the first time.
• Every meal in Norway is concluded with a *takk for maten* (thank you for the food) and, if it's dinner, a general *skål*.

Emergency Numbers

Fire 110
Police 112 (911 from mobile phones)
Ambulance 113
Emergency at sea 120
Medical problems For emergency medical treatment in Oslo *(legevakt)*, ring 22 93 22 93.
Internal directory enquiries 1881/1880
International directory enquiries 1882

Canada
Wergelandsvn 7
Tel: 22 99 53 00
www.canadainternational.gc.ca/norway-norvege/
UK
Thomas Heftyesgate 8
Tel: 23 13 27 00
http://ukinnorway.fco.gov.uk/en
US
Henrik Ibsensgate 48
Tel: 21 30 85 40
http://norway.usembassy.gov

G ay and Lesbian Travellers

In common with the rest of Scandinavia, Norway has a very relaxed attitude to homosexuality. There is very little open hostility to gays and lesbians in general society and, partly as a result, the commercial gay scene is relatively small. Tourist offices *(see page 370)* carry details of the main places and events, including the Gay Pride celebrations in Oslo and Bergen and the annual Oslo Gay Film Festival. The main bars and clubs include:
Elsker, Kristian IVs Gate 9, Oslo. Tel: 22 41 66 08.
London Pub, Hambros Plass 5, Oslo. Tel: 22 70 87 00.
Finken Café and Bar, Nygardsgate 2a, Bergen. Tel: 55 32 13 16.
Contact the Norwegian LGBT for more information:
Valkyriegaten 15
Tel: 23 10 39 39
Email: post@llh.no; www.llh.no

H ealth and Medical Care

The are no major health hazards in Norway. No vaccinations are necessary to enter Norway and the tap water is (generally) good. A degree of common sense is required when travelling in remote areas, especially during the winter. When hiking/skiing in the mountains always let someone know of your travel intentions, and use guides wherever possible. Mosquitos can be a problem in the north in summer, particularly inland near bogs and swamps. Bring repellent and keep legs and arms well covered.

Treatment

Norway has reciprocal treatment agreements with the UK and many other European countries; your own National Insurance should cover you to receive free treatment at public hospitals. EU citizens should obtain the relevant documentation to entitle them to this (for British citizens an EHIC, European Health Insurance Card, is available from post offices). People from countries without such agreements, and those without an EHIC card, will have to pay a small fee.

If you are concerned whether you need extra cover, check in your own country before you go. The EHIC card only covers the basics and does not include the cost of medicine, so it is advisable to take out additional medical insurance.

You will need to take out extra cover if you are going skiing or doing any other dangerous sports.

Doctors and Hospitals

The standard of health provision in Norway is very high, and even in remote areas you should have no problem getting medical help. Just about all doctors and nurses speak good English, and if they don't they'll soon find someone who does.

In medical emergencies EU members will receive free treatment at state hospitals *(see above for reciprocal arrangements)*, but have to pay towards the non-hospital costs and for prescriptions.

If you are ill, ask your hotel, tourist office or a pharmacy for the address of an English-speaking GP. Private doctors are listed in the directory under *Leger* (doctors). Make sure you keep receipts if you have medical insurance.

Pharmacies

For minor problems, head for a pharmacy, or *Apotek (for opening hours, see page 369)*. Most larger cities have all-night pharmacies *(see below)*. In other cities enquire at your hotel, or try the emergency number in the phone book under *Legevakt* (doctor on duty).

Where there is a rota of 24-hour pharmacies in a city, a list will usually be posted on the door of each one.

Oslo

Jernbanetorvets Apotek, across from Central Station, Jernbanetorget 4B. Tel: 22 41 24 82. 24 hours.
Bergen
Apotek Nordstjernen, Strømgata 8. Tel: 55 21 83 84. Mon–Sat 8am–midnight, Sun 9.30am–midnight.
Stavanger
Vitus Apotek Løven, Olav Vs gt. 11. Tel: 51 91 08 80. Daily until 11pm, Christmas, New Year, Easter and Whitsun 9am–8pm.
Trondheim
Ditt Apotek Solsiden, Beddingen 4. Tel: 73 88 37 37. Mon–Sat 8.30am–midnight, Sun 10am–midnight.

Dentists

Emergency dental treatment in Oslo, outside regular dentists' office hours, is available from:
Oslo Kommunale Tannlegevakt, Schweigaardsgate 6, 3rd floor (near Sonia Henies Plass station). Tel: 22 67 30 00.
Mon–Sat 7am–10pm, Sun and public holidays 11am–2pm.
Please note that emergency treatment is very expensive.

I nternet

Free internet access is available at most public libraries in Norway. Screen time is limited, and you may need to reserve your slot in advance. The Oslo Tourist Information Service, Oslo Promotion, publishes a list of internet cafés in the capital. These include:
Arctic Internet, Oslo Central Station. Daily 9am–11pm. Tel: 22 17 19 40; www.arcticinternet.com.
Qba, Olaf Ryes Plass 4. Tel: 22 35 24 60; www.qba.no. Mon–Fri 8am–1am, Sat–Sun 11am–1am.

BELOW: newspaper kiosk.

Maps

For tourist maps, contact:
Den Norske Turistforening
Postboks 7 Sentrum, 0101 Oslo
Tel: 22 82 28 00
www.turistforeningen.no

Media

Newspapers

Most larger kiosks (like the *Narvesen* chain) and some bookshops sell English-language newspapers.

Deichmanske Bibliotek, the main public library, is at Henrik Ibsens gate 1 in Oslo; you'll find a selection of international papers and periodicals in its reading rooms, as well as free internet access.

Radio

English broadcasts on short wave can be picked up if atmospheric conditions are favourable. Best results can usually be heard on short-wave frequency 9410.

During the winter months **BBC Radios 1, 2, 3** and **4** can sometimes be received on AM but reception is often distorted. **Radio 5** can be picked up on 909 and 693 medium wave (best reception in the evening). On Sundays **Radio Norway** (93 FM) broadcasts the news from Norway in English in *Norway This Week*, a 30-minute programme at 5pm.

For local frequencies of the **BBC World Service**, enquire at the nearest tourist office.

Television

Norway has five main television stations: **NRK1, NRK2, NRK3** (public broadcaster), and **TV2** and **TV Norge** (TVN). Cable TV is common here and allows you to pick up a variety of channels, including **BBC Prime, BBC World, CNN, Swedish TV1** and **TV2, Discovery, MTV, French TV5, Eurosport, TV3** and so on, depending on the distributor. Most hotels have pay channels in addition to the above. English films on Norwegian television are subtitled, not dubbed.

Money

The Norwegian krone (NOK) is divided into 100 øre. Notes come in denominations of NOK 50, 100, 200, 500 and 1,000, and coins are 50 øre and NOK 1, 5, 10 and 20.

You can change currency at post offices, the Oslo S train station, international airports, some hotels and commercial banks. FOREX offices have good rates and no fees.

ABOVE: Norwegian kroner.

It is always useful to carry a certain amount of cash with you in case of emergency.

Credit Cards/Travellers' Cheques

Use of credit cards is widespread in Norway, with Eurocard, Visa, MasterCard, American Express and Diner's Club the most common. Check with your own credit-card company about acceptability and other services.

ATMs are widely available, and it is possible to pay for even small amounts (such as parking and toll fees) by credit card.

Travellers' cheques are not very widely used now, but they are accepted in the bigger hotels and should be purchased before travelling to Norway. In most banks you can generally get cash on a debit card or a Visa or MasterCard.

Tipping

Tipping is quite straightforward in Norway. Hotels include a service charge and tipping is generally not expected. Restaurants usually have the service charge included, in which case it's your choice to add anything (5–10 percent is customary). The same applies to taxis. Table service in bars (particularly outdoor tables) requires tipping.

With hairdressers a tip isn't quite as customary, but again 5–10 percent would be appropriate – and appreciated.

Cloakrooms usually have a fixed fee of about NOK 5–10; if not, leave a few crowns for the attendant.

Opening Hours

Office hours are 8 or 9am–4pm; lunch is taken early, usually 11.30am–12.30pm, or noon–2pm for a restaurant lunch or lunch

Public Holidays

1 January New Year's Day
March/April Easter: Thursday to Monday inclusive
1 May Labour Day
17 May National Independence Day
May/June Ascension Day
May/June Whit Monday
25 December Christmas Day
26 December 2nd Christmas Day

meeting, which are always business-like affairs.
Shops Mon–Fri 9am–5pm, Thur until 8pm, Sat 9am–1, 2 or even 3pm.
Shopping centres Mon–Fri 10am–9pm, Sat 9am–6pm. Shops and shopping centres are closed on Sundays.
Banks Mon–Fri only 8.30am–4pm.
Pharmacies Mon–Fri 9am–5pm, Sat mornings and on a rota basis in larger cities.

Postal Services

Post offices in Oslo open Mon–Fri 9am–5pm and Sat 9am–3pm.

Letters and postcards cost the same price to send to the UK and Continental Europe, slightly more to send to North America. Post takes 2–3 days to Europe and 7–10 days to North America.

Religious Services

The Lutheran Church is Norway's state Church, with around 86 percent of the population registered as Lutherans. Oslo has many Lutheran places of worship, including one American Lutheran church (Fritzners g. 15; tel: 22 44 35 84; www.alcoslo.org).

Services are held in English at the **American Lutheran church** and the **Anglican/Episcopalian church** (St Edmund's, Møllergate 30; tel: 22 69 22 14; www.osloanglicans.net).

Minority religious groups are Pentecostalists, Baptists, Seventh Day Adventists, Evangelical Lutherans, Methodists, Catholics, Jews (the **synagogue** is at Bergstein 13, near St Hanshaugen; tel: 22 69 65 70) and Muslims.

Oslo Cathedral (Domkirke; Protestant) at Storgate (tel: 23 62 90 10) puts on an interesting programme of concerts throughout the year. For up-to-date information about what's on, consult the daily press, the tourist office or the *Oslo Guide* at www.visitoslo.com.

ABOVE: glaciers are awe-inspiring.

Student Travellers

There are numerous opportunities for reduced student rates, especially for travel; contact the following for more information:
Ung Info (Young info)
Møllergata 3, N-0179 Oslo
Tel: 24 14 98 20
Fax: 24 14 98 21
Email: mail@ung.info
www.unginfo.oslo.no

Telephones

Calls abroad can be made from hotels – but usually with a hefty surcharge – or from phone booths or the main telegraph office at Kongensgate 21 (entrance Prinsensgate), Oslo.

Norwegian payphones take 1, 5, 10 and 20 kroner pieces. Phonecards, which can be used in the green phone booths, can be bought in *Narvesen* kiosks and at post offices. Credit cards are accepted in card phones.

When calling from Norway to foreign countries always dial 00 first. Cheapest calling times are outside business hours: 5pm–8am. Extra-cheap international calling cards, such as Eurocity, can be purchased from a variety of kiosks (corner shops) in most major towns.

Telephone directories have a page of instructions in English in the index. When looking up names, remember the vowels æ, ø, and å come at the end of the alphabet, in that order.

Some US phone companies have their own international access numbers, to allow US citizens cheaper calls, as follows:
Sprint 800-19 877
AT&T 800-19 011
WorldPhone 800-19 912

Tourist Information

There are around 350 local tourist offices around Norway, as well as 18 regional tourist offices.
For general information contact:
The Norwegian Tourist Board
PO Box 448 Sentrum, NO-0158 Oslo
Tel: 22 00 25 00
Fax: 22 00 25 01
www.visitnorway.com
For business-related information contact:
Innovation Norway (Trade Council)
(Innovasjon Norge)
PO Box 448 Sentrum, N-0158 Oslo
Tel: 22 00 25 00
Fax: 22 00 25 01
www.innovasjonnorge.no

Regional Information
Regional tourist offices are experts in the county they cover. They are usually open to personal callers, and will also supply advice and information in writing or over the phone.

Oslo/Oslofjord
In Oslo, there are three tourist information offices: one by the Central Station and one by City Hall (both are open all year), and one at the cruise-ship terminal (open when cruise ships call).
Visit Oslo
Tel: 81 53 05 55
Fax: 22 17 62 01
Email: info@visitoslo.com
www.visitoslo.com

Tourist Info Abroad

Australia
The embassy deals with tourist information.
17 Hunter Street, Yarralumia,
Canberra ACT 2600
Tel: 2 6273 34444
www.norway.org.au/travel
UK
Norwegian Tourist Board
Charles House
5 Regent Street
London SW1Y 4LR
Tel: 020 7389 8800
Fax: 020 7389 6014
Email: info@visitnorway.co.uk
www.visitnorway.co.uk
US/Canada
Norwegian Tourist Board
Scandinavian Tourism Inc.
655 Third Avenue, Suite 1810
New York, NY 10017-5617
Tel: 212 885 9700
Fax: 212 885 9710
Email: info@goscandinavia.com
www.goscandinavia.com

Østfold Visit Oslofjord
Phonixbrygga, NO-1606 Fredrikstad
Tel: 69 30 14 30
www.visitoslofjord.no
Vestfold
www.visitvestfold.com

South Norway
Destinasjon Sørlandet
Kristiansand Tourist Office
Radhusgate 6, NO-4611 Kristiansand
Tel: 38 12 13 14
Fax: 38 02 52 55
Email: info@sorlandet.com
www.regionkristiansand.no
Visit Telemark
PO Box 3133 Handelstortget
NO-3707 Skien
Tel: 35 90 00 20
Fax: 35 90 00 21
Email: info@telemarkreiser.no
www.visittelemark.com

Fjord Norway
Bergen
Bergen Convention Bureau –
Bergen Tourist Board
PO Box 4055, Dreggen
NO-5023 Bergen
Tel: 55 55 20 10
Fax: 55 55 20 11
Email: mail@visitbergen.com
Fjord Norge AS
Lodin Leppsgt 2B
NO-5003 Bergen
Tel: 55 30 26 40
Fax: 55 30 26 50
Email: info@fjordnorway.no
www.fjordnorway.com
Visit Hordaland
PO Box 416 Marken
NO-5828 Bergen
Tel: 55 33 23 54
Fax: 55 55 20 11
Email: ingunn@visitbergen.com
www.visithordaland.no
Hardangerfjord – Destination
Hardanger Fjord
Hardanger Brygge, NO-5600
Norheimsund
Tel: 56 55 38 70
Fax: 56 55 38 71
www.hardangerfjord.com
Aurland – Flåm – Lærdal
PO Box 53, NO-5741 Aurland
Tel: 57 63 33 13
Fax: 57 63 11 48
www.alr.no
Stavanger Region
Vågsgte 22, NO-4306 Sandnes
Tel: 51 97 55 55
Fax: 51 62 82 14
Email: info@regionstavanger.com
www.regionstavanger.com
Sogn and Fjordane Tourist Board
PO Box 370
NO-6782 Stryn
Tel: 57 87 40 40

Time Zone

Central European Time, 1 hour
ahead of Greenwich Mean Time,
6 hours ahead of Eastern Standard
Time. The clock is set forward an
hour to summer time at the end
of March, and back an hour at the
end of September.

Email: info@sognefjord.no
www.sognefjord.no
Destination Møre og Romsdal
Torget 4, NO-6413 Molde
Tel: 71 20 10 00
Fax: 71 20 10 01
Email: info@visitmolde.com
www.visitmolde.com

Central Norway
Hallingdal Reiseliv AS
Gamlevegen 6
NO-3550, Gol
Tel: 32 02 99 26
Fax: 32 02 99 28
Email: info@eventyrveien.no
www.eventyrveien.no
Lillehammer
Lillehammer Tourist Office
Jernbanetorget 2
NO-2609 Lillehammer
Tel: 61 28 98 00
Email: info@lillehammer.com
www.lillehammer.com
Trøndelag Reiseliv AS
PO Box 65
N-7400 Trondheim
Tel: 73 84 24 40
Fax: 73 84 24 50
Email: turistinfo@trondelag.com
www.trondelag.com
Visit Trondheim AS
Visitors and Convention Bureau
Munkegate 19, PO Box 2102,
NO-7411 Trondheim
Tel: 73 80 76 60
Fax: 73 80 76 70
Email: touristinfo@visit-trondheim.com
www.trondheim.no
Nordland Reiseliv AS
PO Box 434
N-8001 Bodø
Tel: 75 54 52 00
Fax: 75 54 52 10
Email: bodo@visitnorthernnorway.com
www.visitnordland.no
**Lofoten Islands – Destination
Lofoten**
PO Box 210, NO-8301 Solvær
Tel: 76 06 98 00
Fax: 76 07 30 01
Email: lofoten@lofoten.info
www.lofoten.info
See also www.lofoten.com
Visit Tromsø
Kirkegate 2, PO Box 311,
NO-9253 Tromsø

Tel: 77 61 00 00
Fax: 77 61 00 10
Email: info@destinasjontromso.no
www.destinasjontromso.no

North Norway
Finnmark Tourist Board
NO-9515 Alta
Tel: 78 44 90 60
Fax: 78 44 90 79
Email: post@finnmark.com
www.finnmark.com
Svalbard Reiselivsråd
PO Box 323, N-9171 Longyearbyen
Tel: 79 02 55 50
Fax: 79 02 55 51
Email: info@svalbard.net
www.svalbard.net

Websites
Norway's official travel website
State tourism officials compile
this portal offering information on
everything from attractions to special
events to accommodation, with links
to regional sites all over the country.
www.visitnorway.com
Oslo's official travel website
The capital's visitors' bureau
compiles this site full of information
about what's happening in Oslo,
accommodation and tourist tips.
**The Norwegian Trekking
Association (DNT)**
This organisation manages hiking and
skiing trails all over the country, runs
lodges and cabins in the mountains
and other scenic areas, and its staff
are experts on hiking and outdoor life.
www.turistforeningen.no/english/
**Foundation Norwegian Heritage
(Norsk Kulturarv)**
The foundation seeks to preserve
Norway's history through "historical
vitality", that is, opening historic farms
and other sites to the public. It offers
listings of historic sites, lodging and
attractions around the country, using
the St Olav's Rose as its symbol for
quality. www.olavsrosa.no/en.
Det Historiske
Characterful hotels in historical
buildings throughout Norway, the
perfect alternative to chain hotels.
www.dehistoriske.com.
Hurtigruten
Norway's famous coastal voyage from
Bergen in the south to Kirkenes in
the north, and back. One of the most
beautiful cruises anywhere in the
world. www.hurtigruten.com.

Tour Operators
Specialist Tour Operators in the UK
Norway Specialists
Norsc Holidays
The Court, The Street, Charmouth,

Dorset, DT6 6PE
Tel: 01297 560 033
www.norsc.co.uk
Taber Holidays
PO Box 176, Tofts House, Tofts
Road, Cleckheaton, West Yorkshire,
BD19 3WX
Tel: 01274 875 199
www.taberhols.co.uk
Hurtigruten in the UK
3 Shortlands, London W6 8NE
Tel: 0844 448 7654
www.hurtigruten.co.uk
Arctic Voyages
Arcturus
Tel: 01837 840640
www.arcturusexpeditions.co.uk
Discover the World
Tel: 01737 214 250
www.discover-the-world.co.uk

Activity Holidays
Crystal Holidays
Tel: 0870 166 4971
www.crystalholidays.co.uk
Exodus Travel
Tel: +47 22 44 00 73
www.exodus.co.uk
Explore Worldwide
Tel: 0845 013 1537
www.explore.co.uk
Inntravel
Tel: 01653 617001
www.inntravel.co.uk
Scantours
Tel: 01206 708888
www.scantours.co.uk

V isas and Passports

A valid passport is all that is
necessary for citizens of most
countries to enter Norway. Visas are
not required. Norway is a member of
the Schengen agreement, allowing
citizens of other Schengen countries
to enter without passports. If you
enter from another Nordic country
(Denmark, Finland, Iceland, or
Sweden), you won't get a new entry
stamp. Tourists are generally limited
to a three-month visit; it is possible to
stay longer, but you must apply for a
visa after the initial three months or if
you plan to work in Norway.

Weights and Measures

Norway uses the metric sytstem.
Distances are given in kilometres
(km), but Norwegians often refer to
a *mil* which is 10km (thus 10 mil =
100km). When talking about land
area you will often hear the word
mål. This old measure of 984.34
sq metres has been rounded up to
1,000 sq metres (or 1 decare).

L ANGUAGE

UNDERSTANDING THE LANGUAGE

Introduction

Germanic in origin, Norwegian is one of the three Scandinavian languages, and is closely related to Danish and Swedish. There are two official forms of Norwegian, *bokmål* and *nynorsk*. The former reflects Norway's 400 years of Danish domination, while *nynorsk* is built on native Norwegian dialects. The Sami population (Lapps) in north Norway speak Sami. English is widely understood.

Useful Words and Phrases

Yes *Ja*
No *Nei*
Good morning *God morgen*
Good afternoon *God ettermiddag*
Good evening *God kveld*
Today *I dag*
Tomorrow *I morgen*
Yesterday *I går*
Hello *Hei*
How do you do? *Hvordan står det til?*
Goodbye *Adjø/Ha det bra/Hadet*
Thank you *Takk*
How much is this? *Hvor mye koster det?*
It costs *Det koster...*
How do I get to...? *Hvordan kommer jeg til...?*
Where is...? *Hvor er...?*
Right *Høyre*
To the right *Til høyre*
Left *Venstre*
To the left *Til venstre*
Straight on *Rett frem*
Money *Penger*
Can I order please? *Kan jeg få bestille?*
Could I have the bill please? *Kan jeg få regningen?*
What time is it? *Hvor mye er klokken?*

It is (**The time is...**) *Den er (Klokken er...)*
When? *Når*
Where? *Hvor?*
Could I have your name please? *Hva er navnet ditt?*
My name is *Mitt navn er...*
Do you have English newspapers? *Har du engelske aviser?*
Do you speak English? *Snakker du engelsk?*
I only speak English *Jeg snakker bare engelsk*
May I help you? *Kan jeg hjelpe deg?*
I do not understand *Jeg forstår ikke*
I do not know *Jeg vet ikke*
It has disappeared *Den har forsvunnet*
Chemist *Apotek*
Hospital *Sykehus*
Doctor *Lege*
Police station *Politistasjion*
Parking *Parkering*
Department store *Hus/Stormagasin*
Toilet *Toalett/WC*
Gentlemen *Herrer*
Ladies *Damer*
Vacant *Ledig*
Engaged *Opptatt*
Entrance *Inngang*
Exit *Utgang*
No entry *Ingen adgang*
Open *Åpent*
Closed *Stengt*
Push *Skyv*
Pull *Trekk*
No smoking *Røyking forbudt*
Breakfast *Frokost*
Lunch *Lunsj*
Dinner *Middag*
Eat *Spise*
Drink *Drikke*
Cheers! *Skål!*
Hot *Varm*
Cold *Kald*
Aircraft *Flymaskin*

Car *Bil*
Train *Tog*
Ticket *Billet*
Single/return *En vei/tur-retur*
To rent *Leie*
Free *Ledig*
Room to rent *Rom til leie*
Chalet *Hytte*
Can we camp here? *Kan vi telte her?*
No camping *Camping forbudt*
Grocery store (**in countryside**)
Landhandel
Shop *Butikk*
Food *Mat/kost*
To buy *Kjøpe*
Sauna *Badstue*
Off licence/liquor store *Vinmonopol*
Clothes *Klær*
Overcoat *Frakk*
Jacket *Jakke*
Suit *Dress*
Shoes *Sko*
Skirt *Skjørt*
Blouse *Bluse*

Days and Months

Sunday *søndag*
Monday *mondag*
Tuesday *tirsdag*
Wednesday *onsdag*
Thursday *torsdag*
Friday *fredag*
Saturday *lørdag*
January *januar*
February *februar*
March *mars*
April *april*
May *mai*
June *juni*
July *juli*
August *august*
September *september*
October *oktober*
November *november*
December *desember*

FURTHER READING

Fiction

Classics

Knut Hamsun: Norway's best-known novelist. His works *Hunger* and *Growth of the Soil* are his most famous, although *Mysteries* is a more accessible title for novices.

Henrik Ibsen: Norway's most famous playwright, whose works have been performed the world over. Try *A Doll's House* or *Peer Gynt*, two of his most famous plays.

Snorri Sturluson: Any of the Icelandic historian, politician and poet's sagas are worth reading, but *The Prose Edda* and *Heimskringla, History of the Kings of Norway*, are a good place to start.

Sigrid Undset: The only female Norwegian author to have been awarded the Nobel Prize for Literature (in 1928), for her trilogy *Kristin Lavransdatter*.

Other

Knut Faldbakken: Many of Faldbakken's novels focus on the changing role of men in society. *Sleeping Prince, Honeymoon* and *Insect Summer* are among those that have been translated into English.

Jostein Gaarder: *Sophie's World*, a novel about the history of philosophy, has sold millions of copies, and been translated into more than 50 languages. It's an unusual introduction to Western philosophy as seen from the eyes of a teenage girl.

Garrison Keillor: Lake Wobegon series: a fun account of life in a fictional small farm town populated by Norwegian immigrants in the American Midwest.

Erlend Loe: One of the most exciting new literary talents to come out of Norway in recent years. Astonishingly, only one of his novels, *Naiv.Super*, has so far been translated into English, but look out for more.

Per Petterson: *Out Stealing Horses* is a touching novel by one of Norway's best authors. The book won several literary prizes in both Norway and abroad.

Lars Saabye Christensen: Award-winning writer, two of his most famous titles are *Beaties* and *Half-Brother*, both about growing up in 1960s Oslo.

Crime

Karin Fossum: The Norwegian queen of crime has enjoyed huge success at home and abroad. Her most popular books include *Don't Look Back*, *Calling Out for You*, and more recently *The Water's Edge*.

Jo Nesbø: Crime is a popular genre in Norway and Jo Nesbø, with titles such as *The Redbreast* and *The Snowman*, has established a solid reputation.

Gunnar Staalesen: Hailing from Bergen, Staalesen is the man behind the private investigator Varg Veum series, whose adventures have been adapted for TV in Norway. *The Consorts of Death* is his latest title in English, but you could also try *The Writing on the Wall* or *Yours Until Death*.

Comic Strip

Nemi, by Lise Myhre. A comic strip character that maybe appeals more to women than men. She made her

Send Us Your Thoughts

We do our best to ensure the information in our books is as accurate and up-to-date as possible. The books are updated on a regular basis using local contacts, who painstakingly add, amend and correct as required. However, some details (such as telephone numbers and opening times) are liable to change, and we are ultimately reliant on our readers to put us in the picture.

We welcome your feedback, especially your experience of using the book "on the road". Maybe we recommended a hotel that you liked (or another that you didn't), or you came across a great bar or new attraction we missed.

We will acknowledge all contributions, and we'll offer an Insight Guide to the best letters received.

Please write to us at:
   Insight Guides
   PO Box 7910
   London SE1 1WE
Or email us at:
   insight@apaguide.co.uk

appearance in the UK in the *Metro* newspaper, but three book versions are also available for dedicated fans.

Non-Fiction

Architecture

Made in Norway: Norwegian Architecture Today, presents some of the most exciting examples of Norwegian architecture in recent years. Published by the National Association of Norwegian Architects.

Art

Edvard Munch: Behind the Scream, by Sue Prideaux, is an interesting account of Munch's life, and how it shaped Norway's most famous artist. *They Painted Norway*, by Arvid Bryne is informative and has high-quality reproductions. This is an excellent introduction to Norwegian art.

Cookery Books

Kitchen of Light, by Andreas Viestad, one of Norway's most famous chefs. A great mix of recipes, essays and photos based on the *New Scandinavian Cooking* TV series, which he co-hosted.

Famous Explorers

Farthest North, in which Fridtjof Nansen recounts his epic polar exploration, is a classic of the genre. *The South Pole: An Account of the Norwegian Antarctic Exploration in the Fram, 1910–1912*, by Roald Amundsen, is a riveting first-person account of the race to the South Pole. *Kon Tiki: Across the Pacific by Raft*, in which Thor Heyerdahl recounts the journey that made him a household name in Norway, was a bestseller, and casts light on one of modern times' most daring exploration expeditions.

Other Insight Guides

Europe is comprehensively covered by over 200 books in Apa Publications' three series of guidebooks.
Insight Guides provide the reader with full cultural background and top-quality photography. Titles in this part of Europe include: *Denmark, Finland, Iceland, Sweden* and *Scandinavia*.

ART AND PHOTO CREDITS

Aslak Aarhus 100
AKG Images 26TR, 62T
Alamy Images 102, 104, 168L,
168R, 172, 186T, 196, 224, 277,
297L
The Art Archive 33, 40, 44, 49R,
80B
© Aulestad Fotoarkiv, De
Sandvigske Samlinger 123
AWL Images 7CL, 185T
Bergen Tourist Board 352T
Mick Bernard 253
Jan Sølve Borlaug 153T
John Erling Blad 195
John Brunton 86
Trygve Bølstad 37, 108
Fritz Dressler 308/309, 329
Tor Eigeland 265T
Fjord Norway Tourist Board 124,
215T, 217, 218, 225T, 278T
Fotolia 93
Fylkestinget i Nord-Trøndelag/
Informasjonsavdelinga NTFK/
Flickr 297R
Getty Images 27T, 103B
Glen Gening/Apa 2/3T, 3BL, 4B, 4T,
5B, 5T, 6CR, 7BL, 7BL, 7CR, 7TL,
7TR, 8B, 8T, 9T, 11CL, 12/13, 14.15,
16,17, 18, 19all, 20, 22, 24L, 24R,
26BR, 28, 55L, 65, 70, 72L, 72R,
74T, 75, 76, 84B, 85, 90/91, 95B,
95T, 112/113, 115, 116, 116B,
117, 119, 121, 130, 132/133,
134/135, 136/137, 138, 139all,
142/143, 144, 145, 147, 148BL,
149, 156BL, 156BR, 157BL, 160,
161, 162/163, 171BL, 171R, 173,
188/189, 192, 198/199, 200, 201,
204B, 205BL, 205BR, 208B,
210/211, 212, 213, 219, 221, 222,
223, 225, 226/227, 228, 229,
232BR, 232T, 235, 236B, 236T,
237, 238/239, 240, 241, 243, 244,
245, 246L, 246R, 247all, 248B,
248T, 249L, 249R, 250, 251, 252L,
254/255, 256, 257, 259L, 259R,
260, 262, 267, 270/271, 272, 275,
278L, 278R, 279B, 279T, 280,
281B, 281T, 282B, 282T, 283,
284/285, 286, 287, 289, 294/295,
299, 300B, 300T, 301B, 304, 305all,
313, 316, 316T, 318L, 319, 320,
321R, 322, 323, 324, 326, 340,
342, 343, 344, 345, 348T, 348B,
350, 354, 357, 358, 365, 372

Paul Gogarty 191
Blaine Harrington 148T, 261, 303,
314T
Stefan Hauberg 291, 310, 311,
312, 315, 317, 318R, 328
Marie Holstein 46
Hordaland Tourist Board 233
Ibsen Museum 152
Innovation Norway 1, 3BR, 6BL, 6T,
9B, 9C, 11TR, 21, 23L, 23R, 26TL,
27B, 56/57, 67, 68/69, 71, 73,
74B, 84, 87, 92, 94L, 94R, 96, 97,
99, 101, 103L, 103R, 105, 106,
107, 109, 128, 129, 131, 150, 151,
156BR, 159B, 159T, 167, 176, 180,
181, 187, 194, 197, 207, 232BL,
252R, 263, 264L, 264R, 265B, 268,
276, 330, 339, 347, 349, 360,
363T, 363B, 364B, 364T, 366, 370
iStockphoto.com 6BR, 6C, 185B,
190, 193
Jensen & Skodvin Arkitektkontor
353
Gerold Jung 291T, 321T
Janos Jurka 301T
Oskari Kettunen 216
Øystein Klakegg 98B
Hans Klüche 266T, 333, 335, 335T,
336
Arne Knudsen 303T
Kobal Collection 62B
Kokonis 182
Kvikne's Hotel 352
Leslie Garland Picture Library
156T, 209, 269, 289T, 323T, 325T,
327
Mats Linden 314R
Ola Matsson 183
Anna Mockford & Nick Bonetti/
Apa 10TR, 11BR, 359, 368, 369
Martin V Morris 25
Mary Evans Picture Library 45, 48,
49L, 61R, 186B, 293
Michael Mortensen 94B
© Munch Museum/Munch -
Ellingsen Group, BONO, Oslo/
DACS, London 2010 122, 153
National Museum for Art, Oslo 39
Norway Tourist Office 180T
Norwegian Literature Abroad 125
Morten Oddvik 83
Anita Peltonen 165
Press Association Images 77
Rex Features 66, 120
Richard Nowitz 31

Robert Meyer Collection 32, 34,
51, 52, 54, 55R, 58, 118
Rogaland Tourist Board 38, 214
Jostein Ryan 170
Sigborn Sandsmark 169
Sindre Skrede 10B
Robert Spark 296
Stavanger Tourist Board 220
Telemarktreffen 206
Tips Images 332, 334, 337
Topfoto 29, 30, 36, 41, 42, 43, 47,
50, 53, 59, 60, 61L, 63, 64, 78, 79,
80, 81, 82, 114, 158, 174/175,
184, 204T, 249T, 292, 297T, 321L,
325B
Ernst Vikne 148BR
Voss Tourist Board 234
Werner Forman Archive 26BL, 35
Sindre Wimberger 177
WittyName32 302
Ålesund Tourist Board 273

PHOTO FEATURES

Pages 88–89: Glen Gening/Apa
88CB; Mary Evans Picture Library
88BR; AKG Images 88/89T, 89TR;
Corbis Images 89BL; Innovation
Norway 89CL; Werner Forman
Archive 89BR, 89CB

Pages 110–111: Tore Urnes 110BL;
Glen Gening/Apa 110BR; Innovation
Norway 110/111T; Troms
Arbeiderparti 111CL; Michael
Mortensen 111BL; Courtesy Torfinn
Jåsund/norwegiancollector.com
111TR, 111BR

Pages 306–307: Tormod Sandtorv
306BL; Innovation Norway 306,
307BR; Getty Images 306/307T,
307BL; Zicasso.com 307TR

Map production: original
cartography Lovell Johns Ltd,
updated by Apa
Cartography Department

© 2011 Apa Publications UK Ltd

Production: Linton Donaldson and
Rebeka Ellam

INDEX

Note that we have listed Å under A and Ø under O, unlike in Norwegian where they are placed at the end of the alphabet.

N

Oslo T-bane

Oslo

Inset map (top left)

Strømsdammen Lake
Tryvannstårnet
Øvresetertjern
Lillevann
Frognerseteren
Voksenkollen
N
Skogen
500
Tryvann
Borgenveien
Diakonveien
Voksenlia
Voksenkollveien
Holmenkollveien
Sørkedalsveien
Bogstad camping-plass
Matrostveien
Holmenkollen bakken
Holmenkollen
Midstuen
Holmenkollen kapell
Ankerveien
Besserud
Oslo

Main map labels

Grefsen, Holmenkollen
Fysikk
Diakonhjemmet
Barnekunstmuseet
Lille Frøens vei
Fjernsynshuset
N.R.K.
BLINDERN
Kringkastingen
Frøen
Gydas vei
Gardeveien
Majorstuen
Suhms
Truckvegkollen
Hammerstads
Borgen
Aalls
Suhms gate
Colosseum senter
Sporveismuseet
Schønnings gate
168
Fritjof Nansens vei
Sørkedalsveien
Misjons-kirken
Ole Vigs gate
Sørgenfri-stads gate
Døvekirken
Colosseum kino
Essendrops gate
Majorstuen
Jacob
Industrigata
Vibes gate
Bogstadveien
Fagerborggata
Kirkeveien
MAJORSTUEN
Gjørstads gate
168
HEGDEHAUG
VIGELANDS-PARKEN
St Dominikus
Jacob Aalls gate
Majorsveien
Industrigata
Rosenborggata
Bogstadveien
Monolitten
Frogner stadion
Professor Dahls gate
Munthes gate
Fearnleys gate
HOMANSBYEN
Prof. Dahls gate
FROGNERPARKEN
Oslo Bymuseet
Fuglehauggata
Uranienborgveien
Oscars gate
Gyldenløves gate
Briskebyveien
Josefines gate
Frogner
Nordraaks gate
Tidemands gate
Sundts
BRISKEBY
Ullt
Uranienborg
Hegdehaugsveien
Vigeland-museet
Eckersbergs gate
Arno Bergs plass
Camilla Colletts vei
Uranienborgveien
FROGNER
Solheimgata
Løvenskiolds gate
President Harbitz gate
Skovveien
Oscars gate
Inkognitogata
Kristinelundveien
Thomas Heftyes gate
Gimleveien
Briskebyveien
Josefines gate
Grøners
Wergs
Halfdan Svartes gate
Nobels
Odins
Niels Juels gate
Ridderolds plass
Werg
Olav Kyrres plass
Bygdøy allé
Elisenbergveien
Frognerveien
Skovveien
Ridderolds gate
SLOTTSPAR
Thunes vei
Gustav Vigelands vei
Jonsrudveien
Drammensveien
Sandakerveien
Tostrups gate
Frogner
Gimle kino
Niels Juels gate
Meltzers gate
Slottet
Drammensveien
Olav Kyrres gate
American Lutheran Church
Sophus Lies gate
Bygdøy allé
Colbjørnsens gate
DRONNINGS-PARKEN
Frøyas gate
E18
Thomas Heftyes gate
Mogens Thorsens gate
Oslo Energi
Drammensveien
Båthavn
Nobels
Thomas
Slangs
Niels Juels gate
Bygdøy allé
Frognerveien
Inkognitogata
Parkveien
Hydro
RUSELØKKA
BYGDØY
Drammensveien
Frederik
Gabels gate
Universitets-biblioteket
Solligata
Hansteens gate
Observatorie terrasse
Parkveien
Observatoriegata
Munk
Oscarshall slott
Frammensveien
Drammensveien
Rikstrygdeverket
Munkedamsveien
Reichweins
Oscarshallveien
SKILLEBEKK
Munkedamsveien
Oslotunnelen
Wedels vei
Frognerkilen
Båthavn
Munkedamsveien
AKER BRYGGE
Dronninghavnveien
Båthavn
Kongen
Ferry port
Filipstadkaia
B y g d ø y
Meilibyedalen aveny
The Holocaust Center
Dronningen
Hjortneskaia
Filipstadveien
FILIPSTAD
Tjuvholmen
Langviksveien
Huk
Christian Benneches vei
Filipstadutstikker
Langviksbukta
Kon-Tiki Museet
Frammuseet
N
Oslofjorden
Norsk Sjøfartsmuseum

Oslo

0   500 m
0   500 yds

Denmark, Germany
Hellviktangen Manor, Nesoddtangen